Political Attitudes
over the Life Span

POLITICAL ATTITUDES OVER THE LIFE SPAN

The Bennington Women after Fifty Years

Duane F. Alwin
Ronald L. Cohen
Theodore M. Newcomb

THE UNIVERSITY OF WISCONSIN PRESS

The University of Wisconsin Press
114 North Murray Street
Madison, Wisconsin 53715

3 Henrietta Street
London WC2E 8LU, England

Library of Congress Cataloging-in-Publication Data
Alwin, Duane F. (Duane Francis), 1944–
Political attitudes over the life span: the Bennington women
after fifty years / Duane F. Alwin, Ronald L. Cohen,
Theodore M. Newcomb.
452 pp.   cm. — (Life course studies)
Includes bibliographical references and index.
ISBN 0-299-13010-X   ISBN 0-299-13014-2 (pbk.)
1. Attitude change—Longitudinal studies.   2. College graduates—
United States—Attitudes—Longitudinal studies.   3. Bennington
College—Alumni—Attitudes—Longitudinal studies.   4. Women in
politics—United States—Longitudinal studies.   I. Cohen, Ronald L.
(Ronald Lee), 1944–   II. Newcomb, Theodore Mead, 1903–1984.
III. Title.   IV. Series.
HM291.A4895   1992
306.2—dc20   91-50319

To Mary

Contents

Illustrations

Figures

Tables

Preface

In this book we present the third in a series of studies of the sociopolitical orientations of a group of women who attended Bennington College in the 1930s and 1940s. The first in the series, published by Theodore M. Newcomb as *Personality and Social Change: Attitude Formation in a Student Community* (1943), documented the importance of the social environment in the development of sociopolitical orientations during early adulthood. This work was one of the first empirical demonstrations of the importance of the *reference group* to the individual and the developmental impact of the college environment. That work was one of the earliest studies showing that political orientations and social attitudes more generally were still quite malleable and open to change in early adulthood. Newcomb's study continues to be an important reference regarding early political socialization.

The second study in the series, published by Newcomb, Koenig, Flacks, and Warwick in 1967 as *Persistence and Change: Bennington College and Its Students After Twenty-Five Years*, documented the importance of supportive social environments in the stability and/or change of sociopolitical attitudes, suggesting a mutually interdependent relationship between attitudes and those environments. The central finding that emerged from this restudy of the Bennington women was that their political orientations of the 1930s and 1940s remained relatively stable, even 25 years later. Women who maintained their college attitudes were, by and large, those who selected social environments congruent with those attitudes; those whose orientations changed the most were those who inhabited postcollegiate environments that were less congruent.

The purpose of this, the third study, was to trace the subsequent trajectory of the political orientations of these women from their development in college, sustained through mid-life, and on to late adulthood and old age. In 1984 we were able to obtain interviews with 335 surviving members of the original cohorts of students for whom addresses were available from Bennington College, and we were able to combine data from this follow-up study with the earlier data obtained by Newcomb and colleagues. This

Theodore Newcomb on the Bennington College campus, circa 1940. Photo courtesy of Bennington College.

research, funded by the National Institute on Aging (R01-AG04743-01 through R01-AG04743-04), was motivated primarily by a desire to assess the persistence and change in attitudes over the life cycle. In this study we investigate the various paths taken by the sociopolitical orientations of Newcomb's original research participants. With the view that investigations of individual persistence and change must confront the potential impact of several types of factors—those tied to the processes of aging, the unique influences of cohort experiences, and those influences of sociohistorical (or period) factors—we supplemented our study with data from the National Election Study series, which provides data on political orientations in every presidential and congressional election since 1952.[1] In so doing we contribute to the continuing debate about the stability of sociopolitical attitudes over the life span and the role of aging and cohort influences on political attitudes.

Theodore Newcomb and his wife, Mary, initiated the idea for doing some follow-up interviews with the original Bennington women, and they, with Ron Cohen, who has for some years been on the faculty at Bennington, began formulating a design for conducting such a survey during 1982–83. They brought Duane Alwin into the research as they began to prepare a proposal for funding to the National Institute on Aging. Once the research proposal was reviewed and eventually approved for funding by the NIA, Newcomb, Cohen, and Alwin became the principal members of this collaborative venture, along with several others.

In addition to the great debt this work owes to Ted and Mary Newcomb who both encouraged and participated in the early phases of this restudy, a number of other persons contributed in important and diverse ways to this research. We particularly want to thank Pat and Jerry Gurin, who first suggested the collaboration among the three of us. We acknowledge the early involvement of Judy Cohen, who participated in discussions of research design and meetings to draft questionnaires, and who helped provide the inspiration for carrying out the research. Merilynn (Lynn) Dielman provided expert assistance in study design and implementation, and in the analysis of data. Lynn's great talents and energy for conducting large-scale survey projects made the data collection portion of this research possible on a relatively tight production schedule. Lynn also assumed major responsibilities for coding, data management, file construction, and data analysis. This project would not have been completed without her indefatigable assistance. We also wish to acknowledge the milieu of researchers at the Institute for Social Research who in various and diverse ways created a supportive environment for our research, especially Angus Campbell, Charlie

1. There was no NES survey in 1954.

Cannell, Philip Converse, Jim House, Arland Thornton, Joe Veroff, and Bob Zajonc.

Professor Donald Kinder and the staff of the Institute for Social Research's National Election Study were very helpful in allowing us access to the 1984 NES preelection study questionnaire when it was being developed and finalized. The contemporary administration of exact replicas of the NES questions in our Bennington study provided us the opportunity to compare our Bennington respondents with other subgroups in the population. We also acknowledge the assistance of the Inter-University Consortium for Political and Social Research for providing access to the Election Studies data used here.

Many people at Bennington College gave us assistance. Diane Hart provided information that initially enabled us to contact most of the original participants in Newcomb's Bennington studies. Joanne Schultz provided very able secretarial assistance throughout all phases of the planning and execution of this project. Becca Stickney provided important suggestions and wise counsel at many points along the way.

The 1984 reinterview data were collected through the facilities of the University of Michigan's Survey Research Center. Joan Peebles was the SRC Field Section's study manager, and we wish to acknowledge her important role in coordinating the work of the interviewers on the study. We also wish to recognize the high professional standards of the SRC interviewers who worked on this study, and we acknowledge their important contributions. Mark Glaza and Frank Mierzwa provided able library assistance, help in the coding and documentation of the data, and help in the construction of tables. Naomi Levan, whose honors thesis in the Department of Psychology focused on the analysis of some of the Bennington follow-up data and won the Eita Krom Prize in the Department of Sociology, contributed measurably to the articulation of some of the issues addressed in these chapters. Jon Krosnick assisted in the analysis of the NES data and provided important advice on both technical and substantive matters connected with this project. We also gratefully acknowledge the comments and suggestions made by Ronald Abeles, Richard Campbell, Phillip Converse, Norval Glenn, M. Kent Jennings, Glen Elder, David Featherman, Gerald Marwell, Stanley Presser, Jacqueline Scott, David Sears, and Roberta Simmons, who were kind enough to devote time to reading previous drafts of material included in this monograph. We especially wish to acknowledge the help of Jeylan Mortimer, who gave extensive comments on multiple drafts of the entire manuscript. We also extend deep gratitude to David Featherman for his advice in preparing this manuscript and his continuing support of our work.

Marion Wirick and Evelyn Caviani provided very able text preparation and editorial assistance in the early phases of the study. Lynn Dielman provided assistance with the final preparation of the text, assembling study materials and references for publication, and assisted with the final analyses (and documentation thereof) presented herein. Brian Labadie, Donna Read, and Susan Sherry assisted by making innumerable trips to the library and by checking bibliographic material.

We also wish to acknowledge the great cooperation and assistance of the women who participated in the Bennington Studies at several points in their lives. Although these women may not have benefited directly from our research, their participation has provided the basis for significant contributions to the pursuit of knowledge about socialization processes and their role in human development. Our respondents expressed great interest in our subject matter. Their assistance is warmly appreciated. We especially wish to thank those women who participated in the alumni meeting which Ron Cohen held for our respondents and interested others at Bennington College in the summer of 1986. Our thinking about the extent and nature of the changes in the attitude orientations of these women was assisted by those discussions and the feedback that occurred as a result.

Ted Newcomb died in December 1984, after suffering a stroke. His death prevented him from seeing even the first set of preliminary results of this follow-up study, although all the interviews had been completed, and we were in the process of entering the data into the computer at that time. In the last months of his life, Ted was actively involved in the research, continually nudging us along and seeing to it that the study was completed. There is no question that, had Ted lived longer, our research aims would have been completed much sooner. In our memories of Ted, he is constantly looking over our shoulders with great affection for our ideas and efforts and with an intellectual curiosity that compels us beyond the data to find the most plausible explanation of our results. If Ted were alive, he would have been a contributor to this work, just as he was an active participant in its inception and nurturance over these years. With Ted's family's permission, therefore, we have included him as an author. Ted deserves much of the credit for whatever contribution this work represents, and we absolve him of any responsibility for its weaknesses. The work is dedicated with deep love and affection to Mary Newcomb, who has continually been a great source of sustenance and support for carrying out Ted's vision.

Because of Newcomb's death, this monograph was prepared by Alwin and Cohen, again with the assistance of a number of others. Although we consider this book a truly collaborative effort, we feel an obligation to ourselves and to others to record our own separate contributions: Cohen made the primary contribution to chapters 2, 3, 4, and 6, and Alwin contributed chapters 1, 5, 7, 8, 9, and 10.

Finally, our families have provided love and support throughout our work on this project, but, of course, not only during this period. None of the work reported here would have been possible without them and without their encouragement, their help, and their confidence in us. For all this, but also for much more, we thank Anne Alwin and Judy Cohen, and our children: Abby, Becky, and Heidi Alwin, and Becky, Jessie, and Hannah Cohen.

Political Attitudes
over the Life Span

1

Sociopolitical Orientations over the Life Span

INTRODUCTION

The research to be reported here focuses on the development of sociopolitical orientations over the entire adult life span. We analyze data from three periods in the adult lives of a cohort of women who attended Bennington College in the 1930s and 1940s. The first two studies of these women are well-known contributions to the literature in social psychology (Newcomb, 1943; Newcomb et al., 1967). In due course, we will describe the results of the third in this series of studies. Conducted over a span of fifty years, this sequence of studies not only describes the orientations of the members of a specific sample at three points in their adult lives, but also attempts to explain why the orientations remained the same or changed and to suggest the extent to which these explanations might be helpful in understanding the process of lifelong development more broadly conceived. In pursuing this broader task, we also rely on other resources: specifically, data from the National Election Study series.

Newcomb's first study of these women demonstrated significant change in their sociopolitical orientations during the college years: a movement toward endorsing the policies of the New Deal and away from the attitudes of their parents, who were relatively well-established, conservatively oriented families from the Northeast. Twenty-five years later, Newcomb and three of his students—Kathryn Koenig, Richard Flacks, and Donald Warwick—demonstrated that these orientations had remained relatively stable. In trying to understand both the early changes during college and their subsequent stability, Newcomb emphasized the role of reference groups in mediating the impact of historical events and social change on the sociopolitical orientations of this group of women as it moved from early adulthood through middle age.

In designing the third study in this series, undertaken in 1984 when the respondents were in their 60s and 70s, and in trying to understand what we can now see as the lifelong development of their sociopolitical orientations,

3

we not only focused on the kinds of factors Newcomb had originally emphasized—those associated with reference groups and social support—we
also drew upon the literature on life span development that has emerged
during the past twenty years. Specifically, we wondered whether the initial changes Newcomb found in young college students merely reflected
the unique susceptibility of adolescents confronting freedom from parental
authority and constraint, a type of pattern that could have been replicated
at other colleges at other times, or if these changes were the result of the
interaction of this *age-related susceptibility* and the *unique historical circumstances* of the 1930s. Further, was the stability Newcomb observed
later the result of a relatively universal trend in the aging process, that
is, the persistence and strengthening of sociopolitical orientations over the
life cycle, or was it the result of an interaction between the orientations
developed in early adulthood and the particular historical period in which
these women later confronted familial and occupational choices? And what
would be the fate of these orientations in the sixth and seventh decades of
life, when these women faced other choices in another historical setting?

Our primary approach to these questions, using a study of a single cohort
through time, has several limitations, not the least of which is that these
several explanations cannot easily be disentangled empirically. Ultimately,
in order to make sense of our results, we will need additional information to
identify some of the processes at work. This is what Philip Converse (1976)
calls *side-information:* assumptions about the nature of certain historical
and generational processes. We rely on the existing empirical literature
and prevailing theoretical perspectives, as well as some of our own analyses
of the National Election Study data, in order to supply some basis for these
assumptions. In any case, there are a number of complexities involved in
trying to understand the historical, the life-cycle, and the generational factors in the development of sociopolitical orientations, but we have not let
this keep us from trying to sort out the various processes involved.

LIFE SPAN DEVELOPMENT OF SOCIOPOLITICAL ORIENTATIONS

In *The Sociological Imagination*, C. Wright Mills (1959) describes the
sociological imagination as an orientation to the intersection of biography
and history in social structure. He suggests active examination of questions about how the individual and the structural positions intersect—the
biographical factors that brought the person to the position and the set
of historical factors that brought the position to the person. Our present
perspective translates these concerns into a research question aimed at
trying to understand *all* the processes that have an impact upon human

4

development, with a special interest in the processes that contribute to the development of political orientations in adult life.

The understanding of human development is difficult because the factors shaping it are a complex mixture of events that occur along two time lines: *biographical time,* which includes events involving biological/maturational changes over the life span of the individual as well as changes in social roles and experiences, both anticipated and unanticipated, and *historical time,* which includes events that affect large numbers of persons but are unrelated, in theory, to individuals' positions with respect to their own biographies. If one notices changes over the lifetime of an individual, or a group of individuals, the understanding of these changes is complicated by the confounding of events in biographical and historical time. In short, it is difficult to separate aging/life-stage explanations of change from historical explanations—those referring to the period in which particular biographies are embedded.

Furthermore, the study of human development is even more complicated because of the intersection of historical and biographical time in people's lives. The fact that people pass through certain stages in their development at a specific point in historical time, the events of which have unique influences on the course of individual development, presents an even more complex picture of the factors shaping experience through time. Some have referred to these unique influences of the intersection of historical and biographical time as *generational* (Mannheim, 1952) or *cohort* effects (Ryder, 1965). Thus, aging/life-stage explanations are confounded not only with historical, or period, explanations, but also with explanations referring to unique cohort experiences.[1]

The inexorable processes inherent in individual movement through the life cycle in the context of a particular set of social circumstances, themselves continually changing, reflect the intertwining of the processes of social change and individual change. Their separate influences on human development are thus extremely difficult, if not impossible, to disentangle (Riley, 1973), and this means that several plausible explanations potentially exist for any one set of observations. This is particularly apparent in research inquiry aimed at the study of the development and course of sociopolitical orientations over individual life cycles. Past research has shown how difficult it is to understand changes in the sociopolitical orientations

---

1. Notice that in cross-sectional data, age and cohort are confounded, except in replicated cross sections, where it is possible under certain conditions to separate them. Also note that aging and history are confounded in data on a single cohort over time (see Riley, 1973). Below we discuss more fully the theoretical and interpretational issues that make it difficult, if not impossible, to separate the influences of age, period, and cohort factors in the analysis of such data.

of individuals using the types of data which commonly form the basis for inferences about the meaning of change. These difficulties have not, however, presented an obstacle to the creative interpretation of processes of individual change over the life cycle; the existing literature on political socialization contains an array of explanations for these processes (see Converse, 1976; Cutler, 1970, 1974; Cutler and Kaufman, 1975; Glenn, 1969, 1974, 1980; Glenn and Grimes, 1968; Glenn and Hefner, 1972; Jennings and Markus, 1984; Jennings and Niemi, 1981; Kinder and Sears, 1985; Sears, 1975, 1981, 1983, 1987; Sigel, 1989).

ATTITUDE STABILITY AND CHANGE OVER THE LIFE SPAN

The dynamics of attitude stability and change have been the focus of a substantial amount of research in social psychology since the early 1900s. McGuire (1985: 235–37) charts several peaks of interest in attitude research over the past century. With origins as diverse as the behaviorist writings of J. B. Watson (1925) and the interactionist orientations of Thomas and Znaniecki (1918), the interest in attitudes and attitude change over this century may have fluctuated, but it has clearly been a central topic of research, at least since the 1940s. Indeed, Newcomb's (1943) early work, to which the present work is intimately linked, was one of the first to raise questions about life-cycle variations in the stability of attitudes.

The Study of Attitude Change

There are three basic approaches to the quantitative study of attitude change: experimental (or laboratory), quasi-experimental (or field studies), and nonexperimental (or survey) approaches. This variety is due to the amount of cross-disciplinary interest in the topic of attitudes and attitude change. Social psychologists from the disciplines of psychology, sociology, and political science have all contributed to research on attitudes and attitude change. This has spawned a healthy diversity in methods of research, although it is perhaps fair to say that most research on attitude change has been confined to the laboratory. As a consequence, most attitude change studied in these settings has been, by definition, short-lived.

Sears (1987) has recently argued that social psychologists studying attitude change have relied too heavily on a narrow experimental data base, primarily involving the study of college students. He warns that the overuse of this narrow data base may have biased the field's substantive propositions regarding human nature. Interestingly, Sears's argument is quite revealing in the context of the life span developmental perspective. Given

6

that the young are much more vulnerable to attitude change than older members of society because they have affectively weaker and generally uncrystallized attitudes (Glenn, 1980; Sears, 1981, 1983, 1987), it is risky to draw general conclusions about human behavior from an exclusive reliance on studies of the young.

As Glenn (1980:605) notes, however, experimental studies are needed to inform the question of differences in *susceptibility* to attitude change as basic aspects of human functioning. Such experimental studies of attitude change in the laboratory have focused on the impact of "persuasive" communications on the extent and nature of attitude change—specifically, on the impact of their source, the content of the message, and the characteristics of the recipient. However, such research designed to study changes in susceptibility to change due to aging is virtually nonexistent. Laboratory research cannot focus directly on the processes by which people acquire their basic attitudes and the processes by which attitudes develop and change over the life course.

It is noteworthy, however, that most experimental research relevant to these issues has focused on the effects of persuasion. Evidence exists regarding cognitively relevant processes of conservatism—resistance to cognitive change—that bear on hypotheses of susceptibility to change over the life span. Greenwald (1980:611) notes that the tendency to resist change of prior judgments "is especially strong when the topic is important to the person and there is some commitment to (ego-involvement in) the prior position." However, very little of this experimental literature has addressed the question of life-cycle or aging differences in relation to the extent of susceptibility to attitude change.

There is some evidence from studies of persuasion that chronological age is negatively related to the amount of attitude change (e.g., Clos, 1966). Taken as a whole, the experimental evidence suggests a monotonic decline in attitude changeability throughout the life span (Glenn, 1980:606). However, the absence of systematic work on this topic and the diversity of findings have contributed to a certain amount of skepticism regarding the evidence supporting these conclusions (e.g., Oskamp, 1977). Still, if one were to accept the existing laboratory research at face value, one would conclude that aging contributes to the persistence of attitudes (Glenn, 1980).

Sears (1981:95) laments that studies of the linkage of personal life to public attitudes have paid little attention to life-cycle processes. In particular, nonlaboratory research on the stability of attitudes has either ignored life-cycle considerations (e.g., Converse and Markus, 1979; Krosnick, 1988), or has been relatively limited in selection of cohorts, and/or has used relatively primitive methods that are unable to deal with problems of attitude

7

measurement (Capel, 1967; Guest, 1964; Hoge and Bender, 1974; Jennings and Niemi, 1981; Kelly, 1955). As will be revealed later in this book, even the most sophisticated analyses of life-cycle factors and attitude change reported to date (Alwin and Krosnick, 1991a; Glenn, 1980; Krosnick and Alwin, 1989) have been limited to synthetic cohort data and have not examined issues of attitude change over long periods of the life course.

The Study of Attitude Change over the Life Span

Researchers using survey data to address questions of attitude change over the life span have focused on two types of data: replicated cross-sectional surveys and panel studies. Glenn (1980) demonstrates an ingenious approach to studying the *aging-stability* hypothesis using replicated cross-sectional surveys, in which the same cohorts (or, typically, groups of cohorts) are observed over time. If the youngest birth cohorts change more than the older birth cohorts, as assessed over time in repeated cross-sectional surveys, then this is taken as support for the persistence hypothesis (see below). Glenn (1980) reviews a number of studies using this approach, concluding that the available evidence seems to support the aging-stability hypothesis that young cohorts are more vulnerable to change than are older ones.

A second type of data used for studying change and stability in attitudes over the life course arises from more of a "developmentalist" research strategy: observing *the same individuals* over time, rather than members of *the same cohorts* over time. This approach has been actively applied to the study of the stability of cognitive skills (e.g., Bloom, 1964; Schaie, 1983) and the study of the constancy of personality (e.g., Moss and Susman, 1980; Nesselroade and Baltes, 1974). This design has also been applied to the study of political attitudes (e.g., Fendrich and Lovoy, 1988; Lang and Lang, 1978; Marwell, Aiken, and Demerath, 1987; Newcomb et al., 1967; Roberts and Lang, 1985).

Both of these survey designs have certain advantages, but they also have some disadvantages. *Intracohort* trend studies of the type summarized by Glenn (1980) provide data on large representative samples of cohorts, sampled at a particular historical time period, in which excellent estimates can be obtained regarding the *levels of net change*. However, these data do not allow one to study the processes of change for individuals; that is, they do not permit the study of the individual-level components of *macro-level* cohort change. So, while they represent highly valid data from the point of view of *representativeness*, they falter in terms of providing evidence of individual-level processes of change.

For the study of *gross change*, one needs data on the same individuals

8

over time; that is, one needs *panel data* (see Campbell, 1988). And while panel studies of cohorts over time do permit a more precise assessment of the components of change, the typical study is lacking in a number of ways. First, such intracohort studies of the same individuals typically rely on purposive, nonrepresentative samples (e.g., Fendrich and Lovoy, 1988; Hoge and Bender, 1974; Marwell, Aiken, and Demerath, 1987).[2] But even if some effort is made to obtain representative samples, they are often representative of the population at one single time and limited in this sense to particular cohorts during particular historical times (e.g., Jennings and Niemi, 1981). A second problem is that there is typically no *periodic* measurement of such cohorts, and the few measurements that do exist (usually from two or three time points) are also purposive rather than uniform and representative of critical stages in the life cycle.

An emerging literature has relied on a type of research design that combines the best qualities of both of these approaches. This is the set of studies relying on measurements of panels from large representative samples of populations of interest. The first such study that we are aware of is Sears's (1981, 1983) analysis of the National Election Study (NES) 1970s (1972–74–76) panel, which was a large, representative four-year, three-wave panel study. Our own research, presented in subsequent chapters, also makes use of these NES data.[3] Unfortunately, because of the limited number of such national panel studies and because they typically cover no more than four-year periods of time, there are serious limitations to generalizations drawn from such data.[4]

Certain parallels exist between these studies of large representative panel studies (Sears, 1981, 1983) and the repeated cross-sectional data sets relied upon by Glenn (1980) and others. In both cases the researchers must rely on what are known as *synthetic cohort* models of persistence and change. Since in neither case is the same cohort followed over a long period of time, data from the cohorts studied are (implicitly or explicitly) arrayed along an age continuum, and levels of change or persistence are

---

2. One of our main sources of data in the present study is just such a single-cohort study. Although we present these data in the examination of the aging-stability hypothesis, we continually emphasize the need to interpret them within a framework that recognizes their limitations.

3. We rely on this type of data in the analysis presented in chapter 7.

4. A few studies of phenomena outside of the realm of political socialization also use a panel design for studying the relation of age to the stability of attitudes. Lorence and Mortimer (1985) and Mortimer, Finch, and Maruyama (1988) studied the stability of commitment to work and job satisfaction in relation to age using panel data from Michigan's Quality of Employment Survey. They found that stability measured over a four-year period increases with age, and the youngest group shows the most attitudinal instability.

attributed to the age differences in the cohorts studied. Rarely is it possible to separate aging, cohort, and period influences on levels of persistence and change.

EXPLANATIONS OF INDIVIDUAL CHANGE

Given our primary interest in understanding the nature and processes of changes in the sociopolitical orientations of Newcomb's Bennington College subjects over nearly 50 years of their lives, our work has been shaped by a consideration of several explanations of variation in attitudes over the life course. It is thus appropriate that we locate our study within the framework provided by this literature. We turn first to a review of several major hypotheses that have been advanced to explain change and stability in sociopolitical attitudes over the life course and to a review of evidence pertaining to several central issues that arise from these hypotheses. This discussion provides the theoretical background for our presentation of findings from the study of the Bennington women.

Life-Cycle Explanations

One of the early attempts to understand variation in sociopolitical orientations over the life cycle referred to movement through periods of development in which experiences were an important function of age.[5] Lipset, Lazarsfeld, Barton, and Linz (1954), for example, portray the life course in terms of a succession of clearly identifiable life stages.[6] They maintain that people's common experiences at certain stages in their lives help shape their political orientations, and that it is important to specify "the points at which people are likely to have experiences which affect their political behavior" (1143). In specifying these experiences, they point to the great influences of the family in childhood and adolescence, long before the age of voting, and to the tendency of attitudes and values formed in childhood to persist into adulthood, "unless upset by fundamentally different sets of experiences and social relations" (1144).

A second stage in the development of sociopolitical orientations, accord-

---

5. Since *aging, life course,* and *life stage* explanations all refer to regular patterns of development through the life cycle, we use these terms more or less interchangeably, although we acknowledge that changes that are causally linked to age are inevitably a product of biological, psychological, and social aging.

6. This type of explanation is similar in certain ways to other stage-theory approaches to human development more generally (cf. Erikson, 1950, 1959; Gilligan, 1982; Kohlberg, 1966; Piaget, 1932).

10

ing to Lipset and his colleagues (1954), occurs during adolescence, which is "the period in the life cycle where the individual first encounters strong influences outside of his family and must proceed to define his adult role" (1145). This period is characterized as the time of transition from nearly complete dependence on the parent to "a few crucial years" in which important decisions are made. And while they admit that the sociopolitical context in which a child grows up can vary significantly in the extent to which political choices are salient, they argue that the experiences of adolescence can permanently structure political attitudes and behavior in later life.[7] Even in young adulthood, a third stage accompanying the opportunity for one's "first vote," the important role of the family is a major factor in their view. Young adults typically exhibit "hereditary" voting patterns.[8]

Lipset and his colleagues (1954:148–49) suggest that, while there are no inherent political predispositions associated with the experiences of adolescence and young adulthood, in the later experiences of adulthood, there are.[9] They note that increasing age is often associated with changes on several variables, for example, income and social position, which may lead to somewhat more conservative attitudes, although they present little evidence that this is in fact the case. Finally, they address the question of whether old age, a fifth stage in their analysis, brings a conservative influence into social and political affairs. They suggest that since older persons reflect the orientations of an earlier period, stably maintaining the influences of their youth, their sociopolitical orientations may reflect a resistance to change. They also note, however, that many contradictory examples exist across several different sociocultural contexts, and that it is difficult to interpret old age as inherently a time of greater conservatism.

Before continuing our discussion of life course approaches to sociopolitical development, it is important to distinguish between two different uses of the term *conservative* in this literature. Conservatism as a *stability of beliefs over time* should be distinguished from conservatism as *a set of political beliefs that center around the policies and platforms of the Republican party*. In a time of increasing pervasiveness of conservatism (of the second type), older people may hold beliefs that are nonconservative,

7. In the decades following the Lipset and colleagues (1954) analysis of life-stage factors in political behavior, the thesis that the family maintains one of the strongest influences in the socialization of sociopolitical orientations has dominated much of the field (e.g., Davies, 1965; Easton and Dennis, 1969; Greenstein, 1965; Hess and Torney, 1967). We return to these issues later in our discussion of the "impressionable years."

8. Lipset and colleagues (1954) present an extensive analysis of the idea of "political generations," to which we return in the following discussion of cohort explanations.

9. They do, however, subscribe to the view that "no one is more 'conservative' or conformist than the young child" (1149).

even though these beliefs may persist and therefore reflect a conservatism of another type (the first). Thus, in the following pages we are careful to distinguish these two meanings. For the most part we use the term *conservative* to refer to a set of political beliefs that are identified with the Republican party, choosing the term *stability* or *persistence* to refer to the unchanging quality (or even the strengthening) of attitudes, be they "conservative" or "liberal."[10]

Hyman (1959) also advances a life-stage explanation of variation in sociopolitical orientations over the life course. Hyman argues that the family is "foremost among agencies of socialization" (69), and that the "individual's political *orientation* is a product of socialization essentially within the family" (85). He reviews a variety of results that reveal quite strong relationships between the political orientations of parents and children.[11] At the same time, Hyman also articulates the view that the influence of the family declines with age and that "the influence of parental norms declines as peers and other agencies exert their influence on the growing child" (105). This view, that the appearance of additional socially structured socialization influences during adolescence and early adulthood act upon the individual to produce departures from parental orientations, is consistent with the view of Lispet and his colleagues (reviewed above) and with the dominant view of socialization during these life stages (e.g., Campbell, 1969). As the influence of school settings and peer groups increases, the family exerts less of an influence on the child's development. According to such a view, it is not simply the weakening of early family experiences that is tied to the sociopolitical orientations of offspring; in later life other nonfamily factors come into play. Thus, it is argued that during adolescence the social composition of the school and peer group have a somewhat more powerful impact on some aspects of development than the child's family of origin, or at least that family influences occur with greater subtlety.[12]

Prominent among the studies Hyman (1959) reviewed regarding the attenuation of parental influence over time was Newcomb's 1943 volume reporting the results of his Bennington studies. Newcomb had noted that the voting preferences of parents and children were similar during their first year at Bennington, but among sophomores the preferences between parents and children were more divergent, and by the senior year the two sets

10. In chapter 5 we discuss this distinction in somewhat greater depth, and in chapter 8 we offer some evidence concerning the relationship between the two.

11. Hyman noted, however, that relationships with partisanship (party preference) were generally stronger than relationships involving policy attitudes (75).

12. For a review of perspectives on the role of socioeconomic characteristics of the family at different points in the life cycle of the child, see Alwin and Thornton (1984:786–88).

of marginals were markedly different. In fact, as we report below, based on reports obtained from the reinterviews with the Bennington women in the 1960s, while there was some tendency toward similarity between the political orientations of these women during their later college years and those of their parents, the apparent influences of the parental generation were modest. Hyman referred to Newcomb's research as providing some "inferential" support for the hypothesis that parental influence is attenuated "as the child comes into contact with new groups through age and independence" (102).[13]

These early theoretical and empirical discussions of life course patterns in political orientations provided an impetus to an "aging" interpretation of the relationships between chronological age and partisanship in cross-sectional surveys. Specifically, the hypothesis was advanced that *people tend to become more conservative with age.* Indeed, Glenn (1974) opens his essay "Aging and Conservatism" with the assertion that this assumption "is prevalent among social scientists, as well as the lay public," and that "there seem to be few other generalizations about human behavior and thought processes on which there is such widespread agreement" (177). Such a relationship has been very difficult to establish using survey data. Crittenden (1962), for example, contrasts the aging and cohort (or generational) explanations for correlations between age and partisanship in survey data. Concerned to show that "the aging process has an impact on party affiliation . . . independent of any such generational factors" (648), he examined the patterns of party affiliation by age/cohort in four nationwide surveys conducted in 1946, 1950, 1954, and 1958. Crittenden's conclusion, which was essentially refuted in further analyses by Cutler (1970, 1974) and Glenn (1974), was that there was support for the idea that "aging seems to produce a shift toward Republicanism in the period 1946 to 1958" (1962: 654).[14] Evidence and opinion on this issue continue to be mixed (Converse, 1976; Cutler, 1970, 1974; Knoke and Hout, 1974). As Converse (1976) illustrates, however, aging (life stage) may affect some aspects of political orientations, such as intensity of partisanship, but not others, such as partisanship itself.

The life course perspectives, such as those reviewed here, give impor-

13. Hyman notes the difficulty with any inference about the correspondence or similarity of parent and child orientations on the basis of the similarity of marginals (1959:79), and that given the lack of the appropriate cross-tabulation, such a conclusion is not warranted (90). We return to this issue in a subsequent analysis.

14. Further research on this issue generally does not support Crittenden's claim (e.g., Converse, 1976; Glenn, 1974; Glenn and Grimes, 1968; Glenn and Zody, 1970; Glenn and Hefner, 1972). Below we discuss some of the problems with the separation of age and cohort effects (see Glenn, 1977, 1981a, 1981b).

tant emphasis to the periods of openness to change and the periods of greatest vulnerability to the influence of the family and other agencies of socialization. At the same time they offer little information about the stability of sociopolitical attitudes over the life course. It is clear that the family plays a strong role in shaping the orientations of young people in their early years, particularly their party identification; and as Hyman (1959) suggests, with increasing age, the role of the family is lessened. Indeed, Newcomb's (1943) Bennington research provided evidence for the suggestion that under certain conditions the departure from parental orientations could be quite dramatic. What is less clear is the extent to which this kind of vulnerability continues throughout life, or, in the more limited case, how long it lasts. One view is that adult development is a process of continued change, and that social and historical experiences continue to stimulate change and the formation of new attitudes. The idea that there is a *lifelong openness to change* (Kinder and Sears, 1985) suggests that such "influenceability" continues throughout the life course, or that later periods of vulnerability to change reappear (Sears, 1981). The first follow-up study by Newcomb and his colleagues (1967), however, suggests that there is substantial stability of sociopolitical attitudes during early adult life. We return to issues of "the impressionable years" and "attitude persistence" in subsequent sections. For the moment we return to our enumeration of explanations of individual change, briefly considering cohort and historical explanations.

Cohort Explanations

One of the most intriguing hypotheses regarding changes in individual sociopolitical orientations over the life course is not linked to aging, but simply to age. Indeed, the idea that unique cohort experiences (the intersection of biographical and historical time) produce important differences in sociopolitical orientations across age groups is referred to in the majority of discussions of political socialization (e.g., Campbell, Converse, Miller and Stokes, 1960; Cutler, 1970, 1974; Glenn, 1974; Hyman, 1959: 39–47; Lipset et al., 1954:147–48).

Mannheim (1952) is frequently credited with the origin of this thesis in his discussion of the concept of "generations," although the argument is frequently articulated (e.g., Ryder, 1965; Carlsson and Karlsson, 1970). This thesis states that historical events are systematically experienced differently by different age-cohorts, or *generations*, and that this leads to subsequent differences among them. Mannheim makes it relatively clear that such an effect is to be distinguished from an effect of aging per se (1952:293–96). Examples of cohort explanations of sociopolitical orienta-

14

tions are (1) the influence of World War I and its aftermath on the youth of Germany and the appeal of fascist movements among the young in Europe generally in the 1930s (see Lipset et al., 1954); (2) the effects of exposure to the New Deal on persons reaching political awareness in the United States at this time who had gone through the depression of the 1930s (Centers, 1950; Knoke and Hout, 1974); and (3) the effects of political protest and youthful rebellion during the period of the Vietnam War (Lang and Lang, 1978; Roberts and Lang, 1985).

To Mannheim (1952) the concept of the *generation* is a concept of social position as important for the sociopolitical orientation of the individual as that of membership in a particular class or status grouping. The similar location of members of a generation means not only that they are born into the world at the same time, but also that their youth, adulthood, and old age coincide. This "chronological contemporaneity" does not, however, by itself produce the effects of generational location, according to Mannheim (1952:297–98), unless it involves participation in "the same historical and social circumstances." Even though older and younger generation groups experience the same historical processes, they do not have the same "generational location."

This intersection of personal biographies with sociohistorical time is described by Mannheim (1952:298) as follows:

> The fact that their location is a different one, however, can be explained primarily by the different "stratification" of their lives. The human consciousness, structurally speaking, is characterized by a particular inner "dialectic." It is of considerable importance for the formation of the consciousness which experiences happen to make those all-important "first impressions," "childhood experiences"—and which follow to form the second, third, and other "strata." Conversely, in estimating the biographical significance of a particular experience, it is important to know whether it is undergone by an individual as a decisive childhood experience, or later in life, superimposed upon other basic and early impressions. Early impressions tend to coalesce into a *natural view* of the world. All later experiences then tend to receive their meaning from this original set, whether they appear as that set's verification and fulfilment or as its negation and antithesis. . . . This much, however, is certain, that even if the rest of one's life consisted of one long process of negation and destruction of the natural world view acquired in youth, the determining influence of these early impressions would still be predominant. . . . If we bear in mind that every concrete experience acquires its particular face and form from its relation to this primary stratum of experiences from which all others receive their meaning, we can appreciate its importance for the further development of the human consciousness.

The reality of these social processes, with each new cohort or generation experiencing sociohistorical events from its own unique perspective,

15

forms a basis for continuous societal-level change. So, in addition to "cohort effects" on individuals, the natural "succession of generations" represents an aspect of the dynamic of social change that helps in the understanding of the historical process. The dying off of cohorts with one type of early social experiences and the entrance into adulthood of people with a very different sort of socialization reflects a "rejuvenation" of society. And given the assumption articulated above, that *"members of any one generation can only participate in a temporally limited section of the historical process"* (Mannheim, 1952:296), a theoretical model exists for understanding social change in a particular sociocultural heritage as a gradual process involving the succession of cohorts. Indeed, with respect to birth-cohort differences in political and social attitudes, this issue has been the subject of considerable speculation and empirical investigation (e.g., Abramson, 1976, 1979, 1983; Abramson and Inglehart, 1986, 1987; Davis, 1975; Firebaugh and Davis, 1988; Inglehart, 1971, 1977, 1986; Stouffer, 1955).

One would expect that such gradual processes of social change due to cohort replacement could be very difficult to separate from the effects of historical events, since the influence of historical events may be thought of as a weighted average of its effects on different generations. The effects of common experiences that are unusual—such as economic depressions, wars, periods of prosperity, or political upheaval—at critical periods in biographical time are somewhat easier to detect. For example, growing up during the Great Depression, it has been argued, produced a generation of individuals who were different from those going before and those following them through the life cycle (see Centers, 1950; Elder, 1974, 1981).

Lipset and his colleagues (1954:148) note that this type of cohort or generational hypothesis represents a plausible alternative explanation for the ostensible link between aging and sociopolitical orientations. They observed, on the basis of studies of the 1948 and 1952 national elections, that the new political generation (those voting for the first time) was more Republican than that which preceded it. On this basis they reasoned that "persons who came of age during the depression or war have developed Democratic ties, whereas those who know these events only as history and whose first vote was cast in periods of prosperity are turning toward the Republican party." More recently, a number of researchers have reported the existence of a pro-Democratic residue among birth cohorts entering the electorate during the years of the Great Depression, presumably exposed to a greater extent than other cohorts to the political orientations exemplified by the social programs of the New Deal (e.g., Converse, 1976; Knoke and Hout, 1974; Oppenheim, 1970).

Like the aging hypothesis, the cohort, or generational, hypothesis involves changes in biographical time (Crittenden, 1962). Unlike the aging

16

hypothesis, the class of cohort explanations involves macro-level historical influences. Most generational models explicitly specify that it is the young adult who is most vulnerable to the impact of social change, and thus these influences are theorized to affect only one segment of the population: the young (e.g., Campbell et al., 1960:54–56). In cases where such historical factors affect the aggregate to a greater extent, and more uniformly with respect to age, we tend to think of them as historical, or "period," effects. We turn briefly to such influences as a third category of explanations for individual change.

Historical Explanations

Societal-level changes, both in the social and political events that shape history and in changes in technology and social organization, also may produce individual-level changes in sociopolitical attitudes. Often analysts seek longer-term explanations that transcend the unique effects of cohort experiences, and which influence people from many different cohorts over a longer period of time. Such interpretations of change typically concentrate on macro-level social processes and are likely to focus on factors explaining individual stability and change, although, as we pointed out earlier, and as we emphasize throughout this monograph, processes of social and individual change are intimately intertwined.

Historical effects are represented by two basic types of processes: *episodic events* and *social change*. The effects of episodic events, such as political crises, natural disasters, economic fluctuations, and other events of short-term duration which affect large numbers of persons in a dramatic way, are emphasized in one type of historical explanation. The cohort, or generation, effect (as we have described it above) can be thought of as a historical effect of this type, but one affecting only the most vulnerable in the population, the young. Social change, the second type of historical effect examined here, refers to a process that is more incremental; such change reflects processes thought to be very gradual and almost undetectable, once population compositional factors are taken into consideration. These effects are the results of macro-level social changes, such as changes in technology and social organization—a gradual set of causal processes bringing about fundamental shifts in the nature of society. In contrast to episodic historical fluctuations, social change is best conceptualized in the context of relatively long periods of time.

With regard to the evolution of aggregate sociopolitical attitudes, which impinge upon individual attitude change, there are at least two theoretical views. One prominent view, referred to earlier, is expressed by Mannheim (1952) and others (e.g., Bengtson, 1989; Carlsson and Karlsson, 1970;

17

Cutler, 1974; Delli Carpini, 1989; Ryder, 1965) as the *cohort replacement* model of social change. This theoretical perspective assumes that individuals are relatively stable once they reach adulthood. When it comes of age, each successive cohort is affected by the sociohistorical events of the time, and this influence is registered in the aggregate social trend. Because of the assumed stability of individual orientations over time, each cohort affects aggregate levels in proportion to their representation in the population. The *succession of cohorts* produces a dynamic *social metabolism* (see Ryder, 1965), which is reflected in gradual social change. Occasionally such conclusions result from the examination of data on several cohorts studied over long periods of time (e.g., Converse, 1976; Glenn and Hefner, 1972; Knoke and Hout, 1974).

A second view of social change is that the succession of cohorts does not necessarily produce such gradual movements of aggregate levels of sociopolitical orientations because it cannot be assumed that persons' attitudes are stable over time. From this perspective, individual attitudes are continually susceptible to change over the life course. People's attitudes are assumed to be responsive to changes in their immediate social and political environments. Technological innovations, changes in economic welfare, and changes in the quality of life are examples of factors that influence various individuals vulnerable to change, regardless of age. In this sense attitudes are *event-graded* rather than *age-graded* (see Featherman and Lerner, 1985).

Interestingly, each of these two perspectives makes different assumptions regarding developmental processes. According to the first perspective, the cohort replacement view of social change, individual sociopolitical orientations which are acquired in young adulthood become resistent to change and persist over time. By contrast, the event-graded view of individual change emphasizes the inherent flexibility of individuals, their continual vulnerability to disturbances in the distribution of orientations over the life course (see Sears, 1981). This view would find the study of political socialization processes in childhood to be tangential to the understanding of sociopolitical orientations in adulthood, since, according to this view, attitudes have very little stability over time. By contrast, the cohort replacement model of social change argues for the inherent stability of basic sociopolitical orientations over the life course. According to this view, differences between birth cohorts in terms of "intellectual, social and political circumstances" (Cutler, 1974:441) produce different attitudinal perspectives.

The processes of gradual social change are frequently studied using data on several cohorts (e.g., Converse, 1976). The analysis of such data is very useful in charting gradual social change by plotting the data on relevant measures for different cohorts over time. Here we follow Converse's (1976)

18

principle that the kinds of "period" effects of broad theoretical interest are not just those which produce dramatic oscillations because of short-term historical events, such as the assassination of a national leader or the fall of the stock market—that is, the types of episodic factors discussed above. Rather, the effects of "period" in the classical three-ply designation of age-period-cohort effects, are most often characterized by gradual shifts in variables of interest.

Of course, as we noted above, the roles of cohort factors and period factors are often difficult to disentangle conceptually. Converse's (1976) cohort analysis of dynamic interpretations of observed empirical relationships involving the direction and strength components of party identification, which we review in some detail below, illustrates the interdependence between historical and cohort/generational explanations. Indeed, Converse's analysis reminds us of the fragility of either type of explanation as a unidimensional theory of individual and social change.

Theoretical Issues in the Analysis of Change

It is likely that all three of the above explanations of individual change in sociopolitical orientations over the life cycle are ultimately valuable to our present purposes. It seems reasonable, for example, that processes of aging produce changes in orientations to life that affect one's sociopolitical attitudes. Similarly, it is reasonable to expect that those social and historical events occuring at a time when one is open to change, especially during late adolescence and early adulthood, when one is establishing an autonomous existence away from one's parents, are also potent influences on individual attitudes. And it is clear that, regardless of age, historical events produce variation in individual attitudes and behavior. Moreover, a number of additional influences on sociopolitical attitudes fall into none of the above categories. These are the factors which Featherman and Lerner (1985) include under the category of event-graded explanations of individual change.

These several explanations raise a number of theoretical issues regarding political socialization which have important implications for the predictions one might make about the trajectories of the sociopolitical attitudes of the Bennington women as somehow typical of issues of human development more generally. As noted above, three of the crucial issues in understanding the development of sociopolitical attitudes over the life course involve (1) the question of when such attitudes are formed, (2) the extent of stability or persistence in attitudes over time, and (3) the patterns of change in levels of stability. In the remainder of this chapter we discuss each of these issues in the context of the research literature that has examined them. We also summarize the currently prevailing view that combines elements of these results into a single theoretical model, which we refer to as the *generational/persistence model*. This model, due to Sears (1981), represents a process in which the younger cohorts are highly vulnerable to the influences of social and political events in their environments, but once the period of vulnerability ceases, attitudes become relatively stable, persisting over the life course. We turn now to a discussion of the three elements of this theoretical model: (1) *the impressionable years hypothesis*, (2) *the persistence thesis*, and (3) *the cohort replacement model of social change*.

The Impressionable Years

When do people develop their sociopolitical orientations, and what are the factors that shape them? Do children simply reproduce their parents' sociopolitical orientations, or are they vulnerable to the influences of social and political factors in their environments? Or, to put it another way, when do the events of the social and political world outside the family of origin begin to play a role in the child's experience? And are the early years of social and political awareness a period of great sensitivity to all of these various influences; that is, might early adulthood be characterized as the *impressionable years*?

The answers to these questions depend in large measure on the type of orientation which is the focus of study. If one focuses on the ideological or partisan nature of political orientations, one typically finds a great deal of similarity between the orientations of parents and children; if one focuses on more specific policy preferences, the correspondence is less strong. The fact that researchers often have focused on different policy issues at different points in historical time makes it difficult to study attitudes toward these issues over a long period in biographical time. It is therefore of somewhat greater interest to study more central values and orientations.

Measures of party identification typically have defined one endpoint on the spectrum of the strength of intergenerational transmission of sociopolitical orientations. For example, in *The American Voter*, Campbell, Converse, Miller, and Stokes (1960:47) report a strong resemblance between the party identification of their respondents and that which respondents report for their parents. This varies somewhat by the level of political activity of parents—it is weaker when neither parent was politically active than when one or both parents were active. The message from this research is relatively clear: "party identification has its origin in the early family years" (1960:48). This is, of course, consistent with the earlier interpretations of Lipset and his colleagues (1954) and Hyman (1959), re-

20

viewed above, regarding the importance of the family (see also Abramson, 1979; Cutler, 1974; Davies, 1965; Easton and Dennis, 1969; Greenstein, 1965; Hess and Torney, 1967; Jennings and Niemi, 1968, 1981; Jennings, 1979; Sears, 1975).

Kinder and Sears (1985:718–19) suggest that young children acquire "primitive partisan attitudes to a number of political and social objects in the early and middle grade-school years." They mention the early development of strong positive affective ties to their own nationality, race, and party; and of negative affect expressed toward objects involving different social categories. Although "cognitively barren," they write, the early commitments of young children are clearly present. Kinder and Sears cite a number of studies that indicate increasing likelihood of endorsement for a political party with increments in age. They conclude that, although young people are definitely capable of political choices, their commitment may be relatively weak, and "it is quite possible that these adolescent attitudes are potentially highly vulnerable to change" (1985:719).

The work of Sears and his colleagues is very helpful in clarifying the nature of sociopolitical orientations early in the life cycle. Sears's (1975) earlier work indicates that younger children are much more positive toward the various symbols of party identification than are older children. As children begin to develop partisan identifications, their acquisition of negative evaluations of objects in the sociopolitical environments increases (Kinder and Sears, 1985:719). As we note throughout this monograph, the predominant view of sociopolitical development over the life cycle assumes a particular vulnerability to the influences of the social environment during the early years, culminating in late adolescence and early adulthood. This model, referred to as the *generational/persistence model*, assumes that a period in the life cycle exists in which the individual is particularly vulnerable to attitude formation and change. This period we refer to as the *impressionable years*.

The extensiveness of this vulnerability during this early period in the life cycle is less clear. There is a great deal of speculation in the literature reviewed in the discussion above suggesting that vulnerability exists at least into late adolescence. It seems likely that, although individual differences definitely exist, the openness to attitude formation and/or change persists even into early adulthood, that is, into the early twenties. Newcomb's Bennington research clearly supports such a perspective. Sears's model (1981), which we review in somewhat greater detail subsequently, also suggests a period of relative stability following this period of vulnerability. Prior to a review of this generational/persistence model, however, let us turn to a discussion of the theoretical question of persistence.

The Persistence Thesis

Regardless of when sociopolitical orientations are formed in biographical time, there is the additional question of the stability of these orientations once they are developed. One view, reflected in a substantial amount of literature on political socialization, is that sociopolitical orientations are quite stable over the adult years. There is considerable support for the idea that sociopolitical orientations are still quite malleable into late adolescence and early adulthood (e.g., Jennings and Niemi, 1978, 1981). But, according to the *persistence thesis*, there is a point at which orientations gain in strength and become relatively stable thereafter (Glenn, 1980). Campbell and his colleagues (1960:48), for example, suggest that partisanship is relatively stable.[15] Converse (1964, 1970), on the other hand, shows that responses to policy issues often appear to be quite unstable.

As Sears (1983:89–90) indicates in reviewing the question of the temporal persistence of orientations over the life cycle, it is important to specify the particular orientations of interest. Responses related to dimensions which are more *ideological* in nature, and closer to what Sears (1983:83) refers to as *symbolic predispositions*, may be more highly stable over time, whereas attitudes on issues that are less tied to these ideological dimensions may not necessarily persist over time. Sears (1983:89–91) reviews several studies, assembling estimates of the relative stability of various measures of sociopolitical orientations, ranging from partisanship to such things as political efficacy and trust, using four-year panel data from the National Election Studies. He finds that the stability of orientations over the life cycle varies depending upon the particular aspect of orientations which is assessed.[16] His review is consistent with the principle suggested here; over short intervals of time (four years) the more ideological responses, such as party identification and liberal/conservative orientation, are highly stable, whereas those responses reflecting policy orientations and diffuse subjective orientations, such as political trust, political efficacy, and political interest, are much less stable over similarly short intervals (see also Abrahamson, 1979; Achen, 1975; Converse, 1964; Converse and Markus, 1979; Markus, 1982a, 1982b).

---

15. The research of Campbell and his colleagues has been criticized because of the use of retrospective questions (see Himmelweit, Jaeger–Biberian, and Stockdale, 1978; Niemi, Katz, and Newman, 1980). We discuss this issue in chapter 6.

16. Many of the studies reviewed by Sears take unreliability of measurement into account, which is critical to any approach to the assessment of stability (see chapter 4). We refer primarily to these studies in our summary of Sears's review. More recent research results (see Alwin and Krosnick, 1991a) suggest that the distinction between "symbolic" and "nonsymbolic" attitudes in terms of their stability over the life course is somewhat overdrawn. In chapter 8 we return briefly to these questions.

The conclusion Sears (1983:93) draws from the existing research is that people "show high levels of persistence after late adolescence and early adulthood." Moreover, the level of persistence seems to increase with age (Sears, 1981). Such a conclusion is consistent with Jennings and Niemi's (1981) longitudinal study of a national sample of high school seniors and their parents from 1965 to 1973. Their study produced higher estimates of attitude stability over eight years among the parental cohorts than among the young in virtually all the measures they considered (Jennings and Niemi, 1974, 1978, 1981). Glenn (1980) comes to the same conclusion, based on his examination of the persistence thesis using available repeated cross-sectional data.

In assessing the validity of the persistence thesis, it is important to keep several potentially complicating factors in mind. First, what is the nature of the sociopolitical orientation on which stability or change is being examined? As indicated in the foregoing, some evidence suggests there may be more persistence for measures of ideological orientation than for policy orientations. Is there a relationship, for example, between the "symbolic" nature of attitudes and life-cycle stabilities? Second, over how long a period of (biographical) time is persistence being assessed? Do more ideological dimensions of orientations persist over longer periods of time than aspects of orientations linked to policy issues? And third, at what stage of life is persistence being examined? Does persistence of a particular type of orientation, defined in terms of a specified length of biographical time, vary as a consequence of different stages of life?

One issue not entirely adequately addressed in the existing literature is the extent to which age and the stability of attitudes are linked. Do attitudes gain in their strength with age; that is, do levels of assessed stability suggest greater persistence with increasing age? Or do they at some point achieve a constant level of stability, remaining relatively persistent regardless of age? Or is there a *lifelong openness to change* in sociopolitical orientations, as suggested by Jennings and Niemi (1978, 1981) and others (e.g., Gergen, 1980; Loott, 1973)? Again, the answer to these questions is likely to depend on the nature of orientations assessed. We will return to this set of issues in subsequent chapters (see also Alwin, 1992).

The Generational/Persistence Model

As indicated in the previous section, substantial evidence exists for the view that the more ideological aspects of sociopolitical orientations, once formed, are relatively stable over the life cycle.[17] When combined with the

17. In chapter 4 we discuss more fully our use of the concept of *ideology* in the present research.

principle of the *impressionable years*, reviewed earlier, the notion of *persistence* subsequent to early periods of vulnerability suggests a process in which the younger cohorts are highly influenced by the social and political events in their environments. Once the period of vulnerability ceases, attitudes become quite stable over time. Sears (1981:87, 1983:93) refers to this set of ideas as the *generational/persistence* model. He argues convincingly that, while the process of political socialization may begin in childhood, the acquisition of important attitudes and orientations does not occur until later. In fact, he cites Newcomb's Bennington study as evidence of the "resocialization" of young people in late adolescence and early adulthood.

Such a generational/persistence model can be formulated in at least three versions. A simple version suggests a period of vulnerability in which young people's attitudes and orientations are changing, but once past a particular period, distributions of attitudes in relevant populations of interest are highly stable. This model is consistent with Ryder's argument that "the potential for change is concentrated in the cohorts of young adults who are old enough to participate directly in the movements impelled by change, but not old enough to have become committed to an occupation, a residence, a family of procreation or a way of life" (1965:848). Once people establish important role commitments through marriage and family formation, the transition to adulthood is considered accomplished, and the potential for attitude change is considerably diminished.

A second, somewhat more complicated version of the model argues that changes in attitudes tend to taper off; attitudes are thought to become more stable but not dramatically so after a period of vulnerability. This we refer to as the *increasing persistence* version of the generational/persistence model. This is consistent with the view expressed by Carlsson and Karlsson that "with increasing age people become less likely to change" (1970: 710), with each cohort reflecting the conditions prevailing during its early formative years. Their results, derived from a Swedish voting study, show a decrease in openness to change after ages 20–24, such declines occuring monotonically throughout the remainder of the life course.

A third version, due to Sears (1981:85–86; see also Kinder and Sears, 1985) is even a bit more complicated. Sears posits the basic principles of the model presented here, that is, a period of vulnerability, followed by increased strengthening of attitudes, eventually leveling off at a relatively high degree of persistence. It is in considering the nature of attitudes among the elderly that this version of the model becomes particularly complex. Specifically, Sears considers a theoretical argument (1981:95) suggesting that the attitudes of the elderly may be particularly resistant to change; however, he presents some empirical results which cause him to conclude the opposite. He reports results from a Gahart and Sears study of the stability of whites' racial attitudes, which uses data from the National

24

Election Study 1972–76 panel. These results indicate that the "stability coefficients" across age cohorts are of increasing magnitudes from age 21 to age 60, but that the magnitude then declines dramatically.[18] Sears (1981:86) results suggest that the period of vulnerability to attitude shifts is not entirely limited to categories of the young, citing a number of studies of event-graded experiences which suggest attitudinal adaptation among persons undergoing changes in old age. This, then, represents a distinct version of the generational/persistence model, one positing a later stage of vulnerability of the attitude structure to change in old age.

SOCIAL CHANGE AND SOCIALPOLITICAL ORIENTATIONS

The preceding set of models reflects current theory and research findings in the area of political socialization and the development of sociopolitical orientations over the life course. The main problem with these models is that they do not specify the way in which processes of social change interact with the life-cycle experiences of individuals. That is, they do not directly address the way in which individual patterns of stability and change might vary as a function of the level of social development or with the occurrence of sociopolitical events. For the most part, these models ignore the sociohistorical context, particularly the role of social change. They refer only to the level of stability of individual attitudes and fail to articulate the link between individual attitudes and aggregate sociopolitical orientations, especially the role of such a link in sociopolitical development over the life course.[19]

18. There are serious difficulties with the form in which Sears (1981) presents these results. Attitude stability is estimated using bivariate correlations of overtime measures, without corrections for measurement error. It is well known that unreliability of measurement attenuates correlations of measures over time (Alwin, 1973, 1989; Heise, 1969; Wheaton, Muthén, and Summers, 1977). Thus, true attitude change is confounded with unreliability of measurement, which is known to be greater among older respondents (see Andrews and Herzog, 1986). In fact, Sears (1981:98) reports reliability coefficients by age cohorts, showing that older respondents generally exhibit lower reporting reliability. Thus, Sears's own analysis of reliability belies the substantive interpretation given to correlational differences among age groups in overtime measures (see Alwin and Krosnick, 1991a, 1991b).

19. Elder (1980) develops an interesting argument regarding social changes in the definition of adolescence. In a society characterized by a lengthy youthful stage in which the individual experiences a great deal of independence and a period of flexibility and openness to change, it may be reasonable to speak about the "impressionable years." On the other hand, in a society characterized by a rather abrupt transition to adulthood, with fewer choices open to the individual, there may not be such a youthful stage during which the individual is preoccupied with the pursuit of the value of autonomy. Elder's argument illustrates recent theorizing regarding the importance of considering the interaction of social change and life course development (see also Elder, Caspi, and Burton, 1988; Neugarten and Datan, 1973).

It is interesting to note in this regard that Newcomb began his first monograph (1943) by discussing the profound social changes sweeping the United States in the 1930s. Newcomb was interested in the extent to which people were influenced by these changes and why. Rejecting what he saw as a simplistic association of socioeconomic status with the willing acceptance of the progressive changes of Roosevelt's New Deal, Newcomb suggested that change and resistance to change were likely to be the result of the pursuit of individual values. He argued that since such values were mediated through the reference groups with which the person identified, the understanding of the individual's environment was crucial to an understanding of individual adaptation and change. Newcomb's view was that social events and processes of social change were interpreted for the individual through the "groups with which an individual has direct contact" (1943:3).

Newcomb's (1943) theoretical insights into the processes by which social change is mediated by the individual's environment have since become incorporated in social psychological perspectives on human development and their linkage to social change. It is now quite commonplace to assume that an individual's *reference groups*, their composition and their associated characteristics, mediate the influences of social and political events of "the times." In other words, it is commonly assumed that the effects of social change are mediated by the environmental interpretation of those changes (e.g., Bronfenbrenner, 1979; Inkeles, 1955). Environmental events are thus often interpreted *for* individuals, especially those seeking such meanings and interpretations, by the groups and individuals with whom they have contact.

THE PRESENT RESEARCH

Just as Newcomb (1943) demonstrated the role of reference groups in his Bennington College studies, and just as Newcomb and his colleagues (1967) again reinforced the importance of this notion in their analysis of change and persistence in the lives of these women through mid-life, we sought through the current research to examine the validity of this thesis over the entire life course. The present research attempts to relate patterns of individual-level change and stability over the biographies of individuals to the contextual influences on those biographies stemming from historical and social circumstances. Thus, we consider the *reference group* as the critical feature of the historical and social environment that transmits these influences to the individual. In so doing, our research deals with *both* persistence and change, and the critical role of the reference group in producing them. The first major objective of our research is to describe processes of change over the individual biographies of the women in our study. The second major objective is to try to account for persistence and change through the application of what we consider to be the two major mechanisms responsible for producing both stability and change: the extent to which individuals are susceptible to change, and the extent of environmental support for change or stability. In the latter category we pay particular attention to reference-group phenomena by examining the role of social support in the development and maintenance of attitudinal perspectives.

Research Strategy

Because of the limitations of our research design, we planned to evaluate the extent of persistence and change in several ways. This approach allowed us to address our research questions from multiple perspectives, therein strengthening our inferences. Alone, any one of our measures of change is limited. Taken together, they will provide a more complete picture of the nature of the changes the Bennington women experienced over the course of their lives. We briefly summarize each of these in the following paragraphs and discuss the outline of the book.

We first gauge the 1984 political attitudes of the former Bennington collegians against those of the American population. Using comparable data from the 1984 National Election Study for various subgroups in the U.S. population, including women of the same age and educational level, we assess the extent to which the Bennington women have remained stable in their political orientations. Also, using the full set of NES data since 1952, we compare our Bennington respondents to relevant subgroups in the population.

Second, we use the restrospective accounts of the individual members of our sample to help assess the extent of change in attitudes over their lives. Several of our questions asked the Bennington women for assessments of their own attitudes and how they might have changed over their lives. These self-assessments of stability and change are interesting in their own right and might also provide an important kind of control for many of the factors left unmeasured in our own statistical analyses.

Third, using correlational techniques, we assess the extent to which the Bennington women have remained the same relative to each other over time. This measure of change and stability is somewhat more sensitive to individual-level attitudes and behavior because it assesses members of our sample relative to their Bennington contemporaries. Even if the Bennington sample changed in one direction or another because of historical or life-cycle events, their relative positions with respect to one another, that is, their correlational stability, should tell us something about the persistence of their attitudes over time.

Outline of the Monograph

In this chapter we have provided a theoretical framework for understanding the developmental processes by which sociopolitical orientations are formed and modified over the entire life course. In the remainder of the monograph we bring a number of diverse sources of information together to articulate an empirical perspective on this developmental life course process. We begin the organization of these various fragments of empirical data by reviewing the central aspects of the original Bennington studies. In chapter 2 we provide a relatively detailed presentation of Newcomb's earliest research at Bennington College. This detailed summary is provided both as a benchmark against which to compare the Bennington women in later life, and as a summary of the early research for those who may not be as familiar with it.

In chapter 3 we review the results of the first follow-up study conducted by Newcomb and his students (Newcomb et al., 1967) in the 1960s. Following the same general outline as in chapter 2, we present and interpret in some detail the findings of the previous research on this cohort of women that resulted in some of the early evidence on life-cycle processes. This review is intended to provide a life course context for this, the third Bennington study, in that it again provides an important benchmark for the attitudes and orientations of the Bennington women during mid-life, a point at which they had already settled into their careers and family lives. In this context, at the end of chapter 3, we present a brief statement of the substantive issues we felt were left unaddressed by the first follow-up study because it was limited in its possible coverage of the later years. These issues, linked to those theoretical matters already reviewed in the present chapter, provided the motivational basis for this, the third study of the Bennington women.

In chapter 4 we describe the design of our 1984 follow-up study of the Bennington cohort, including a detailed presentation of the methods we used to obtain further information on the political orientations of the surviving participants in Newcomb's original research. We summarize the characteristics of our research design; the limitations of this design and the obstacles we faced in implementing a more elaborate design; the sample and response rates; the development of measurement strategies; our procedures of data collection; and our approach to the analysis of change and stability in sociopolitical orientations over the life span. In that chapter we also describe the additional archival data we use from the National Election Study series.

The remainder of the book presents our main findings in five chapters which collectively embody the several research strategies we articulated earlier in this section, plus a final concluding chapter. Chapters 5 through 7 present several analyses relevant to the question of persistence and change in sociopolitical orientations. Our focus in these chapters is on the magnitude of change and persistence, rather than on their causes. We examine a variety of different indications of persistence, including comparisons of the Bennington women with their contemporaries then and now (chap. 5), comparisons of their retrospective attitudes over time (chap. 6), and the analyses of our reinterview data that correlate their responses over time (chap. 7). In chapters 8 and 9 we examine two main sets of explanations of stability and change in attitudes over the life span. Chapter 8 considers the role of personality, or *personological*, explanations of differences in susceptibility to attitude change and stability. Chapter 9 presents an investigation of the role of the social environment in promoting attitude change and stability over the life span—explanations that are more *sociological* in nature. In chapter 9 we analyze the characteristics of the sociopolitical environments of our subjects; and to the extent our measurement of these environments is to be relied upon, we examine the principal environmental construct Newcomb used, the reference group, in its role in promoting both attitude change and stability. This chapter also considers life course factors in the development of sociopolitical orientations, including aspects of the family and work. Finally, chapter 10 concludes our work with a discussion of the major results and a recapitulation of the major themes of interpretation. Chapter 10 also considers the extent to which our findings regarding life course patterns in the stability of attitudes has any degree of "historical durability" in the sense that they reflect more or less uniform patterns of life-cycle stabilities (see Gergen, 1973, 1980). That chapter concludes with a discussion of future directions which research on life-cycle variations in the development of sociopolitical orientations might profitably take.

2

Newcomb's Bennington Studies: The Impressionable Years

INTRODUCTION

In this chapter we review in some depth Newcomb's early work at Bennington College.[1] In this account we try to capture both the findings of his research at Bennington and the theoretical outlines of reference-group interpretations of attitude development and change. We begin with a brief review of the sociohistorical setting in which the research was embedded. We then review the early Bennington research from a perspective of the sociohistorical and political circumstances in which these women lived their lives. In the next chapter we review the 1960s follow-up research conducted by Newcomb, Koenig, Flacks, and Warwick (1967) and the sociohistorical context in which it occurred.

THE SETTING

Established in 1932, Bennington College from its inception was (and is) a self-conscious experiment in liberal education.[2] From the beginning, students were provided considerable social freedom, without ostensible externally imposed social rules. The curriculum was also experimental, with minimal requirements beyond general basic studies, and the faculty fos-

1. Newcomb's early monograph, *Personality and Social Change* (1943), analyzed changes in the sociopolitical orientations of young women attending Bennington during the 1930s and 1940s. Briefer summaries of the original Bennington work were published elsewhere by Newcomb (1946, 1947, 1952).
2. The best and most detailed account of the establishment of Bennington College and of its early years is undoubtedly Brockway's (1981) *Bennington College: In the Beginning*. Barbara Jones's (1946) *Bennington College: The Development of an Educational Idea* gives an interesting account of changes in the educational policies and programs of the College over the first decade of its existence. More recently, Horowitz (1984) provides a brief summary of the College's origins, locating them in the context of other nineteenth- and twentieth-century women's colleges in the United States.

30

tered an intellectual atmosphere based on an intense personal association with students. Located in rural Vermont, the newly founded Bennington campus of the 1930s formed a largely self-contained, geographically isolated, and highly integrated community of young women and their teachers.

Like other women's colleges of the nineteenth and twentieth centuries, Bennington was also an experiment in breaking down the intellectual barriers to women, extending to them the skills and knowledge that American society had previously extended only to men. Horowitz's (1984) *Alma Mater* describes Bennington and other women's colleges as part of the social process of redefining and reinterpreting, generation by generation, the popular conceptions of womanhood in both public and private life. Fashioned after women's colleges of the nineteenth and early twentieth centuries, especially Mount Holyoke, the founders of Bennington strove for a form of higher education, not based on the traditionally masculine subjects of mathematics and the classics, but toward what they defined as the contemporary needs of women, which included art, music, literature, the social sciences, and social problems (Horowitz, 1984:330–31). And although the founders of the college struggled with whether Bennington should be molded in the tradition of existing women's colleges, the early college was distinct in a number of ways. Entrance was based on the entire academic history rather than on specific requirements or examinations (Horowitz, 1984:332). Academic work at Bennington was individualized, in the upper division courses, but its general educational philosophy was experimental in nature.

Bennington as Reference Group

On hand for this social experiment, Newcomb decided to study the processes by which students were socialized into the college community, a community characterized by a unique set of values. Using the concept of the *reference group*, a term coined at that time by Hyman (1942), Newcomb focused on the nature of the student's adjustment to the Bennington environment.[3] He began with the now commonplace social psychological premise that "whatever the manner in which public issues come to be related to individual values, the relationship will be established through the medium of whatever group or groups of which the individual is a member" (Newcomb, 1943:12). Newcomb's work addressed the nature of this

3. As Hyman (1960:384–85) would later clarify, while Newcomb (1943) sought to understand the ways in which individuals were affected by the groups of which they were members, it was not until later that Newcomb summarized and rephrased the results of the Bennington study in terms of the concept of the reference group (see Sherif, 1948, and Newcomb, 1952).

An aerial view of Bennington College, 1935, facing southeast toward the towns of Old Bennington and Bennington. Photo by C. G. Scofield, courtesy of Bennington College.

adaptation to group membership and the factors associated with patterns of value orientations in the college community.

Newcomb identified the most important of these values as those involving independence from parents and the establishment of independent, personal status within the community (1943:4). The most important community for those who became his participants was the Bennington College community. How did the young women attending Bennington pursue the value of achieving their own identity and independence from their parents? And how did the pursuit of these values intersect with the values Newcomb identified as prevalent in the Bennington College community? The college administration and faculty were clearly committed to open intellectual debate and artistic exploration, and the climate of the community was one in which a majority of the faculty themselves willingly accepted the New Deal.

Newcomb recognized the distinctiveness of the setting, noting that "each year some ninety young women, most of them seventeen or eighteen years old, leave homes in which they have led a relatively sheltered existence . . . [and] families whose opinions about contemporary public issues are [with individual exceptions] definitely conservative" (1943:10). There were exceptions, as we discuss more fully below, but for most of the women "both home and school influences have been such that there was little or no necessity for them to come to very definite terms with public issues" (1943:10–11).

One of Bennington's most distinctive characteristics at that time was the commitment of its faculty to progressive ideals of fostering students' personal development and autonomy. While at once achieving personal status within the College and loosening the parental bonds, these young women confronted "unprecedented levels of personal freedom and personal responsibility for their own conduct" (Newcomb, 1943:11). In the words of one of the members of the class of 1936, the College was "very liberating, in the sense of right off the bat our autonomy was recognized by the faculty. . . . They were encouraging us to take a hand in our education. The faculty was so new and young. We were building the college together. They were not set up as authorities."[4]

From such backgrounds and with such preoccupations, these young women came into a setting where community life was intense, and "where there is much more pressure to come to terms with public issues, and where there are people of intelligence and good breeding (upper-class students and faculty, in the main) who do *not* agree with their families and their families' friends regarding contemporary public affairs" (Newcomb, 1943:10–11).

These unique aspects of the Bennington setting at that time made it a particularly valuable "natural" experiment. As noted, the students came primarily from upper-class, conservative family backgrounds, whereas the faculty "was rather young and given to friendly informal relationships with the students . . . [and] almost universally described as liberal concerning then-current public issues" (Newcomb, 1943:8). Reflecting on this period much later, Newcomb recalled that the College's president at the time, Robert Leigh, had been trying to recruit teachers who would be open to educational innovation and "ended up with lots of New Deal types, some even farther left. . . . So while none of us said, 'We have got to make good little liberals out of these gals,' we did say, 'By God, they are going to know how the other half lives'" (Newcomb, quoted in Brockway, 1981:206–7).

It was probably not only in direct contact that members of the faculty provided a liberal orientation, but by example as well. Bennington College historian Thomas Brockway (1981:207) notes that Newcomb himself "did what he could to encourage unionization in town . . . organized a teachers' union at the College against [President] Leigh's wishes . . . [and] from time

4. "The Bennington Girl: Fifty Years Later," *Ann Arbor News*, F1–F2, 27 July 1986.

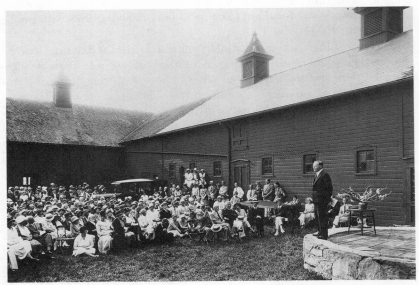

Robert Leigh, president of Bennington College from 1928–1941, at the groundbreaking ceremony, 16 August 1931. Photo courtesy of Bennington College.

to time attempted to influence United States foreign policy, particularly during the Spanish Civil War." In addition, Brockway suggests that Leigh's decision to leave Bennington's presidency was directly related to his feeling that members of the faculty during the late 1930s were turning away from him. With respect to Newcomb in particular, he had two grievances: the previously mentioned organization of a teacher's union and the fact that "he had ignored Leigh's remonstrance against publishing a summary of his study [i.e., the Bennington study] which showed that Bennington students moved leftward politically while in college" (212).

This was the institutional setting in which the original research was undertaken. Young women primarily from privileged and conservative families entered a new college dedicated to educational innovation and employing a faculty largely open to such innovation and concerned to expose their students to the other side of privilege. The wider historical context was no less volatile: severe economic depression, international instability, widespread and intense potential for societal upheaval, and (partly in response to the volatility of the times) fundamental institutional changes. These factors not only gave shape to the particular historical period in which the original Bennington study was conducted; they also helped define the specific social and political issues which were the vehicles Newcomb used to mount his investigation.

34

Table 2.1. Mean PEP Scores by Entering Cohort and Time of Measurement

Class Entered	Fall 1935	Fall 1936	Fall 1937	Spring 1938	Fall 1938	Spring 1939
1932	65.8 (45)					
1933	68.6 (47)	60.1 (27)				
1934	66.5 (74)	62.3 (37)	58.9 (27)	59.9 (37)		
1935	74.5 (88)	68.5 (55)	64.1 (45)	63.7 (50)	63.2 (40)	62.7 (45)
1936		75.8 (69)	72.3 (72)	69.1 (85)	68.4 (37)	68.5 (58)
1937			71.9 (64)	70.6 (86)	69.5 (40)	70.0 (62)
1938					75.9 (55)	72.8 (73)

Source: Newcomb, 1943:23.

THE EARLY BENNINGTON RESEARCH

In the fall of 1935, Newcomb began to collect the data for this first study. The central findings of Newcomb's research were expressed in terms of changes in levels of *progressivism*, as measured by his *Political and Economic Progressivism* scale (the *PEP* scale). The items of this scale originated with Stagner (1936), who fashioned them as reflecting what was the essence of attitudes on the key political issues of the time.[5] To Newcomb, these items dealt with issues "which were then alive in the Bennington community, and bid fair to continue so . . . issues made prominent by the New Deal administration, then in its first term of office" (1943:20). The PEP scale primarily assessed attitudes toward public relief, the role of labor unions, and the legitimacy of private and corporate wealth. The PEP score was a 26-item, Likert-type measure of attitudes toward these political-economic public issues (see Newcomb, 1943:178–79; Newcomb et al., 1967:242–45).

In addition to these self-administered questionnaires, Newcomb used written reports on individual students prepared by different College offices, and interviews conducted with individual students.[6] All students enrolled in the fall term, 1935, received a letter explaining the research, and later they completed a questionnaire which included the PEP scale. Then, in each of the succeeding three fall terms (of 1936, 1937, and 1938) and in the spring of 1938 and 1939, each enrolled student received a similar

5. The items in the PEP scale are reproduced in appendix A.

6. In addition to the PEP scale, the questionnaires included several other scales, but only two were repeated more than twice. The first was a scale of international attitudes, the other a scale of attitudes toward Loyalist Spain. Other scales dealt with more specific issues of the time (e.g., the Spanish civil war, FDR's Supreme Court proposals, and the Munich settlement). Sociometric questions were also included, but the responses to those questions, and to the questionnaire scales other than PEP, were not useful, nor in most cases available for our present purposes (see chapter 4).

The entire student body and faculty posed as Bennington College opened in September 1932. Photo courtesy of Bennington College.

reminder letter and a questionnaire. Table 2.1 presents the dates on which questionnaires including the PEP scale were collected from each of the classes, the numbers of students from whom data were obtained at each point in time (in parenthesis), and the mean PEP scale scores. High scores on the PEP scale reflect greater sociopolitical conservatism.

Aggregate Change in PEP Scores

Newcomb (1943) documented systematic and meaningful changes of attitudes during the four years at Bennington for the average young woman participating in his research. These attitudes generally moved away from those of their parents and toward the "liberal" orientation of the college environment. He showed that, for most cohorts, the longer the stay at Bennington, the more liberal the score on his principal measure of political orientation, the PEP scale. On the basis of his other measures, he noted that the main shift was in attitudes on domestic issues (e.g., the CIO, the Supreme Court, the New Deal) rather than on international issues (e.g., the Soviet Union, the Munich settlement, and American isolationism) (1943:205). One exception to this pattern was the shift in attitudes toward Loyalist Spain, which we discuss at greater length below.

Newcomb's data, presented in table 2.1, suggest aggregate change in PEP scores both cross-sectionally and longitudinally. At any one point in time (and with minor exceptions), mean scores for younger students (freshman and sophomores) are higher, that is, more conservative, than mean

Table 2.2. Mean PEP Scores by Class and Year

Class	Fall 1935	Fall 1936	Fall 1937	Fall 1938	Total
Freshman	74.5	75.8	71.9	75.9	74.2
	(88)	(69)	(64)	(55)	(276)
Sophomore	66.5	58.5	72.3	69.5	69.4
	(74)	(55)	(72)	(40)	(241)
Junior	68.5	62.3	64.1	68.4	65.9
	(47)	(37)	(45)	(37)	(166)
Senior	68.5	60.1	58.9	63.2	62.4
	(45)	(27)	(27)	(40)	(155)
Total	68.1	67.4	66.7	68.7	
	(254)	(188)	(208)	(172)	

Source: Newcomb, 1943:23.

scores for older students (juniors and seniors). And scores for any one class generally become markedly less conservative over historical time.[7]

Newcomb also combined the PEP scores for all freshman, all sophomores, and so forth, regardless of the date of their initial enrollment. These results, shown in table 2.2, depict these same data another way, demonstrating the relative conservatism of younger as opposed to older students. Newcomb concluded that, at least in terms of aggregate scores, there was evidence of substantial and significant change from the first to the fourth year of attendance at Bennington in the direction of increasing liberalism.

One of the methodological criticisms often leveled at the interpretation Newcomb gave the Bennington results is that selection processes instead of processes of socialization were at work. It could have been that students who did not feel at ease in the liberal Bennington climate left the College for settings in which there was less pressure to adopt the predominant orientation of the college community.[8] Or, it could be that more conservative students, familiar with Newcomb's personal views, avoided continued participation in the study, thus producing a bias toward greater progressivism in the estimated means for older cohorts at any given time.[9] There was

7. Slightly weaker effects, as registered in this table, are seen for the cohorts entering in 1937 and 1938, but it is important to note that these two cohorts did not make it to the upper classes during the time period of the study.

8. See Campbell and Stanley (1963) for a discussion of selection factors as threats to the internal validity of the type of research design employed by Newcomb.

9. On the hypothesis that students not comfortable with the sociopolitical climate at Bennington left, Brockway (1981:207–9) quotes a number of the Bennington women, commenting in essence on the possibility of selection bias. The most prevalent view was that, while some women did not thrive in the Bennington environment, their numbers were few, and it was doubted that the Bennington norms were the reason. Brockway cautions, however,

The senior class procession at Bennington College's first commencement, 6 June 1936. Photo by Rotzel, courtesy of Bennington College.

clearly attrition from the student ranks, as seen in the diminishing numbers of cases on which the average PEP score was based for each cohort over time. Both of these alternative explanations are plausible, and neither can be sufficiently ruled out to clarify the true nature of the processes generating these data.

In anticipation of the selection argument, Newcomb (1943:199–200) presented mean PEP scores for the continuing groups within each of the four classes entering 1933 through 1936. These results, shown in table 2.3, are very similar to those given in table 2.1, and since they are based on the same people across the four years, Newcomb was led to conclude "that the year-to-year changes appearing in [this] table cannot be attributed to the fact that different subjects are involved in the year-to-year

that the sampling of opinion regarding this issue was "conspicuously lacking in testimony from dropouts who might well have opposite views" (1981:209).

Table 2.3. Mean PEP Scores for Individuals in Four
Classes Who Responded on All Occasions

Class Entered	N	1935	1936	1937	Spring 1938
1933	26	68.0	60.0		
		(68.6)	(60.1)		
1934	21	62.1	59.9	57.4	58.7
		(66.5)	(62.3)	(58.9)	(59.9)
1935	35	73.7	68.0	63.3	64.3
		(74.5)	(68.5)	(64.1)	(63.7)
1936	51		73.9	70.8	67.5
			(75.8)	(72.3)	(69.1)

Source: Newcomb, 1943:199.

Note: Corresponding mean scores, taken from table
2.1, representing all subjects, appear in parentheses
beneath each score in this table for purposes of ready
comparison.

comparisons" (Newcomb, 1943:199). Further comparison of those who
dropped out of the study, either because of nonresponse or because they
left Bennington, revealed differences that were by and large negligible and
not likely to distort the results (Newcomb, 1943:201).

Divergence from Parental Orientations

In addition to comparing PEP scores over time and among cohorts in a
given year, Newcomb compared political preferences of the Bennington
women with those of their parents, in order to show the divergence of the
attitudes of students away from their parents' attitudes. In the fall of 1936
students were asked their preferences among the five presidential candidates. They were also asked which candidate each of their parents would
choose. Table 2.4 presents these results.[10] These data show that in the
aggregate the freshman students were quite similar to their parents, sophomores were somewhat divergent from the parents, and the preferences of
the juniors and seniors were dramatically different from those of their parents. In Newcomb's words: "A gradual process of political divergence from
parents is here revealed" (1943:28).

Newcomb presented no bivariate data to substantiate this claim in *Personality and Social Change*, and it has become a matter of some serious

10. In the 1936 election, Landon and Roosevelt were the Republican and Democratic candidates, respectively. Thomas was the Socialist candidate, and Browder was the Communist
candidate. Lemke, the fifth candidate, received no support among the students.

Theodore Newcomb's psychology class, McCullough House living room, 9 June 1935. Photo by C. G. Scofield, courtesy of Bennington College.

speculation. For example, at least one student at Bennington during those times has come forward with the observation that, while the atmosphere at Bennington was one that promoted independence and self-direction, many students actually came from liberal backgrounds, which took many of the tenets of the New Deal for granted. For these women, Bennington may have been "liberating" in terms of a sense of self, but little divergence from the parental generation was actually experienced.[11]

Such observations raise the question of whether there were such sharp parent-child cleavages in sociopolitical questions for all students. Newcomb (1943) presented only the univariate distributions of parents and children, and as Hyman (1959:90 n. 18) correctly observed, little can be deduced from patterns of divergence over time. Some of these data can be reconstructed, although any conclusions one might draw from such an exercise are not free of assumptions. In any event, we can arrive at

11. See "The Bennington Girl: Fifty Years Later," *Ann Arbor News*, F1–F2, 27 July 1986.

Table 2.4. Percent Preference for Presidential Candidates: Fall 1936, Bennington Students and Parents, as Reported by Students

Candidate	Freshmen		Sophomores		Juniors–Seniors	
	Students	Parents	Students	Parents	Students	Parents
Landon	62	66	43	69	15	60
Roosevelt	29	26	43	22	54	35
Thomas-Browder	9	7	15	8	30	4
n	52		40		52	

Source: Newcomb, 1943:28.

a speculative basis for Newcomb's conclusion with regard to divergence from parental orientations. We now turn to this analysis.

On the basis of responses to inquiries made in the 1960s, it is possible to reconstruct some information regarding the bivariate relationships between the political preferences of the Bennington students and their parents in the 1930s and 1940s during the college years. These relationships are shown in tables 2.5 and 2.6. These tables give the cross-tabulation of respondent and parent party preference in 1936 (panel A of table 2.5 for fathers and of table 2.6 for mothers), and the cross-tabulation of respondent's 1940 political preference with parent party preference in 1936 (panel B of tables 2.5 and 2.6 for fathers and mothers, respectively).[12]

These tables present a very interesting picture regarding the pattern of relationship between the political preferences of the Bennington women and their parents. First, about 75 percent of the Bennington women originated in families with some Republican identification. About 60 percent of these women retained this Republican or conservative orientation; roughly 30 percent identified with the Democratic party; and slightly more than 10 percent preferred socialist or communist candidates. At the same time, nearly 90 percent of those women from liberal (Democrat or Socialist) backgrounds retained this identity—Bennington simply reinforced this orientation.

The relationship identified here is generally the same whether we look at mother's or father's political preference, and with respect to either measure of the student's political orientation—either 1936 party preference or 1940 candidate preference (obtained retrospectively in the 1960s). Unfortunately, we have no direct purchase on the relationship that presumably existed at entry to college, but it is possible to arrive at a reasonable esti-

12. The data on parents and students in these analyses were collected in the 1960s from respondents in both the interview and mailed-questionnaire samples.

Table 2.5. Relationship of Father-Child Political Preference

Panel A	Student's Party Identification, 1936		
Father's Political Preference, 1936	Democrat/ Socialist	Republican	Total
Democrat/Socialist	93.1% (54)	6.9% (4)	100% (58)
Republican	40.5% (60)	59.5% (88)	100% (148)
Total	55.3% (114)	44.7% (92)	100% (206)

Panel B	Student's Party Identification, 1940		
Father's Political Preference, 1936	Liberal	Conservative	Total
Democrat/Socialist	88.4% (38)	11.6% (5)	100% (43)
Republican	48.4% (45)	51.6% (48)	100% (93)
Total	61.0% (83)	39.0% (53)	100% (136)

A: $df = 1, \chi^2 = 46.58\ p = .000$
B: $df = 1, \chi^2 = 19.79\ p = .000$

Table 2.6. Relationship of Mother-Child Political Preference

Panel A	Student's Party Identification, 1936		
Mother's Political Preference, 1936	Democrat/ Socialist	Republican	Total
Democrat/Socialist	92.8% (64)	7.2% (5)	100% (69)
Republican	39.9% (59)	60.1% (89)	100% (148)
Total	56.7% (123)	43.3% (94)	100% (217)

Panel B	Student's Party Identification, 1940		
Mother's Political Preference, 1936	Liberal	Conservative	Total
Democrat/Socialist	82.4% (42)	17.6% (9)	100% (51)
Republican	52.1% (45)	47.9% (49)	100% (94)
Total	60.0% (87)	40.0% (58)	100% (145)

A: $df = 1, \chi^2 = 53.61\ p = .000$
B: $df = 1, \chi^2 = 16.35\ p = .000$

Table 2.7. Hypothetical Bivariate Relationship between
Student and Parent Party Preferences at the
Time of Entry to College

| | Student Political Preference | | |
Parent	Liberal	Conservative	Total
Liberal	90%	10%	100%
	(45)	(5)	(50)
Conservative	23%	77%	100%
	(35)	(115)	(150)
Total	40%	60%	100%
	(80)	(120)	(200)

mate of what this relationship would have been like, given the other data we have.

We carried out some speculative exercises regarding the relationship between student and parent political preferences at the time of entry to college. For example, one can inquire about what relationships would exist in these tables if the marginal distributions of political preference for students were constrained to reflect those marginals reported by Newcomb for freshmen students in 1936 (1943:28). Such marginals are compatible with the distribution of party preferences for mothers and fathers, which is about 60 percent conservative and 40 percent liberal. If we constrain the student marginals to have this pattern, and we fix the distribution of students from liberal backgrounds, then we find a pattern something like that given in table 2.7. This result suggests that there may have been substantial movement away from parental political orientations, principally for those from conservative backgrounds.

By this accounting, when students from a liberal background entered Bennington, some 90 percent of them remained liberal. Similarly, some 77 percent of students from a conservative background were conservative at the time of entry to Bennington. Putting these observations together with the actual relationships (given in tables 2.5 and 2.6) observed between students and their parents in the later years of college, the distribution of political orientations for those entering with liberal orientations had not changed, but the distribution for those from conservative backgrounds had been dramatically altered. Nearly 20 percent of those from conservative backgrounds had shifted to the liberal point of view.

Further Evidence

In order to verify further the nature of these influences, Newcomb also compared the PEP scores of Bennington students and the differences in those scores among entering classes to similar responses collected at reasonably similar colleges. Data collected in 1938 from 322 Williams College students in history, government, and economics classes were compared with the scores of Bennington social studies majors that same year. In 1939 data were collected from 252 Skidmore College students in classes in psychology, philosophy, and English and were compared with the scores of Bennington students obtained the same year. These results are given in table 2.8. For both comparisons, the mean PEP scores of Bennington students of every class year were lower than the corresponding scores at Williams and Skidmore. In addition, the freshmen-to-senior differences, in the direction of increased liberalism, were greater at Bennington than at either Williams or Skidmore. Thus it appears that, while the transition Newcomb witnessed at Bennington occurs with some consistency across other environments, there is little question that Bennington's influence was somewhat more pronounced.

One could argue that the experiences of the Bennington women in the 1930s and 1940s were not all that unique, but were in fact widespread, well beyond the confines of a single women's college in Vermont. There was widespread opposition to the nationalist government in Spain, and Roosevelt's New Deal was quite popular among the young (Allen, 1939). Although it has never been investigated as a plausible alternative explanation to the Bennington findings, the trends observed over time may not have been unique to the Bennington environment. Instead such patterns might have been widespread among college students. We pursue this possibility to a greater extent in chapter 5.

In any event, results concerning attitudes on the Spanish civil war, which began in the summer of 1936, also support Newcomb's (1943:25–26) hypothesis of socialization into the college community and further clarify the nature of the effect. This issue was unique, according to Newcomb (1943:26), because it came up suddenly. Women in the junior and senior years were more liberal on this subject than were first- and second-year students, despite the fact that they had not been exposed to discussion of these issues for longer periods of time, the opposite of which may have been true for some of his other measures. He concluded that

> the only possible conclusion to be drawn is that other already existing attitudes and allegiances were responsible for the almost immediate differentiation between the upper and lower classes [26] [and that]. . . . it seems necessary to

Table 2.8. Mean PEP Scores of Williams, Skidmore, and Bennington Students

Class	Williams 1938		Bennington 1938		Skidmore 1939		Bennington 1939	
	N	$\overline{X}$	N	$\overline{X}$	N	$\overline{X}$	N	$\overline{X}$
Freshmen	95	76.1	23	66.1	83	79.9	73	72.8
Sophomores	114	69.4	24	68.1	53	78.1	62	70.0
Juniors	74	70.7	19	61.1	70	77.0	58	68.5
Seniors	36	71.2	12	55.0	46	74.1	45	62.7

Source: Newcomb, 1943:31.

explain this in terms of loyalties built up to institutions, persons, or ideologies, which gave direction almost immediately to new issues not previously subsumed under the particular loyalty involved. (147–48)

Newcomb (1943:39–40) further demonstrated that the amount of information the student had about the Spanish civil war was predictive of her attitude. He obtained data on this issue at Williams College, as well as Bennington, finding that at both colleges the upper classes (juniors and seniors) were better informed on the issue.[13] Those Williams College students in social studies classes were highly informed about the issue; however, all students at Bennington seem to have been exposed to it. His description of Bennington bears this out:

Lectures, discussions, movies, and money-raising campaigns for Loyalist Spain were repeatedly held. More than enough money was raised to purchase an ambulance. Only a tiny minority were opposed to the Loyalists, and the favorable attitudes of many students were extreme. Both information and attitudes were of course influenced by all of these activities, but whatever their relationship, the general conclusion seems unavoidable that interest in the issue was a community-shared one at Bennington and scarcely at all so at Williams.

The students' information regarding this political issue, then, was almost entirely defined by the community norms, strongly suggesting a link between the sociopolitical environment and individual orientations.

Newcomb (1946) later returned to an analysis of attitude shifts regarding the Spanish civil war in terms of the informational environment, comparing both the Bennington and Williams data with an environment in which a pro-Nationalist climate existed, Catholic University. His analysis of this issue revealed further support for the thesis that the local climate of opinion was dynamically linked to attitude change, regardless of direction.

13. Eighty-two percent of the Bennington women ($n = 174$) agreed with the statement "I hope the Loyalists win the war," compared to 64 percent of the Williams students ($n = 312$).

45

Individual Change

In order to establish further the strength of Bennington's influence on its students, Newcomb (1943:29) also examined levels of change in individuals' attitudes over time. To investigate this question, he correlated PEP scores obtained by the same individuals at various time intervals for all participants in the study who remained in college for two or more years. The mean correlation for an interval as short as 7 months was .86; for an interval of 1 year it was .70; for 2 years, it was .60; and for 3½ years, it was .42 (1943:29). Thus, the longer students remained at Bennington, the more likely their attitudes (as assessed by the PEP) were to change, and the lower were the correlations over longer time periods.

In addition, Newcomb divided the PEP scores of participants in the entering classes of 1935 and 1936 (the only classes for which both freshman and junior or senior data were available) into five groups, from least to most conservative. He concluded as follows: "Each of the five groupings in both classes maintains the same relative standing in the junior or senior year that it had in the freshman year" (1943:29–30).

Newcomb (1943:74–80) also investigated the extent of attitude stability by obtaining mail questionnaire responses from women after they had left Bennington. The relation between PEP score when leaving college and that obtained later was substantial, although rather than observing regression to the mean for the extreme scores, he concluded from these analyses that those with low PEP scores changed the least with time, whereas those with intermediate scores actually changed the most.

PERSONALITY AND SOCIAL STRUCTURE

Having established the systematic behavior of attitudes in several successive cohorts, Newcomb then set out to understand how personality interacted with social structure in encouraging these changes. Many of the students at Bennington between 1935 and 1939 had changed, and changed in the direction of accepting policies associated with the New Deal. Thus, consistent with the theoretical premises he had advanced, the liberalizing effect of Bennington seemed to operate through the normative influences of their predominant reference group, the Bennington College faculty and student community.

Values and Interests

Newcomb (1943:38–46) first examined the role of *values and interests* in attempting to account for his findings. He reasoned that students in a few of the academic divisions of the College might be responsible for the effects he observed, and he thought that students in the social sciences in particular might be predisposed to attitude change. After a detailed analysis of this question, he concluded that there were few differences in these processes between academic divisions; rather, the processes at work were community-wide. He did, however, conclude that PEP scores between academic divisions—differences mainly between literature and the social sciences versus science and music—tended to diverge over time. This he deduced by comparing the divisional differences over classes; the differences were higher among juniors and seniors than among freshmen and sophomores.

Newcomb also explored this issue in other ways. He used the Allport-Vernon scale of values, a measure of personal interests and values which was in wide use at that time (see Allport and Vernon, 1931), to learn more about those students who were "most and least affected" by the Bennington College community influence on attitudes (1943:41–42). Among 40 members of the 1939 graduating class, he found that theoretical and aesthetic values were unusually high and that political and religious values were especially low.[14]

Asking whether these value scores were linked to attitudes, Newcomb was somewhat surprised to find that those low on the PEP scale (that is, more liberal in political attitudes) were higher in theoretical and aesthetic values, and those with higher scores on the PEP (more conservative in attitudes) were those highest in economic and political values. As assessed by this research instrument, economic values reflect an interest in what is practical and useful, and political values refer to an interest in power. From these results he concluded that political interests and orientations were related to those whose values reflected an interest in power and leadership, rather than those concerned with theory and harmony in life. He asserted: "It may sound perverse that those highest in these [economic and political] values are more conservative and less concerned about public affairs in the politico-economic arena, but such is the fact" (1943:42). What he found most interesting in relation to this, which would shape his later understanding of the social structural influences at Bennington, was that many

---

14. The "political" values referred to here have to do with an interest in *power* rather than an interest in politico-economic affairs. This scale is discussed in greater detail in chapter 3.

of those more successful in achieving leadership positions at Bennington were those who placed less value on power.

It was in social values (human relationships and love, interest in human beings for their own sake) that those high and low on his PEP scale were the most different. He considered this "convincing testimony to his general thesis that nonconservative social attitudes are developed at Bennington primarily by those who are both capable and desirous of cordial relations with their fellow community members" (1943:43). From these findings he then turned to an examination of the critical elements in the community of faculty and students.

The Informational Environment

It was in his consideration of the role of interests and values in attitude change that Newcomb (1943:39–40) discovered the relationship between political interests and information. We have already alluded to Newcomb's measurement of class differences in attitudes toward the civil war in Spain. It was in that context that he discovered that the informational environment "tends to support whatever attitude is held." He showed that at Bennington students in social studies classes were not that different from students with other majors. On the other hand, students in social studies classes at Williams College were distinctively less conservative than other Williams students. He concluded, as we noted above, that the Spanish civil war was, at Bennington, "an affair of the community, rather than of courses pursued."

The key elements Newcomb identified as contributing to the impact of the informational environment of the Bennington women's attitudes were two:

1. The closely integrated nature of the college community.
2. The relatively homogenous faculty with predominantly nonconservative social attitudes.

These factors contributed to the uniformity and intensity of experience within the Bennington community.

Although Hyman must be credited with originating the concept of the reference group, Newcomb's early Bennington work gave substantial consideration to the role of the college community as a "frame of reference." He argued that the extent to which a person will be influenced by the community-as-a-whole depends upon "her relationship to it," and "how she looks at it" (1943:45). Using a modified version of his PEP scale, he showed that Bennington seniors viewed first-year students as more conservative, themselves as more liberal, and the faculty as most liberal of all; and

Table 2.9. Mean PEP Scores of Former Students, Classified According to Time Spent in College and since College

Years since College	3–4 Years in College			1–2 Years in College			Total	
	N	Last Score in College	1939	N	Last Score in College	1939	Last Score	1939
3	42	66.7	68.0	26	71.3	77.5	68.4	71.6
2	39	62.1	60.5	8	68.3	66.1	63.1	61.5
1	43	59.2	57.2	27	69.2	71.1	63.0	62.6
Total	124	62.6	61.9	61	70.0	76.4	65.1	65.6

Source: Newcomb, 1943:77.

Note: Scores obtained at last possible opportunity; all scores included for each group, except in *total* column, were obtained at the same time.

he showed that Bennington first-year students viewed themselves as more conservative, the juniors and seniors as more liberal, and the faculty as most liberal. However, the differences observed by seniors were greater, and first-year students underestimated the differences between classes and between students and faculty. In short, seniors overestimated the actual class differences and freshmen underestimated them. In contrast to this, students at Skidmore did not see very many differences in sociopolitical orientations by class, and they perceived students and faculty to be roughly equivalent.

Thus, the Bennington College community seemed distinctive. In Newcomb's words:

> Seniors do respond less conservatively than freshmen at Skidmore, but apparently the fact is not advertised. It seems to be overadvertised at Bennington. The longer one remains at Bennington the more one is convinced of the magnitude of this difference. At both institutions the degree and the direction of error in estimated attitudes provides a useful indicator, if not an accurate measure, of community influences at work in modifying those attitudes. . . . [These data] afford us certain glimpses into the community, a picture of attitude toward attitudes, as it were. (1943:52–53)

He observed a pull of attitudes in the direction of the juniors and seniors, who embodied more liberal values and orientations, and who also held positions of status and leadership in the community. These observations, then, formed the basis for Newcomb's further investigation of the status and leadership structure at Bennington and the role of reputation in these aspects of the community norms and standards.

To further establish this last point, Newcomb sent a questionnaire by mail to all students who, since the fall of 1935, had participated in the earlier Bennington research, and who were no longer in college. Table 2.9

presents the relationship of PEP scores upon leaving college with length of time at Bennington (1–2 vs. 3–4 years). This table shows that for all categories of time since leaving Bennington, those who spent more time at Bennington were less conservative, as measured by the PEP score. We return to this issue in chapter 7.

Personal Status and Community Reputation

The study of individual interrelations within the community, Newcomb argued, was needed in order to understand the nature and extent of attitude change at Bennington. Changes in attitudes had to be "mediated by individuals." He predicted that in the Bennington community, upper-class, prestige-endowed women would be characterized by less conservative social attitudes (1943:54).

Half-way into his study, Newcomb indicates, he discovered the importance of *personal status* for understanding the influences on attitudes (1943:54). He developed the instrumentation for a sociometric study of "community prestige," and in 1938 and 1939 he administered this to the Bennington students. He classified students according to their popularity as "worthy representatives" of the College, relating this to their PEP scores. These data are given in table 2.10. Reputational status was clearly related to sociopolitical orientations: the most popular students in all classes had distinctively lower scores on the PEP scale. Further, students chosen more frequently in a standard sociometric friendship question were more likely to have lower PEP scores (1943:60–61, 72–73).

Newcomb's fascination with the dynamics of social interaction led him to ask why certain students seemed impelled toward leadership positions, and why their social attitudes seemed to become less conservative as a result. He was convinced that it was social influence that brought about this change. The more certain students "were impelled, with varying degrees of awareness, toward varying degrees of leadership . . . the more it is necessary for them to fit in to what they believe to be the college pattern" (1943:59). Thus, motivated by success in the competition for status and leadership, women adapted the attitudes of the Bennington community, which were (correctly) perceived to be liberal in orientation. Moreover, he found those students with less conservative attitudes to represent a somewhat more cohesive friendship group than those with more conservative attitudes (1943:62–64).[15]

15. If the nonconservative students were more cohesive and in charge, it may have been difficult for a conservatively oriented student to feel integrated into the college community. Such students may have chosen to leave Bennington for another, more compatible environ-

Table 2.10. Mean PEP Scores, Classified According to Frequency of Being Chosen as Representative

Frequency of Choice	Freshmen		Sophomores		Juniors–Seniors		Entire College	
	N	Mean	N	Mean	N	Mean	N	Mean
1938								
40–89	—	—	3	60.3	5	50.4	8	54.1
12–39	—	—	5	65.6	15	57.6	20	59.7
5–11	—	—	5	65.3	18	62.2	23	62.7
2–4	10	64.6	18	68.6	19	61.6	47	65.3
1	12	63.4	17	68.6	15	62.1	44	65.0
0	61	72.8	39	71.3	14	69.0	114	71.7
Total	83	70.5	87	69.2	86	61.5	256	67.1
1939								
40–90	—	—	—	—	6	59.5	6	59.5
12–39	—	—	2	48.0	16	63.2	18	61.5
5–11	2	60.5	4	57.2	15	63.8	21	62.4
2–4	8	69.5	2	74.5	16	64.4	26	66.7
1	10	71.0	20	68.9	16	69.9	45	69.3
0	53	74.1	58	72.8	34	70.0	145	72.5
Total	73	72.8	86	70.6	103	66.0	261	69.5

Source: Newcomb, 1943:55.

Personality Factors

Newcomb believed that personality interacts with social change through the medium of social structure. Thus he felt compelled to demonstrate, not only that social norms influenced the development of social attitudes, but that some students were more susceptible to the influence of community reference groups and some women were more capable of shielding prior attitudes from change. Using a measurement technique he called the Guess-Who task, a device for obtaining personality ratings for individuals relying on a subset of 24 students as "expert" raters, Newcomb assessed the extent to which each student in each of several classes possessed each of 28 different personality characteristics (1943: appendix A, 183–85).

Although he granted certain weaknesses of the method, he was able to extract some plausible hypotheses regarding the types of people most likely to be influenced by the norms of the Bennington community. Through this approach he found that those individuals who were "most resistant to com-

___

ment. This, of course, raises again the question of whether Newcomb's effects were due to socialization or selection. While Newcomb's results are somewhat helpful in ruling out the hypothesis of selection, the issue is unfortunately not easily settled with the data at hand.

munity codes" and to "faculty authority" had the highest PEP scores, and those rated as "most influenced by faculty authority" tended to have lower PEP scores (1943:72).

These observations, while supportive of Newcomb's general thesis, did not specify which personality traits made some individuals more vulnerable to community influence, and because of the limitations of his measures, he reserved this question primarily for speculation. In his final chapters he argued that those who were more susceptible to change were those who were relatively more independent of their parents, those with a high sense of personal adequacy, and those whose personalities were "supple enough to permit modification in the means of achieving social ends." In chapter 8 we return to the issue of personality factors and their role in promoting or discouraging individual change.

SUMMARY

In summary, the key elements Newcomb identified as influential aspects of social structure in affecting the extent of attitude change among his subjects were the *informational environment* of the community and the *status structure* embedded in that environment. The closely integrated nature of the college community and the relatively homogenous faculty with predominantly nonconservative social and political attitudes were two of the main aspects of the informational environment encountered by the Bennington women as they experienced a changing and expanding environment. Whatever the uniformity and intensity of experience within the Bennington community, Newcomb concluded that the longer a person's stay at Bennington, the more likely it was that she would be exposed to and influenced by this informational environment.

3

Persistence and Change:
The Bennington Women at Mid-Life

INTRODUCTION

The results obtained in Newcomb's (1943) original Bennington study became widely known and contributed to the early literatures on college impact, attitude development and change, and the relationship between life stage and political orientation. But because it was a study of a single cohort that was in many ways unique, it was limited in its ability to provide solid evidence on many of the questions it posed. Perhaps the most central of the questions concerned the importance of the changes in individuals' attitudes that Bennington seemed to produce in its students of the 1930s. Despite the degree to which the political attitudes of these young women were susceptible to change and rooted in the new community norms of Bennington, Newcomb felt at the time he published his findings that new attitudes in most cases acquired considerable autonomy as values and meanings were reorganized in line with them. Thus, new attitudes should gain stability and persist over time.

Were these changes permanent, or were they simply the result of immersion in a relatively closed and historically specific environment? If permanent, these newly formed cognitive structures would be expected to persist over time; if not, would it be reasonable to expect that once the environment changed, the attitudes would change as well? It was partly in an attempt to answer these questions that Newcomb returned in the early 1960s to the former participants in his research at Bennington, approximately 25 years after he launched *Personality and Social Change*. Newcomb and three of his graduate students, Kathryn Koenig, Richard Flacks, and Donald Warwick, decided to pursue the question of persistence and change in the attitudes of the Bennington College women of the 1930s and 1940s.

Newcomb and his students had several different concerns as they approached the second study. In their words, they hoped to satisfy our own and many others' curiosity as to the persistence of rather remarkable individual changes incurred . . . in a special historical and institutional setting, . . . study the durability of that institution's effectiveness in facilitating such changes, . . . contribute to the social-scientific understanding of the interplay of public, institutional, and personal factors in the modification of attitudes and in the persistence of those modifications, . . . and refine their knowledge of those features, in one small college, that seem essential to its function of stimulating and supporting students' systems of values. (1967:9)

While the present study has benefited from the information Newcomb and his colleagues collected with reference to all these purposes, we primarily review and focus on those parts of the 1967 volume dealing with individual stability and change over portions of the life course. Given our own present focus, it is interesting to note the way in which Newcomb and his colleagues posed similar questions in this, the first follow-up:

Given such a temporary experience at a susceptible period of life in a somewhat secluded community, what is the subsequent fate of attitudes thus engendered? Under what conditions, if any, would individuals maintain the kinds of attitudes with which they had left the college 20-odd years before, and under what conditions change them, and in what directions? Thus our first problem deals with *individual* change and persistence of attitudes over a relatively long period of time. (1967:6)

The 1960s follow-up study was undertaken to discover the degree to which attitudes adopted during college would remain stable into mid-life, the extent and direction of change, and the conditions linked to those changes.[1] The authors attempted to locate as many as possible of those who had participated in any phase of the original study.[2] Of the 525 women who had participated, 15 were known to have died, and no known address could be found for an additional 24. The Alumnae Office at Bennington College had mailing addresses for 486, and these women became the focus of the follow-up study. This population was divided into two subsets on the basis of the amount of information each had provided in the initial study. One group became the focus of an intensive personal interview. These were the 147 women who were members of the graduating classes of 1938, 1939, and 1940; these women had been studied over at least three and in some

1. The second Bennington study, *Persistence and Change: Bennington College and Its Students After 25 Years* (1967), was undertaken for other purposes as well. Some of the most important of these are discussed in chapter 4, where we also explain why we were unable to take advantage of all of the data collected in pursuit of these purposes.

2. Newcomb and his colleagues (1967:13) report that 525 women had participated in the first study. In examining the actual data from that study, we found records of 527 women who had participated (see chapter 4).

cases four years. Face-to-face interviews were completed with 129 of these women; 9 of them later completed questionnaires by mail. Thus, 138 of 147 (94 percent) of the graduates in the classes 1938–40 having known addresses participated.

The interview was extensive, 1–2½ hours in length, and solicited information on respondents' postcollege educational and occupational history, organizational activities and interests, past and present attitudes, attitudes of friends and spouses, and marital and family history. In addition, each respondent completed two self-administered questionnaires during the interview. She was asked to respond to the PEP as she thought she had responded when she was a senior at Bennington, and she responded to 45 items from the Omnibus Personality Inventory (including the entire 20-item authoritarianism scale and 25 items from the liberalism scale, selected because they dealt with political liberalism in the public domain).

Questionnaires were mailed to all other remaining students who had participated in any way in the first study and for whom a current address could be obtained. Some had attended Bennington College for less than three years between 1935 and 1939, and some had graduated (in 1936, 1937, 1941, or 1942) but had participated for less than three years. Questionnaires were mailed to 329 women, and 207 (62.9 percent) were returned in usable form.

The mail questionnaire was constructed along lines similar to the personal interviews and included background information (educational and occupational history, marital status, spouse's education and occupation, and the respondent's organizational interests and activities); political attitudes and conduct (voting preferences for all presidential elections from 1940 to 1960, spouse's voting preferences, current issues, PEP scale, 15 items from OPI scales); and the respondent's evaluation of her educational experience at Bennington College.

POLITICAL ATTITUDES AND ACTIVITIES IN 1960

As a group, respondents in the interview sample retained their liberal political attitudes a quarter-century later. Newcomb and his colleagues described them in the following way:

> The picture obtained from the interview sample [including the nine who responded by questionnaire] is that of a group of women who favor a "liberal" political philosophy, are interested in public affairs, have become involved enough to have worked in some political capacity, prefer the Democratic Party to the Republican Party, and think of themselves as "liberal" rather than "conservative." (1967:25)

55

Further, as a group, the interview sample preferred Democratic party positions on national issues (62 percent) to Republican positions (38 percent). Sixty percent preferred John Kennedy in the 1960 presidential race; 38 percent preferred Richard Nixon. A short follow-up questionnaire mailed in 1964 found 90 percent of this sample preferring Lyndon Johnson in that year's presidential race, while only 8 percent preferred Barry Goldwater.

A majority (57 percent) of this interview subsample believed they had not significantly changed their points of view or political attitudes since graduating from Bennington. Of those who thought they *had* changed, about equal proportions said they had become more liberal or more conservative. A majority expressed nonconservative attitudes on several crucial political issues of the day (school desegregation, Eisenhower's handling of the U-2 spy plane incident, the admission of China to the United Nations, and sit-ins and picketing for racial integration). A majority expressed favorable opinions of Franklin Roosevelt, Adlai Stevenson, Walter Reuther, John Kennedy, Harry Truman, and Dwight Eisenhower; and a majority expressed unfavorable opinions of Joseph McCarthy, Richard Nixon, Douglas MacArthur, and Robert Taft. Sixty percent had worked for a candidate or a political organization at some time since graduating. Democrats and other parties and candidates of the Left received help from the most (66 percent of those active), whereas many fewer (27 percent of those active) aided the Republicans and parties of the Right. Two-thirds of the interview sample reported participating in at least one "liberal cause" or "liberal" organization.

Results from the mailed questionnaire were consistent with those obtained in the direct interviews, but they were less pronounced. Though still a minority, a higher percentage of the questionnaire sample described themselves as conservative (34 percent as opposed to 17 percent in the interview sample). More reported voting for Nixon in 1960 (48 percent as opposed to 38 percent), and fewer reported having worked for a political party or candidate (31 percent as opposed to 60 percent). The questionnaire sample included women who had attended but had not graduated from Bennington. Newcomb suggests that the nongraduates may have left Bennington because they were uncomfortable in what was clearly a liberal atmosphere in the 1930s.[3] Whatever the reason, graduates (in both the interview and questionnaire sample) tended to give fewer conservative responses than did nongraduates.

Overall, then, the majority of the women in the interview sample and of

3. As we noted above, such a plausible explanation actually militates against the socialization interpretation Newcomb gave his original findings.

the graduates in the questionnaire sample had liberal political attitudes in 1960. The majority of the nongraduates were more conservative than the graduates.

STABILITY AND CHANGE SINCE COLLEGE

Several techniques were employed to assess the degree of stability and change in the respondents' political attitudes since leaving college. Once again, these analyses were conducted separately for the interview and questionnaire samples. One general strategy was to take the respondents' final scores on the PEP scale as a measure of political liberalism upon leaving Bennington and relate them to various measures of political attitudes in 1960.

For interview respondents, the 1960 *Political Conservatism Index*, which assessed opinions on seven then-current political issues (such as the Supreme Court's desegregation decision, use of the Fifth Amendment before congressional committees, and admitting China to the United Nations), correlated .47 with final college PEP scores. Political conservatism upon leaving college (as assessed by the PEP) was also correlated with indices of favorability to conservative ($r = .42$) and nonconservative ($r = -.45$) political figures. Women who were conservative when they left Bennington were much more likely to be favorable to McCarthy, Nixon, Taft, Eisenhower, and MacArthur, and unfavorable to Stevenson, Roosevelt, Truman, and Reuther than were women who left college with liberal orientations.

Final college PEP scores for interview respondents (split at the median) were also significantly related to voting in the 1960 presidential election. Only 18 percent of those below the median (liberal) voted for Richard Nixon, while 61 percent of those above the median (conservative) did so. Self-reported voting patterns for presidential elections between 1940 and 1960 show the same pattern. The correlation between final PEP score and the number of Republican presidential candidates voted for in this time span was .48. Political party preference assessed in 1938 also related significantly to party preference in 1960, to the 1960 conservatism index, and to opinions of conservative political figures.

Finally, interview respondents were divided into four groups in terms of change while at Bennington. Employing median splits of the final PEP distribution of interviewees as the criteria for defining conservatism and liberalism, Newcomb and his colleagues identified those who remained conservative, those who remained nonconservative, those who became more liberal, and those who became more conservative. As suggested by

Table 3.1. Relationship between Change in Attitude in College and
1960 Political Conservativism Index

| | 1960 Political Conservativism Index | | | |
Attitude Change in College	Above Median	Below Median	Total	Mean
No change; remained conservative	67% (36)	33% (18)	100% (54)	24.8
No change; remained nonconservative	30% (6)	70% (14)	100% (20)	19.0
Became less conservative	37% (15)	63% (26)	100% (41)	19.7
Became more conservative	67% (4)	33% (3)	100% (7)	21.0
n	61	61	122	

Source: Newcomb et al., 1967:37.

the results shown in table 3.1, women who became less conservative at Bennington were significantly less conservative in 1960 than women who remained conservative in college. This same measure of attitude change while in college was also significantly related to political party preference in 1960 and to candidate preference in the 1960 presidential election.

Overall, then, interview respondents who were relatively conservative when they left Bennington in the 1930s tended to be conservative approximately 25 years later; women who were liberal when they left the College tended to remain liberal. These results are paralleled in all but one instance for the questionnaire respondents. For both graduates and nongraduates, those who left the College conservative remained conservative, and those who left liberal remained liberal. The one exception is that larger proportions both of graduates (32 percent) and of nongraduates (43 percent) in the questionnaire sample described themselves as conservative than did the women who were interviewed (23 percent).

FACTORS ASSOCIATED WITH CHANGE

Newcomb and his colleagues had expected to observe significant stability over the 25 years that separated their two assessments of political attitudes, particularly for those women who had experienced significant change while in college. They reasoned that large changes "were likely to have been accompanied by a significant reorganization of important values to support persistence." This reorganization was expected to have led these women to create "a social environment which would nurture and reinforce the value systems with which they left college" (1967:53).

In examining these hypotheses, Newcomb and his colleagues focused initially on those women in their interview sample who had experienced a large change in political attitudes while in college. Of the 43 women in the interview sample whose PEP scores while in college had become less conservative by at least one standard deviation, 28 (65 percent) scored below the median for conservatism in 1960; 15 (35 percent) scored above the median. This finding reinforces the findings described earlier. In addition, however, 11 of the 15 (73 percent) women whose college move toward nonconservatism had been "reversed" in 1960 were either married to someone who was relatively conservative or, if unmarried, had primarily conservative friends. Of the 28 women who had "retained" the college move toward nonconservatism, 24 (86 percent) had either nonconservative spouses or, if unmarried, nonconservative friends. Here was the initial indication of the importance of social support for long-range stability or change in political attitudes.

Newcomb and his colleagues were forced to rely on respondents' reports of the attitudes of spouses and friends (the one important exception to this is noted below). Thus, the possibility of distortion exists. Notwithstanding that possibility, the correlation between the 1960 conservatism index reported for the spouse and the index for the respondent was .85. Several measures of spouse's reported political attitude in 1960 were examined (including 1960 conservatism index, favorability to conservative figures, spouse's choice in the 1960 presidential election).

Among those whose last PEP score in college was conservative (above the median), women who had remained conservative in 1960 had husbands who were significantly more conservative than the husbands of those who had become less conservative by 1960. Data employing the husbands' scores on the 1960 *Political Conservatism Index*, as reported by their wives, appear in table 3.2.

But does this evidence mean that the women changed their political opinions after marriage toward those of their husbands, that the husbands changed their political opinions after marriage, or that the women simply married men of the same political orientation as themselves? Sufficient data were not available in the 1960 study to test these different possibilities.[4] We return to this issue in chapter 9.

---

4. Similar results were obtained with reported attitudes of friends. However, the close friends of some of the respondents were respondents themselves, and so it was possible to conclude that there was both a perceived *and an actual* congruence in political attitudes among respondents and their close social environment.

Table 3.2. Relationship of Wife's Change in Attitude and Husband's Political Conservatism

Final PEP Score in College[b]	1960 Conservatism Index[b]	Husband's 1960 Conservatism Index[a]			
		Above Median	Below Median	Total	Mean
Above median	Above median	29	1	30	29.8
Above median	Below median	1	13	14	17.2
Below median	Above median	15	1	16	27.2
Below median	Below median	6	24	30	18.1
n		51	39	90	

Source: Newcomb et al., 1967:55.

[a]The husband's attitudes were reported by the wife.

[b]The median of final PEP scores is that of the total population of students replying in college. The median for the 1960 conservatism index is that of interviewees only.

The interdependence among respondents' political attitudes, change and stability in those attitudes, and the attitudes of significant others in their immediate social environment is clear. What is much less clear are the processes through which this interdependence operates. Newcomb and his colleagues concluded that husbands' influence on their wives' attitudes appeared to be indirect, providing a supportive social environment for existing attitudes, rather than directly producing change. With respect to friends as well, they concluded that these women "selected and moved into—and perhaps in some degree, created—a social environment which tended to support and reinforce the value systems with which they had left college" (1967:64).

SUMMARY OF PERSISTENCE AND CHANGE

Data from both samples suggest that very little major change in relative standing on a liberal/conservative dimension of political attitude had taken place in the attitudes of the respondents between the first study in the 1930s and the follow-up study in 1960–61. Whether measured by their attitudes toward political issues, their voting preferences, their opinions toward various public figures, or their party identifications, Bennington women who were relatively conservative while in college remained relatively conservative a quarter-century later, and those who were relatively nonconservative while in college remained nonconservative in 1960–61. We would echo the caution issued by Newcomb concerning the role that particular historical, period factors may have played in this attitude stability. And we would emphasize, as he did, the apparent importance of interdependence among individuals' own attitudes, the environment they select and help shape, and the degree and quality of social support they encounter in it. We return to these issues in chapter 9.

AGING, PERSISTENCE, AND CHANGE: UNRESOLVED ISSUES

Subsequent to the work of Newcomb and his colleagues (1967), several studies have dealt with the relation between age and the stability of socio-political orientations. These studies have focused on a number of research issues, all related in some way to life-cycle variations in attitude stability. The issues raised by this literature can be summarized by the following three questions. First, at what point in the life cycle do attitudes achieve their greatest strength, and thus their highest point of durability in the face of social change and other experiences that would potentially induce changes in attitudes? Second, do attitudes grow in strength over the life course and become more resilient with age, or is there an openness to change that characterizes the development of attitudes over the life span? Third, if attitudes grow in persistence over the life course, does this growing persistence achieve some pinnacle of stability, with a fall-off in persistence after some point in later life (and at what point), or does inertia in attitudes provide for continued persistence over the life span?

Students of political socialization now generally agree that most political attitudes are quite malleable and susceptible to change into late adolescence and early adulthood (e.g., Kinder and Sears, 1985). This is in sharp contrast to the earlier predominant view that ideological orientations stabilized even before adolescence (e.g., Campbell et al., 1960; Davies, 1965; Greenstein, 1965; Hess and Torney, 1967). Newcomb's (1943) research at Bennington demonstrated that the political attitudes of young, college-age adults can be quite open to change. Subsequent theory and supportive research findings have led to the formulation of a view of late adolescence and early adulthood as particularly "impressionable years" (Kinder and Sears, 1985). However, it has been theorized that after some point of crystallization, attitudes begin to grow in strength with age, due to both biological processes of aging and life-cycle variations (Glenn, 1974, 1980; Sears, 1981, 1983).

As we shall describe in greater detail, most of the extant research on the topic of aging and its relation to political attitude strength does not adequately address issues of attitude change and stability. Cohort effects on party identification have been estimated, and efforts to separate aging and cohort effects on mean levels of variables have created a virtual cottage industry.[5] By contrast, the examination of aging and cohort factors in the extent of attitude change over the life course is nonexistent. Discussion has instead focused primarily on the relationship of aging and the "intensity" or "strength" of political orientations, and even within this context the primary focus has been on political party identification. The key issues discussed in this literature are whether "aging" and "life-cycle" factors versus "cohort" or "generational" factors are primarily responsible for empirically observed relationships between age and the intensity of party loyalties (e.g., Abramson, 1976, 1979, 1983; Converse, 1969, 1976, 1979). As we discuss below, while this literature is suggestive of possible aging/attitude-stability relations, most of this work is limited in its ability to address these issues.

Assuming a period of continuing attitude formation and change during early adulthood and the potential for growth in levels of attitude stability with age, the remaining important question concerns the nature of this age/stability function.

Models of Attitude Stability Over the Life Course

Most discussions of *cohort effects* on attitudes and the behavioral orientations they reflect assume a high degree of individual stability after some early point in the life cycle, either after childhood or early adulthood (e.g., Mannheim, 1952; Ryder, 1965). If individuals were unstable in their orientations over time, there would be little purpose in hypothesizing that such cohort effects might persist over time. Early discussions of the development of political orientations over the life course (e.g., Campbell et al., 1960) assumed that some aspects of political orientations were highly stable after the period of childhood and adolescence, and such models of individual persistence form the basis for many *generational* explanations of social change. Although there has been little subsequent support for what others have called the *primacy principle* (Searing, Wright, and Rabinowitz, 1976), this model of persistence (see model A in figure 3.1) serves as a worthwhile conceptual baseline with which to contrast other theoretical ideas. This baseline is depicted by a constant and high level of stability throughout the life cycle.

5. In fact, the study of cohort factors in mean levels of party loyalty by political scientists interested in public opinion and electoral behavior has been one central focus for discussion and debate within that discipline, and the terrain is well known in those circles (e.g., Abramson, 1976, 1979, 1983; Claggett, 1981; Converse, 1969, 1976, 1979; Converse and Pierce, 1987; Franklin, 1984). Sociological attention to this subject has been rather sparse, although several serious treatments of the subject do exist (see Cutler, 1970, 1974; Glenn, 1974, 1980; Glenn and Hefner, 1972; Knoke, 1976; Knoke and Hout, 1974).

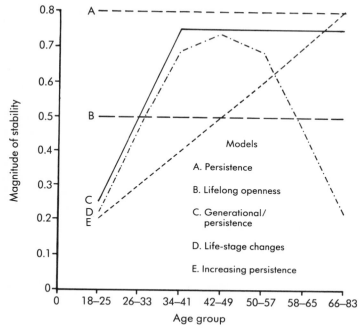

Figure 3.1. Models of Attitude Stability over the Life Span

A second model of the age/attitude-stability relationship portrays a process of linear increases in attitude stability with age (see model E in figure 3.1).[6] This *increasing persistence* model is suggested by a naive psychological view of the development of attitudes as a self-contained individual process. To our knowledge, this model actually has no contemporary supporters, but, again, it represents another extreme case that can be viewed conceptually for purposes of comparisons with other, perhaps more realistic models.

A third view of the relation between age and attitude change is that social change occurs relatively independently of the birth-cohort composition of the population and that compositional shifts in the population are endogenous rather than exogenous factors in processes of social change. This

---

6. Although we describe such a model as linear, it need not be so. The model might be best thought of as having a variety of forms, all showing essentially a monotonic relationship between attitude stability and age. Sears and his colleagues (Sears and Weber, 1988) suggest that political socialization may actually proceed in "fits and starts," reflecting a more jagged, or steplike, relationship with time, but the net relationship with age would be monotonically increasing.

perspective is compatible with a viewpoint that has emerged recently with great force in developmental psychology: that attitudinal flexibility is maintained well beyond early socialization experiences, potentially extending beyond early adulthood into mid-life and through the mature years. Recent work in adult developmental psychology, focusing on the entire life span, suggests that there may be a *lifelong openness to change* apparent in many areas of life (e.g., Brim and Kagan, 1980; Lerner, 1984).

This perspective on individual adult psychology suggests that one critical assumption of the cohort replacement model, namely, the assumption of high degrees of attitude stability after early adulthood and/or an increasing degree of stability with aging, is potentially erroneous (see model B in figure 3.1). If individuals are vulnerable to attitude change at all stages of the life cycle, then the age distribution of the population per se may indicate little about the potential for aggregate social change.

The generational/persistence model (see model C in figure 3.1) suggests that through late childhood and early adolescence, attitudes are relatively malleable, with many experiencing increases in strength through early adult socialization, but with the potential for dramatic change possible in late adolescence or early adulthood (Newcomb, 1943). With time, an "affective mass" is developed, "making attitude change progressively more difficult with age" (Sears, 1981:186–87). According to this model, among more youthful cohorts, all else being equal, attitudes are less stable than among older ones, but greater stability sets in at some early point, and attitudes tend to be increasingly persistent as people age. As we noted in chapter 1, Sears has developed a theoretical argument regarding why we should expect growing persistence of attitudes over time. One element of this thesis involves the inherent nature of attitudes to grow in strength with time (Sears, 1983). Another involves the nature of life-cycle changes that support the growing rigidity of attitudes (Sears, 1981).

This model converges nicely with results from panel studies of single cohorts that show high levels of attitude persistence over most of the adult life cycle (Jennings and Niemi, 1981; Marwell, Aiken, and Demerath, 1987; Newcomb et al., 1967), and with results from panel studies of attitudes in cross-sectional samples that examine differences in stability by age (Sears, 1981, 1983). This model is also compatible with the recurrent theoretical suggestions of the existence of cohort effects on means, since the detectability of such cohort effects requires the substantial persistence of attitude orientations over time. On the other hand, those cohort effects identified in the literature are typically quite weak, a finding more consistent with the lifelong openness hypothesis. Still, the faintness of these impulses does not necessarily signal the existence of weak individual stabilities. Attitudes may be persistent over time without containing the historical remnants of early adult cohort experiences.[7]

Sears (1981) also suggested that attitude stability may decline after age 60 to levels achieved in young adulthood, constituting yet a *fifth* model of age-related changes in attitude stability. Thus, there may be more than one critical period of vulnerability to attitude changes across the life span. What is unclear from this work is the actual trajectory of stability in old age. Sears (1981) reported some empirical evidence suggesting that in old age attitudes may become vulnerable again to change, a second period of increasing flexibility across the life span (model D in figure 3.1). However, the analyses on which this speculation is based contain some serious methodological limitations that preclude a strong inference regarding such a second major period of attitudinal flexibility (see Alwin and Krosnick, 1991a).

In chapter 7 we address this general question using longitudinal data assessing individual attitude stability. In addition to our Bennington re-interview data, we also use panel data from the 1956–58–60 and 1972–74–76 National Election Study panel studies, which permit some estimates of the degree of stability in measures of political attitudes (see also Alwin and Krosnick, 1991a). In this regard we focus most of our attention on political party identification as a central political orientation. Using this measure, we address the question of whether political attitudes grow in strength, as assessed by gains in attitude stability over the life course. By linking data on birth cohorts across the two four-year NES panels, we are able to assess the potential changes in levels of individual stability within the same birth cohorts across a period of sixteen years.

---

7. Mannheim's (1952) theoretical argument regarding the importance of the concept of *generation* in understanding social change did not suggest that such cohort effects would be present for all cohorts. Some generations would be particularly affected by the historical events influencing them when they came of age, but others would not be. Thus, part of the difficulty of isolating cohort effects is their potential scarcity.

4

The Bennington Women Revisited:
The Present Study

INTRODUCTION

Our ultimate interest in pursuing this research was consistent with that of Newcomb and his colleagues (1967), namely, to address the question of whether young people's sociopolitical attitudes are developed as they make the transition to adulthood and then remain relatively stable over the remainder of their lives, or whether such attitudes are open to change over the life cycle. Because our research involves the study of a single cohort over time, our analysis is limited in critical respects, and we cannot provide a definitive test of various models of attitude change over the life course (see Riley, 1973).[1] However, by supplementing these data with information from the National Election Study series, we can address several questions empirically for which there are few answers in the available research literature.

The present analysis addresses the issue of the stability of sociopolitical attitudes among the Bennington women in three ways. First we examine the current political orientations of these women in relation to their contemporaries. We compare them with members of a national sample, obtained from the National Election Study in 1984, and within this context we compare them with women who would otherwise be similar in terms of life circumstances. In this latter regard we compare them with other women over the age of 60 and with such older women who are college-educated. In this context we also rely on data from past National Election Studies in order to address the question of whether the uniqueness of the Bennington women transcends any possible cohort or generational difference common to all members of the particular age groups involved. Second, we analyze

---

1. We should note, however, that there have been several worthy attempts to make sense out of panel data on single cohorts. Elder (1981), for example, makes a fairly convincing case for intra-cohort research in his work with data from cohorts experiencing the Great Depression (see also Elder, 1974, 1975, 1978a, 1978b, 1979).

the retrospective subjective assessments of the Bennington women themselves. Following similar methods employed in the 1960s follow-up, in 1984 we asked these women to assess the extent of their attitude change over various parts of their lives, and we examine those retrospections. We also examine their retrospective accounts of voting preferences as registered in both the 1960s studies and in 1984. Some interesting disparities exist which can be explained against the background of the sociopolitical context of the period in which these studies were carried out. Third, we examine the stability of attitudes by asking whether the correlation of these measures over time among the Bennington women increases or decreases with age. This we address by analyzing the relationships among measures of sociopolitical attitudes gathered at critical times during the life course: young adulthood (age 21), the middle years (ages 40–45) and the mature years (65–70).[2]

Finally, we focus attention on the processes that help explain the consistency or lack of consistency of attitudes among these women over these various periods of their lives. Of particular importance in this regard, again consistent with the research goals of the 1960s follow-up, is the study of the political orientations of spouses and friends. However, one additional contextual factor which we consider in the present context is the set of orientations of the womens' children and the degree of consistency with those of their mothers. Of course, because of the nature of our data—again we rely on the reports of the Bennington women regarding the sociopolitical orientations of their children—we are not able to make a strong argument regarding the direction of this influence. Our goal is to find evidence that would test the reference-group interpretations of consistencies which may exist among our respondents and significant others in their environments.

RESEARCH DESIGN

The research reported here focuses on a purposive sample of women who were students at Bennington College in the 1930s. Available data from the two previous studies of this sample, collected in approximately 1938 and 1961, provided us with the opportunity to collect a third wave of data in 1984. They also provided us with the opportunity of taking advantage of statistical techniques available for assessing and interpreting relationships

2. Assuming an average graduation age of 22, the women in the Bennington class of 1936 were roughly 47 in 1961 and 70 in 1984, and the women in the class of 1942 were 41 in 1961 and 64 in 1984. Thus, our occasions of measurement reflect qualitatively different stages of life, as well as different historical times.

in longitudinal data over three widely separated periods of time covering between 45 and 50 years of our respondents' lives. However, it is clear that the nature of our design is limited by the uniqueness of the sample and the focus on a single cohort.

Several features of the second Bennington study (Newcomb et al., 1967) might suggest the ability to recoup some of these lost advantages. This might have been done by collecting a second wave of data from those women who were enrolled at the College in 1959–62, and for whom attitude data may exist. Even more desirable would have been the collection of a first wave of data from students currently (1984) enrolled at the College. Such a design would have provided us with longitudinal data over 45–50 years and at three points in time for the original 1938 cohort, longitudinal data over 23 years and at two points in time for the second (1961) cohort, and cross-sectional data for a current (1984) sample of Bennington students.

Desirable as such a research strategy would have been, we did not pursue it for two reasons. First, we were unable to locate anything but aggregate-level data for the second cohort. Despite the cooperation of those most directly involved in the collection of data in the second study (Newcomb, Flacks, Koenig, and Warwick), and despite extensive searches in the files of the Institute for Social Research, only aggregate-level data for the 1961 cohort could be located. This would have seriously limited our ability to employ data that we might have collected in 1984 to assess longitudinal change within that cohort or to use those data in assisting us to disentangle the relative importance of age, cohort, and period effects.

Second, as a consequence, the usefulness of data from Bennington students enrolled in 1984 for these specific purposes, though not for others, would have been minimal. Even if the individual-level data for the second (1961) cohort had been available, and even if we had included the third (1984) cohort in the design, generalizing from the results generated would have been risky.

We mention these considerations both to explain why we did not employ what might first appear to be a natural and more compelling design, and to acknowledge the limitations in the design we have employed. We have instead focused sole attention on the original cohort, the members of which attended Bennington College in the late 1930s and early 1940s.

The research to be reported here has several unique features. It is rarely possible to follow even a limited sample for as long as members of the original Bennington cohort have been involved in this work, and thus to be able to collect data on the questions we will be addressing. Our sample has provided data over a 45–50 year period, through historical periods covering the depression and New Deal, the Second World War, the McCarthy

Era, the development of atomic energy and atomic weaponry, the civil rights movement, political assassinations, the Vietnam War, and the re-emergence of feminism and the emergence of ageism as social and political issues.

This half-century has "caught" the original cohort of Bennington women at three different life stages: late adolescence, mid-life, and the mature years. During that period of time, these women have confronted most of the major life course transitions and crises that are associated with adult development: marital transitions (marriage, divorce, remarriage, widow-hood); familial transitions (parenthood, "empty nest," grandparenthood); occupational transitions (family-career conflict, work entry and reentry, semi- and full retirement), and educational transitions. The ability to ex-amine this admittedly unique and thus limited sample as it traverses the life course should contribute a great deal to an understanding of the devel-opment of political orientations and social orientations more generally.

DATA AND PROCEDURES

The Sample

The Bennington College Alumni Office provided us with lists of all stu-dents enrolled at the College from 1936 to 1942. From these lists, we were able to identify 399 women (76 percent of the 527 who had in some way participated in the initial research) who were still living, and for whom a code number had been assigned in the original (1930s) research.[3] Of the 527 who participated in the original Bennington studies, 77 were known to be deceased, 31 had requested that the College not give out their ad-dresses, and the College had lost contact with another 20. Thus, we began the present research with current addresses for 399 women who were alive and who had participated in some way in the initial study. Of these we were able to locate 383 successfully.[4]

Members of this sample of 383 (residing throughout the United States) were recontacted using a combination of face-to-face and telephone inter-views. In-depth face-to-face interviews of two hours duration were at-tempted with 31 randomly selected women in the sample; 28 of these inter-views were completed. These interviews provided extensive biographical

3. As mentioned earlier, Newcomb et al. (1967: 13) report that 525 women had partici-pated in the first study. In examining the actual data from that study, we found records of 527 women who had participated (see chapter 3).

4. Twelve of the 399 were not locatable, 1 was deceased, 2 were institutionalized, and 1 was living in Europe.

and qualitative data on this subset of respondents and provided a basis for pretesting the core questions that were included in a telephone interview protocol used with the remaining members of the sample.

The remaining 352 members of the sample who were alive and locatable within the contiguous United States were contacted by telephone to complete a one-hour interview. These contacts yielded 307 completed interviews, resulting in a total response rate of over 87 percent. Respondents in the telephone interview were sent a respondent booklet containing visual presentation of response categories and response scales prior to conducting the interview. Respondents in the telephone interview were also sent self-administered questionnaires, 95 percent of which were returned completed. The respondents were interviewed between September and November, before the 1984 presidential election, concurrent with the 1984 NES preelection survey.

Response Rates

In summary, of the 527 women for whom we had some information from the 1930s (including a PEP score), we were able to identify and locate 383 women. Of these, 335 (or 87.5 percent) agreed to participate in the study. Table 4.1 presents the numbers of cases in several categories of participants in the Bennington studies. Specifically, this table cross-classifies categories of participation in the 1984 and 1960 surveys. These figures show that 266 women participated in both the 1960 and 1984 studies, allowing us to analyze correlational data on the stability of attitudes for a subset of our respondents. About one-half of those not contacted in 1960 were also not contacted in 1984, and vice versa. However, it is noteworthy that in 1984 we were able to reach a sizeable number of people for whom there was no evidence of contact in 1960. A similar number of people participated in the 1960 study, but were not contacted in 1984.

Potential Sampling Biases

We have pointed out with some regularity the fact that the original Bennington "sample" was not a sample in a technical sense; that is, it was not a sample of some known population of interest. It therefore presents difficulties as a basis for generalization. We were nonetheless concerned that our follow-up data be at least representative of this original group of Newcomb's research participants. This issue is especially acute with respect to the 1960s data because the interview subsample was, as we noted in chapter 3, made up exclusively of the graduating classes of 1938, 1939, and 1940.

Table 4.1. Frequencies of Respondents/Nonrespondents for Various Categories of Participation

		1960–61		
		Participants	Refusals	No Contact
1930 (PEP)	527	350	19	151
1984				
Participants	335	266	7	62
Refusals	48	21	8	19
No contact	144	63	11	70

Note: The "no contact" category includes women who had died, could not be located, and so forth.

Table 4.2 presents the distributions for the Bennington samples on four variables for which information is available from the earliest Bennington study records, specifically, the year the student entered Bennington College, the number of years the student attended Bennington, and the political party affiliation of the mother and father.[5] The table displays the distributions of these variables for the 527 cases representing the original Bennington research participants, designated the *total sample,* for the respondents in the 1960s surveys and for the respondents in the 1984 survey. These data show rather convincingly that, at least insofar as these distributions are concerned, the 1960s mailed-questionnaire respondents and the 1984 respondents differ only trivially from the original group who had participated in the research while at Bennington. Understandably, because of the way they were selected, the 1960s interview respondents were located mainly in the entering classes of 1934, 1935, and 1936, and virtually all of them spent four years at Bennington. Despite the over-representation of these classes in the 1960s follow-up data, these interview respondents are very similar to the other respondents with respect to parental party preference. Thus, the overall picture is that, except for the explicit over-sampling of the graduating classes of 1938, 1939, and 1940, the follow-up data from both the 1960s and 1984 studies are broadly representative of the Bennington students who participated in Newcomb's original research.

As one further check on the representativeness of the follow-up respondents, we examined the 1930s PEP scores for respondents and nonrespondents in the 1960 and 1984 studies. Table 4.3 presents an analysis of the potential response biases in our ultimate set of 1984 respondents. Here we present average PEP scores from when the women left Bennington for

5. These data were available from the early Bennington records and supplemented in some cases with responses to the 1984 questionnaire when early information was missing.

Table 4.2. Distribution of Bennington Sample on Four Indicators of Early
Political Environment

	Total Sample (527)	1960		1984 Respondents (335)
		Interview (129)	Mail[a] (221)	
Year entered Bennington College				
1932	9.2%	—	13.0%	9.5%
1933	9.2	0.8	12.7	9.5
1934	14.1	22.5	9.6	15.3
1935	17.2	32.6	10.7	15.3
1936	18.2	44.2	8.2	20.2
1937	16.6	—	23.1	15.6
1938	15.5	—	22.8	14.7
Total	100.0	100.0	100.0	100.0
N	(523)	(129)	(221)	(329)
Number of years at Bennington				
One	10.0%	—	11.1%	7.8%
Two	21.5	—	22.6	20.5
Three	14.6	1.6	15.6	13.9
Four	53.9	98.4	50.8	57.8
Total	100.0	100.0	100.0	100.0
N	(519)	(129)	(215)	(333)
Parental political affiliation				
Mother				
Republican	66.4%	64.3%	68.5%	65.0%
Democrat/Socialist	31.0	34.3	29.3	31.8
None/independent	2.1	1.4	1.3	2.6
Other	0.5	—	0.9	0.6
Total	100.0	100.0	100.0	100.0
N	(451)	(111)	(201)	(311)
Father				
Republican	71.9%	70.7%	72.4%	70.5%
Democrat/Socialist	25.9	27.8	25.3	26.8
None/independent	1.7	1.5	1.4	2.0
Other	0.6	—	0.9	0.7
Total	100.0	100.0	100.0	100.0
N	(433)	(106)	(198)	(295)

[a]Ten women who did a pretest interview also completed a mail questionnaire and are included in this column.

Table 4.3. PEP Score Means for Various Categories of Bennington
Respondents and Nonrespondents

	1930	1960s			
		Interview	Mailed Questionnaire	Both	No Contact
1984 interviews					
F-T-F	(28)	(9)	(17)	(26)	—
PEP	59.000	57.667	61.941	60.462	—
Phone	(307)	(89)	(151)	(242)	—
PEP	67.524	65.664	66.937	67.495	—
Total	(335)	(98)	(168)	(266)	(62)
PEP	64.890	65.453	67.887	66.995	—
1984 Refusals	(48)	(7)	(14)	(21)	(24)
PEP	68.083	—	—	—	—
1984 No contact	(144)	(24)	(40)	(64)	(70)
PEP	68.999	—	—	—	—
Sample total	(527)	(168)	(353)	(521)	—
PEP	67.568	64.190	68.829	67.609	—

Note: The "no contact" category includes women who had died, could
not be located, and so forth.

several categories of participants. Specifically, we cross-classify the various participant categories in the 1960 and 1984 surveys and compute the
average PEP score for when the women left Bennington. These data show,
as we observed in chapter 3, that the interview subsample from the 1960
study is slightly less conservative than those in the mailed-questionnaire
subsample. Also, these data show that those who refused and were not
contacted in 1984 were somewhat more conservative, as reflected in their
PEP scores from the time they left Bennington. Finally, our face-to-face
(F-T-F) interview subsample in 1984 was somewhat less conservative than
the telephone subsample, but this difference is likely due to chance, since
we used random selection procedures to obtain the face-to-face subsample.

These results lead to the conclusion that in assessing individual change
since leaving Bennington (in chapter 7), it will be important to control
statistically for the year entering Bennington College and the amount of
time spent there. This will reduce the over-representation of the entering
classes of 1934, 1935, and 1936 in the 1960s follow-up data. We entertain
these controls for a second important reason as well. Our study "inherited"
only one PEP score on each of the original participants—the last PEP
score gathered by Newcomb. Thus, these PEP scores come from a variety
of different times (both biographic and historic) and reflect varying degrees

of influence of the Bennington College environment. As we point out at greater length in chapter 7, these scores can better represent the residue of the Bennington experience, a baseline against which later scores can be evaluated, if we examine them while controlling for the year the individual entered Bennington and the number of years she attended the College.

The 1984 Questionnaire

In order to answer the research questions we had posed, we structured the 1984 interview and questionnaire with two things in mind. First, we replicated, or tried to replicate, many of the items Newcomb had employed in the first and second Bennington studies. This enabled us to assess stability and change in individuals' political orientations over time. Second, we included a range of questions that were oriented toward more contemporary social and political issues of the early 1980s. These issues (listed later in this chapter) were those assessed by selected questions from the 1984 National Election Study (Miller and Traugott, 1989). This enables us to compare the political orientations of our sample to those of similar groups in the population as a whole, and thus to suggest how the results of this research might apply to other groups in the population.

The 1984 questionnaire (this phrase will be used to refer generally to both the interview schedule and the questionnaire schedule) included items in six different areas (the actual questionnaires appear in appendix B):

1. background and demographic variables: age, education, occupation, marital and family status, residence, and religious preference
2. retrospections on past political attitudes: retrospective response to PEP scale of 1930 and 1960
3. self-assessed change in political attitudes and interests: self-assessed change in amount, direction, and cause for the periods 1938–60, 1960–84, and 1938–84
4. current political attitudes, interest, and participation: party identification, presidential voting record, current PEP response, affective orientations to the political system, evaluation of current political figures, policy preferences on current issues, interest in politics and public affairs, and current participation in political organizations
5. perceptions of the current political attitudes of others: spouse, children, grandchildren, age peers, former Bennington classmates, and current Bennington students
6. other measures: health status, subjective well-being, attitudes on women's issues, sex-role attitudes, politics of age, and social integration

AVAILABLE DATA OVER TIME

The research reported here employs certain data collected in the first two Bennington studies. Data collected from Bennington students during 1935–39 were reported in *Personality and Social Change* (Newcomb, 1943). Approximately 527 students took part in some phase of that original project. Data from that study were available to us in two ways. First, we had access to some of the original data in their original form (via code sheets produced and retained over the 50-year period by Newcomb, college personnel office reports, and individual autobiographies). Second, and more important for purposes of systematic comparison over time, at the time of the second study (1960), portions of the large data set collected in the initial study had been transferred to computer cards. These data were made available to us by Kathryn Koenig and include the following information:

1. scores on the Political and Economic Progressivism Scale in 1938–39, or when the student left Bennington College
2. the year of entry into Bennington College
3. the student's own political party preference in the 1930s
4. father's political party preference in the 1930s
5. mother's political party preference in the 1930s

At the time of the first follow-up, Newcomb and his colleagues (1967) tried to contact all of those who had participated in any way in the original study. Of the 527 original participants, there were 486 still living for whom addresses could be found; these 486 constituted the focus of the first follow-up. An intensive interview was completed with 129 of the 147 graduates of the classes of 1938, 1939, and 1940, and 9 later completed a mailed questionnaire; this subgroup had been studied for at least three years in the initial research. A mailed questionnaire was sent to the remaining 329 former students, and 207 were returned in usable form. Thus, of the 527 participants in the initial research, data were collected from 345 (63 percent) in 1960–61, either by personal interview or mailed questionnaire. The second wave of data, a substantial portion of which was available to us, includes the following information:

1. postcollege history: education, occupation, work reasons, leisure interests
2. organizational activities and interests: current and while at Bennington
3. attitudes and interests: self-assessed changes and reasons for change while at Bennington; self-assessed change from Bennington to present; current political opinions; voting record in presidential elections; atti-

tudes toward public figures and issues; estimated attitudes of spouse and friends

4. personality assessments: the Allport-Vernon scale of values, and the Omnibus Personality Inventory scores (the OPI liberalism score and the OPI nonauthoritarianism score)

5. other measures: identification and involvement with Bennington College, and family background

We have made two different kinds of comparisons with the longitudinal data that we have. First, there are two assessments of political orientations that have been taken at all three points in time: responses to the PEP scale and political party preference. Second, there are several other measures of political orientation that were employed twice: for example, self-assessed change, estimated orientations of spouses and friends, and so forth.

PROBLEMS OF COMPARATIVE MEASUREMENT

In using data from three sources—Newcomb's (1943) original study of Bennington women during the 1930s and early 1940s ($n = 527$), the 1960–61 follow-up study of a subsample of the original subjects ($n = 345$), and our 1984 follow-up of locatable survivors from the original study ($n = 335$)—there are important methodological issues associated with the comparison of measurement over time. There is considerable support in the methodological literature for what Lykken (1968) called literal replications in studies over time (see Duncan, 1975b; Presser, 1982). At the same time, there are strong arguments in favor of "conceptual replications," especially in a domain of measurement where the events and issues change from year to year.

As Newcomb and his colleagues (1967:22) note, a major problem in attempting to compare sociopolitical attitudes over a long interval of time is in finding comparable measures of attitudes. Measures of attitudes that were "appropriate and valid in 1935" may not be meaningful in the early 1960s or in the 1980s "because so many of the issues have changed" (1967: 22). In their judgment it was not possible to replicate measures of attitudes in an exact way, but to replicate them conceptually. They attempted to use similar measures based on the contemporary issues of the 1960s, rather than those of the 1930s and 1940s. Similarly, our measures of 1984 sociopolitical attitudes are, at least in part, based on the contemporary issues of the early 1980s. At the same time, we had the advantage of being able to include several exact replicas of the questions used in the 1930s and the 1940s and in the 1960s. In general, while we were able to replicate some questions exactly, we attempted to replicate the concept being measured rather than its indicator(s) (see Lykken, 1968).[6]

THE CONCEPT OF POLITICAL IDEOLOGY

We conceive of sociopolitical orientations in terms of cognitive and affective beliefs about social and political systems, the institutional structures they constitute, and the individual and collective actors that populate these systems and institutions. In part because of the problems of comparative measurement referred to above, and in part because we seek a deeper understanding of public opinion, we distinguish such sociopolitical orientations from less fundamental aspects of attitudes. We try to avoid reference to object-specific attitudes tied to particular political issues and political actors. Theoretically, this is important because our substantive concerns about life span development transcend such particularistic issues and actors, referring instead to more ideological aspects of the individual's orientation toward the social and political system.

Although we refer throughout this book to *sociopolitical orientations*, we consider these as indicators of more fundamental belief systems, often referred to as elements of *political ideology*. This is the term Sniderman and Tetlock (1986:63) refer to as the coherent set of cognitive and affective beliefs that are weakly organized, or at least minimally connected. While there is evidence that individuals in general may not pay much attention to political issues (e.g., Converse, 1964), know very little about them, and do not seem to organize their responses to issues and actors in terms of the ideological categories "liberal" and "conservative" as used by political scientists, there is support for the view that individuals tend to carry around "a set of root likes and dislikes," which provide the basis for figuring out "a relatively coherent set of opinions, covering many of the major issues of the day" (Sniderman and Tetlock, 1986:63).

There are detractors from the conventional viewpoint that, despite some variation in the extent of connectedness, attitudes on political issues are at least minimally linked to an ideological core. Kinder and Sears, for example, argue that "citizens are innocent of ideology" (1985:670). After a thorough review of the history of the debate between those espousing an "ideological innocence" argument (e.g., Converse, 1964, 1970, 1975) and

6. In some instances, particularly those involving shorter time intervals, it is desirable to replicate indicators exactly, given an interest in assessing social trends; however, this was not possible in the present case, and we focus on correlational analysis of these data rather than simply a comparison of marginals.

those who have challenged this view, Kinder and Sears suggest that few Americans "make sophisticated use of sweeping ideological ideas," and few express "consistently liberal, conservative, or centrist positions on policy" (1985:670). Still, they concede (with Converse) that there is some minimal coherence that exists in the place of "ideological innocence." And while "ideological coherence" may not be widespread, the terms *liberal* and *conservative* are not entirely meaningless. In the words of Sniderman and Tetlock: "People's likes and dislikes of strategic political groups provide them with the clues they need in order to understand politics in terms of liberal versus conservative" (1986:89).

Thus, we organize our measures of sociopolitical orientations around the concept of ideology, and more specifically around the ideological categories of liberal and conservative. We impose this distinction on many of our measures, which do not explicitly relate responses to either category; in other cases, we directly assess the ideological self-placements of our respondents using these terms. In either instance, as we make explicit below, we use the distinction between *liberal* and *conservative* to refer to the principle dimension of contrast in assessing persistence and change in sociopolitical orientations over the life span.

MEASURES OF SOCIOPOLITICAL ORIENTATIONS

The central findings of Newcomb's original study and many findings in the first follow-up study in 1961 were expressed in terms of changes in levels of *progressivism*, as measured by his PEP scale (Newcomb, 1943:178–79; Newcomb et al., 1967:242–45). The 26 Likert-type items making up this scale are presented in appendix A, and a perusal of these questions shows clearly that they measure one's stance on issues made prominent by Roosevelt's New Deal: public relief, the role of labor unions, and the legitimacy of private and corporate wealth, as against socialized control of industry. These issues represent in many respects the social meaning of the terms *liberal* and *conservative*, which we use to refer to the contrasts embodied in this scale.

PEP scores for the time the subjects left Bennington College were available from the sources of the 1930s and 1940s. Also available from these sources were data on the party identification of the respondent and her parents, the year the student entered Bennington, and the number of years she attended Bennington.

These PEP measures were replicated for respondents to the 1960s mail questionnaire. In 1984 a subset of the original PEP items was used to refer

78

to public issues in the 1980s, as follows (numbers of the comparable original items are given in parentheses):

— The prosperity of the nation as a whole must be based upon the prosperity of working class people. (1)
— Some form of socialist society is preferable to our present system. (3)
— Most labor trouble happens only because of radical agitators. (6)
— Any able-bodied person could get a job right now if he or she tried hard enough. (10)
— The budget should be balanced before the government spends any money on social programs. (12)
— Our government has always been run primarily in the interests of big business. (13)
— Labor unions are justifiable only if they refrain from the use of strikes. (14)
— Most employers think only of profits and care little about their employees' welfare. (17)
— Organizations of the unemployed are just a group of chronic complainers. (19)
— We have no true democracy in this country, because only business and industrial concerns have economic opportunity. (20)
— If the government did not meddle so much in business, things would be all right. (21)
— You can't expect democracy to work very well as long as so many uneducated and unintelligent people have the vote. (22)
— The vast majority of those in the lower economic classes are there because they are stupid or lazy, or both. (23)

A second scale, the *Political Conservatism Index* (PCI) was used by Newcomb and his colleagues in the 1960–61 restudy of the Bennington women. It was based on a set of six items in the interview subsample (1967:238) and a set of four items in the mailed-questionnaire subsample (1967:250). The interview subsample items asked about favorability (on a four-point scale) to the following: the Supreme Court's decision about desegregation of schools, the government's handling of the U-2 incident, increasing social security taxes for medical needs of the aged, the admission of the People's Republic of China to the United Nations, the use of the Fifth Amendment in refusing to answer congressional committees' questions about allegedly subversive activities, and making greater concessions than the United States had then offered toward nuclear disarmament. The mailed-questionnaire subsample items asked about approval regarding "Negro" student sit-ins and picketing, the Eisenhower administration's handling of the U-2 incident, increasing social security taxes for medical needs of the aged, and admitting China to the United Nations. Only the four overlapping items were used in our analysis.

The 1984 study included a variety of attitude questions dealing with social and political issues, including the respondents' subjective assessments of changes in their attitudes over different periods of their lives. The 1984 sociopolitical-issues measures assessed attitudes toward the reduction of government spending for services in areas such as health and education, governmental efforts to improve the social and economic position of blacks and other minority groups, the involvement of the United States in the internal affairs of Central American countries, spending money for defense, cooperation with Russia, and improvement in the social and economic position of older Americans.

A third central measure of political orientations was the respondent's self-placement on a unidimensional *liberalism/conservatism* scale. We were not able to replicate directly the 1960s five-point version of this scale used by Newcomb and his colleagues (1967), as we placed somewhat greater importance on being able to furnish our analysis with an exact replica of the question used in the National Election Study since 1972. This question from the NES series, which we replicated conceptually in our 1984 questionnaire, is as follows:

> We hear a lot of talk these days about Liberals and Conservatives. Here is a seven-point scale on which political views that people might hold are arranged from extremely liberal to extremely conservative. Where would you place yourself on this scale?

The categories used by the NES were: "extremely liberal," "liberal," "slightly liberal," "moderate, middle of the road," "slightly conservative," "conservative," and "extremely conservative." As appendix B shows, our measure (D3 to D9 series) of liberalism/conservatism is comparable to this measure, although we use slightly different category labels.

A fourth measure of political orientation, which is perhaps the most common measure in the modern era, is a measure of *party identification*. The question measuring *partisanship* in the NES surveys is the following:

> Generally speaking, do you usually think of yourself as a Republican, a Democrat, an Independent, or what? (If Republican or Democrat) Would you call yourself a strong (Republican/Democrat) or a not very strong (Republican/Democrat)? (If Independent, No Preference or Other) Do you think of yourself as closer to the Republican or to the Democratic party?

This measure can be used to assess both the direction and strength of partisanship (e.g., Converse and Pierce, 1987). The directional component of partisanship (i.e., liberal/conservative), is indexed by this measure, as well as the "strength," or intensity, of party loyalty.

Retrospective Measures of Sociopolitical Orientations

As indicated earlier, our 1984 studies included retrospective reports of several variables. The 1960s study included retrospective measures of two attitude measures from the 1930s and 1940s study: retrospective reports of PEP-scale items, item by item, and a 1960s estimate of self-placement on the liberalism/conservatism scale. In the 1984 questionnaire we were able to supplement this information in two ways. First, we were able to ask the respondent to respond again to the PEP-scale in the way she would have responded at the time she left Bennington College, and we were again able to obtain an assessment on a liberalism/conservatism rating scale. Second, in addition to this we were able to focus their retrospections on the 1960s and points along the way. Specifically, we asked our 1984 respondents to respond to the PEP-scale in the way they would have in the 1930s and 1940s, when they left Bennington College, and in the 1960s. Also, in addition to obtaining retrospective self-placements on the scale measuring ideological liberalism/conservatism (LC scale) for the 1930s, our 1984 instrument asked for assessments for the 1960s and 1972, as well as the current placement (see questions D3 through D13 in appendix B).

We have a third source of retrospective data that overlaps importantly across the two follow-up studies. In both 1960–61 and 1984 the Bennington respondents were asked to report their candidate preferences in all presidential elections since 1940.

Finally, we also asked our respondents to provide retrospective estimates of their changing interest in political and social affairs since college (questions D14 through D21), and their retrospections regarding the "general political viewpoint" of their Bennington College contemporaries from the 1930s and 1940s (see questions D22 through D26). All of this information will assist us when we evaluate the usefulness of retrospective reports of attitudes in chapter 6.

Constructed Measures of Sociopolitical Orientations

We thus approach the question of the relative persistence of attitudes over the lives of the Bennington women using a combination of direct and retrospective measures of attitudes. We employ a variety of indicators of sociopolitical orientations in an effort to improve the measurement of such orientations at each stage of the life course. We rely on the principal assessments of attitudes registered by Newcomb (1943) and Newcomb and his colleagues (1967), in addition to some measures heretofore omitted from previous analyses and a variety of measures gathered in our 1984 restudy.

Our direct measures of attitudes for the early period, that is, the time of a woman's departure from Bennington, are two: Newcomb's PEP score,[7] and a measure of electoral preferences. These indicators are as follows:

1. *1930s Political and Economic Progressivism (PEP) Scale.* A linear composite variable consisting of the sum of the 26 items given in appendix A. (PEP30)
2. *1936–40 Electoral Preferences.* An index combining the electoral preferences from the 1930s data (1936 candidate preference) and the 1960s report of the 1940 candidate preferences. (PID30)

For the mid-life period, assessed during the early 1960s, we have a somewhat greater direct purchase on levels of sociopolitical orientations and rely less on retrospective reports. In addition to having a score for the 26-item PEP scale from respondents to the mailed questionnaire for this period, we make use of Newcomb and his colleagues' (1967) *Political Conservatism Index*, consisting of responses to public issues important in the 1960s (see above), obtained in both the interview and mail questionnaire subsample. Also, the 1960s interviews and mailed questionnaires included a five-point, single-item scale assessing the subject's position on the dimension of liberalism/conservatism, and there is a measure of electoral preferences for this middle period. These measures are as follows:

3. *1960s Political and Economic Progressivism (PEP) Scale.* A 1961 version of the PEP composite variable consisting of the same 26 items assessed in the original study. (PEP60)
4. *1960–84 Reports of Electoral Preferences for 1956–64.* A combined measure of the number of conservative candidates preferred in the 1956, 1960, and 1964 elections. (PID60)
5. *1960s Political Conservatism Index (PCI).* A four- to six-item scale based on items obtained in 1961 dealing with the support of liberal versus conservative positions on public issues. (PCI60)
6. *1960s Five-Point Liberalism/Conservatism Scale.* A 1960s single-item measure involving a five-point liberalism/conservatism scale with labeled scale points. (LC60)

7. Although this composite score was available for participants in the early studies, data for the individual component items were unavailable. For simplicity we refer to this measure as gathered in the 1930s, although it could have been gathered anywhere from 1936 to 1942. Below we discuss some of the problems with bolstering our early measure of the PEP with retrospective reports in order to identify the latent factor in the 1930s and 1940s.

Measures of 1984 sociopolitical attitudes are even more plentiful than attitudes assessed in earlier periods. As described earlier in this chapter, we obtained a version of the PEP scale relevant to the social issues of the 1980s, and a version of the PCI for 1984 using items connected to current public affairs. Also, we have the seven-point, single-item scale measuring liberalism/conservatism referred to in our review of subjective assessments of attitude change, and there is a measure of electoral preferences. Our measures of sociopolitical attitudes for 1984 are as follows:

7. *1984 Political and Economic Progressivism (PEP) Scale.* A 1984 version of the PEP composite variable made up of 12 of the 26 items assessed in the original study. (PEP84)
8. *1984 Reports of Electoral Preferences for 1976–84.* A measure of the conservative electoral preferences in the 1976, 1980, and 1984 elections. (PID84)
9. *1984 Political Conservatism Index.* An eight-item scale based on the items obtained in 1984 dealing with the support of liberal versus conservative positions on public issues. (PCI84)
10. *1984 Seven-Point Liberalism/Conservatism Scale.* A 1984 single-item measure involving a seven-point liberalism/conservatism scale with labeled scale points. (LC84)

Although we make considerable use of other information in describing and interpreting changes in attitudes over the time period covered by this study, we make important use of these 10 measures in the following chapters. Future discussions of the results of our research will refer the reader to the preceding variable descriptions.

THE NATIONAL ELECTION STUDY

One of the important elements of our research strategy is the comparison of our Bennington respondents with various subgroups within the National Election Study (NES). Our exact replication of several of the 1984 NES questions provides a comparative benchmark against which we can evaluate our Bennington sample. In addition, our search for cohort or generational interpretations of Newcomb's "Bennington effect" (see chapter 2) led us to consider data on selected indicators from the NES series since its beginning in 1952. And finally, we found it important to report research using the NES panel studies (in chapter 7). Thus, some background on the NES is perhaps valuable.

Every two years since 1952, the Center for Political Studies at the University of Michigan's Institute for Social Research has interviewed a representative cross-section of Americans to track national political participation.[8] On the years of presidential elections, a sample is interviewed before the election and is reinterviewed immediately afterward. Only postelection interviews are conducted on congressional election years. The preelection interviews typically take place between September and November, and the postelection interviews usually continue through February of the following year.

The sampling design of the National Election Studies is as follows, as described by Miller and Traugott (1989). Data are obtained from personal, face-to-face interviews with national full-probability samples of all citizens of voting age in the United States. The Survey Research Center's multistage area sample was used in all studies. It is designed to represent dwelling units in the contiguous United States exclusive of those on military reservations. In 1978 the primary sampling unit specifications for sampling were changed from SMSAs and counties to fit lines of congressional districts. This change should have no appreciable effect on the representativeness of the full sample, though it does facilitate certain subsample analyses. The sample sizes for each year are as follows:

1952: $n = 1,899$
1956: $n = 1,762$
1958: $n = 1,450$
1960: $n = 1,181$
1962: $n = 1,297$
1964: $n = 1,834$
1966: $n = 1,291$
1968: $n = 1,673$ (includes supplement of 116 black respondents)
1970: $n = 1,694$ (includes supplement of 114 black respondents)
1972: $n = 2,705$
1974: $n = 1,575$
1976: $n = 2,248$
1978: $n = 2,304$
1980: $n = 3,587$
1982: $n = 1,418$
1984: $n = 2,257$
1986: $n = 2,176$
1988: $n = 2,040$

The 1984 design was somewhat more complicated. In addition to the 2,257 cases in the regular pre- and postelection survey, the NES also conducted a survey conducted by telephone of several small consecutively-administered cross-sections from January through November ($n = 3,496$). This "continuous monitoring" survey was intended to understand the dynamics of the election campaign (see Miller and National Election Studies, 1985). For our purposes, we combined the data from both the regular pre- and postelection survey and the "continuous monitoring" survey where both were available, although in some cases data were available from the

8. There was no such survey in 1954.

regular pre- and postelection survey only. In the case of comparisons of the Bennington respondents to national samples on measures of "political affect," data were available for approximately 1,600 respondents in the NES preelection portion of the study.

Because of the differences in attitudes of blacks and whites (see Abramson, 1983), and because our Bennington respondents are almost uniformly white, we restrict our analyses of the NES cross-sectional data to whites only. This will limit the generality of our conclusions regarding cohort differences and population changes, but it will exercise control over one possible difference between our Bennington sample and the larger population of which they are a part.

Finally, detailed descriptions of the NES measures are omitted here, because some of the key measures were described in the foregoing (see the discussion of our measures of sociopolitical orientations), and because a full description of the measures we use from the NES series is provided within the context of those analyses that make use of them.

NES Panel Studies

Of the respondents interviewed in 1956, 1,256 (or 71 percent) of them were reinterviewed in 1958 and again in 1960. The interview schedule for the 1958 survey of these respondents was the same as the 1958 cross-section received, and the schedule for the 1960 interview was the same as the 1960 cross-section received. These respondents are referred to subsequently as the *1956–60 panel.* Of the respondents interviewed in 1972, 1,320 (49 percent) were reinterviewed in 1974 and again in 1976. The interview schedules for these follow-ups were the same as the cross-sectional sample received at that time. This group of respondents is referred to as the *1972–76 panel.*

These NES panel data are useful for assessing the generality of conclusions we reach from our analyses of the Bennington data. The existence of such panel data, however, does not solve all of our methodological problems. While panel data are useful, unfortunately, simple correlations of measures replicated over time confound attenuation due to unreliability of measurement and true attitude change. Thus, some method must be employed to attempt to separate unreliability from attitude change (see Alwin, 1988c).

STRATEGY OF ANALYSIS

For the most part we use the same data-analysis tools used by Newcomb and his colleagues in the two previous research reports from this project. That is, we base our inferences primarily on a detailed examination of the data, beginning with marginal distributions, going on to the display of frequencies, averages, and percentages across categories of additional variables, and including the presentation of cross-tabulations of data and the calculation of "zero-order" or "bivariate" associations in the data. Although Newcomb and associates did not rely on the techniques of multiple regression or structural equation modeling, which were not then the routine analytic tools they are today, they did rely on Pearsonian correlation coefficients routinely. From that point of origin, the more sophisticated research tools of today involve just one or two more levels of complexity. We make use of regression and structural modeling techniques, which are described briefly below, but the basic inferential base in this monograph is very similar to that used by our forerunners.

The problems of reliably measuring attitudes make it difficult to assess the nature of true attitude change over time. Unreliability of measurement, a source of error which occurs quite regularly in the measurement of attitudes, is confounded with true attitude change in data gathered on the same population over time (Alwin, 1973, 1976, 1988b; Heise, 1969; Wheaton et al., 1977). Thus, it is important to confront directly the issues of measurement reliability in examining issues of attitude stability. In our analyses of intertemporal correlation in subsequent chapters, we present results that reflect an effort to adjust or control for the influences of these random sources of error.

Structural Equation Methods of Analysis

Serious flaws exist in previous attempts to estimate the stability of sociopolitical attitudes at different stages in the life cycle. In Sears's (1981) work, for example, attitude stability is estimated using bivariate correlations of over-time measures, without corrections for random measurement error. It is well known that unreliability of measurement attenuates correlations of measures obtained on the same individuals over time (e.g., Heise, 1969). True attitude change is confounded with unreliability of measurement, which is known to be greater among older respondents (see Andrews and Herzog, 1986). In fact, Sears (1981:198) reported reliability coefficients by age cohorts, showing that older respondents generally exhibited lower reporting reliability. And because reliability of measurement varies as a function of age (see Alwin, 1989b; Alwin and Krosnick, 1991b), it is necessary to examine attitude stabilities free of random measurement error to the extent possible.

In chapter 7 we employ a class of simple models that specify the relationships among measures in terms of two general types of structural equations for the processes at work, one for measures, y_{it} (measure i at time t), and one for the latent variables assessed by the y_{it}, denoted here as τ_t. The two equations are given as follows:

$$y_{it} = \tau_t + \epsilon_{it}$$

$$\tau_t = \beta_{t,t-1}\tau_{t-1} + v_t$$

The first equation represents a set of measurement assumptions, indicating that the over-time measures are thought of in terms of measuring the underlying attitude at that particular time. Indeed, the measures are thought of as directly assessing the latent attitude, except for errors of measurement, and over-time correlations of measures are thought to represent attitude stability to the extent that these errors of measurement can be minimized and controlled. The second equation specifies the causal processes involved in attitude change over time.

In our application of these modeling strategies to the data assembled here, we approach the specification of a measurement model by including a minimum of two measures of the latent variable representing sociopolitical orientation at each time point. A minimum of two measures of this latent construct permitted us to identify the parameters associated with both aspects of the model given above—the measurement model and the model for change in the latent attitude variable over time. For the 1930s we have just two measures of sociopolitical orientations, but for the 1960s and 1984 we have four measures at each time point. In chapter 7 we analyze several different models involving differing sets of measures in order to investigate the robustness of our results with respect to alternate sets of measures. Appendix E provides a more detailed discussion of structural equation methods, and appendix F presents a discussion of how we organize the estimates of structural coefficients in the NES panel data into "synthetic" cohort models for analyzing life course development.

5

Generations and the Stability of Sociopolitical Orientations over the Life Span

INTRODUCTION

Newcomb's work on the change and stability of sociopolitical attitudes among the Bennington students of the 1930s and 1940s has been widely cited as evidence of the relative plasticity of such attitudes in adolescence and young adulthood, and at the same time as evidence of the relative stability or persistence of attitudes in later life (e.g., Kinder and Sears, 1985). With its emphasis on the importance of early experiences in adulthood, Newcomb's work seemed at odds with the literature on political socialization that developed in the mid-1960s, which emphasized the formation of relatively stable orientations early in life. The latter work emphasized substantial "inheritance" of sociopolitical orientations from the parental generation (e.g., Campbell et al., 1960; Cutler, 1974; Davies, 1965; Greenstein, 1965; Hess and Torney, 1967; Sears, 1975). Newcomb's research indicated the potential for significant openness to change in political orientations even into late adolescence and early adulthood. His work reinforced the idea that there are "impressionable years," a time in early adulthood when people are probably the most vulnerable to change. At the same time, as we saw in chapter 3, Newcomb's later work emphasized the stability of orientations in the middle years. This later work is in line with more recent panel studies that suggest substantial stability of some sociopolitical orientations over the life course (e.g., Converse and Markus, 1979; Jennings and Neimi, 1981; Niemi et al., 1980; Sears, 1981).

This view of the powerful influences of formative experiences on sociopolitical attitudes early in adult life that persist later in life is also consistent with Mannheim's (1952) *generational* model of social change, which suggests that each new generation is exposed to a unique set of sociohistorical experiences when it becomes politically aware. The different experiences of each generation, or birth cohort, then produce social change, which occurs via a succession of generations, or cohorts. One assumption underlying such models of *cohort replacement,* often left implicit, is that people's political orientations are relatively stable after some point early in their lives. If such stable tendencies emerge soon after the early adult experiences of a particular cohort, then *cohort effects* may be quite durable in the face of social change. In chapter 7 we explore more thoroughly the question of individual persistence over the life course; the present chapter focuses on the stability of the Bennington cohort in the aggregate and the extent to which its patterns of political orientation reflect the cohort or generation of which they are a part.

The idea that these early experiences shape the values and orientations which people carry with them throughout their lives, thus, not only has implications for the study of individual persistence and change over the life course; it presents implications for the study of social change as well. As an explanation of social change, the cohort replacement ideas of Mannheim (1952) have been relatively popular (e.g., see Abramson, 1983; Abramson and Inglehart, 1986; Bengtson, 1989; Carlsson and Karlsson, 1970; Davis, 1975; Delli Carpini, 1989; Fendrich and Lovoy, 1988; Firebaugh and Davis, 1988; Inglehart, 1971, 1977, 1986; Ryder, 1965; Stouffer, 1955). At the same time there is only fragmentary evidence that cohort, or generational, differences are responsible for social changes in sociopolitical orientations. For example, a number of researchers have reported the existence of a pro-Democratic residue among birth cohorts entering the electorate during the years of the Great Depression, presumably exposed to a greater extent than other cohorts to the political orientations exemplified by the social programs of the New Deal (Crittenden, 1962; Knoke and Hout, 1974; Oppenheim, 1970).[1] This pattern is consistent with what is known about the relative ascendence of the Democratic party in the late 1930s and 1940s, when it reached a level of popularity among the voting electorate which has been reached in only two presidential elections since: 1960 and 1964 (see Abramson, 1975:5). If cohorts entering adult life during these early periods were more "liberal" or Democratic as a result of their exposure to these Democratic regimes during the impressionable years, this might help account for the "Bennington effect" described in chapter 2. And if the cohort replacement process depends on the relative stability or persistence of individual attitudes over the life span, the patterns of stability witnessed in chapter 3 might be viewed as confirming this part of such a *generational/persistence* model.

1. Also consistent with this generational thesis is a recent study by Roberts and Lang (1985; see also Lang and Lang, 1978), who show, using a large sample of 1,321 former Woodrow Wilson fellows, that those who reached age 20 during the middle of the 1960s reveal a somewhat stronger sensitivity to the sociopolitical issues of that period.

AGING, COHORTS, AND CONSERVATISM

Cohort effects are, of course, difficult to establish given the confounding of age and cohort in cross-sectional studies and the confounding of aging and history in longitudinal, single-cohort designs. Despite these problems, the research literature is filled with discussion about the relative importance of aging and cohorts (or generations) in accounting for age-related differences in political conservatism.[2] Crittenden (1962), for example, contrasted aging and cohort explanations for an observed association between age and partisanship in survey data. Concerned to show that "the aging process has an impact on party affiliation . . . independent of any such generational factors" (648), he examined the effects of age/cohort in four nationwide surveys conducted in 1946, 1950, 1954, and 1958. Crittenden concluded that support existed for the idea that "aging seems to produce a shift toward Republicanism in the period 1946 to 1958" (654).

Further research on this issue generally does not support this conclusion (e.g., Abramson, 1983; Converse, 1976; Glenn, 1974; Glenn and Grimes, 1968; Glenn and Hefner, 1972). Glenn, for example, concludes that "although the evidence suggests that attitudes probably become somewhat less susceptible to change as people grow older, there is scant evidence for any other contribution of aging to (political) conservatism" (1974: 176). Rather than aging making people ideologically conservative, and hence more likely to identify with the Republican party, Glenn argued that people of different ages reacted differently to the liberalizing (or Democratic) influences of the 1930s—a thesis consistent with the generational/ persistence model of Sears (1981, 1983), which indicates that people become less susceptible to change as they grow older.

On the basis of election surveys carried out in 1952 and 1956, Campbell and his colleagues (1960) found that younger cohorts had weaker party loyalties than older ones, which has since become one of the best documented findings on political attitudes (Abramson, 1983:106). Campbell and his colleagues further proposed that the relationship between age and partisanship observed in cross-sectional studies had two different, but compatible interpretations. The directional changes in political partisanship in the

2. There are two types of conservatism referred to in this literature, and they are some-sometimes confused. The term is often used to refer, on the one hand, to *conservatism* defined in terms of a political ideology and, on the other, to *conservatism* defined in terms of rigidity with respect to the acceptance of change, that is, the extent of attitude stability over time. In the present chapter we focus primarily on the former type of political conservatism— the contrast between conventional notions of liberal and conservative political ideologies. In chapter 7 we deal with political conservatism in the sense of the growing resistance of attitudes to change.

United States, that is, historical shifts in Democratic-Republican choices, were interpreted as the product of a cohort phenomenon akin to Mannheim's notion of generations. At the same time, attitudes were seen to grow in "strength" or "intensity" as a function of aging and life-cycle changes, rather than through the phenomenon of the succession of generations.

This thesis was further investigated by Converse (1976) and found to hold up well to the data for the period from 1952 to 1964, a period of relative stability in American politics.[3] Following Campbell and his colleagues (1960:161), Converse acknowledged "the fundamental dilemma of interpretation" of cohort analysis based on replicated cross-sections, suggesting that "any substantive case must rest on contentions of relative plausibility, rather than iron-clad proof." He noted that both components of party identification—the direction and intensity components—suffer an interpretational ambiguity. Concerning direction, he notes that "older people may be relatively more Republican in the United States as a function of life-cycle changes," that is, that "aging breeds increased conservatism," or the age-partisanship relationship may be a "reflection of the known succession of political periods in our electoral history: older people were socialized in a period of Republican ascendancy before the Great Depression and Roosevelt's New Deal, whereas younger cohorts matured in a period of relative Democratic popularity" (1976:11). With regard to the strength component of party identification, Converse noted that older people might be more "staunchly partisan due to a variety of factors . . . likely to reinforce the strength of any initial party preference progressively over the life cycle." Or, he notes, the stronger partisanship of the old may reflect the "political ethos of grass-roots politics in an earlier epoch . . . more ardently and unquestionably partisan than it has been in recent years" (1976:12).

Converse's (1969, 1976) independent examination of this issue supported Campbell and his colleagues' (1960) two-ply argument—that age differences in the directional component of partisan attitudes may be traceable to cohort factors, unrelated to aging, but that aging, or life-cycle, processes are responsible for the age-intensity aspect of the broader relationship of age to party identification. Analyzing long-term, U.S. and international survey data (29 national samples of the adult U.S. population conducted by the Survey Research Center between 1952 and 1975, and a number of other data sets), Converse found some support for the growing intensity of party affiliations over the life cycle as an aging process, net of cohort differences, for the 1952–64 period.

3. Converse (1976) refers to the 1952–64 period as a *steady-state period*, whereas the years following 1964 were viewed as an *era of political crisis*. It is important to be able to assume no major historical disturbances exist for purposes of sorting out life-cycle versus generational factors in the development of party loyalties.

Changes in cohort composition, on the other hand, were seen as responsible for the historical changes in the direction of partisan shifts. More recently, in response to criticism (see Abramson, 1979), Converse argues that "under the simplifying assumptions" necessary for his assessment, "the test for the pure-generational hypothesis is negative, and life-cycle gains account for roughly all of the age-strength relationship" (Converse, 1979: 100).

Evidence and opinion on this issue continue to be mixed. Glenn and Hefner (1972) and Glenn (1974) studied age differences in "political conservatism" as measured by questions about party identification. They found no support for the idea that people become more resistant to change in old age. More recently, Abramson (1983:130) concluded that "when cohorts are tracked over time, there is virtually no increase in partisan strength as cohorts age, although there is some support for the life-cycle thesis if we restrict the analysis to the years between 1952 and 1964." He further argues that Converse mistook purely generational effects for life-cycle (or aging) effects. Abramson claims that Converse's evidence for life-cycle effects in his data is weak and that the main decline in party loyalty reflects a succession-of-cohorts phenomenon. He notes that Converse's analysis fails to take account of the strengthening of black partisan loyalties during the period of 1952–64, and that he "mixed period effects with life cycle effects" (Abramson, 1979:78). He shows that there was little gain in partisan strength among young whites during the period in which Converse identified an aging effect, 1952–64, whereas black partisan strength increased dramatically after 1960. He concluded that, by including blacks in the analysis, Converse confounded period effects with life-cycle effects, mistaking the former for the latter, and "by failing to disentangle these effects, he interpreted period effects as if they were the result of life-cycle forces" (Abramson, 1979:90).[4]

Abramson's (1983) analysis of the intensity of party identification is unusual in its joint reliance on a cohort analysis of the repeated cross sections contained in the SRC-NES data set (from 1952 through 1980) *and* panel data from the Michigan student-parent study (Jennings and Niemi, 1981).[5]

4. We find considerable merit in Converse's (1979) argument that Abramson's point about analyzing results separately by race is a trivial matter, since it primarily involves southern blacks, who represent one-twentieth of the electorate.

5. The Jennings and Niemi study was based on a two-wave panel study of a national sample of 1965 high school seniors ($n = 1,348$) and their parents ($n = 1,179$), observed in 1965 and 1973. Interestingly, Abramson (1983:109) rejects the utility of the 1950s and 1970s NES panel data, which we use in chapter 7. He states that these panel surveys "do not prove very helpful, since, as we shall see, the predicted gains in partisan strength are so small that they would be difficult to detect during a mere four-year period." Apparently, Abramson did not envision the use to which these data could be put in cohort analysis of attitude stability over time (see chapter 7).

Such simultaneous consideration of both types of data is important for at least two reasons. First, as we mentioned in the foregoing, conclusions regarding the presence of cohort succession or cohort replacement hinge on the assumption that such generation effects persist in the affected individuals. In other words, it is important to verify the existence of high degrees of individual-level stability of relevant variables in order to make such cohort interpretations plausible. Second, aging (or life-cycle) interpretations of attitude stability, to the extent that they can be induced from replicated cross-sectional data, are not based on an adequate empirical referent. The extent of individual change *cannot* be inferred from aggregate changes in cohort data; that is, gross change cannot be inferred from net change.

Abramson (1983:114–15) observes a weakening of party support in the Jennings and Niemi (1981) student cohort between 1965 and 1973, a period of extraordinary volatility on the American political landscape. He concludes that this decline provides a compelling argument for a generational interpretation of the intensity of party loyalties, providing "no support for a life-cycle formulation" (1983:115). This, of course, depends upon the assumptions one is willing to make in interpreting such results. As indicated above, the study of a single cohort tells us little about the life-cycle trajectory of political attitudes. Moreover, while Abramson notes that the parental sample in the Michigan parent-student panel also shows a "small decline in partisanship" (1983:119), he fails to report the fact that the levels of attitude stability in the parental sample over the eight years covered are considerably higher than comparable estimates in the student sample (see Jennings and Neimi, 1981:48–75). This might lend some support to the life-cycle thesis, in that attitudes in the older parent sample are more persistent than those of the student sample. Despite this Abramson concludes that the Michigan student-parent panel "provides compelling evidence that partisan strength has not increased with age" (1983:115).

The Michigan data, of course, provide no such "compelling evidence," either in favor of a life-cycle or cohort interpretation. The apparent decline in party loyalty among the 1965 youth into the mid-1970s may simply be a reflection of the type of "impressionable years" phenomenon identified in the wider literature, which relies on both sets of ideas. Indeed, the comparison of the eight-year stability figures for the student and parent samples would seem to suggest a growing level of attitude persistence with age. Thus, Abramson's use of panel data to examine the question of the stability of political attitudes is inadequate. Patterns of change for the Michigan student-parent samples over the eight-year period studied are limited because they involve a somewhat restricted range on the age distribution, and they involve a single, unique eight-year period, so that life-cycle and historical factors are perfectly confounded. Moreover, Abramson (1983) focuses entirely on average levels of party loyalty, ignoring the comparison

93

of stability information across the student and parent samples. We return to a consideration of issues of individual stability and change in chapter 7.

PATTERNS OF SOCIOPOLITICAL ORIENTATIONS
IN THE BENNINGTON SAMPLE

At this point we turn to an analysis of one aspect of the generational/persistence thesis, reviewed in chapter 1, using the data from the Bennington women in 1984 as well as data from the National Election Study series of cross sections since 1952. Specifically, we ask whether the change Newcomb (1943) witnessed at Bennington could be accounted for in terms of a generational phenomenon. In addition to presenting the marginal distributions for the Bennington women's responses to our questions concerning their sociopolitical attitudes in 1984, we also compare their 1984 responses with those of respondents in the 1984 preelection National Election Study (see Miller and Traugott, 1989). Then we probe somewhat more deeply into the NES series by analyzing cohort differences in several different measures of partisan loyalty and political liberalism/conservatism.

We begin by describing the general orientations of our respondents in 1984, how they may have changed, if at all, in their aggregate responses over the roughly 45–50 years since leaving Bennington. In chapter 6 we compare these patterns with what we learned from our respondents' own retrospections of their sociopolitical attitudes over the time since they left Bennington College. And in chapter 7 we add to this overall picture through a comparison of the 1984 attitudes to those registered by these women at the end of their Bennington years and in the early 1960s, when Newcomb and his colleagues reinterviewed them for the first time. In the present context we compare their 1984 responses to several categories of respondents in the 1984 NES data. We then turn to an analysis of the extent to which their 1984 responses can be thought of in terms of part of a generational (cohort) effect.

Political Orientations in 1984

Table 5.1 presents the distribution of responses to our series of questions (C1–C6) dealing with party identification.[6] This table shows that about 44 percent of respondents in our 1984 survey classified themselves as Democrat, some 24 percent as Republican, and another 30 percent as indepen-

---

6. When we refer to the questions used in the 1984 study, we give the question numbers (e.g., C1–C6) that correspond to the actual questionnaire (see appendix B).

Table 5.1. Univariate Distributions for Questions about Political Preference

A: 1984

C1. Generally speaking do you usually think of yourself as a Republican, a Democrat, an independent, or what?

Republican	Democrat	Independent	Other	No Preference	Total
24.2% (81)	44.2% (148)	30.4% (102)	0.3% (1)	0.9% (3)	100% (335)

C2. Would you call yourself a strong (Republican/Democrat) or a not very strong one?

Republican		Democrat	
Strong	Not strong	Strong	Not strong
56.3% (45)	43.8% (35)	81.6% (120)	18.4% (27)

C5. Do you think of yourself as closer to the Republican party or to the Democratic party?

Republican	Democrat	Neither
16.2% (17)	61.9% (65)	21.9% (23)

C6. Do you think of yourself as much closer or only a little closer to the (Republican/Democrat) party?

Republican		Democrat	
Much closer	Little closer	Much closer	Little closer
35.3% (6)	64.7% (11)	68.8% (44)	29.7% (19)

B: 1960s Party Preference

Republican	Democrat	No preference	Total
37% (58)	58% (90)	5% (7)	100% (148)

C: 1984 Reports of Party Preference—Common Respondents 1960–84

Republican	Democrat	Independent	Other	No preference	Total
19% (23)	52% (63)	27% (33)	0% (0)	2% (2)	100% (121)

D: 1960 Reports of Party Preference: Common Respondents 1960–84

Republican	Democrat	No preference	Total
39% (47)	56% (68)	6% (6)	100% (121)

dent. The latter designation, while compatible with current categories of political preference, introduces some ambiguity in making comparisons with the past, given that such categories were not used in Newcomb's earlier research.

Note, however, from this table that of the 102 respondents identifying themselves as independent, some 62 percent viewed themselves as closer to the Democratic party, 22 percent felt closer to neither major party, and 16 percent identified more closely with the Republican party. If we allocate these independent respondents to the major party they feel closest to, we surmise that about two-thirds identify themselves with the Democratic end of the political spectrum, while slightly fewer than 30 percent identify themselves with the Republican side. A small residue of about 6 or 7 percent declined either designation.

Somewhere between the figures of 60 and 70 percent seems appropriate, then, as a rough designation of the proportion of the Bennington respondents on the liberal side of the ideological continuum represented by party identification in 1984. This is reinforced further in their responses to our question about candidate preferences in the impending 1984 election (C11). Seventy-one percent of our respondents preferred the Democratic candidates, Walter Mondale (68.3 percent) or Gary Hart (2.5 percent), whereas some 25 percent expressed support for Ronald Reagan.

The aggregate results with respect to partisanship are roughly similar to those obtained in the 1960 reinterview, as reported by Newcomb and his colleagues (1967), although close comparisons are not possible because, as noted above, the 1960s surveys did not present *independent* as a response choice. If we consider just those respondents who participated in both the 1960s and 1984 studies (see sections C and D of table 5.1), it is clear that the percentage choosing *Democrat* has remained about the same. As we suggest, however, it is difficult to draw firm conclusions about aggregate shifts in party identification in this group because of the differences in the questions used. We tentatively conclude, however, that the study population as a whole has experienced little *net change* in party loyalty since the 1960s; if anything, it may have become slightly more liberal. As a group these women certainly have not become more politically conservative with age.

Interest in Public Affairs

One of the major differences Newcomb described between the experiences of Bennington students during the early years of the College's existence and those of students attending other colleges at that time was in the approach to education. Newcomb described the Bennington approach to education as emphasizing a "contemporary" rather than "historical" orientation, making students "aware of their contemporary world" (1943:175).

A large number of our Bennington respondents continue to be interested in public affairs. As shown in table 5.2, about 75 percent of the Bennington respondents said that they "followed what's going on in government and public affairs" most of the time (C9). Similarly, 75 percent of these women

Table 5.2. Univariate Distributions for Questions about Interest in Politics

C9. Some people seem to follow what's going on in government and public affairs most of the time, whether there's an election going on or not. Others aren't that interested. Would you say you follow what's going on in government and public affairs most of the time, some of the time, only now and then, or hardly at all?

Most of the time	74%	(248)
Some of the time	21%	(70)
Only now and then	4%	(13)
Hardly at all	1%	(4)
Total	100%	(335)

C10. How about the presidential campaign in 1984? Would you say that you are very much interested, somewhat interested, or not much interested in following the presidential campaign in 1984?

Very much interested	75%	(252)
Somewhat interested	19%	(62)
Not much interested	6%	(21)
Total	100%	(335)

C12. Would you say that you personally care a good deal which party wins the presidential election in the fall of 1984, or that you don't care very much which party wins?

Care a good deal	88%	(289)
Don't care very much	12%	(38)
Total	100%	(327)

Table 5.3. Univariate Distributions for Questions about Political Interest since College

	More Interested	Remained the Same	Less Interested	Total
Obtained in 1984				
For the period *1940–60*, did you become more interested, remain the same, or become less interested in public affairs than when you were in college?	65% (218)	30% (100)	5% (15)	100% (333)
From the period *1960–72*, did you become more or less interested in public affairs?	51% (169)	44% (146)	5% (18)	100% (333)
From the period *1972 to the present*, did you become more or less interested in public affairs?	47% (156)	45% (149)	9% (28)	100% (333)
Obtained in 1960s				
Have you become more interested in public affairs since college?	63% (232)	32% (119)	5% (17)	100% (368)

97

indicated that they "were very much interested" in the 1984 presidential campaign (C10), and over 85 percent said they "personally cared" about "which party wins the presidential election in the fall of 1984" (C12).

As we shall explore in somewhat more detail in the next chapter, this present interest in public affairs, as illustrated in the foregoing tables, has increased since their days at Bennington. Sixty-five percent of the sample indicated in 1984 that they had become more interested in public affairs since college. These data are given in table 5.3. Most of this interest seems to have occurred between the period marked by their college days (1940s) and the 1960s, and it is remarkable that the 1960 and 1984 estimates of this phenomenon are virtually identical. Still, substantial numbers reported becoming more interested in public affairs during the 1960s and 1970s.

Involvement in Politics

Table 5.4 reveals yet another dimension to the distinctiveness of the Bennington women, one that reflects some change from their earlier lives. While nearly 80 percent of these women were *not* active in political organizations in 1984 (F2), the large majority of them (60 percent) reported having "worked for a political party or candidate since leaving Bennington" (F16). At the same time, 25 percent reported that they had "personally been involved in activities and organizations whose major purpose was a change in the status of women" (G21). We do not have comparable data for the U.S. population as a whole from the Election Studies, but we surmise that these figures reflect a level of political involvement that is considerably higher than that of comparable others.

The comparison of these estimates of involvement over the decades given in the question suggests some substantial change in certain aspects of

Table 5.4. Univariate Distributions for Questions on Political Involvement (1984, $n = 335$)

Response to Question	Since Leaving college?	1980s	1970s	1960s	1950s	1940s
F16. Have you worked for a political party or candidate. . . ?						
Yes	60%	31%	34%	36%	32%	22%
G21. Have you personally been involved in any activities or organizations whose major purpose was a change in the status of women?						
Yes	23%	15%	17%	10%	3%	3%
F17. Have you been involved in other political activities or public issues?						
Yes	58%	36%	57%	36%	21%	15%

involvement. Generally, involvement in political activities gradually rose over time among these women, peaking in the 1970s. In the 1980s their involvement in politics began to taper off, presumably because of increased difficulties presented by aging. But it is remarkable that as many as 63 percent indicated that they had become more interested in public affairs since college. This might be interpreted as an *accentuation* effect (see Feldman and Newcomb, 1969; Feldman and Weiler, 1976); that is, the distinct influence of Bennington College on these women might have continued its impact over the years, producing an even greater disparity between this group and those who attended other colleges at that time. We explore this to some extent later in the chapter.

Electoral Preferences

Another area in which the distinctiveness of the Bennington women can be seen is the area of electoral preferences. In our 1984 questionnaire, we asked respondents to provide candidate preferences in all presidential elections beginning in 1940 (C18 and C19).[7] The elicitation of these retrospective reports was designed to replicate a similar series of questions obtained in 1961 for presidential elections occurring from 1940 to 1960. Table 5.5 presents the percentage figures for the liberal/conservative distinction for both series of questions, those gathered in 1984 and those gathered in the 1960s.

These results, based on the 1984 data, show that in most elections since 1940 the Bennington respondents predominantly preferred liberal (Democratic and independent) candidates. Most of the time 60–70 percent of the sample reported a preference for liberal candidates. There are some interesting exceptions to this pattern. Only slightly more than one-half of the respondents reported a preference for Roosevelt in 1940—this is actually the lowest percentage having a liberal preference in the entire series. Recall, however, that in 1940 a sizeable portion of the Bennington sample was still in its early years at Bennington, and the full effect of the Bennington environment may not have run its course. Thus, this lower percentage identifying with the New Deal administration may simply reflect their family origins and not the influence of the Bennington environment. About 75 percent of the Bennington sample preferred Kennedy rather than Nixon in 1960, and nearly 80 percent preferred Johnson rather than Goldwater in 1964. Similarly high support for the more liberal party is seen in 1980.

The 1984 series, then, is relatively stable over this period of more than

7. This allows us to tabulate preferences, regardless of whether the individual voted in the election.

Table 5.5 Univariate Distributions for Candidate Preferences
(Conservative vs. Liberal)

Election Year	Obtained in 1984		Obtained in 1960s	
	Conservative	Liberal	Conservative	Liberal
1984	27%	72%		
	(81)	(220)		
1980	24%	76%		
	(78)	(253)		
1976	31%	69%		
	(103)	(227)		
1972	31%	69%		
	(101)	(229)		
1968	33%	67%		
	(108)	(218)		
1964	21%	79%		
	(67)	(253)		
1960	26%	74%	46%	56%
	(86)	(245)	(159)	(203)
1956	37%	63%	50%	50%
	(124)	(205)	(174)	(174)
1952	43%	57%	52%	48%
	(139)	(187)	(183)	(171)
1948	32%	68%	47%	53%
	(102)	(213)	(155)	(175)
1944	32%	68%	36%	64%
	(101)	(219)	(122)	(221)
1940	45%	54%	52%	48%
	(145)	(168)	(167)	(153)

40 years. If there is any change reflected in this series, it is a gradual move-ment in the direction of greater liberalism. The 1960s data also reflect relative stability; but interestingly, these data suggest greater conservatism among the participants in the 1960s studies. In most years roughly one-half of the 1960s respondents preferred the conservative candidate.[8] In chapter 6 we return to the apparent disparity between these two series of reports. We do so by exploring the fact that these responses are retrospec-tive reports and by considering the possible response biases that might help account for the differences between the two.

8. We should point out that the two series of retrospective reports of candidate preferences presented in table 5.5 are based on the same respondents.

BENNINGTON EFFECT OR GENERATIONAL EFFECT?

All the information we have summarized above suggests that for the most part the Bennington women maintained their collegiate orientations; they continue to be intensely interested in political and social issues, and their responses are significantly in the liberal direction. The Bennington respondents overwhelmingly revealed themselves to be interested in the 1984 presidential campaign, which was then underway, and significantly attentive to political news, and their responses to most political issues favored a liberal orientation.

In chapter 2 we raised the possibility that the changes witnessed by Newcomb (1943) in the 1930s and 1940s among these women were due, not to the unique influences of the Bennington College environment, but to the larger historical environment affecting young people, especially those in college, at the time. If there is any strength in the type of arguments suggested by Mannheim and others that, potentially at least, the sociopolitical orientations of each new generation are affected in a distinctive way by events occurring at the time they reach political maturity, then we should find remnants of this type of orientation in data from others growing to maturity at that time. Our earlier discussion of this hypothesis made reference to the possibility that students at other colleges might have been similarly affected, or (more generally) that people of the same age and educational level might be so affected.

We also noted in chapter 2 that Newcomb had anticipated this hypothesis by examining the generality of the Bennington effect by surveying students at other colleges. In so doing, Newcomb found some evidence of a move toward greater liberalism in colleges similar to Bennington, but changes involving somewhat less intensity than at Bennington (see Newcomb, 1943:30–31). We also noted earlier that Newcomb found similar "reference-group effects," but in a direction ideologically different in a college whose faculty was more conservative in orientation (Newcomb, 1946). Thus, he established a stronger basis for the reference-group effect he had found at Bennington but was not able to address the more general question of whether this was part of a larger generational phenomenon.[9]

Thus, we have the advantage of hindsight when we "second-guess" the original interpretation which Newcomb (1943, 1946) gave his results. And using a somewhat broader-gauged assay of empirical evidence, we can investigate the extent to which a generational explanation for the Bennington

9. We should note that reference-group and generational interpretations are not necessarily incompatible.

results might be plausible. We are mindful, however, that little in the way of "ironclad proof" (to use Converse's term) may be generated from this exercise, because in cross-sectional designs, it is virtually impossible to separate the effects of aging and cohort experiences. It is only in the presence of reasonable theoretical assumptions about the nature of some of these influences that certain plausible hypotheses can be launched. In any case, our focus will be on more or less testable consistencies or inconsistencies, the nature of which can and will lead to plausible interpretations only in the presence of "side information" (see Converse, 1976).

COMPARISONS WITH THE 1984 NATIONAL ELECTION STUDY

To this point we have offered no benchmark against which to compare the Bennington women. One such comparison, incorporated in the design of our study, is a comparison of our Bennington sample with various subsets of respondents to the 1984 National Election Study. Here we compare the responses of our Bennington respondents on many of our questions assessing political orientations and interest to four subsets of respondents from the 1984 preelection National Election Study: (1) the total NES sample, (2) the total NES subsample of women, (3) the NES subsample of women aged 60 or over, and (4) NES women aged 60 or over who also had attended college.[10] These several subsets were used to provide some control over relevant differentiating factors linked to political response.[11]

Party Identification and Candidate Preference

Table 5.6 presents the comparisons for party identification and candidate preference in 1984. These results indicate that the Bennington women are somewhat more likely to choose the Democratic party than is the general population. They are more similar to other women and to older women, but they are, relatively speaking, unlike college-educated women of their own age. The Bennington women were much more likely to pre-

10. Because of the small samples in the upper age-ranges, we include respondents older than age 60 in 1984. Such persons were born prior to 1924, which coincides exactly with the youngest of the Bennington sample. Later in this chapter, when we have more cases within our grasp, we will restrict the sample to those members of the cohorts into which the Bennington women were born.

11. Despite the obvious merits of interethnic comparisons, we here limit our comparisons to the NES data to white respondents because there were almost no minority group members in the Bennington sample. Thus, all of the following tables based on tabulations from the NES data pertain only to white respondents.

Table 5.6. Comparison of 1984 Bennington Respondents to 1984 National Election Study Respondents

Response to Question	1984 NES White Respondents				
	Total NES	Women	Women 60+	Women 60+ w/College	Bennington
C1. Party identification?					
Democrat	32.3%	35.6%	41.0%	35.7%	44.2%
Republican	30.1	28.9	32.3	37.1	24.2
Ind. other/none	37.6	35.5	26.7	27.3	31.6
n	4,990	2,750	471	143	335
C11. Candidate preference?					
Mondale	30.8%	33.0%	32.9%	35.0%	68.3%
Reagan	60.8	57.1	51.5	53.0	25.4
Other	0.8	0.6	1.1	1.0	2.5
DK	7.6	9.3	14.7	11.0	3.8
n	2,892	1,582	375	100	319
D13. Liberal/conservative?					
Liberal	25.1%	24.5%	23.4%	15.2%	72.8%
Moderate	32.8	37.0	42.3	45.5	12.0
Conservative	42.0	38.4	34.2	39.4	15.1
n	1,392	711	111	33	324

fer Mondale than their educated female contemporaries (older, college-educated women), and this was one of their distinct tendencies. The majority of respondents in the population subgroups assembled in table 5.6 preferred Ronald Reagan to continue as president, but only 25 percent of our Bennington sample were so disposed. Thus, with respect to some aspects of sociopolitical orientations, the Bennington women are quite unlike their contemporaries and even more unlike their educated peers (e.g., see the results for the liberal/conservative scale and our measures of candidate preferences), whereas in terms of party loyalty the differences are smaller, but they are present nonetheless.

Political Interest and the Mass Media

Table 5.7 presents comparisons with the NES data for political interest and orientation to news regarding public affairs. Older, highly educated women tend to follow government affairs. This may be suggestive of a cohort effect. However, the Bennington women continue to be more extreme. The Bennington women and the NES category of educated women

Table 5.7. Comparison of 1984 Bennington Respondents to 1984 National Election Study Respondents (Political Interest)

Response to Question	1984 NES White Respondents				
	Total NES	Women	Women 60+	Women 60+ w/College	Bennington
C9. Follow government affairs?					
Most of time	38.3%	32.3%	49.4%	66.2%	74.0%
Some of time	33.1	35.4	28.5	24.6	20.9
Now and then	19.4	21.1	13.7	7.7	3.9
Hardly at all	9.3	11.3	8.3	1.4	1.2
n	4,728	2,599	445	142	335
C10. Interest in 1984 presidential campaign?					
Very much	40.8%	38.7%	52.9%	64.1%	75.2%
Somewhat	41.6	43.2	32.6	29.6	18.5
Not much	17.5	18.1	14.6	6.3	6.3
n	5,009	2,759	473	142	335
C12. Care who wins?					
Good deal	67.7%	67.3%	72.6%	75.4%	88.4%
Not very much	32.3	32.7	27.4	24.6	11.6
n	4,921	2,697	456	138	327
C14. Watch TV national news?					
Every day	45.1%	45.4%	72.0%	76.2%	53.2%
3–4 times/week	20.7	20.1	14.5	11.9	22.1
1–2 times/week	18.5	18.5	7.5	7.1	9.6
Less often	15.8	16.0	5.9	4.8	15.1
n	1,940	1,072	186	42	312
C14a. Attention to political news?					
Great deal	35.6%	29.2%	41.3%	46.3%	67.9%
Some	51.2	56.4	47.8	48.8	31.1
Not much	13.2	14.3	10.9	4.9	1.0
n	1,872	1,040	184	41	305

aged 60 or over appear to be the most involved: they are more likely to follow government affairs, show more interest in the 1984 presidential campaign, care more about who wins, and pay more attention to political news. The Bennington women exceed their age and education peers in all areas of involvement except one: the category of "watching TV national news." The Bennington women are much less involved in television news than are other older women. This may help explain their greater resistence to change.

Stance on Political Issues

Table 5.8 presents comparisons with the NES data for several political issues. Again the Bennington women are distinctive. They exceed all groups in their liberal orientation. Nearly 40 percent of these women are concerned that the United States might get itself into a conventional war (C24), and over 60 percent are "worried . . . about our country getting into a nuclear war," (C25) and concerned that the strength of the U.S. position in the world is weaker than it should be (C23). Few of the Bennington women (13 percent) felt that the national government should spend less on health and education (C26), and over one-half felt the federal government should be working to "improve the social and economic position of blacks and other minority groups" (C27), as well as that of older Americans (C31). Very few (5 percent) think that the "United States should become more involved in the internal affairs of Central American countries" (C28), and a large majority (72 percent) thinks we "should spend less money for defense" (C29). There is great support for the importance of "cooperating more with Russia" among the Bennington respondents (68 percent)—almost twice that registered by any other subgroup (C30).

In all these contrasts the Bennington women seem to be most aligned with other women of their own age, and they are least similar to other college-educated women of their own age. Several contrasts bear this out, for example, in the areas of government spending, defense spending, and the likelihood of nuclear war. At the same time, the Bennington women are quite different from most categories on virtually all the political issues measured in the 1984 National Election Survey. These findings can be used to reinforce the observation that the Bennington women of the 1930s and 1940s are distinct in the sense that, on the whole, they are extremely well-informed in the area of public affairs and decidedly liberal on most social and political issues.

Political Affect

Although we do not summarize them in detail, we also present comparisons of our Bennington sample with the NES subgroups on several measures of affective response to political figures and social categories (see appendix C). In general, the Bennington women respond most favorably to liberals, with about 70 percent identifying highly (a rating above 60) with this

105

Table 5.8. Comparison of 1984 Bennington Respondents to 1984 National Election Study Respondents (Political Issues)

Response to Question	1984 NES White Respondents				
	Total NES	Women	Women 60+	Women 60+ w/College	Bennington

C23. During the past year, would you say that the United States' position in the world has grown weaker, stayed about the same, or has it grown stronger?

Weaker	27.8%	29.8%	33.4%	36.2%	63.1%
Stayed same	40.4	45.1	43.2	44.0	22.2
Stronger	31.8	25.2	23.4	19.9	14.8
n	4,927	2,702	461	141	325

C24. At this time, how worried are you about our country getting into a *conventional war*, one in which nuclear weapons are *not* used?

Very	18.9%	22.3%	22.5%	18.9%	39.0%
Somewhat	45.9	49.9	49.4	50.3	47.1
Not	35.2	27.8	28.2	30.8	13.9
n	4,995	2,752	472	143	331

C25. At this time, how worried are you about our country getting into a *nuclear war*?

Very	26.9%	31.8%	28.9%	22.2%	62.4%
Somewhat	36.9	39.9	41.4	41.0	30.7
Not	36.2	28.2	29.7	36.8	6.9
n	4,993	2,751	471	144	335

C26. Some people think the government in Washington should provide fewer services, even in areas such as health and education, in order to reduce spending. Other people feel it is important for the government to provide more services, even if it means an increase in spending. Do you think the government should reduce spending, provide more services, or is your position somewhere in between?

Reduce	32.8%	26.4%	29.1%	36.2%	13.3%
Between	35.2	36.2	39.7	36.2	50.3
More services	31.9	37.4	31.3	27.5	36.4
n	4,061	2,138	348	127	324

C27. Some people feel that the government in Washington should make every effort to improve the social and economic position of blacks and other minority groups. Others feel that the government should not make any special effort to help minorities because they should help themselves. Do you feel the government should help improve the position of minorities, that minorities should help themselves, or is your position somewhere in between?

Govt. help	30.2%	30.7%	27.5%	26.6%	53.7%
Between	29.1	30.6	31.7	37.5	38.2

106

Table 5.8. Comparison of 1984 Bennington Respondents to 1984 National Election Study Respondents (Political Issues) *(continued)*

Response to Question	1984 NES White Respondents				
	Total NES	Women	Women 60+	Women 60+ w/College	Bennington
Help selves	40.7	38.7	40.8	35.9	8.1
n	4,210	2,271	375	128	330

C28. Some people think that the United States should become more involved in the internal affairs of Central American countries. Others believe that the United States should become less involved in this area. Do you feel that the United States should become less involved in Central America, become more involved in this area, or is your position somewhere in between?

More involved	22.3%	14.1%	11.3%	15.8%	5.3%
Between	19.8	19.3	21.0	23.3	32.1
Less involved	57.9	66.5	67.7	60.9	62.6
n	4,210	2,022	353	120	324

C29. Some people believe that we should spend less money for defense. Others feel that defense spending should be increased. Do you feel the government should decrease defense spending, increase defense spending, or is the government spending about the right amount?

Decrease	35.9%	38.0%	34.0%	30.4%	75.2%
Right amount	31.0	30.4	36.0	36.8	20.3
Increase	33.2	31.6	29.9	32.8	4.5
n	4,313	2,234	364	125	311

C30. Some people feel it is important for us to try to cooperate more with Russia, while others believe we should be much tougher in our dealings with Russia. Do you feel that we should try to cooperate more with Russia, get tougher in our dealings with Russia, or is your opinion somewhere in between?

Cooperate	34.5%	33.9%	31.7%	34.4%	68.3%
Between	22.4	23.9	27.5	27.9	25.6
Get tougher	43.1	42.1	40.9	37.7	6.1
n	4,204	2,155	360	122	328

C31. Some people feel the government in Washington should make every effort to improve the social and economic position of older Americans. Others feel that the government is already doing as much as it can, and families should do more to care for their older adults. Do you feel that the government should do more to improve the position of older Americans . . . ?

Govt. help	36.1%	38.3%	34.3%	31.6%	34.4%
Between	26.7	25.9	22.2	21.4	44.4
Help selves	37.1	35.8	43.5	47.0	21.2
n	3,988	2,202	347	117	326

category. Their responses tended to be similar to those of other women, but not necessarily to those of similar age and education, yet these respondents are clearly distinct. Relative to all other categories considered, they respond positively to civil rights leaders, people on welfare, blacks, and women's liberation. They respond negatively to evangelical groups active in politics, such as the Moral Majority, conservatives, the military, the present Supreme Court, and big business. These findings simply confirm the general findings emerging from our foregoing analyses that the Bennington women remain liberal in orientation, rejecting what they see to be conservative forces within society.

COMPARISONS TO PRE-1984 NES SURVEYS

In order to gauge more finely the exact nature of the disparity between the Bennington women and their female contemporaries, we compared them with data we could glean from the entire National Election Study series since its inception in 1952. Specifically, we were interested in whether stronger evidence could be brought to bear on the question of the political distinctiveness of the Bennington women. We wished to extend our grasp of the available archival record beyond the small samples of these birth cohorts from the 1984 study. For party identification and self-rated liberalism/conservatism, we were able to extend our reach beyond the 1984 database, because the party identification variable has been assessed in all NES cross-sections since 1952, and the self-rating of liberalism/conservatism has been included since 1972.

In table 5.9 we present relevant tabulations of the Bennington sample across birth years. Because of the need for flexibility and greater ease of comparison, and because the bulk of the sample lies in the 1915–24 cohort, we partition our cohort variable differently depending upon the focus of our analysis. First, as above, for purposes of comparison of the Bennington sample with a comparable NES cohort, we use a wider span of years—specifically, 1910–24. Second, later on for purposes of intercohort comparisons, a smaller range of birth cohorts is more useful. Thus, in our subsequent analyses of intercohort patterns in sociopolitical orientations, we use the 1915–24 category.

Inspection of tables 5.10 and 5.11 permits a comparison of the Bennington women with the NES sample women composing the birth cohorts of which our Bennington women were members. Table 5.10 presents these comparative data for the NES measure of party identification obtained in the presidential election years since 1952 (nine surveys). For this table we obtained the percentage of the NES subgroups in each survey year who

Table 5.9. Distribution of Bennington Sample
by Birth Year

Year Born	Age in 1984	Number of Women	Percent
1912	72	1	0.3%
1913	71	10	3.0
1914	70	22	6.6
1915	69	30	9.0
1916	68	52	15.5
1917	67	53	15.8
1918	66	53	15.8
1919	65	50	14.9
1920	64	47	14.0
1921	63	13	3.9
1922	62	3	0.9
1923	61	1	0.3
Total		335	100.0%

Table 5.10. Comparison of Bennington Sample to Subgroups within the National Election
Presidential Year Surveys, 1952–84

	Percent Republican Party Preference				
Year	NES Total Sample	NES Women	NES Women Born 1910–24	NES Women Born 1910–24 w/College	Bennington Women
1952	58.4%	58.4%	58.0%	75.0%	42.6%
	(1,417)	(764)	(262)	(44)	(326)
1956	63.1%	66.5%**	62.9%	72.1%	37.7%
	(1,562)	(855)	(326)	(61)	(329)
1960	51.3%	53.7%	51.3%	75.6%***	26.0%
	(969)	(525)	(197)	(45)	(331)
1964	33.5%	32.9%	32.2%	51.2%**	20.2%
	(1,255)	(681)	(208)	(41)	(321)
1968	64.0%	62.6%	63.9%	74.4%	32.9%
	(1,177)	(661)	(191)	(43)	(328)
1972	69.4%	67.2%*	75.3%**	68.9%	30.6%
	(1,436)	(781)	(194)	(45)	(330)
1976	53.4%	53.5%	52.4%	52.9%	31.2%
	(1,194)	(665)	(185)	(51)	(330)
1980	58.3%	55.0%**	54.4%	65.2%*	23.4%
	(1,850)	(1,012)	(228)	(66)	(133)
1984	66.4%	57.1%	61.0%	60.2%	26.4%
	(2,649)	(1,425)	(316)	(88)	(307)

Note: Asterisks (*) refer to the degree of significance of the difference of the particular NES
subsample from the remainder of NES respondents.
*$p < .05$ **$p < .01$ ***$p < .001$

Table 5.11. Comparison of Bennington Sample to Subgroups within the National Election Presidential Year Surveys, 1960–84

	Percent Conservative				
Year	NES Total Sample	NES Women	NES Women Born 1910–24	NES Women Born 1910–24 w/College	Bennington Women	
1960	—	—	—	—	26.7% (251) 16.1% (324)	actual recalled
1972	38.8% (1,411)	37.8% (752)	44.1% (161)	50.0% (42)	15.9% (321)	recalled
1976	41.7% (1,356)	38.7% (714)	45.3% (172)	44.8% (58)		
1980	45.8% (1,143)	44.4% (585)	56.8% (111)	54.5% (33)		
1984	42.0% (1,392)	38.4% (711)	34.2% (38)	39.4% (33)	15.1% (324)	actual

selected the Republican party. Table 5.11 presents similar data for the NES seven-point liberalism/conservatism scale, namely the percentage in each year describing themselves as slightly to very conservative.

All these figures show rather convincingly that the Bennington sample is systematically different from the women in the NES surveys who are most similar to them in other important respects. The Bennington women are significantly less conservative than NES women born between 1910 and 1924 who obtained some college experience. In virtually all of the presidential election years since 1952, the Bennington women preferred liberal candidates to a significantly greater degree than did all groups available for comparison in the tables. Moreover, they are more similar to women in general, although still considerably more liberal, than they are to women of similar age and education. This general finding creates some doubt about whether the Bennington women are part of a larger generational phenomenon.[12] They hardly resemble other women of their own generation and

12. In appendix D we present data for all of the 1984 Bennington study measures which were replicated in the 1952–84 election series enough times to make their inclusion here warranted. In addition to the party identification and ideological self-placement questions, the appendix gives the distributions of responses for the four groups of NES respondents by year for the following variables: whether the respondent follows government affairs (since 1964); the extent of the respondent's interest in election campaigns (since 1952); the extent to which the respondent cares who wins the election (since 1952); whether the respondent follows national television news (since 1974); whether the respondent gives attention to political

110

seem most different from other women of that generation who attended college.

All of these results show that whether one compares the Bennington women to their educated age-mates using the 1984 data, or whether the comparison is extended to all their contemporaries in NES surveys since the early 1950s, there is little basis for the contention that their liberal attitudes and liberal party affiliation arise from the generational milieu in which they acquired them. There are some interesting exceptions to this conclusion, which we do not attempt to dissect fully here, but which represent some possible leads for future research.

This analysis, however, does not go far enough in the search for evidence of a generational effect. It shows only that the Bennington women as a group are relatively dissimilar to their age-peers and even more unlike their educated generational contemporaries. It says nothing about how similar or different that generation is to others coming before and after. Our answer to this question is still incomplete; our conclusion at this juncture, therefore, is that unless we introduce comparisons among cohorts (see the next section), we cannot determine the nature of the Bennington phenomenon.

INTERCOHORT DIFFERENCES IN POLITICAL ORIENTATIONS

Our final foray into birth-cohort terrain involves an even more exhaustive search for a generational explanation of the original Bennington effect. The analysis we summarized above (contained in tables 5.10, 5.11, and appendix D) left us with three general questions. First, is there any evidence that generational differences in fact exist? Second, if the Bennington women were not that much like their comparable contemporaries (educated women of the same age), would this necessarily question the existence of a generational phenomenon? And third, what other social influences might have contributed to the sample's uniqueness and stability over the several decades involved?

To address the first of these questions, we created several categories of birth cohorts for comparative purposes: those born between 1895 and 1904, those born between 1905 and 1914, between 1915 and 1924, between

---

news on television (only for 1980 and 1984); attitude about the strength of the U.S. position in world affairs (since 1958); whether the respondent is worried about whether the United States will get into a conventional war, that is, one that does not involve the use of nuclear weapons (since 1956); attitude toward government spending (only for 1982 and 1984); the respondent's attitude toward aiding minorities (since 1970); and her attitude regarding defense spending (since 1980).

1925 and 1934, between 1935 and 1944, between 1945 and 1954, and between 1955 and 1964.[13] Tables 5.12 and 5.13 present differences among these cohort categories for the party identification and liberal/conservative measures respectively. Table 5.12 presents intercohort comparative data for the NES measure of party identification involving both the percentage Republican of all respondents in these surveys and the percentage Republican of those respondents identifying with either political party. This table also presents the mean of the party identification variable, ranging from a score of 7 for strong Republicans to 1 for strong Democrats (see the discussion of this measure in chapter 4). Table 5.13 presents similar data for the NES seven-point liberal/conservative scale—both the percentage describing themselves as conservative and the simple average of the variable, scaled such that a 7 is assigned to "very conservative" and a 1 to "very liberal."

The figures in table 5.12 present a very interesting picture of generational differences in political orientations. The 1915–24 cohorts are less conservative than older and younger ones, except among college-educated women. Among the latter group there seems to be a rather linear decline, whether one looks at party loyalty or self-ratings on the liberal/conservative scale (table 5.13). The figures in table 5.12 indicate that among women generally and among the total population, the 1915–24 cohort is definitely less conservative than both older and younger groups. The 1945–54 cohort, the group achieving political maturity during the 1960s, is the major exception to this, since this group—the Vietnam generation—is the most liberal in orientation, whatever measure one uses or whatever subsample one considers. This finding is of interest, since the children of the Bennington women were mainly born between 1940 and 1959. The potential concentration of liberal attitudes among this generation of offspring might have assisted in producing their mothers' attitude stability over the life cycle. We return to this issue in chapter 9.

In contrast, table 5.13 does not reproduce this pattern. Here, based on the NES seven-point liberal/conservative rating scale, the 1915–24 birth cohorts have among the highest conservative ratings. Indeed, as noted above, among women with some college education there is a fairly regular decline in the percent conservative with age. This is approximated among women in general. We suspect that these ratings better reflect the intensity rather than the direction of partisanship. Indeed, these ratings produce results that are very similar to those presented in the following section

13. In the later NES surveys some members of post-1964 cohorts were sampled. In these last few surveys we include these youngest respondents in the 1955–64 category. Similarly, those born prior to 1895 are included in the 1895–1904 category.

Table 5.12. Comparisons of Party Identification by Birth-Cohort Categories in the National Election Studies, 1952–84

Birth Cohort	N	Percent in Cohort	Mean (1–7)	Percent Republican		N
				All	Party	
All Whites						
1895–1904	2,434	9.5%	3.79	42%	46%	2,245
1905–14	4,016	15.7	3.59	37	41	3,651
1915–24	4,918	19.3	3.53	36	39	4,450
1925–34	4,367	17.1	3.59	36	41	3,904
1935–44	3,726	14.6	3.81	39	45	3,227
1945–54	3,990	15.6	3.77	35	43	3,292
1955–64	2,089	8.2	3.96	40	48	1,718
Total	25,540	100.0%	3.69	37%	42%	22,487
F			18.37**	8.96**	12.32**	
White Women						
1895–1904	1,405	10.0%	3.86	44%	47%	1,302
1905–14	2,177	15.5	3.73	40	44	1,988
1915–24	2,714	19.3	3.50	35	39	2,472
1925–34	2,427	17.3	3.56	36	40	2,169
1935–44	2,008	14.3	3.80	39	45	1,760
1945–54	2,166	15.4	3.70	34	40	1,821
1955–64	1,137	8.1	3.80	37	44	942
Total	14,034	100.0%	3.68	37%	42%	12,454
F			8.62**	9.38**	7.26**	
White Women with College						
1895–1904	267	6.4%	4.42	56%	59%	256
1905–14	459	11.0	4.34	54	57	433
1915–24	574	13.7	4.17	50	54	537
1925–34	668	16.0	4.09	49	52	620
1935–44	697	16.7	4.07	47	51	640
1945–54	1,006	24.1	3.83	39	43	909
1955–64	510	12.2	3.88	42	47	457
Total	4,181	100.0%	4.06	46%	50%	3,852
F			5.67**	8.41**	6.38**	

**$p < .001$

Table 5.13. Comparisons of Liberal/Conservative Self-
Identification by Birth-Cohort Categories in the
National Election Studies, 1952–84

Birth Cohort	N	Percent in Cohort	Mean (1–7)	Percent Conservative
All Whites				
1895–1904	446	4.1%	4.49	45%
1905–14	1,119	10.2	4.48	44
1915–24	1,503	13.7	4.48	46
1925–34	1,602	14.6	4.46	46
1935–44	1,892	17.2	4.38	46
1945–54	2,861	26.0	4.09	37
1955–64	1,565	14.2	4.14	36
Total	10,988	100.0%	4.31	42%
F			31.86**	14.4**
White Women				
1895–1904	263	4.6%	4.58	46%
1905–14	587	10.2	4.61	46
1915–24	788	13.7	4.44	43
1925–34	797	13.9	4.38	41
1935–44	981	17.1	4.30	40
1945–54	1,499	26.2	4.05	34
1955–64	816	14.2	4.11	33
Total	5,731	100.0%	4.28	39%
F			22.92**	9.41**
White Women with College				
1895–1904	73	2.9%	4.82	51%
1905–14	182	7.1	4.72	53
1915–24	250	9.8	4.44	46
1925–34	337	13.2	4.28	42
1935–44	458	17.9	4.28	43
1945–54	817	32.0	3.97	35
1955–64	435	17.0	4.12	36
Total	2,552	100.0%	4.22	40%
F			14.33**	5.70**

$**p < .001$

regarding attitude intensity. Suffice it to say at this point that these results point to a conclusion that would place the Bennington cohort in the context of a generation that identified to a greater extent with Democratic political parties and candidates, while at the same time placing them in an age group (or generation, for that matter) which holds these party loyalties more intensely.[14]

Cohort Differences in Attitude Intensity

In the literature reviewed at the beginning of this chapter, there are references to the idea of attitude intensity—in the sense of the resistance of attitudes to change. Little of the above-reviewed research on "aging and conservatism" has actually addressed this question adequately using panel data, which we undertake in chapter 7. Despite methodological limitations involved in using repeated cross sections for this purpose, interpretations about the persistence of individual attitudes and their age-related resistance or susceptibility to change abound in this literature. Thus, it is of some value in the present context to examine cohort differences in attitude intensity as indexed by the "strength" of party identification.[15]

Table 5.14 presents data based on our cohort categories for the intensity of party identification. We measure intensity of this dimension in two ways: (1) using a 1–3 scale of intensity for persons identifying (in some degree) with either of the major political parties (i.e., excluding independents and any others), and (2) using a 0–3 scale that includes the independents or those otherwise neutral, who are coded as having 0 intensity.

These results show rather persuasively that, regardless of the measure used, intensity of party loyalty declines monotonically in virtual linear fash-

---

14. It has occurred to us that respondents to the NES liberal/conservative rating scale may actually use more than one meaning of the term *conservative*, as we discussed above, referring to rigidity of personality as well as political conservatism. If this is true, then this scale is substantially less useful for our purposes than we proposed.

15. We recognize that the term *attitude strength* is used in at least three different ways in the relevant literature. First, we have followed one conventional meaning, which uses the term to refer to the degree to which attitudes are resistent to change. Strong attitudes are, by this definition, much less likely to change than weak ones. The term *attitude strength* has also been used to refer to the "intensity" with which attitudes are held (see Converse, 1976). In the measurement of partisan identifications, for example, "strong" attitudes are those that are held with greater "intensity" of identification. Thus, party identification has been viewed as having two components—direction and intensity of support—and the intensity component is often discussed as an aspect of "attitude strength." Finally, the concept of attitude strength often arises in the discussion of the salience or centrality of attitudes (Rokeach, 1968). Attitudes that are more central to cognitive organization are viewed as shaping the development of other attitudes and behaviors, and are thereby considered to reflect greater "strength."

Table 5.14. Comparisons of Intensity of Party Identification by Birth-Cohort Categories in the National Election Studies, 1952–84

Birth Cohort	N	Percent in Cohort	Mean Intensity (0–3)	Mean Intensity (1–3)	N
			All Whites		
1895–1904	2,434	9.5%	2.103	2.324	2,245
1905–14	4,016	15.7	2.025	2.253	3,651
1915–24	4,918	19.3	1.918	2.149	4,450
1925–34	4,367	17.1	1.827	2.069	3,904
1935–44	3,726	14.6	1.667	1.949	3,227
1945–54	3,990	15.6	1.516	1.869	3,292
1955–64	2,089	8.2	1.493	1.878	1,718
Total	25,540	100.0%	1.802	2.079	22,487
F			197.2**	170.3**	
			White Women		
1895–1904	1,405	10.0%	2.115	2.344	1,302
1905–14	2,177	15.5	2.034	2.264	1,988
1915–24	2,714	19.3	1.943	2.174	2,472
1925–34	2,427	17.3	1.849	2.103	2,169
1935–44	2,008	14.3	1.714	1.985	1,760
1945–54	2,166	15.4	1.591	1.933	1,821
1955–64	1,137	8.1	1.511	1.880	942
Total	14,034	100.0%	1.836	2.110	12,454
F			94.12**	88.46**	
			White Women with College		
1895–1904	267	6.4%	2.243	2.340	256
1905–14	459	11.0	2.170	2.300	433
1915–24	574	13.7	1.969	2.108	537
1925–34	668	16.0	1.969	2.124	620
1935–44	697	16.7	1.859	2.025	640
1945–54	1,006	24.1	1.726	1.922	909
1955–64	510	12.2	1.751	1.969	457
Total	4,181	100.0%	1.905	2.073	3,852
F			23.61**	21.78**	

**$p < .001$

Table 5.15. Bennington Cohort Comparisons of Party Identification, Strength, and Conservativism

	Birth Cohort			
	1905–14	1915–24	Total	F
Party ID				
N (all)	31	297	328	
% in cohort	9.5%	90.5%	100.0%	
Mean (1–7)	3.26	3.23	3.23	0.01 ns
% Republican (all)	26%	30%	30%	0.20 ns
N (party only)	28	277	305	
% Republican (party)	29%	32%	32%	0.12 ns
Strength of party				
N (all)	31	297	328	
Mean (0–3)	1.90	2.13	2.11	1.44 ns
N (party only)	28	277	305	
Mean (1–3)	2.11	2.28	2.27	1.10 ns
Liberal/conservative				
N (all)	32	295	327	
Mean	2.88	2.68	2.70	0.40 ns
% Conservative	19%	15%	15%	0.33 ns

ion from the oldest birth cohorts to the youngest. Thus, the Bennington women were in a set of birth cohorts exhibiting more intensely held party loyalties compared with those who followed, but less intensely held than those of their forerunners. The smoothness of this relationship hints very strongly at a more or less "pure" aging effect. This is, of course, the type of observation that has been interpreted both in terms of aging and cohort processes (e.g., Converse, 1979; Abramson, 1979, 1983).

We do not attempt a resolution of the aging versus cohort debate with regard to the apparently strong relationship of age/cohort and the intensity of party support. Our main interest is in being able to locate the Bennington sample within an appropriate historical/generational context. In this regard, table 5.15 presents data on these various measures of party identification and *liberalism/conservatism* and their intensity for the two Bennington cohort categories that are comparable to those used in the foregoing. Both of these cohorts are distinctively more liberal and hold more intense attitudes than comparable women from these cohorts. Thus, as we observed earlier in this chapter with regard to political involvement and interest, the Bennington women seem to have more intensely held attitudes than women of similar age and educational experience. In this regard they resemble their elders, those born in pre-1905 birth cohorts. This was the generation that taught them at Bennington—a generation which

117

held an intense sense that the policies of the New Deal were a positive, progressive force in American society.

Although it is commonly assumed that attitude intensity is related to attitude persistence and that more intensely held attitudes are more difficult to change, we see these as two separate issues. At the same time this type of interpretation of the age/attitude-stability relationship is based on some plausible empirical assumptions. There is, for example, reason to expect a relationship between the persistence or stability of attitudes and their centrality, or ego-relatedness (e.g., Krosnick, 1988). It might be profitably assumed that such attitude strength, as indicated by the extent of attitude persistence over time, is correlated with attitude strength, as indicated by the intensity or extremity of partisan identification. In such a case, then, Converse's (1976) findings of a relation between aging and intensity may also imply a relation of age and attitude stability. In addition, Abramson's (1983) finding of a decline in the intensity of party loyalty among the Michigan student panel may also indicate a weaker level of attitude persistence in the young.

On the other hand, there may be no necessary relation between attitude stability, as defined here, and attitude intensity. Intense attitudes may be just as volatile or stable as less intensely held ones, depending in part on the time period in which they are observed. Furthermore, growing attitude stability with age may reflect the time periods covered by the available cohort survey data, and growing stability may not necessarily be related to life-cycle dynamics themselves, but rather to the historical epochs involved. In any event, we return to the issue of attitude persistence in chapter 7.

SUMMARY AND CONCLUSION

With the possible exception of the 1960s generation (see Gitlin, 1987), the generation from which the Bennington College women of the 1930s and 1940s came was clearly more liberal in its orientations than either earlier or later ones. And interestingly, regardless of the direction of party loyalty, the 1930s and 1940s generation appears to hold more intense loyalties than the younger cohorts. At the same time, the Bennington women were themselves even more intensely liberal than women of their own generation. Thus, in order to fully understand these patterns, we need an interpretation which explains the distinctiveness of the 1915–24 generation and at the same time explains the deviation of the Bennington women even further in that direction.

One interpretation is that the Bennington women were more a part of the New Deal generation than many of their peers, and in some sense they were more intensely affected by the events of the 1930s and 1940s than their collegiate contemporaries. Interestingly, educated women of that generation are likely to carry allegiances to the Republican party to a much greater extent than their age-mates, so even on this score the Bennington women were deviants. Their attachment to the New Deal and to Democratic political loyalties since the 1930s and 1940s could scarcely be more distinct from that of other educated women of comparable maturity. Thus, they may in a sense be seen as more typical of their generation than other older, educated women. Other women receiving an education in the 1930s and 1940s were probably more likely to be shielded from social events and social change, whereas the Bennington experience was one in "contemporary" education amidst a set of actors who had shaped a particularly progressive informational environment (see chapter 2).

Thus, we favor both generational and "Bennington" interpretations. That is, we believe there was a generational milieu to which the Bennington students were exposed, but perhaps more intensely exposed than most of their contemporaries, particularly more so than their contemporaries at other colleges. Of course, our comparison of the Bennington women with these cohort categories cannot readily resolve the confounding of age and cohort in these comparisons. One line of reasoning that may give some better definition to the nature of aging and cohort effects in these contrasts is that aging as a phenomenon related to conservatism is probably monotonically increasing, if it is related at all. Thus, the irregularities in the cohort comparisons may be the basis for generational contrasts. And, given the fact that the younger cohorts are even more conservative than those preceding them, and the fact that the "Vietnam" cohort is even less conservative than all others—which makes sense in terms of the character of the dominant political regimes during the times corresponding to that group's greatest vulnerability to political socialization—we may be more secure in a cohort interpretation of these data than in one relying purely on an aging process. In other words, there are too many nonlinearities in the data to wholly prefer the latter interpretation. On the other hand, the intensity of party loyalty may reveal a systematic monotonic increase that is attributable to aging. But partisan attitude "strength," as Abramson (1983) has argued, might also be explained by cohort factors. So, even though we cannot claim on the basis of these analyses to have arrived at an understanding of aging and cohort processes more generally, we have at least tentatively secured a plausible interpretation of our Bennington results.

119

6

Retrospective Accounts of Sociopolitical Orientations over the Life Span

INTRODUCTION

The primary purpose of this research is to understand the development of sociopolitical attitudes over the adult life span. To achieve this understanding we have here assembled several sources of information, including repeated assessments of current attitudes at various points in the life cycle (see chapters 5 and 7), and we have been in the fortunate position of being able to compare many of these attitudinal reports with similar reports by members of the U.S. adult population from 1952 onward, until the 1984 survey, in which a rich set of questions was available. In addition to these external benchmarks for comparison, another rich source of comparative information involves our respondents own assessments of the trajectories of their attitudes over their entire life course.

In a recent study, Converse, Schuman, and Scott (see Schuman and Scott, 1989) found that when people are asked to recall important events or changes over the past half-century, the most frequently reported memories come from late adolescence and early adulthood. For the majority of the 12 or more major world or national events and/or changes reported in a national sample of some 1,400 Americans, Schuman and Scott report that "the memories refer back disproportionately to a time when the respondents were in their teens or early 20s" (1989:377). This finding provides further support to the idea that there are "impressionable years" (see chapter 2), but it also provides some basis for the assumption that memories of that distant period of adolescence and early adulthood might be particularly vivid. Such is our assumption as we explore the retrospective terrain of our Bennington respondents.[1]

---

1. We should note that retrospective data can be quite distorted; in the words of Yarrow, Campbell, and Burton (1970:36), "the data of such research are perhaps as much the products of the informants and instruments as they are of the phenomenon being investigated." The analytic task thus becomes one of attempting to clarify the nature of consistency and its sources.

The availability of the multiple sources of comparison of the "objective" data we obtained from our Bennington follow-up respondents prompted us to speculate about how they would understand the life course trajectory of their attitudes. Would these more "subjective" understandings coincide with our more "objective" time-specific assessments? Would those whose attitudes, as assessed by the questions asked in the earlier research at Bennington, became more liberal while at college describe themselves as having changed in this way? And would such self-understandings themselves change or remain stable over time according to some set of understandable set of processes? Some of these same questions obviously prompted Newcomb and his colleagues in the first follow-up study (Newcomb et al., 1967) to engage in the same type of query. In that study respondents were asked to describe their attitudes when they were students at Bennington 25 years earlier. Due to these similar interests in the value of retrospective reports of attitudes, we have available these retrospective data from the 1960s, and we felt compelled to include a similar set of questions about our respondents' memories of the development of their sociopolitical attitudes at earlier points in their lives and about their beliefs concerning the trajectory of those attitudes through their lives.

In addition, we thought such data might also bear on the presumed validity of retrospective attitude data employed as objective indicators of attitudes or events at earlier points in time. For this purpose we asked our respondents to complete some of the same questionnaires which Newcomb had used in his research of the 1930s and 1940s *in the way they would have answered at the time they left Bennington College.*[2] Thus, the data we report in this chapter not only provide a more subjective or qualitative estimate of the nature and extent of attitude change in our sample; they permit us to address the question of the validity of retrospective data.[3] We first inspect these retrospections, gauging the extent to which they are compatible with our more objective assessments. We then consider the potential biases that may be inherent in such retrospective exercises. In so doing we encounter strong evidence that our respondents' self-assessed changes are relatively accurate, which adds further validity to the consideration of these self-reports.

2. Specifically, on the self-administered questionnaire we mailed to our respondents, we asked them to complete Newcomb's 26-item PEP scale in terms of how "in the 1930s you think you agreed or disagreed" with the statements *at that time.*

3. In the absence of prior data on actual attitudes, respondents are sometimes asked to report what their attitudes were at earlier points in time. Investigators then use those retrospections as reference points from which currently assessed attitudes are argued to have changed or not changed (e.g., Moss and Goldstein, 1979; Smith, 1984; Smith and Klaeser, 1983).

RETROSPECTIVE ACCOUNTS OF ATTITUDES AND ATTITUDE CHANGE

In order to clarify the extent of net attitude change over the life span as well as to examine the utility of retrospective reports of past orientations we supplemented our objective measures of attitudes in the 1984 follow-up with a variety of retrospective assessments. One of these attempts is reflected in questions to respondents asking about their "general political viewpoint at various points in your life from the 1930s until the present." The question continued as follows:

> Please just try to remember and describe your general political viewpoint as best you can. In the questions that follow, please describe your general political view on a scale of 1 to 7 where 1 is very conservative, 2 is somewhat conservative, and 3 is moderate, but leaning toward conservative. Four would be moderate. Five is moderate, but leaning toward liberal, 6 is somewhat liberal and 7 is very liberal.

Respondents were provided a card showing a visual representation of the scale points and these labels. They were asked to record a response for their general political viewpoint (1) when they entered Bennington College, (2) when they left Bennington College, (3) in the year 1960 ("the year Kennedy and Nixon ran for president"), (4) in 1972 ("the year McGovern and Nixon ran for president"), and (5) their general political viewpoint today. Some of these questions had also been asked in the surveys carried out in 1960–61. The mail questionnaire respondents were asked items 1 and 2, and provided their then-current estimate of the 1960 position (3), using a five-point liberal/conservative scale. Also, the 1961 respondents from the personal interview subsample responded to the five-point scale with regard to their 1960 liberal/conservative position. These results are presented in table 6.1.

The characterization of our Bennington follow-up respondents that emerges from their self-placement on our retrospective scale of liberal versus conservative identifications confirms our earlier observations. Some 70 percent of our respondents identified themselves with the liberal side of the continuum in 1984, but with varying levels of strength. As we explore more fully below, there is considerable self-assessed change along this continuum during the impressionable years, but an amazing level of stability during the remainder of the life course. In both the 1960s and 1980s our respondents express substantial identification with the liberal direction of these scales.

These retrospective reports tell a very interesting story about the Bennington women's past experiences. Table 6.2 presents the means and standard deviations for the responses to these inquiries on the seven- and five-

Table 6.1. Univariate Distributions for Political Viewpoints

Viewpoint		1984	1972	1960	Left Bennington	Entered Bennington
Obtained in 1984						
Very conservative	1	3.0%	1.5%	1.2%	2.1%	10.1%
		(10)	(5)	(4)	(7)	(32)
Somewhat conservative	2	5.5%	6.1%	4.2%	7.0%	18.6%
		(18)	(20)	(14)	(23)	(59)
Tending toward conservative	3	6.7%	8.6%	10.0%	7.9%	12.3%
		(22)	(28)	(33)	(26)	(39)
Moderate	4	12.1%	11.6%	15.2%	12.4%	19.2%
		(40)	(38)	(50)	(41)	(61)
Tending toward liberal	5	13.0%	15.0%	15.5%	18.2%	12.6%
		(43)	(49)	(51)	(60)	(40)
Somewhat liberal	6	35.5%	31.2%	29.7%	24.2%	12.3%
		(117)	(102)	(98)	(80)	(39)
Very liberal	7	24.2%	26.0%	24.2%	28.2%	14.8%
		(80)	(85)	(80)	(93)	(47)
Total		100%	100%	100%	100%	100%
		(330)	(327)	(330)	(330)	(317)
Obtained in 1960s						
Conservative	1	—	—	9.0%	14.0%	36.8%
				(30)	(29)	(74)
Somewhat conservative	2	—	—	19.1%	18.8%	19.9%
				(64)	(39)	(40)
Moderate	3	—	—	10.4%	4.8%	5.5%
				(35)	(10)	(11)
Somewhat liberal	4	—	—	30.4%	24.6%	14.4%
				(102)	(51)	(29)
Liberal	5	—	—	31.0%	37.7%	23.4%
				(104)	(78)	(47)
Total				100%	100%	100%
				(335)	(207)	(201)

Table 6.2. Subjective Assessments of Change: 1961 and 1984 Follow-up
Respondents

Item	5-point scale			7-point scale		
	$\overline{X}$	S.D.	n	$\overline{X}$	S.D.	n
Entered Bennington College	3.32	1.63	201	3.97	1.94	314
Left Bennington College	2.47	1.49	207	2.70	1.65	327
In 1960	2.45	1.34	335	2.74	1.54	335
In 1972	—	—	—	2.70	1.60	324
In 1984	—	—	—	2.70	1.62	327

123

point scales.[4] In their retrospections of their own political orientations over the life course, these women verify the strong impact of their collegiate years, witnessed so keenly in Newcomb's quantitative data (1943). Also, the results confirm in the aggregate the overall stability of this group in terms of these scales. These women see themselves as having changed dramatically during college, moving from a *moderate* political position on the 1984 scale to one described as *leaning toward liberal* at the time they left Bennington. And this aggregate position persists relatively unchanged over their lives to the present.

Does this apparent level of stability in aggregate attitudes also indicate high levels of individual stability? That is, to what extent does the distribution of attitudes remain stable over time? There is no necessary link between these two types of stability, although, in a strict sense, individual stability across all persons does logically imply aggregate stability. However, aggregate stability can exist in the absence of individual stability. Further, it is possible for a high level of individual stability, defined in correlational terms rather than in an absolute sense, to coexist with aggregate change. In such a case, all persons change in a similar direction, producing an aggregate shift, while individuals remain in the same distributional position relative to other members of the group or population. In chapter 7 we consider the stability of individual sociopolitical orientations.

Retrospective Estimates of Bennington Contemporaries

The notion of *collective ignorance* is prominent in interpretations of history and public opinion polls. For example, Noelle-Neumann's (1984) trenchant account of how individual opinion is often molded by (sometimes inaccurate) perceptions of group opinion is an example of how collective ignorance may operate. But—more to the point—our Bennington respondents, presumably more or less aware of Newcomb's studies and their main hypotheses, may have thought that they were much less affected by the events and experiences of their college years than their contemporaries. Or, on the contrary, they may have thought that while their outlooks changed dramatically during the 1930s and 1940s, because their autonomy was reinforced by those events and experiences, their Bennington contemporaries were held back from development in a liberal direction by the

---

4. In our summary of these data here we have reversed the scoring, so that a high score reflects conservatism. In other words, in our coding scheme for 1984, 7 = very conservative, 6 = somewhat conservative, 5 = leaning toward conservative, 4 = moderate, 3 = leaning toward liberal, 2 = somewhat liberal, and 1 = very liberal; and for 1961, 5 = extreme conservative, 4 = moderate conservative, 3 = middle point, 2 = moderate liberal, and 1 = extreme liberal.

Table 6.3. Subjective Assessments of Change in the Bennington
Contemporaries: 1984 Follow-up Respondents

	1984 Respondents			Classmate Recall		
Item	$\overline{X}$	S.D.	n	$\overline{X}$	S.D.	n
Entered Bennington College	3.97	1.94	314	4.12	1.39	247
Left Bennington College	2.70	1.65	327	2.68	1.15	253

conservative forces within society. These issues caused us to inquire about the perceptions on the part of the Bennington sample of the trajectories of the political attitudes of their classmates over time.

Our 1984 questionnaire delved into this topic very briefly, by asking our respondents to rate on a seven-point scale, from very liberal to very conservative, how they would place their "Bennington contemporaries" when they entered Bennington College and when they left (whether they graduated or not). These figures are given in table 6.3, along with similar ratings of themselves, using the same scale. Interestingly, these figures suggest that the Bennington women thought that their contemporaries at the beginning of their Bennington years were slightly more conservative ($p <$ .05), but that there was no difference by the time of leaving Bennington. In other words, there was a tendency for these women to see the "Bennington effect" to have happened to others more than themselves. They clearly thought that there was a major transformation in their own lives (see tables 6.1 and 6.2), but it appears that they saw their contemporaries as even more conservative than themselves initially, changing more over the course of their college years.

This may be an example of Noelle-Neumann's (1984) "spiral of silence," in which, due to collective ignorance, individuals' opinions may be affected by the "perceived majority's opinion." Attitude change is thought to occur because the individual is fearful of the insecurity of being alone, as a part of a small minority. In the Bennington case, it might be argued that people were influenced by the sociopolitical milieu at Bennington, but were not aware that it was happening to the extent that it was. They saw it happening "collectively" more to others than to themselves.

There is an interesting similarity among Noelle-Neumann's (1984) "perceived public opinion," Newcomb's concept of the "informational environment," and Hyman's description of the (1942) "reference-group" phenomenon. All refer to the opinions of other people (as perceived by the individual) and how these opinions affect the individual. In the case where the "comparative" and "normative" functions of the reference group (to use Kelley's [1952] distinction) *overlap* in the sense that they are served

125

by the same "others," there may be an even more powerful influence of the other actors who make up the reference group. Thus, an important normative system for these young women, as described by Newcomb (see chapter 2), was located "ecologically" within the confines of the Bennington College community—a small rural community, several miles from the nearest town. And because of their "impressionable" status in life—they were there to learn from their professors—this community also provided a powerful informational environment. But perhaps they were not aware that it was happening to them.[5]

THE VALIDITY OF RETROSPECTIVE ATTITUDINAL REPORTS

There is little in the way of explicit theory or convincing data to guide the exploration of the validity of subjective accounts of attitudes. However, in a recent empirical investigation of these issues, Markus (1986) suggests the relevance of at least one strand of recent theorizing from cognitive psychology that may help us understand the retrospective data we collected. Markus argues that to the extent the attitudes being examined have only tangential importance for one's self-identity, and to the extent they are not "linked to readily available memories of salient events or experiences," there is little reason to expect such retrospections to be accurate (1986: 28). Of course, we have already suggested, on the basis of Schuman and Scott's (1989) research, that young adulthood is an impressionable time, one clearly and importantly linked to one's self-identity. Furthermore, we have every reason to believe that there is a particular salience attached to the early experiences of our Bennington women, and thus our respondents may not manifest the more general processes described by Markus.

Several theoretical arguments and sets of experimental results from the laboratory study of attitude change seem to bear out Markus's pessimistic claims. Bem's (1972) well-known *self-perception* theory of attitude formation suggests, for example, that people often do not know their own attitudes and are forced to infer them from their behavior. Bem's theory

5. Although Noelle-Neumann (1984) does not explicitly make the connection, this phenomenon of reference-group behavior in the formation of individual and public opinion can also be applied to the rise of the Nazis to power in Germany in the 1930s, to the Salem witch trials, and to the rise of McCarthyism and "Red-baiting" in the 1950s in the United States. There is some experimental evidence that suggests individuals are not aware of attitude change. For example, Bem and McConnell (1970) report an experiment in which subjects who changed their attitudes did not perceive themselves as having changed. An important difference between their results and ours, however, is that their subjects were not able to accurately recall their premanipulation attitudes.

and the results of other researchers (e.g., Nisbett and Wilson, 1977) suggest that people are often forced to rely on the same inferential processes and implicit causal theories to discover their own attitudes as they employ to estimate others' attitudes. The results of some experimental work on attitude change (e.g., Bem and McConnell, 1970; Goethals and Reckman, 1973) suggest that individuals are unaware of change in their attitudes; that is, they inaccurately report their prior attitudes over as short a period as a week. Moreover, other research suggests that people are not just inaccurate—they are biased in the direction of making perceptions of past behaviors and attitudes compatible with presently held attitudes (e.g., Ross, McFarland, and Fletcher, 1981; Ross, McFarland, Conway, and Zanna, 1983).

Of course, any interpretation of such experimental results must come to grips with issues of attitude salience and importance. For example, as Converse (1964, 1970) pointed out, some people may not have previously thought about a given topic or may have little familiarity with it. Thus, with respect to that topic or attitude issue, they could be said to have no attitude. However, they often report attitudes because they feel pressure to do so, when in fact they have none. This might be the case because people assume that researchers expect them to offer opinions and because our culture affirms the view that opinionated persons are more respected than those without many opinions. Because they wish to conform to these expectations and project positive self-images, Converse suggested, such people might frequently concoct attitude reports during studies of the type reviewed above. Such attitudinal responses are, he hypothesized, essentially random choices from among the response alternatives offered. If some people select answers randomly when they actually lack attitudes on the topics studied, it would be no surprise that they might not be able to remember them at some later time. We would expect that the greater the salience of the attitudes measured, the more aware respondents would be of attitude change over time and the less subject the attitudes would be to processes of random reporting.

There are other reasons to expect attitudinal retrospections to be inaccurate. The "implicit causal theories" (cf. Nisbett and Wilson, 1977) on which people rely to infer their own and others' attitudes might affect retrospections in a number of ways. Beliefs about the general stability of certain types of attitudes over biographical time, or over certain stages of the life course, should have an impact on retrospections assessed at different stages of life. For example, in Markus's (1986) research, younger respondents were less likely than older respondents to recall their past positions as identical to their current ones. This might have been the case because "younger respondents believed they had just experienced a life stage of changing basic political views" (1986:32).

In addition, it is conceivable that respondents may wish to appear "consistent," either to themselves or to their interrogators. As their current attitudes are more salient, or more readily tied to recallable overt behavior, discrepant past attitudes are more likely to be assimilated to current attitudes. Respondents would, thus, report less change than the objective assessments would indicate, and stability over time would be seriously overestimated. Thus, there are several reasons to expect retrospective reports of attitudes, such as the ones we used earlier in this chapter, to be inaccurate, though as Markus (1986:36) reports, there is likely to be less distortion in more salient attitudes.

Convergences in Retrospective Reports

Tables 6.4 and 6.5 present cross-tabulations between the original PEP score (PEP30) and the 1960 and 1984 retrospective reports of these original scores. Recall that the retrospective task was an item-by-item task, and the scores used here are summed over these items. In this case it is difficult to measure the agreement between the two measures because it is not possible to compare the raw data. Here we divide the sample at the median on the summed scores and present the frequencies of joint occurrence within these categories. These tables show a relatively high level of

Table 6.4. Consistency of 1960 and 1984 Retrospective Reports
with the Original 1930s PEP Score

	1960 Recall		1984 Recall	
1930s PEP	Below Median	Above Median	Below Median	Above Median
Below median	87.9%	32.8%	77.9%	27.7%
Above median	12.1%	67.2%	22.1%	72.3%
Total	100.0%	100.0%	100.0%	100.0%
N	91	58	145	137

Table 6.5. Consistency of 1960 and 1984 Retrospective Reports of Liberalism/Conservatism
Scores with the Original 1930s PEP Score

	1960 Recall			1984 Recall		
1930s PEP	Liberal	Moderate	Conservative	Liberal	Moderate	Conservative
Below median	66.7%	62.5%	12.5%	65.9%	28.2%	9.4%
Above median	33.3%	37.5%	87.5%	34.1%	71.8%	90.6%
Total	100.0%	100.0%	100.0%	100.0%	100.0%	100.0%
N	96	8	49	232	39	53

Table 6.6. Relationship of 1960 Liberalism/Conservatism Score to 1930s PEP Score Using Actual and Retrospective Measures

1930s PEP	1960 Actual			1984 Recall		
	Liberal	Moderate	Conservative	Liberal	Moderate	Conservative
Below median	67.5%	44.4%	31.3%	63.1%	34.0%	20.4%
Above median	32.5%	55.6%	68.7%	36.9%	66.0%	79.6%
Total	100.0%	100.0%	100.0%	100.0%	100.0%	100.0%
N	157	27	67	225	50	49

agreement between the original attitude and the retrospective reports, but it is difficult to gauge correlational consistency from these tabulations. We take up this issue in a subsequent section.

An additional step in validating these retrospective reports of attitudes involves the examination of the pattern of relationships between the 1984 retrospective report of the 1960s liberal/conservative score and the actual relationship. In table 6.6 we present two cross-tabulations of interest. On the left side is the table categorizing (above and below the median) the 1930s PEP score by categories on the seven-point liberal/conservative scale (the liberal region, moderate, and the conservative region); on the right side is the same table expressing the relationship between the recalled 1960 attitude and the 1930s PEP score (again, split at the median). These relationships are almost identical.

Finally, we calculated Pearson product-moment correlations among selected variables involving retrospections of earlier attitudes. These results again provide a good showing for our retrospective data (table 6.7). The correlations are not extremely high, but it is reassuring that they occur in the .7 range of association between actual attitudes and recollections of those attitudes. It can also be seen that recalled attitudes often reproduce fairly well the actual correlation between variables. For example, taking the focus of table 6.6, that is, the relationship between the 1930s PEP and the 1960s liberal/conservative scale, the actual relationship is .378, whereas the 1984 recalled 1960s L/C score correlates .45, roughly in the same range of association. Another example of this is the correlation of 1930 PEP scores with the 1960s PEP scores. The correlation of 1930s and 1960s PEP scores is .60, whereas using the 1984 recollections of 1960s item-by-item scores produces a correlation of .625! There are several other examples of this in the table.

Despite what appears to be the rather high quality of retrospections made by our Bennington respondents, there are also some important divergences or biases in recollections. These we consider in the following section. Before turning to these results, we should note also that even though

Table 6.7. Correlation Matrix among Selected Recall Variables: Bennington Women ($N = 335$)

	PEP40	1960 Recall PEP40	1984 Recall PEP40	Party ID40	1960 Recall L/C40	1984 Recall L/C40	PEP60	1984 Recall PEP60	L/C60	1984 Recall L/C60
PEP40	1.00									
1960 Recall PEP40	.718	1.00								
1984 Recall PEP40	.682	.740	1.00							
Party ID40	.501	.532	.418	1.00						
1960 Recall L/C40	.526	.751	.612	.594	1.00					
1984 Recall L/C40	.526	.689	.711	.409	.626	1.00				
PEP60	.604	.695	.677	.460	.555	.511	1.00			
1984 Recall PEP60	.625	.654	.846	.419	.507	.578	.717	1.00		
L/C60	.378	.496	.514	.328	.562	.517	.688	.597	1.00	
1984 Recall L/C60	.447	.546	.631	.353	.466	.682	.587	.673	.692	1.00

we believe that the retrospective data considered here reveal a high degree of consistency, we rely on them only tangentially in assessing attitude change. Our research strategy was to pursue issues of attitude change using objective measures (see chapters 5 and 7), but to supplement these results where possible with the subjective element of over-time measurement, that is, how our Bennington subjects perceived the "real" change. Thus, while we do not rely principally on the retrospective data as a way of assessing attitude change over the life span, these data may be very valuable and accurate, especially with such politically conscious subjects as our respondents, for whom public and social affairs were (and continue to be) of considerable importance. However, as suggested earlier, there are some critical systematic errors or distortions in retrospective reports that must be given serious attention. This is important because some of our measures (measures of party identification) rely somewhat on retrospective data.[6]

Divergences in Retrospective Reports

When we reviewed the reports of electoral preferences of our Bennington respondents in chapter 5, we noted that there was a sizeable disparity between the 1960s and 1984 reports. In all six presidential elections between 1940 and 1960, the 1960s reports reveal considerably more of our women in the Republican camp than was the case for our 1984 reports. These marginals are reproduced in table 6.8.

The most striking of these is perhaps the comparison of preferences of candidates in the 1960 election. Here 46 percent reported in 1960 that they had preferred Richard Nixon, whereas only 26 percent indicated such a preference in 1984. Presumably, the 1960s report was the more accurate because it essentially involves no retrospection. If so, the 1984 report of the 1960 candidate preference includes some extent of liberal bias. Similar disparities exist throughout these series, with sizeable differences from 1948 onward. There were apparently more Nixon and Eisenhower supporters in the 1960s than were reported to have existed in 1984.

By cross-tabulating the two sets of reports (the 1960s and 1984 reports) for each of the election years, we can get an even better purchase on the sources of the bias in the marginals given in table 6.8. Table 6.9 presents the percentage of those reporting a Democratic preference in 1960 who reported preferences for Democratic and Republican candidates in 1984. For example, of those reporting Democrat in the 1960s for the 1960 election,

6. Specifically, our measures of electoral preferences in past presidential elections for 1936–40, 1956–60–64, and 1980–84 (see chapters 4 and 7) were used in our assessment of attitude change.

Table 6.8. Univariate Distributions of Matching 1960 and
1984 Respondents for Candidate Preferences
(Conservative vs. Liberal)

Election Year	Obtained in 1984		Obtained in 1960s	
	Conservative	Liberal	Conservative	Liberal
1960	25%	75%	44%	56%
	(64)	(194)	(114)	(144)
1956	38%	62%	49%	51%
	(99)	(160)	(131)	(128)
1952	44%	56%	52%	48%
	(112)	(144)	(122)	(134)
1948	33%	67%	47%	53%
	(78)	(161)	(112)	(127)
1944	31%	69%	36%	64%
	(76)	(171)	(90)	(157)
1940	47%	53%	53%	47%
	(109)	(125)	(111)	(123)

99 percent of them so reported in 1984. By contrast, 45 percent of those reporting in the 1960s that they had preferred the Republican candidate in the 1960 election denied that report in 1984, claiming instead that they had preferred the Democratic candidate in 1960. As table 6.9 illustrates, the source of bias in the 1984 reports (assuming the 1960s reports are more accurate) comes from those reporting that they were Republican in 1960. Better than 90 percent (and often many more than 90 percent) of those reporting a Democratic preference in the earlier report repeated that same preference in the 1984 report. On the other side, from one-fifth to one-half of respondents who in the 1960s reported Republican preferences in the 1940–60 elections recalled a Democratic one in the 1984 survey.

A CONCLUDING NOTE ON RETROSPECTIONS

Retrospective data should probably not be the sole basis for information on the past. Indeed, this has been the more or less consistent conclusion of prior research (Markus, 1986; Niemi et al., 1980). For this reason, we are cautious in our use of it in establishing "true" levels of change.[7] At the same

7. In the analyses reported in chapter 7 we use retrospective reports of candidate preferences in several of our measures—the combined measure of the number of conservative candidates preferred in the 1936 and 1940 elections (PID30), in the 1956, 1960, and 1964 elections (PID60), and in the 1976, 1980, and 1984 elections (PID84).

132

Table 6.9. Tabulation of 1984 Retrospective Candidate Preferences by
1960s Reports of Candidate Preferences: Bennington Panel

Election Year	Obtained in 1960		
	Democrat	Republican	N
Obtained in 1984			
1960			
Democrat	99.3%	44.7%	
Republican	0.6%	55.3%	
Total	100%	100%	268
1956			
Democrat	95.4%	27.3%	
Republican	4.6%	82.7%	
Total	100%	100%	259
1952			
Democrat	98.4%	17.9%	
Republican	1.6%	82.1%	
Total	100%	100%	256
1948			
Democrat	99.2%	31.3%	
Republican	0.8%	68.7%	
Total	100%	100%	239
1944			
Democrat	94.9%	24.4%	
Republican	5.1%	75.6%	
Total	100%	100%	247
1940			
Democrat	91.9%	18.7%	
Republican	8.1%	81.3%	
Total	100%	100%	234

time, as we illustrated in the foregoing, there is a considerable amount that can be learned from retrospective data.

One of the important functions served by retrospective data is that they provide a subjective reading on the phenomenon under study, especially when measurements are not exactly comparable over time and there is no precise metric for assessing attitude change over time. A common metric can be established using retrospective data, and differences over time can be *directly* assessed in these units. Thus, as we noted above, the fact that the change and stability of attitudes, as our Bennington respondents remembered them, moved in a parallel fashion in both our objective data and our recall data, provided a confirmatory validation of the interpretations we advanced.

A second value of retrospective data lies in their ability to assist in the interpretation of social processes. The fact, for example, that the Bennington women actually perceived students who were their contemporaries at the College in the 1930s to have been more conservative than they believed themselves to be and thus saw more attitude change in their contemporaries actually sheds some light on the processes of public opinion and attitude change. Collective sentiment is often misperceived. However, whether correctly or incorrectly perceived, our retrospective data further establish the fact that the Bennington women were aware of the environment around them and aware of its effects on them and others. They also point to the ways in which (or the areas in which) they were not aware of what was happening to them.

Finally, the use of retrospective reports in conjunction with actual data or other retrospective reports of the same events, but from a different time point, can help illuminate the errors in retrospective reports. We established above, for example, that the direction of disparities in the 1960 and 1984 reports of candidate preferences in the presidential elections between 1940 and 1960 was predictable. The disparity virtually always occured among those reporting themselves to be Republican in the earlier time frame, and it always erred in the direction of showing greater liberalism in the 1984 reports. Our Bennington respondents did not remember themselves in the same way during the 1980s as they did in the 1960s.

How do we interpret these disparities? During the late 1940s through the 1950s, Republican candidates were much more popular with our Bennington sample than they later claim was the case. This is the essence of the data presented above, suggesting that the 1984 reports are distortions. If so, they are distortions in the liberal direction, and such distortions (if they be that) may reflect a type of denial of a previous actual identification with the Republican party during its ascendency in the 1950s. Such a denial may reflect an unwillingness to admit a previous association with a candidate—Richard Nixon—who led the party and the office of president itself into disgrace in the 1970s. Recall that all 1984 reports of attitudes and preferences for 1964 onward suggest clearly liberal self-assessments. To the extent that identification with one or more conservative candidates in the past suggests to our respondents a lack of consistency or stability in their attitudes, these retrospections may reflect another type of denial—denial of attitude instability (see Bem and McConnell, 1970).

7

Aging and the Stability
of Sociopolitical Orientations

INTRODUCTION

There is an emerging consensus on some aspects of political socialization as related to the life cycle, but a variety of views on other aspects. As we indicated in earlier chapters, there is, in fact, broad consensus on the relative lack of stability of sociopolitical orientations in adolescence and early adulthood, and there is growing support for the idea that these are the impressionable years. Indeed, Newcomb's (1943) early work at Bennington is frequently cited as evidence of such a time of vulnerability to the influences of social and historical events. And, while it is debatable whether the residues of early cohort experiences inscribe an indelible mark on the content of sociopolitical orientations in later life, the cohort effects that have been observed in the research literature seem to fit Mannheim's generational model, wherein people acquire their basic sociopolitical orientations during late adolescence and early adulthood.

Beyond this general agreement regarding the malleability of attitudinal orientations early in adult life, there is a considerable lack of uniformity in interpretations of the potential for attitude change and its actualization after that point. One view, noted at several points in prior discussions, assumes the basic persistence of attitudes, suggesting that once such sociopolitical attitudes are formed, they are relatively immune to social forces that might produce change, remaining relatively stable over the life course. As we noted earlier, Newcomb and his colleagues' (1967) initial follow-up of the Bennington College students provides substantial support for this view. A variant on this perspective refers not only to the tendency for attitudes to resist change but to their inherent tendency to gather strength increasingly with time. Attitudes are thought to become more resistant to change in older age, due to the influences of the biological, psychological, and sociological processes of aging (see Converse, 1976; Glenn, 1974, 1980; Jennings and Niemi, 1981; Markus, 1979; Sears, 1981, 1983).

Support for the persistence of attitudes from early in the life cycle is somewhat mixed. On the one hand, strong arguments aimed at qualifying the scope conditions of the persistence thesis have been advanced. Searing and his colleagues (1973, 1976), for example, argue that the *primacy principle*, that early experiences have a lasting influence on later attitudes and behavior, has been overstated. At the same time, there is some support for the hypothesis of increasing attitude stability in biographical or personal time. Jennings and Niemi's (1974, 1978) national panel study of 1965 high school students and their parents indicates higher stability of attitudes, as assessed eight years later, among the parental cohorts than among the young. Using data from the American National Election Studies, Sears (1981) reports some evidence of higher levels of persistence in racial attitudes among older cohorts. Also, the intensity of party identification appears to grow in the later years (e.g., Converse, 1976; Glenn, 1974).

Another major perspective on attitude persistence and change over the life cycle, inspired by the emergent theoretical perspective of *life span developmental psychology* (see Brim and Kagan, 1980), holds that attitudes have a relatively uniform potential for change at all ages and/or stages of life. This view, the *lifelong openness hypothesis*, suggests that sociopolitical attitudes undergo continual change, reflecting the influences of social events and the individual's adaptation to a changing environment. In other words, changes in attitudes are principally due to historical factors and changes in the individual's sociopolitical environment; they are not necessarily correlated with age.

Such an alternative view is somewhat intriguing in light of several findings which, in fact, suggest that the stability of attitudes declines in older age. Aging may, for example, disrupt one's cognitive commitments, and it may introduce conservatism as an orientation (see Glenn, 1974). Or, it may produce greater alienation from the rest of society in general because of social isolation from other age groups. Sears (1981) reports evidence from the National Election Studies suggesting that stability in attitudes increases with age, but declines after the age of 60.[1]

Except for a relatively few studies such as Sears's (see also Jennings and Niemi, 1974, 1981), little is known about attitude change over the life course. As Sears (1981:195) laments, "Research exploring the connections between personal life and attitudes toward public life has generally not paid much attention to life-cycle considerations." Social psychologists have assembled an almost overwhelming amount of literature about the determinants of attitude change in laboratory studies over very short periods of

---

1. As we have pointed out in chapter 4, this lack of stability could also be due to a decrease in the reliability of measurement, which is known to accompany increasing age, as Sears's (1981:198) analyses hint (see also Andrews and Herzog, 1986; Alwin, 1989).

time. This work reveals some theoretical principles involving the role of the characteristics of the attitude object and of the informational environment (e.g., Kiesler, Collins, and Miller, 1969; McGuire, 1985). As noted above, there is evidence suggesting that sociopolitical orientations are relatively stable over short periods in people's lives, but the available studies which also attempt to deal with measurement errors in attitude measurement typically span less than a decade. In this chapter we confront the question of the individual stability of attitudes across the life span. We first review certain aspects of the initial work by Newcomb and his colleagues (1967) on this subject; we review the existing evidence in that study, and also set the stage for our own continued treatment of these data in the context of the 1984 reinterviews. Then we extend the analysis of these issues of change and stability to include data at three distinct points in biographical/historical time.

INDIVIDUAL STABILITY OF SOCIOPOLITICAL ORIENTATIONS

As indicated in chapter 3, Newcomb and his colleagues (1967) concluded that there was considerable stability in the sociopolitical attitudes between the college years and the time of the interview and mailed-questionnaire responses obtained nearly 25 years later. They concluded that the respondents who were relatively conservative when they left college were relatively conservative in the 1960s, and those who were nonconservative were still nonconservative. In other words, to the extent that changes in attitudes occurred, these changes were on the whole not radical, but lesser changes, perhaps more akin to minor "adjustments" tied to the experiences of the intervening years. Although the PEP scale was replicated in a portion of the 1960s restudy sample (those receiving the questionnaire), Newcomb and his colleagues (1967) do not report the empirical relationship between the 1930s–40s and 1960s PEP scores. The case they make for the stability of sociopolitical attitudes is instead based on the relationship between the 1930s–40s PEP score and a variety of different kinds of indicators assessed among the interview subsample in the 1960s (1967:22–33).

One such relationship reported is the product-moment correlation of .47 between the 1930s PEP score and the 1960s measure of political conservatism (the PCI described in chapter 3) obtained in their interview subsample.[2] Naturally, this correlation is attenuated by unreliability of measurement, and one would expect such a correlation to be higher, espe-

---

2. This relationship is virtually identical in the subsample receiving the questionnaires $(r = .45)$.

cially if it were interpreted as reflecting a high degree of stability. If the reliability of measurement in the two indicators was about .7, the "true" correlation between the 1930s PEP and 1960s PCI scores would be about .67; if the reliability were lower than this, the estimated true score correlation would be substantially higher.[3] In the absence of some concrete indication of the degree of unreliability in these measures, such hypothetical exercises reveal nothing more than sheer speculation. Nevertheless, it was the order of magnitude reflected by the above-reported correlation of .47 which formed the major basis for the conclusion of Newcomb and his colleagues that "with few marked exceptions . . . political attitudes developed or maintained in college by these women persisted over the period between graduation and 1960 without major change" (1967:27). In fact, the empirical basis for the conclusions of Newcomb and his colleagues may have been slightly stronger if they had reported the product-moment correlation between the 1930s and 1960s PEP scores from their mail survey, which is calculated to be nearly .6 (see below).

In order to get a somewhat firmer grasp on the nature of these correlations, we calculated *internal consistency* (see Nunnally, 1978) reliability estimates for the 1960s data, since we had the item-level information. The 1960s PEP score was estimated to have an internal consistency reliability of .90, and the 1960s *PCI (Political Conservatism Index)* score was found to have a reliability of .71. Thus, we can perform some corrections in the reported correlations between the 1960s measures and the 1930s PEP score by removing some of the attenuation due to measurement errors. Assuming that the 1930s PEP score had a reliability of approximately .9 (as estimated for the 1960s PEP score), then the correlation between the 1930s PEP score and the 1960s PEP and PCI respectively would be approximately .59 and .67.[4] Thus, the correlations reported by Newcomb and his colleagues (1967) were somewhat on the low side, but not by much.

By current standards, such a level of correlation may not seem great and may not appear to reflect the persistence of attitudes. Rather it suggests a high degree of attitude flexibility and change. After all, a correlation of roughly .5 indicates that only 25 percent of the variance in the 1960s PCI score is empirically tied to collegiate variation in PEP scores, and an observed correlation of about .6 between the PEP scores of the 1930s–40s and 1960s translates to roughly 35 percent of the variance. The remaining

3. If, for example, the reliabilities were .6, the true correlation would be nearly .8, and in the extreme case of reliabilities of .5, the true correlation would be nearly unity. For an excellent discussion of the role of unreliability and its effects on relationships among observed variables, see Lord and Novick (1968).

4. See Lord and Novick (1968) for a discussion of "corrections for attenuation" of bivariate correlations.

65–75 percent of the variance is either true attitude change, because of the influence of a variety of potential sources of change or because of error variance produced by unreliability of measurement, or both. There is, in other words, considerable ambiguity regarding the relative roles of these influences when looking at a single correlation between two somewhat fallible measures.

REASSESSING THE STABILITY OF ATTITUDES

There are several difficulties with estimating the true level of stability in survey data, but we have confidence that the quality of the present data and procedures will assist this process. One of the first difficulties involves the accurate measurement of change from the early 1930s to later years. We have no direct measurement of the process of attitude development and change from the time these women entered Bennington. Our only measure of attitude from this time is the PEP score Newcomb obtained from these women *when they left Bennington.*[5] Since these women differed in the time they left Bennington—both biographical and historical time—and since they varied in the length of time they had been at Bennington, this measure has some obvious problems. On the one hand, it might reflect the score of a young first-year student, who had entered Bennington in 1934 but had dropped out of school and out of the study. Or it might reflect the score of a seasoned Bennington college graduate, who had entered Bennington somewhat later. One of these hypothetical women would have caught the full force of the Bennington environment and reached her potential for change, whereas the other one would have barely reached the opportunity for experiencing Bennington and therefore may not have been exposed to the potential for change. Two such scores do not equally reflect the full impact of life-cycle factors either. One student at the time the score was available would have been younger and less experienced in the broader world as well. The point here is that our early measure of the PEP is confounded with a number of processes that do not render it a flawless instrument for detecting the early impact of the Bennington experience.

Fortunately, however, we were able to obtain three critical measures which will help in understanding the early PEP score. First, we have a measure of the year the student first entered Bennington College, and

5. There was no direct access to the original Bennington data, and we were forced to rely on computerized records of the early data constructed by our forerunners. The data available from these sources contains only the *last* measure of the PEP obtained by Newcomb in the 1930s and 1940s.

we can thus control for differences in the year she first experienced the Bennington environment. Second, we have a measure of the number of years she attended Bennington, and thus we can control for the number of years before the available PEP measure was obtained. And third, we have a measure of parents' political preferences, so we can control for the direction of the parental influences.[6] The distributions of these variables were presented in chapter 4 for the various samples of the Bennington women studied over time. By holding constant these variables when we assess changes in individual attitudes from the 1930s onwards, differences in attitudes assessed over time will be free of the confounding of the initial measure with the amount of time spent at Bennington, the year entered, and parental attitudes.

A second problem of measuring true attitude change is that measurement errors often masquerade as change. Such measurement errors occur for many reasons, including a number of sources of chance errors as well as systematic errors, and they need to be recognized as a source of bias in bivariate correlations observed over time. To the extent possible we need to rely on correlational techniques that will try to control for these sources of error as well. We begin, however, with somewhat simpler methods, looking carefully at the attenuated bivariate data in some amount of detail before moving to the more complicated and more "sensitive" analytic techniques.

Early Environmental Influences

We begin this analysis by considering the relationship between our early measures of sociopolitical orientation and the three measures of early social and political experiences. In addition to the PEP score, we also have a second measure of the 1938–40 political party preference, obtained from the original Bennington data base. Thus, our direct measures of attitudes for the early period, that is, the time of the woman's departure from Bennington, are two: (1) Newcomb's *Political and Economic Progressivism (PEP) Scale*—a linear composite variable made up of the sum of the 26 items given in appendix A (PEP30);[7] and (2) a measure of the direction of party support, based on *1936–40 Electoral Preferences*—an index combining the electoral preferences from the 1930 data (1936 candidate preference) and the 1960s report of the 1940 candidate preference (PID30).

---

6. Here we use a summary score based on both parents' political party identification.

7. Although this composite score was available for participants in the early studies, data for the individual component items were unavailable. For simplicity we refer to this measure as PEP30, even though it could have been gathered anywhere from 1936 to 1942.

In table 7.1A we present a matrix containing the bivariate (pairwise-present) correlations among all the measures we consider in this chapter.[8] We present all the correlations among our measures here, even though we will be considering only the early (1930s) measures at this point in our analysis. We discuss the later (1960s and 1984) measures in due course, and it is sufficient here to point out that there are strongly positive relationships among all of the measures of sociopolitical attitudes within and between time points. For example, note that the two measures of 1930s sociopolitical orientations correlate in the .5–.6 range. They obviously measure something in common, but somewhat different things as well. In any event there appears to be a strong common factor here, which we take to reflect sociopolitical orientations early in the adult life cycle. Similarly, the measures of sociopolitical orientations at different time points seem to be tapping aspects of the same phenomenon.

It is clear from this table that there are moderately strong relationships among these measures of sociopolitical orientations and the political preferences of parents. These positive relationships indicate considerable similarity between parents and children. In addition, there are also some quite interesting results in this table concerning the two measures of exposure to Bennington College. On the one hand, those entering Bennington relatively later (1938 vs. 1932) seem to have more politically conservative views. This probably results from the fact that those entering later were younger (and had thereby spent less time at Bennington) when their last PEP score was obtained. Also, as expected, these data suggest that the more time spent in the Bennington environment, the more liberal one became—to wit, the negative correlations of the two early measures of political orientations (PEP and PID) with the number of years matriculating at Bennington.[9] These latter correlations are not that sizeable, but they are consistently negative across all measures of sociopolitical attitudes.

Parental Influences

The influence of parental attitudes and values on children's orientations is a well-established finding in the literature on socialization (Acock and Bengtson, 1980; Bengtson, 1975; Dalton, 1980; Glass, Bengtson, and Dun-

---

8. Because of the general scarcity of overlapping data in this relatively small sample of 335 persons, we work with pairwise-present correlations. Table 7.1B presents the number of cases on which each correlation is based.

9. Recall that we have followed the practice of scoring the conservative direction of the partisan and ideological variables with a relatively higher score: 1 versus 0 in the case of party identification, 7 versus 1 in the case of the liberalism/conservatism scales, and the highest score in the case of the PEP and PCI scores reflects a more conservative orientation.

Table 7.1A. Correlation Matrix among Selected Variables: Bennington Women ($N = 335$)

	PEP30	PID30	PEP60	PID60	PCI60	L/C60	PEP84	PID84	PCI84	L/C84	Yr. Enter	# Years	Parents
PEP30	1.00												
PID30	.551	1.00											
PEP60	.572	.606	1.00										
PID60	.496	.590	.701	1.00									
PCI60	.384	.425	.571	.617	1.00								
L/C60	.417	.475	.694	.740	.584	1.00							
PEP84	.342	.295	.390	.395	.323	.333	1.00						
PID84	.457	.496	.588	.772	.499	.653	.442	1.00					
PCI84	.447	.420	.594	.652	.445	.573	.386	.728	1.00				
L/C84	.410	.442	.555	.694	.476	.699	.442	.796	.749	1.00			
Yr. Enter	.218	.201	-.007	.119	.074	.022	.008	.086	.030	.071	1.00		
# Years	-.161	-.112	-.086	-.097	-.163	-.110	-.134	-.098	-.129	-.156	-.300	1.00	
Parents	.418	.534	.448	.451	.278	.392	.178	.324	.283	.291	.079	-.015	1.00

Table 7.1B. Paired Number of Observations in Correlation Matrix among Selected Variables: Bennington Women ($N = 335$)

	PEP30	PID30	PEP60	PID60	PCI60	L/C60	PEP84	PID84	PCI84	L/C84	Yr. Enter	# Years	Parents
PEP30	520												
PID30	450	463											
PEP60	195	195	200										
PID60	407	408	200	420									
PCI60	349	341	199	347	349								
L/C60	335	327	187	332	332	335							
PEP84	324	326	154	332	266	254	332						
PID84	325	332	155	338	267	255	332	338					
PCI84	321	323	152	329	263	251	329	329	329				
L/C84	319	321	152	327	261	249	325	327	325	327			
Yr. Enter	479	420	173	386	321	308	332	335	329	327	488		
# Years	370	306	193	376	317	304	324	325	321	319	378	378	
Parents	387	391	173	335	295	284	322	325	320	317	320	370	395

Table 7.2. Partial Regression Coefficients for Prediction of Over-Time Measures of Sociopolitical Orientations from Indicators of Political Background and Bennington College Environment

Predictor Variable	Dependent Variable				
	(1) PEP30	(2) PID30	(3) PEP60	(4) PID60	(5) PCI60
x_1 Year entered Bennington	.153**	.141**	−.073	.062	.005
x_2 Number of years at Bennington	−.109*	−.062	−.101	−.072	−.158**
x_3 Parental orientations	.405**	.522**	.452**	.445**	.276**
R-squared	.221	.314	.212	.215	.103
	(6) L/C60	(7) PEP84	(8) PID84	(9) PCI84	(10) L/C84
x_1 Year entered Bennington	−.044	−.051	.036	−.033	.003
x_2 Number of years at Bennington	−.117*	−.147*	−.082	−.134*	−.150**
x_3 Parental orientations	.393**	.180**	.320**	.284**	.289**
R-squared	.166	.051	.115	.097	.108

$*p < .05$ $**p < .01$

ham, 1986; Jennings and Niemi, 1968, 1981; Smith, 1983). One can see this influence in the present data by inspecting the simple partial regression coefficients for all of our indicators of sociopolitical orientations across the life span when they are regressed on the measured set of exogenous variables considered above: year entering Bennington College, number of years in attendance, and parental orientations. These regression coefficients are given in table 7.2. These coefficients indicate with amazing clarity and consistency that throughout the life cycle, parental orientations are much more predictive of the later orientations of these women than are the variables linked to the Bennington experience. Of course, one must keep in mind that most aspects of the Bennington experience (those that set it apart from other colleges and other social environments of the time) are a constant in this analysis and can only partially be represented by the set of variables considered. Keeping this in mind, we cannot, thus, conclude from the above that parental influences were "more important" than the Bennington influences. We conclude at this point only that parental influence is strong and consistent throughout the life course, though it appears to weaken with time. We advance these conclusions as tentative here, since we need to take more seriously various aspects of this process not represented in these simple regression models. As noted above, such analyses need to take into account the imperfection of our measures, and, we need to represent more adequately the process of latent attitude change over time.

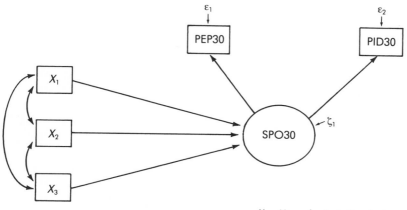

X_1 = Year of entry to Bennington

X_2 = Number of years at Bennington

X_3 = Political orientation of parents

Figure 7.1. Linear Structural Equations Model for Early Sociopolitical Orientations

These findings of the strong influence of parents' sociopolitical orientations may be unexpected, given the type of emphasis Newcomb's original results have received (see chapter 2). Based on the present set of findings, the original results may seem somewhat exaggerated, especially given the overwhelming evidence in the recent research literature that parents' attitudes are significant predictors of children's attitudes in adulthood. We return to this issue below.

The logic of this patterning of relationships suggested a simple causal model that specified three determinants of early attitudes: the year entering Bennington, the length of time at Bennington, and parental political orientation. Following the path-analytic conventions (see Duncan, 1975a) of diagraming such causal models, we present a pictorial representation of this generative process in figure 7.1. This model represents the 1930s sociopolitical attitude in terms of two measures: the 1930s PEP score and the 1930s party identification measure (PID30).[10] This construct depends, according to this model, on three critical factors (among others presumably operating, but for which we have no measures): x_1 = year of entry to Bennington (obtained from our 1984 query), x_2 = number of years at

10. Although these data were collected at points varying from the 1930s into the 1940s, for simplicity (if not accuracy), we henceforth refer to these as *1930s* measures. Likewise for simplicity, we later refer to our 1960–61 data collection point as the *1960s* and our 1984 survey as the *1980s* measures.

Table 7.3. Parameter Estimates for a Linear Structural Equations
Model for Early Sociopolitical Orientations

	Dependent Variable		
	(1)	(2)	(3)
Predictor Variable	PEP30	PID30	SPO30
η_1 1930s sociopolitical factor	.677**	.814**	—
x_1 Year entered Bennington	—	—	.190**
x_2 Number of years at Bennington	—	—	−.101
x_3 Parental orientations	—	—	.628**
R-squared	.458	.662	.473

Note: Based on a model with 2 df and a χ^2 of 2.10 ($p = .350$)
*$p < .05$ **$p < .01$

Bennington (again obtained from our 1984 query), and x_3 = political orientation of parents (obtained from the archived 1930s data).

We can summarize the information from these regressions (in table 7.2) somewhat more compactly by regressing the "common variance" of our two 1930s measures on our three predictors, using somewhat more sophisticated methods. To estimate the parameters of the model given in figure 7.1, we employed estimation strategies contained within the LISREL framework of Jöreskog and Sörbom (Jöreskog, 1973; Jöreskog and Sörbom, 1982, 1986). This general framework permits us to predict the common part of our two 1930s measures of political orientations from the three predictor variables of interest (see the brief discussion in appendix F). Table 7.3 presents coefficients for this equation (model 3) along with coefficients for the regression of the two indicators on the latent common factor (models 1 and 2).[11] We can also get some idea of the relative impacts or influences of these three variables on the early sociopolitical attitudes from the estimates of these model parameters. Again note that in this model the two indicators of early sociopolitical orientations are used to represent a latent factor

11. The parameter estimates reported for this and subsequent models were estimated using Jöreskog and Sörbom's (1986) LISREL program. The pattern matrices for the model should be apparent from the coefficients given in the tables and the accompanying figures. Throughout the following analysis we rely on standard-form structural coefficients, since our primary interest is in the relative importance of variables. In all cases in which we report the estimates for such LISREL models, we report the degrees of freedom, goodness of fit, and model modifications in the stub of the table. We also report approximate levels of significance for the estimated coefficients in our models, although reporting significance levels may not be justified on statistical grounds. In all tables in this and subsequent chapters, coefficient estimates exceeding the .01 level of significance for a one-tailed test are indicated by two asterisks (**) and those significant at the .05 level for a one-tailed test are indicated by one asterisk (*).

146

for the 1930s sociopolitical attitudes, and this latent factor is essentially "regressed" on these three predictor variables. Table 7.3 presents these parameter estimates. All the coefficients in this table can be interpreted as regression coefficients in standardized form for each of the two measures—y_1 = 1930s PEP score, and y_2 = 1930s PID (models 1 and 2)—as well as for the common factor used to represent these indicators (model 3). In the first two equations the coefficients reflect the linkage between the particular indicator and the latent factor. Indeed, the coefficients in those two first columns may be interpreted as correlations of the indicators and the factor. In both cases the linkage is strong, but it is clear that each indicator measures something different as well. The PEP score shares only about one-half of its variance with the common factor, whereas the party preference measure (PID) shares about two-thirds of its variance with the factor. This means (for one thing) that the factor is slightly more defined in terms of the PID measure, which also implies that this indicator is more strongly linked to the exogenous predictors than the PEP score. This can be further verified by inspecting the regression coefficients for these two measures in table 7.2.

As noted, the common part of the PEP score and the party preference (PID) measure is what our model (figure 7.1), the results of which are presented in table 7.3, predicts from variation in the three exogenous variables. These coefficients indicate that the strongest apparent influence among these three variables is parental political preference, with the two predictors representing the Bennington experience having somewhat weaker influences. Here, the result noted above is reproduced in somewhat more robust form. There is little question that parental influences were strong in the Bennington cohort, accounting for most of the explained variation in these measures, regardless of how one constructs the analysis.

Does this finding contradict the original argument of Newcomb (1943), summarized in detail in chapter 2? Does the seeming importance of the Bennington experience pale in comparison with the apparent strength of -parental influences on sociopolitical orientations? And does not the present portrayal of the importance of parental influences undermine one of the essential ingredients in Newcomb's original understanding and interpretation of the "Bennington effect," namely that these young women seemed to do an "about-face" in terms of consistency with their family origins, adopting a much more liberal view of the world—in line with their new reference groups, but in contrast to the attitudes of their parents?

These results do *not* contradict the earlier findings. Rather, they illuminate them somewhat and put them in a larger interpretive context, just as our earlier analyses (chapters 5 and 6) have attempted to place our results in the broadest possible context. What these (table 7.3) results show is

147

that parental influences on political orientations are relatively strong, perhaps as strong as, or stronger than, once believed (e.g., see Davies, 1965;
Greenstein, 1965; Hess and Torney, 1967). But the existence of strong
parental influences does not negate the possibility of the type and magnitude of the "Bennington effect" reviewed above. Indeed, the coefficients in
table 7.3 reveal a significant influence of the year of entry to Bennington,
but not of the number of years spent there. Those youngest women who
had not experienced Bennington for long, and who presumably would still
change further, were more conservative. And by holding constant time of
entry and parental background, the number of years spent at Bennington
had a discernable liberalizing effect. In other words, we think these results simply reinforce the conclusions drawn by Newcomb from his original
studies (see chapter 2).

Recall also our discussion of Newcomb's (1943) analysis of the divergences from parental orientations (see chapter 2). We noted then that
about 30 percent of the Bennington women's parents identified with the
Democratic party and as many as 10 percent or more preferred Socialist
or Communist candidates. Some 90 percent of these women retained their
liberal origins, thus reflecting *no change!* This is a sizeable portion of the
sample, and this contributes to a high level of correlation with the parental background measure. At the same time, we noted that while about 75
percent of the Bennington women's parents were Republican, some 60
percent of these women (or 45 percent of the total sample) changed in
a more liberal direction, with more than one-half changing to a Democratic, Socialist, or Communist political party preference. Thus, whether
one looks at these results as reflecting change within the Bennington population or not, there is ample basis in the transitions summarized here to
suggest considerable overlap between parent and child. Thus, just as with
the development of attitudes over the life span, it is perhaps most produc-
tive to view the relationship between parent and child as involving some
balance of stability and change. While it may be interesting to account
for the similarity between parent and child, either theoretically or empirically, we cannot engage in this effort here. Our focus on the parental
linkage here is primarily a way of controlling for parental influences in our
analysis of change.[12]

12. At several points in our earlier chapters, we have mentioned those accounts that would
discredit the main Newcomb thesis by attesting to exceptional cases, such as Brockway's
(1981) speculation that Newcomb's research did not adequately sample testimony from the
side of those who became disenchanted with Bennington (see chapter 2). We also mentioned
at least one Bennington woman who revealed herself to be another type of exception, one
whose parents were liberally oriented to begin with and for whom Bennington was an environment that supported the political orientations of her parents (see "The Bennington Girl:

These results also further reinforce our stance regarding the necessity to control for these three "prior" variables in assessing attitude change since Bennington. Consistently across both measures of sociopolitical attitudes in the 1930s, these dependencies suggest that we need to assess change only from the perspective of holding these other experiences constant. Thus, in all of our future analyses of stability we control statistically for these three factors: parental background, year entering Bennington, and the amount of time spent there.

Estimating Stability and Change from the Impressionable Years to Mid-Life

Our analysis at this point reexamines the nature of the attitude shifts among the Bennington women from the point of leaving Bennington through the early 1960s, which reflected changes in attitudes over approximately 20–25 years in their lives, from young adulthood to mid-life. As indicated earlier (see chapter 4), for this purpose we have a somewhat richer array of measures of sociopolitical orientations. For the mid-life period, assessed during the early 1960s, we have a second measure of the PEP score. In addition to having a score for this 26-item scale from respondents to the mailed questionnaire for this period, we make use of Newcomb and his colleagues' (1967) index of political conservatism, made up of responses to public issues current in the 1960s (see above), obtained in both the interview and mail questionnaire subsample. Also, the 1960s interviews and mailed questionnaires included a five-point, single-item scale, assessing the subject's position on the dimension of liberalism/conservatism, and there is a measure of electoral preferences for this mid-life period of the life cycle.

The measures we have for the 1960s are thus as follows: (1) *1961 Political and Economic Progressivism (PEP) Scale*—1961 version of the PEP composite variable made up of the same 26 items assessed in the original study (PEP60); (2) *1960–84 Reports of Electoral Preferences for 1956–64*—a combined measure of the number of conservative candidates preferred in the 1956, 1960, and 1964 elections (PID60); (3) *1961 Political Conservatism Index*—a four- to six-item scale based on items obtained in 1961 dealing with the support of liberal versus conservative positions on public issues

---

Fifty Years Later," *Ann Arbor News*, F1–F2, 27 July 1986). It may not seem so to the critical observer, but our use of parental political orientations as a control variable is intended to control for these major exceptional categories, although we can do nothing to make up for the loss of participants due to disaffiliation from the early Bennington study.

Table 7.4. Parameter Estimates for a Linear Structural Equations
Model for the Indicators of Sociopolitical Orientations
at Mid-Life

Predictor Variable	Dependent Variable			
	PEP60[a]	PID60[b]	PCI60[c]	L/C60[d]
x_1 Year entered				
Bennington	−.261**	−.087	−.117*	−.167**
x_2 Number of years				
at Bennington	.004	.009	−.091	−.051
x_3 Parental orientations	−.157	−.049	−.126	−.009
η_1 1930s sociopolitical				
orientation	.966**	.785**	.638**	.639**
R-squared	.694	.539	.315	.380

[a]Based on a model with 3 df and a χ^2 of 3.55 ($p = .314$)
[b]Based on a model with 3 df and a χ^2 of 2.12 ($p = .548$)
[c]Based on a model with 3 df and a χ^2 of 2.32 ($p = .509$)
[d]Based on a model with 3 df and a χ^2 of 2.31 ($p = .511$)
*$p < .05$ **$p < .01$

(PCI60); (4) *1961 Five-Point Liberal/Conservative Scale*—a 1961 single-item measure involving a five-point liberal/conservative scale with labeled scale points (LC60).

Table 7.1 presented the correlations of our 1960s measures of sociopolitical orientations among themselves and their correlations with the earlier variables considered thus far. Each of these 1960s measures is strongly related to the 1930s measures, but especially to the 1930s latent construct reflecting sociopolitical orientations. This was, of course, the central conclusion of the analysis on this point conducted by Newcomb and his colleagues (1967), which we discussed in chapter 3. We can demonstrate this by regressing each of the 1960s measures on the 1930s latent variable, without imposing (as yet) any latent construct on the 1960s measures. This we accomplish using a structural equation model in which sociopolitical orientations in the 1960s are assessed by a single fallible indicator. We present the estimates for this model (separately for each 1960s measure) in table 7.4. These results portray strong relationships of the 1960s indicators to the 1930s latent sociopolitical construct. The relationship of the 1960s PEP to the 1930s construct is especially strong: .966.

These results also show that, independent of the 1930s sociopolitical orientations, the year of entry into Bennington has a significant negative effect on the 1960s measures. This means that the later the student entered Bennington, the more her attitudes changed in a liberal direction between when they were last measured at Bennington and the 1960s study. We suspect this reflects the fact we reported earlier that the PEP measures for students entering Bennington later were obtained when they were relatively younger and had not yet experienced the full force of the Bennington environment. Thus, from the time of measurement in the 1930s and 1940s, there was considerable change yet to occur. This is reflected in a negative relationship between these 1960s measures and the year entering Bennington, when the 1930s assessment of sociopolitical orientations is held constant.

The results in table 7.4 suggest further that parental orientations and the number of years at Bennington have no effect on the amount of attitude change between the 1930s–40s and the 1960s. That is, there is no direct effect of parental orientations on the 1960s measures. Thus, parental influences affect the 1960s indicators only through their effects on early (1930s) sociopolitical orientations. This means that parental influences are a source of stability in 1960s attitudes, rather than a source of change. We pursue a somewhat more refined articulation of this conclusion in the following analysis.

Estimation of Attitude Stability and Change

By capitalizing on our multiple assessments of attitudes in the 1960s, and controlling for the above-referenced background variables, we can approach a somewhat better estimate of the extent of true change and stability in attitudes. Using these multiple measures, we can formulate a simple model, portrayed in figure 7.2, which depicts the process of attitude change over this period. In this model we allow the prior background variables to influence the amount of attitude change; that is, we allow these variables to have an independent influence on the attitude construct represented in the 1960s. Ultimately we will capitalize further on this multiple-occasion approach to measurement. Multiple measures of attitudes at three points in time will permit us to examine the issues addressed here within the even more complete model of attitude change over time. However, at this point we restrict our attention to the data accessible to Newcomb and his colleagues (1967), which can be used to assess the extent of attitude change between the 1930s and 1960s.

In order to estimate the structural equation model represented in figure 7.2, we employed estimation strategies contained within the LISREL framework of Jöreskog and Sörbom (Jöreskog, 1973; Jöreskog and Sörbom, 1982, 1986). This general framework allows the specification of a measurement model linking latent attitude variables to indicators at each point in time, allowing for random and nonrandom errors of measurement in the indicators, and the simultaneous specification of a structural equation model

151

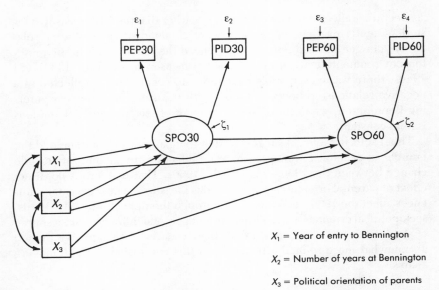

Figure 7.2. Linear Structural Equations Model for Sociopolitical Orientations at Mid-Life

stating the causal relationships among latent variables, in the present case coefficients of stability linking latent attitude variables over time.[13]

Using this approach we focus on the following questions. How stable or persistent are such sociopolitical attitudes estimated to be once some effort is made to control for variation in the exogenous causal factors referred to above (parental background, year entering Bennington, and number of years at Bennington), and when some attempt is made to adjust for imprecision of measurement? How much stability is necessary in order for one to conclude that the experiences of the past, say those tied to early cohort experiences, are responsible for current variation in attitude? And how much relative change in attitudes over time is needed to conclude that an individual's sociopolitical attitudes are inherently flexible, reflecting adaptation to social change and changing social experiences?

In order to maintain as much comparability of measurement as possible between the 1930s and 1960s, we first entertain a model that includes only the same types of indicators across the two time points, namely the PEP

13. Our initial models included correlations among the errors or disturbances of common measures over time. That is, we wanted to allow for the possibility that there were correlated errors of measurement between the PEP scores in the 1930s and 1960s and between the party preference (PID) scores in the 1930s and 1960s. The only one of these correlated errors that proved significant was that between the 1930s and 1960s PEP scores, and the correlation of the errors of the PID measures was deleted in further analyses.

Table 7.5. Parameter Estimates for a Linear Structural Equations Model of Sociopolitical Orientations at Mid-Life—Model 1

Predictor Variable	Dependent Variable					
	PEP30	PID30	SPO30	PEP60	PID60	SPO60
η_1 1930s Sociopolitical orientation	.684**	.808**	—	—	—	.996**
η_2 1960s sociopolitical orientation	—	—	—	.860**	.816**	—
x_1 Year entered Bennington	—	—	.198**	—	—	−.218**
x_2 Number of years at Bennington	—	—	−.102	—	—	−.001
x_3 Parental orientations	—	—	.629**	—	—	−.090
R-squared	.463	.653	.479	.738	.666	.813

Note: Based on a model with 6 df and a χ^2 of 10.10 ($p = .121$). The model assumed all measurement disturbances were uncorrelated over time, except that the disturbances for the PEP30 and PEP60 were allowed to covary.
*$p < .05$ **$p < .01$

measures (PEP30 and PEP60) and the party preference measures (PID30 and PID60). These results are given in table 7.5. These results build upon our prior analyses in several important respects. First, the results here incorporate the earlier findings regarding variation in early (1930s) socio-political orientations—those previous results given in table 7.3. In other words, we are simply carrying forward that part of our model by incre-mentally adding the 1960s measures to the analytic framework (compare figures 7.1 and 7.2). Thus, our conclusions ventured earlier regarding the influences of the exogenous factors on early sociopolitical orientations are embodied in the results presented here. Indeed, the results for PEP30, PID30, and SPO30 in table 7.5 are virtually identical to those presented in table 7.3.

These results also bear out our preliminary speculations, based on our analyses of the separate indicators of the 1960s sociopolitical attitudes (see table 7.4). They reflect an extremely high degree of dependence of the 1960s latent sociopolitical attitude variable on its earlier 1930s counter-part, suggesting a high degree of stability. The year in which the student entered Bennington is a significant predictor of the 1960s latent attitude, holding the 1930s attitude constant. This influence, shown by the signifi-cant negative coefficient in table 7.5, reveals, as above, that those entering the College community later (and whose available PEP scores existed rela-tively early in their college experience) continued to change in a liberal direction between the 1930s and 1960s. This amount of attitude change,

Table 7.6. Parameter Estimates for a Linear Structural Equations Model of Sociopolitical Orientations at Mid-Life—Model 2

Predictor Variable	Dependent Variable							
	PEP30	PID30	SPO30	PEP60	PID60	PCI60	L/C60	SPO60
η_1 1930s sociopolitical orientation	.670**	.792**	—	—	—	—	—	.950**
η_2 1960s sociopolitical orientation	—	—	.832**	.873**	.693**	.830**	—	—
x_1 Year entered Bennington	—	—	.206**	—	—	—	—	−.208**
x_2 Number of years at Bennington	—	—	−.107*	—	—	—	—	−.019
x_3 Parental orientations	—	—	.633**	—	—	—	—	−.102
R-squared	.456	.628	.491	.691	.763	.480	.689	.723

Note: Based on a model with 19 df and a χ^2 of 37.20 ($p = .007$). The model assumed all measurement disturbances were uncorrelated over time, except that the disturbances for the PEP30 and PEP60 were allowed to covary.
*$p < .05$ **$p < .01$

as indicated above, is a spurious result of the fact that our post-Bennington PEP score is actually the last PEP score recorded by Newcomb in his early research.

In order to take full advantage of all four of our available measures of sociopolitical attitudes in the 1960s, we examined this same model using all four of these indicators to represent the latent sociopolitical attitude variable in the 1960s. The model is identical in all respects to the one whose results were presented in table 7.5, except that instead we include all four measures for the 1960s time point. These results are given in table 7.6. Except for an overall poorer fit to the data, which is to be expected given the wider range of measures used, these results lead to exactly the same conclusions we reached above. Specifically, we conclude that once we take into account the possibility of some further attitude change for women who entered Bennington College near the end of Newcomb's study, and who therefore had further change to experience during college (which was not fully reflected in our available measures of attitudes in the 1930s and 1940s), the attitudes of our sample were unbelievably stable over this 20–25-year period. Our standardized estimate of this relationship is in the neighborhood of .95–.99 (compare tables 7.5 and 7.6).

ATTITUDE CHANGE AND STABILITY ACROSS THE LIFE SPAN

This part of our analysis of gross levels of individual stability in attitudes over the life span brings the 1984 measures of attitudes into the picture, looking simultaneously at the changes between the 1930s and the 1960s on the one hand and the changes from the 1960s through the 1980s on the other. Measures of 1984 sociopolitical attitudes are roughly as plentiful as attitude assessments obtained in the 1960s, and are directly comparable as conceptual replicates. As described in chapter 3, we obtained a version of the PEP scale relevant to the social issues of the 1980s, and a version of the PCI for 1984 using items connected to current public affairs. Also, we have the seven-point, single-item scale measuring liberalism/conservatism referred to in our review of subjective assessments of attitude change, and there is a measure of electoral preferences.

Our measures of sociopolitical attitudes for 1984, then, are as follows: (1) *1984 Political and Economic Progressivism (PEP) Scale*—a 1984 version of the PEP composite variable made up of 12 of the 26 items assessed in the original study (PEP84); (2) *1984 Reports of Electoral Preferences for 1976–84*—a measure of the conservative electoral preferences in the 1976, 1980, and 1984 elections (PID84); (3) *1984 Political Conservatism Index*—an eight-item scale based on the items obtained in 1984 dealing with the support of liberal vs. conservative positions on public issues (PCI84); (4) *1984 Seven-Point Liberalism/Conservatism Scale*—a 1984 single-item measure involving a seven-point liberalism/conservatism scale with labeled scale points (LC84). As noted earlier, table 7.1 presented the correlations of our 1980s measures of sociopolitical orientations among themselves and correlations with the earlier variables considered thus far.

By extending the previous model of attitude change, we can use these multiple assessments of attitudes in the 1984 data, coupled with all of our measures analyzed thus far, to model the extent of attitude change and stability of attitudes into later life. There is a strong sense in which the issues of attitude change and persistence are different over this second period of the life course, in that the sources of stability and change differ. As with very young adulthood, in later life there are considerably more disruptions of social roles and activities (Steckenrider and Cutler, 1989). Thus, there may be theoretical reasons for expecting that the level of stability would differ, perhaps even decline, in older age.

Using these multiple measures, we can formulate a final model, shown in figure 7.3, which extends the earlier models of attitude change from young adulthood to mid-life. This model depicts the process of attitude change throughout the life cycle. Indeed, all of the causal specifications

155

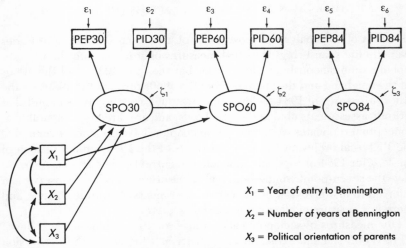

Figure 7.3. Linear Structural Equations Model for Sociopolitical Orientations across the Life Span

made earlier with regard to exogenous influences on early attitudes and the high level of stability in attitudes into mid-life are rendered a part of this model. Since the exogenous factors do not convey any of their effects on 1984 attitudes directly, and since early sociopolitical attitudes do not directly affect attitudes in later life, except through their stabilizing influence on attitudes in mid-life, the only factor in this model contributing to the 1984 sociopolitical attitude construct is the 1960s sociopolitical attitude.[14] These causal specifications are drawn in figure 7.3. They indicate that the latent attitude variable in 1984 is determined directly (in this model) by only one other variable—1960s sociopolitical orientations. Further, they indicate that a single factor represents the covariation among the 1984 indicators.

In a preliminary examination of the correlational data, we can calculate the correlation of each of the 1984 indicators with the 1960 latent sociopolitical attitude construct.[15] Table 7.7 presents these correlations. With one notable exception, these correlations reflect a high level of stability in sociopolitical orientations. The 1984 PEP score, which was an abridged

14. In chapter 8 we consider some of the potential sources of stability and change between the 1960s and 1984. Here we are concerned only with gross levels of stability (i.e., our main concern is the amount of change versus stability there is to explain), and in chapter 8 we consider some of their sources.

15. This is the same strategy we used in assessing levels of association between early attitude constructs and later indicators, as in table 7.4.

Table 7.7. Parameter Estimates for a Linear Structural Equations
Model for the Indicators of Sociopolitical Orientations

Predictor Variable	Dependent Variable			
	PEP84[a]	PID84[b]	PCI84[c]	PID84[d]
1960s sociopolitical orientation	.458**	.811**	.716**	.735**
R-squared	.210	.658	.513	.559

[a]Based on a model with 14 df and a χ^2 of 20.45 ($p = .117$)
[b]Based on a model with 14 df and a χ^2 of 40.57 ($p = .000$)
[c]Based on a model with 14 df and a χ^2 of 31.18 ($p = .005$)
[d]Based on a model with 14 df and a χ^2 of 35.52 ($p = .001$)
*$p < .05$ **$p < .01$

version of the original PEP, does not correlate as highly with the 1960s construct as do the other measurements. This is to be expected, since the original PEP was substantially shortened and reflects only a subset of the item content of the original measures. Otherwise, as shown in table 7.7, there are strong zero-order correlations between the 1984 measures of political attitudes and the 1960s latent political attitude variable.

As before, in estimating the structural equation model implied by figure 7.3, we employed Jöreskog and Sörbom's LISREL framework. As noted above, this set of procedures allows us to estimate a model that includes measurement parameters, linking latent attitude constructs and measured variables, while at the same time estimating the parameters of a structural equation model expressing relationships among the latent variables. Again, our primary interest in estimating this model is in the underlying stability parameters. These tell us how stable or persistent sociopolitical attitudes are over various periods of the life cycle. In our analyses up to this point we encountered an extremely high level of attitude persistence or stability from the early adult years through mid-life. The question at this stage is whether this level of stability is maintained, or whether it grows (if that is possible) or declines in later life. Again, we raise the question of the degree of stability and change in sociopolitical attitudes. How much change in levels of stability would be considered different from the prior levels of stability?

Following our above research strategy, in order to maintain as much comparability of measurement as possible among assessments made in the 1930s, 1960s, and 1984, we first consider a model that includes only the common indicators over the three time points: the PEP score and the party preference indicator (PID). The results for this model, as before in standard form, are given in table 7.8; and, as above, we will also consider an extension of this model which includes more indicators where they are available. In this regard we have some flexibility, since we have a considerable array of measures in both the 1960s and 1984. We pursue a couple of different approaches for inclusion of indicators in the following analysis.

These results incorporate all of our earlier findings: both the earlier findings regarding the influences of the early environment on early (1930s) sociopolitical attitudes, and the earlier findings regarding the extent of stability and change in attitudes between the 1930s and 1960s—from the impressionable years to mid-life. By extending the analysis to include the 1984 measures, we include our earlier conclusions in the model that represents attitude changes into later life. In this regard, the results in table 7.8 that pertain to these earlier aspects of our model are virtually identical to those given before, and we will not review them further.

The results in table 7.8 confirm our expectation that there is a high degree of stability of sociopolitical attitudes into later life. The stability coefficient (in standard form) linking the 1960s and 1984 attitudes is .86. This compares with an estimated .908 for the stability coefficient linking the 1930s and 1960s. This means that the correlation between the 1930s attitude and the 1984 attitude is roughly .781, the product of these two shorter range stabilities. This reflects a very high level of stability in sociopolitical attitudes over the life span, and the magnitude of stability seems to be relatively constant over various periods in the life span. Indeed, whatever differences one may perceive between stability coefficients of .91 and .86 are probably linked to the differing amounts of time involved in the remeasurement intervals.[16]

This model represents an excellent fit to the data, and there is little basis on which to fault the model. It is again clear from these estimates that the 1984 version of the PEP was not as tightly linked to the latent attitude variable as were the other indicators and as were previous PEP measures. But this seems a minor consideration, given the intent to replicate indicators conceptually to the extent possible.

As in our above analysis, we were concerned that these results not be dependent upon the particular set of indicators chosen, and that they would be found consistent over a variety of different choices of indicators. Thus, we estimated two additional models to represent this process: one including four measures of sociopolitical attitudes in 1984, but including just the original two measures in the 1930s and 1960s, and a second model that included all available measures at all time points. The latter model included the PEP score and the party identification measure at all three time points,

16. There were a few more years between the 1960s and 1984 studies than between the early measurement and the 1960s.

Table 7.8. Parameter Estimates for a Linear Structural Equations Model of Sociopolitical Orientations across the Life Span—Model 1

	Dependent Variable								
Predictor Variable	PEP30	PID30	SPO30	PEP60	PID60	SPO60	PEP84	PID84	SPO84
η_1 1930s sociopolitical orientation	.692**	.821**	—	—	—	—	—	—	—
η_2 1960s sociopolitical orientation	—	—	—	.857**	.822**	.908**	—	—	—
η_3 1984s sociopolitical orientation	—	—	—	—	—	—	.529**	.799**	.860**
x_1 Year entered Bennington	—	—	.194**	—	—	-.198**	—	—	0.0f
x_2 Number of years at Bennington	—	—	-.107*	—	—	0.0f	—	—	0.0f
x_3 Parental orientations	—	—	.605**	—	—	0.0f	—	—	0.0f
R-squared	.473	.675	.449	.733	.676	.765	.283	.642	.740

Note: Based on a model with 18 df and a χ^2 of 20.97 ($p = .281$). The model assumed all measurement disturbances were uncorrelated over time, except that the disturbance for the PEP30 was correlated with the disturbances for PEP60 and PEP84, and the disturbance for PID60 was correlated with the disturbance for PID84.

$*p < .05$ $**p < .01$ f = parameter fixed at zero

and the index of political conservatism and the liberal/conservative rating scale at both the 1960s and 1984 points.

The results of our estimation of these two additional models are given in tables 7.9 and 7.10. These results show with amazing clarity and consistency that, regardless of the indicators chosen to represent the underlying processes of attitude change over the life course, the levels of stability are high and roughly equal over the two time periods studied. The two additional models fit the data less well. In both cases the ratio of the χ^2 to the degrees of freedom is less than 2.0, which is our rule of thumb for an adequate fit to the data (see appendix E). It is obvious that when more information is introduced into the system at the level of measurement, the fit to the data declines, but the substantive results are virtually unaltered.

The Stability of Retrospective Attitudes

In order to assess the extent to which our above estimates of the stability of sociopolitical orientations are also reflected in retrospective assessments of attitudes, we also examine the intercorrelations among the retrospective reports of attitudes over the life cycle. We expected that the amount of stability in attitudes would be overestimated via the use of retrospective reports, and we assess the extent to which retrospective reports of attitude produce higher levels of stability than those observed in the above analyses.[17] For this purpose we examine the 1984 reports of attitudes at several points in the life cycle. Recall that respondents were asked to report their "general political viewpoints" for each of several time points: when they entered Bennington; when they left Bennington; in 1960; in 1972; and in 1984. Table 7.11 presents the intercorrelations among these measures.

These results suggest relatively modest levels of correlation between assessments of attitude at the time of college entry and at later points in the life cycle, decreasing in magnitude over time. At the same time, these attitudes seem to gain in strength, becoming more highly correlated with one another with time. These data (table 7.11) reveal an interesting form of the simplex model described by Jöreskog (1970), since attitude measures separated by greater distance show smaller levels of correlations. However, because of the unknown nature of retrospective bias in these reports, the estimation of the parameters of a simplex model, taking such retrospective biases into account, is not straightforward. Nevertheless, we estimated the parameters of several plausible models, which required placing some

17. Some evidence suggests that retrospective attitude measurement overestimates stability of attitudes (e.g., Himmelweit et al. 1978; Niemi et al. 1980).

Table 7.9. Parameter Estimates for a Linear Structural Equations Model of Sociopolitical Orientations across the Life Span—Model 2

Predictor Variable	Dependent Variable										
	PEP30	PID30	SPO30	PEP60	PID60	SPO60	PEP84	PID84	PCI84	L/C84	SPO84
η_1 1930s sociopolitical orientation	.682**	.805**	—	—	—	.871**	—	—	—	—	—
η_2 1960s sociopolitical orientation	—	—	—	.804**	.888**	—	—	—	—	—	.853**
η_3 1984s sociopolitical orientation	—	—	—	—	—	—	.492**	.878**	.833**	.887**	—
x_1 Year entered Bennington	—	—	.203**	—	—	-.168**	—	—	—	—	0.0f
x_2 Number of years at Bennington	—	—	-.115*	—	—	0.0f	—	—	—	—	0.0f
x_3 Parental orientations	—	—	.601**	—	—	0.0f	—	—	—	—	0.0f
R-squared	.478	.648	.450	.648	.793	.704	.247	.786	.694	.786	.727

Note: Based on a model with 35 df and a χ^2 of 56.69 ($p = .012$). The model assumed all measurement disturbances were uncorrelated over time, except that the disturbance for the PEP30 was correlated with the disturbances for PEP60 and PEP84, and the disturbance for PID60 was correlated with the disturbance for PID84.

$*p < .05$ $**p < .01$ f = parameter fixed at zero

Table 7.10. Parameter Estimates for a Linear Structural Equations Model of Sociopolitical Orientations across the Life Span—Model 3

Predictor Variable	Dependent Variable												
	PEP30	PID30	SPO30	PEP60	PID60	PCI60	L/C60	SPO60	PEP84	PID84	PCI84	L/C84	SPO84
η_1 1930s sociopolitical orientation	.682**	.800**	—					.855**					—
η_2 1960s sociopolitical orientation			—	.819**	.885**	.684**	.855**	—					.849**
η_3 1984s sociopolitical orientation			—					—	.492**	.877**	.832**	.887**	0.0f
x_1 Year entered Bennington			.202**					-.175**					0.0f
x_2 Number of years at Bennington			-.121*					0.0f					0.0f
x_3 Parental orientations			.602**					0.0f					0.0f
R-squared	.477	.639	.454	.673	.792	.467	.686	.675	.245	.787	.692	.787	.721

Note: Based on a model with 54 *df* and a χ^2 of 83.66 ($p = .006$). The model assumed all measurement disturbances were uncorrelated over time, except that the disturbance for the PEP30 was correlated with the disturbances for PEP60 and PEP84, and the disturbance for PID60 was correlated with the disturbance for PID84.

*$p < .05$ **$p < .01$ f = parameter fixed at zero

162

Table 7.11. Bivariate Correlations among Subjective Assessments of Change Using a Seven-Point Scale: 1984 Follow-up Respondents ($n = 327$)

Item	(a)	(b)	(c)	(d)	(e)
Entered Bennington College	1.00	.66	.48	.41	.33
Left Bennington College		1.00	.68	.60	.56
In 1960			1.00	.84	.81
In 1972				1.00	.92
In 1984					1.00

Table 7.12. Parameter Estimates for a Simplex Linear Structural Equation Model of Retrospective Sociopolitical Orientations over the Life Span

Predictor Variable	Dependent Variable								
	Observed Variables					Latent Variables			
	L/C36	L/C40	L/C60	L/C72	L/C84	η_2	η_3	η_4	η_5
η_1 1936 latent variable	.974[a]					.695**			
η_2 1940 latent variable		.974[a]					.712**		
η_3 1960 latent variable			.984					.877**	
η_4 1972 latent variable				.971[b]					.970**
η_5 1984 latent variable					.971[b]				
R-squared	.949	.949	.968	.943	.943	.483	.507	.767	.941

Note: Based on a model with 3 df and a χ^2 of 9.60 ($\sqrt{}\approx(p = .022)$.
[a]Parameters constrained equal
[b]Parameters constrained equal
**$p < .01$

constraints on the model reflecting simplifying assumptions regarding the influence of measurement error.[18]

We proceeded by analyzing only the 1984 reports in a model that assumes retrospective reliabilities of reporting early attitudes to be equal and that reliabilities of recent and current attitudes are also equal, but not equal to one another. Thus, the reliabilities of those attitudes pertaining to the time the woman entered and left Bennington College are assumed to be equal, as are those for 1972 and 1984 attitudes. Table 7.12 presents the

18. Specifically, in order to identify the model we needed to place some equality constraints on the disturbances on the measured variables. It seemed realistic that the amount of measurement error in reports of the two early times—when they entered and left Bennington College—in the 1984 survey would be about the same, so we assumed the reliabilities of these measures were equal. Also, it seemed reasonable to assume that the amount of error in reporting 1984 and 1972 political positions would be about the same, and we assumed these reliabilities to be equal. These two assumptions were sufficient to identify the model.

parameter estimates of an overidentified model which incorporates these assumptions.

These results indicate a set of processes quite similar to those suggested in our previous analyses; that is, they demonstrate a high level of stability in attitudes over time. However, these results give the impression of slight increases in the level of stability over the life course. Specifically, at least in the minds of our respondents, the level of stability over time, as shown in table 7.12, appears to increase in more recent periods. We would point out, however, that this is partially deceptive, since the more recent time periods in this analysis are more closely related in time than some of the earlier periods. Also, it is important to note that the stability of .7 for the span of four years, while these women were in college, may not appear to represent a somewhat volatile state of attitudes. However, it should be noted that for (in most cases) a four-year period, such a level of stability reflects considerable attitude change. Taken together, these observations support the notion of increasing stability of attitudes over time. Even if we control for the length of the time period by multiplying the coefficients linking 1960 to 1972 stability and 1972 to 1984 stability, we observe a stability from 1960 to 1984 of .851. Thus, in our respondents' retrospections, we observe the perception that attitudes gain strength over the life cycle, and consequently become more stable with time. While this may be conventional wisdom, as verified by both current theory (e.g., Sears, 1983) and popular belief, the results we presented above suggest a somewhat different set of processes: that after an initial period of vulnerability to attitude change in young adulthood and an increase in attitude stability thereafter, sociopolitical attitudes remain quite stable over the life course. That is, there is little evidence based on our objective assessments of attitudes and attitude change for the view that attitudes *grow* in stability over the entire life course.

These results may be shaped to an unknown degree by the nature of the assumptions we have made to identify the model, but we do not believe these assumptions are that far off the mark. One interesting aspect of these results is that the model's estimate of the degree of correlation between attitudes of the 1960s and attitudes of 1984 is virtually identical to that estimated for our objective indicators of attitudes. Indeed, in tables 7.8, 7.9, and 7.10 our estimate of this parameter is .85 or .86! Thus, however we approach the estimation of the stability of attitudes for this period— from mid-life to the mature years—we get the same result. Where the objective and subjective results differ is in their estimate of the degree of persistence between the time the women left Bennington and mid-life. As noted, our estimate based on retrospective data is somewhat lower, whereas our earlier objective assessment places that stability in the same range as stability in later life.

The Stability of Electoral Preferences

Although there is some risk of doing so, given the considerations articulated in chapter 6 regarding biases in reports of electoral preferences, we calculate the percentage agreement between reported electoral preferences in each of the years since 1936. Table 7.13 presents these figures based on the 1960 reports and table 7.14 presents these figures based on the 1984 reports. The 1960 data suggest that from election year to election year, the similarity of preferences increased from 1940 through 1952 (from 73 percent to 87 percent) and then declined (to 75 percent). The 1984 data suggest a higher degree of similarity between adjacent election years, as well as a gradually increasing level of between-election similarity.

There is clearly some lack of agreement in the 1960 and 1984 figures. Table 7.14 also gives the percentage agreement between the two reports. In general the agreement is very high, averaging 86 percent, although there is some variation. The lowest of these figures, at 80 percent, are from the 1984 and 1960 reports of 1960 preferences. This stems from the fact that in 1960 some 44 percent of the Bennington respondents reported a preference for Nixon, but in 1984 only 26 percent so reported (see our discussion of this issue in chapter 6). Whatever reasons there may be for this disparity, it simply reveals the low ebb of reliable reporting of electoral preferences. Generally the error is small relative to the variation involved.

The results in table 7.14, as mentioned, suggest that similarity in electoral preferences increases with time. Some of this similarity and dissimi-

Table 7.13. Percentage Agreement between Electoral Preferences, 1936–60: Bennington 1960 (N = 266)

1960 Report	Electoral Preferences by Year: 1960 Reports					
	1940	1944	1948	1952	1956	1960
1936	73.2	75.8	72.7	68.2	65.7	72.7
1940		77.3	75.6	77.9	74.2	77.3
1944			84.1	83.2	82.6	80.2
1948				87.3	84.6	76.3
1952					83.2	72.9
1956						75.3
Total % conservative	52%	36%	47%	53%	50%	45%

Table 7.14. Percentage Agreement between Electoral Preferences, 1936–84: Bennington 1984 Respondents ($N = 335$)

	Electoral Preferences by Year: 1984 Reports											
	1940	1944	1948	1952	1956	1960	1964	1968	1972	1976	1980	1984
1936	71.2	70.2	69.3	69.3	68.4	64.9	67.2	70.4	69.6	68.4	64.7	67.0
1940	<u>86.5</u>	84.5	82.7	79.7	78.1	73.6	74.9	74.9	73.5	75.8	71.4	77.9
1944		<u>87.6</u>	89.7	82.7	84.8	84.1	86.9	82.5	82.7	82.2	80.4	86.2
1948			<u>85.2</u>	84.5	88.0	86.0	86.6	84.7	84.0	84.2	81.1	86.5
1952				<u>90.0</u>	91.9	81.9	77.3	84.0	81.2	82.2	76.6	82.3
1956					<u>84.4</u>	86.1	81.2	85.1	85.7	85.8	80.0	86.0
1960						<u>80.1</u>	86.3	83.6	85.4	85.2	81.4	86.0
1964								85.7	86.2	86.3	87.2	90.3
1968									89.0	90.2	85.7	90.8
1972										90.8	88.0	92.9
1976											88.9	94.2
1980												94.9
Total % conservative	46%	32%	33%	43%	38%	26%	21%	33%	31%	31%	24%	27%

Note: Underlined diagonal is 1984 report compared with 1961 self-report.

larity can be understood in terms of the high popularity of some incumbent candidates (e.g., Eisenhower), and some of it can also be considered to represent the inertial pattern of such preferences. To the extent that these tendencies exist at the individual level, they suggest that people become more persistent, that is, increasingly stable in their orientations over the life span.

In addition to examining the extent of stability and change in sociopolitical orientations as indexed by our measures of sociopolitical attitudes, we also investigated the stability of sociopolitical orientations using reports of candidate preferences from presidential elections. Included were two independent reports of major candidate preferences in national elections from 1940 to 1960 (one given in the 1960s studies and one given in our 1984 follow-up) and a single report (given in 1984) of candidate preferences in national elections since 1960. There is error in retrospective reports of candidate preferences, as indicated in chapter 6, and multiple measures of these reports permit us to adjust for the effects of random and nonrandom sources of error. The intercorrelations among these measures and our estimates of stability inferred from them (not presented here) suggest that the ideological component of electoral preferences is quite stable and that there are no major differences in levels of stability over the life course.[19]

19. We used binary variables indicating the liberal/conservative choice by the respondent to represent the ideological component of electoral preferences. We assessed the levels of

RESULTS FROM THE NES PANELS

We can supplement our estimates of individual stability in the Bennington sample by briefly summarizing an analysis of the NES panel studies conducted in 1956–58–60 and 1972–74–76 (see Alwin and Krosnick, 1991a). These panel data provide only "synthetic" cohort data, in that respondents were not reinterviewed at points over the entire life span, but rather only over a four-year interval. These data are representative of the national U.S. population, however, and by analyzing data for subgroups defined by birth cohorts (or age), it is possible to array the data in such a way that they portray a synthetic cohort.[20]

Following the methods of analysis described in chapter 4 for analyzing the stability of attitudes using *simplex* models, we estimated four-year stability coefficients for party identification for groups defined by eight-year age groups: 18–25, 26–33, 34–41, 42–49, 50–57, 58–65, and 66–83 for each of the two NES panel surveys. Totals of 1,088 and 1,309 respondents were available from the 1950s and 1970s panel studies respectively. The breakdown of these samples by age in the two studies is given in table 7.15.

The estimated four-year stability coefficients in standard form are presented in table 7.15 for each of the seven age groups in the two studies for the full range of the party identification variable (a score that ranges from 1 to 7), a measure of the direction of party identification (Democrat = 1, independent = 2, and Republican = 3), and a measure of the intensity of party support. This table also provides standard errors for these estimates in parentheses.

These results demonstrate several interesting convergences with the Bennington studies. First, there is support here for the impressionable years hypothesis for the youngest age group. This group (18–25) shows the lowest level of stability in attitudes over the four-year assessment period in both studies. Second, there is support here for the idea that the stability of attitudes increases with age. This support exists both in the comparison of the stability estimates across age groups (from youngest to oldest) in each study, but also via the comparison of stability estimates for the same set of birth cohorts across the two panel studies.

---

stability of sociopolitical orientations over the life span using these indicators by estimating the parameters of a quasi-Markov model of the process of attitude change over this nearly 50-year period. These estimates uniformly indicate that the ideological component of electoral preferences is quite stable, even more stable than the ideological component underlying our attitude measures. Thus, there appears to be a genuinely high level of stability in the ideological component of the sociopolitical attitudes of these women over the life span.

20. We provide a brief discussion of synthetic cohort models in appendix F.

167

Table 7.15. Estimates of Four-Year Stability Parameters for Party Identification and Direction of Party Identification: National Election Study Panels

Age in:				Party ID 1–7		Dem/Ind/Rep 1–3		Intensity 0–3	
1956	n	1972	n	1956–60	1972–76	1956–60	1972–76	1956–60	1972–76
		18–25	(191)		.664		.656		.597
					(.081)		(.098)		(.128)
		26–33	(219)		1.000		.991		.840
					(.053)		(.089)		(.098)
18–25	(83)	34–41	(181)	.731	.976	.665	.960	.608	.715
				(.101)	(.066)	(.123)	(.078)	(.162)	(.125)
26–33	(212)	42–49	(191)	.798	.963	.789	.904	.690	.804
				(.066)	(.059)	(.078)	(.072)	(.106)	(.115)
34–41	(227)	50–57	(158)	.998	.999	.959	1.000	.813	.934
				(.043)	(.052)	(.054)	(.056)	(.111)	(.197)
42–49	(174)	58–65	(132)	1.000	.954	.988	.932	.810	.899
				(.050)	(.077)	(.055)	(.085)	(.127)	(.296)
50–57	(125)	66–83	(151)	.945	.869	.905	.858	.864	.666
				(.049)	(.072)	(.064)	(.085)	(.107)	(.165)
58–65	(94)			.966		.875		.605	
				(.069)		(.087)		(.154)	
66–83	(92)			.912		.849		.640	
				(.057)		(.066)		(.158)	
Total	(1,045)		(1,237)	.932	.945	.908	.934	.761	.762
				(.025)	(.028)	(.030)	(.035)	(.053)	(.055)

There are some interesting differences between this set of results and our analyses given above of the Bennington data, however, which need some further discussion. Specifically, the results in table 7.15 not only show a difference between the stabilities of the youngest and older groups in these samples; they also reveal a slight decline in stability of the party identification measure in the oldest age group. Indeed, contrary to what we concluded might be true for the Bennington cohort, these synthetic cohort data reveal a small, systematic decline in stability in old age, reflecting what Sears (1981) speculated might be a second period of vulnerability to attitude change. These declines in stability can be seen both in the comparison of age-specific stabilities within each study (both the 1950s and 1970s NES panels) and in the comparison of cohort-specific stabilities over time. The observation of such declines pertains only to the full seven-point party identification scale, *not* to the ideological, or directional, component of that measure. In other words, with regard to the Republican/Democrat preference, there seems to be no declining stability in party loyalty in old

168

age, but there is clearly a destabilization that occurs in the full measure after age 65.

More detailed treatment of these data (see Alwin, 1992; Alwin and Krosnick, 1991a) suggests that the declines in stability in the oldest age group are due to the declining persistence of the intensity, or strength, component of party identification (see chapter 10). Thus, although there appears to be no greater or lesser amount of shifting between the two major political parties that occurs in old age, there does appear to be a weakening of the stability of the intensity of that party loyalty. These results confirm Sears's (1981) speculation that there may be a period of declining stability that accompanies old age that primarily affects the intensity of party loyalty.

Still, while such conclusions may be justified in the synthetic cohort data portrayed above, we find very little evidence of this in the Bennington sample. Of course, we have never indicated that we thought the Bennington cohort was broadly representative of other, more general populations, and it would be relatively easy to dismiss the Bennington results on these grounds. At the same time, our Bennington results are based on only three measurements, widely separated over the entire life span, and it is therefore not possible to test such a hypothesis on the basis of these measurements. In fact, the synthetic cohort data used in table 7.15 span more of the life course than our Bennington data. Thus, one could again easily dismiss the Bennington results as not pertinent to an examination of this issue. On both of these grounds, then, we are not able to use the Bennington results to challenge what appears to be a more pervasive trend in the general population represented by the NES samples. The question for our purposes, which we pursue further in chapter 8, is whether there is any basis for a finding of diminished attitude stability in later life among the Bennington sample, and if not, what might account for their unusual degree of attitude persistence into old age?

Summary and Discussion

We began this chapter by citing the original Bennington studies as providing early evidence for the predominant view of attitude change in adolescence and early adulthood articulated by Sears (1981) and others (see Kinder and Sears, 1985). The attitude changes of the students at Bennington reflected, we argued, the relative plasticity of sociopolitical attitudes in early adulthood; and we noted that the relative stability of these attitudes suggested by Newcomb's later work was consistent with the general findings of a developing literature supporting the view of increasing stability of attitudes over the life cycle. We also contrasted these results with those suggested by the hypothesized process of lifelong flexibility, suggesting developmental changes in attitudes throughout the life course.

Our present set of results lends further support to the major interpretive lines of social psychological theorizing found in Newcomb's earlier work, and it adds to the set of cumulative research findings that exist to provide interpretations of processes of political socialization. We have provided further evidence documenting the importance of Mannheim's (1952) generational thesis in accounting for the attitude changes occurring among Newcomb's Bennington students. Our data in chapter 5 suggested that these changes were in part the effect of the exposure to the liberalizing Bennington environment, and in part a reflection of historical experiences of the generation of which these women were members.

More importantly, perhaps, our follow-up data on the surviving participants in Newcomb's Bennington studies permit some assessment of the extent of the persistence in attitudes over the life course, as well as the relative levels of persistence and change over different periods of the life course. On this point our results are relatively clear. There is strong support in these data for the notion that sociopolitical orientations are highly persistent over the life course and that levels of stability are relatively constant over major stages of the life cycle. These findings seem to provide little support for one version of the persistence thesis, which allows for decreased persistence in old age (see Sears, 1981). The overwhelming finding is that of a high degree of persistence in the *ideological* component of attitudes at all assessed stages of the life course.

There is, then, a perspective on life course persistence and change in sociopolitical attitudes which these data suit very well. This is the emergent perspective which includes aspects of Mannheim's (1952) generational thesis and the thesis of persistence of attitudes over the life cycle. Thus, our analyses are consistent with a generational/persistence model, summarized particularly well by Sears (1981:185–87), which posits that in late adolescence and early adulthood people are substantially flexible and responsive to their social circumstances, but that once sociopolitical attitudes are formed, they gather strength, remaining stable through much of the life course.

In making this interpretation of our most central findings, we should comment on several aspects of the present phenomenon that may argue for caution in accepting the generality of our results. First, while much of our discussion has referred to the persistence of attitudes, our analysis has focused almost exclusively on the more fundamental *ideological*, or directional, orientations underlying individuals' political attitudes. This is due in part to the contrasts built in to most of our measures, but also to the fact that we have analyzed the common core of a diversity of such attitude assessments rather than any one of them in isolation. Thus, specific attitudes tied to unique political events may vary in their levels of stability over time, and in some instances are quite unstable; on the other hand, dispositions that are more central to individuals' cognitive and affective orientations may be considerably more stable and remain quite strong even into late adulthood. The less strongly attitude measures are tied to this ideological core, the more likely they are to change with time; the more central such attitudes are to the individual, the less susceptible they are to change (Converse, 1964; Krosnick, 1988; Rokeach, 1968). In other words, we may have been more likely to discover high levels of persistence in orientations because we focused on the more common (rather than unique) aspects of our attitude measures. We may thus understand the rather high levels of stability ascertained here as due in part to our concentration on this ideological component of our attitude measures, rather than on its more superficial embodiments. We return to this issue in chapter 8.

A related and somewhat complementary qualification on the generality of our findings concerns the unique nature of our subjects, and the several factors that may be plausibly linked to an understanding of our high levels of assessed stability in these terms. Newcomb (1943) pointed out two major differences between the experiences of Bennington students during the early years of its existence and those of students attending other colleges of that time period. One of these had to do with the emphasis on a contemporary rather than historical approach to education at Bennington, in the sense that the faculty placed great emphasis on making their students "aware of their contemporary world" (1943:175). Thus, regardless of their particular ideological orientations to public issues, Bennington students were exposed to an emphasis on the importance of public affairs and the need to be well informed on current issues through the curriculum of the college. They have clearly shown themselves to be interested in political issues. Second, and also critical to Newcomb's interpretation of attitude change, was the link between participation in political discussions and activities, on the one hand, and a woman's standing in the hierarchy of prestige and influence in the Bennington student community. The fact that involvement in political affairs and the possession of "current" attitudes on public issues were criteria of status at that time in the Bennington community made such orientations quite salient and more likely to retain their viability as important values in later life. In this sense, because the Bennington women are not only well educated, but were also socialized into an orientation emphasizing public affairs and social change, the characteristics of their orientations seen in our results more closely approximate those of "informed elites"; therefore our interpretation may be less plausible with respect to the attitudinal characteristics of broader representations of the population at large.

Finally, we noted that data based on such broader representations (see Alwin and Krosnick, 1991a) provide some evidence that supports these conclusions, but also some which is at variance with the Bennington results. These results, summarized above, indicated some destabilization of political attitudes in later life, roughly after the age of 65. However, such declines in attitude persistence in old age were linked to the intensity component rather than the directional component of party identifications; as such, these results tend to complement rather than contradict the Bennington results. As we have already indicated, due to an inability to distinguish these two components in the Bennington data, we have relied on measures that primarily tap the directional component, and in this sense, our Bennington data are in complete agreement with the broader-based, synthetic cohort results insofar as the directional component of political attitudes is concerned.

8

Constancy of Personality, Cognitive Organization, and the Stability of Sociopolitical Orientations

INTRODUCTION

The research reported in the preceding chapters suggests that there is a relatively high degree of persistence, or stability, in sociopolitical attitudes from early adulthood through later life. Support for this conclusion certainly exists in the reinterview data we have assembled from the women in the Bennington sample, but as we have noted at several points, we must be careful not to overgeneralize these results, because the Bennington women may not be representative of other populations to which we may wish to generalize. High degrees of attitude stability are also suggested by the National Election Study panels, although the magnitudes of stability decline somewhat in old age. The limitations of the synthetic cohort design for describing stability and change over the life span, however, are sufficiently great to warrant some caution in drawing conclusions about life-cycle differences in attitude persistence.

The results of the preceding chapters also suggest that, while there is considerable attitude stability over the life course, there is also a substantial amount of *change* in political orientations. Indeed, by our best estimates in the Bennington data, we can attribute about 40 percent of the variation in 1984 sociopolitical orientations to factors linked to attitude change since the 1930s and 1940s rather than to persistence from early adulthood.[1] Thus, even in the midst of what might appear to be high levels of attitude stability in the Bennington sample, there is also support for the obverse interpretation, namely, that considerable attitude change occurs over the life course as well. Our results, then, might suggest a "hybrid" version of the generational/persistence model, one which acknowledges the poten-

---

1. The 1930s latent attitude accounts for some 60 percent of the variance in the 1984 latent attitude—40 percent is unexplained by the 1930s latent attitude. These calculations are based on squaring the standardized reduced-form coefficient linking the 1930s and 1984 latent attitudes.

tial for generational differences and a tendency for these to persist, but at moderate rather than high levels of persistence. In other words, there seems to be much more lifelong openness to change than the generational/ persistence model suggests might be the case.

In this chapter and the next we continue our analysis by systematically investigating the sources of stability and change in the sociopolitical orientations of the Bennington women.[2] It is not a simple matter to disentangle sources of stability and change, because, as we argued in chapter 5, sources of individual change and societal change are inextricably linked. People may change, or they may remain the same, because of aspects of social experience, and the ways in which they collectively change or remain the same may affect the nature of society. Levels of individual stability and change represent more than just a property of individuals—they also reflect something about the nature of society. Thus, such stability coefficients as we have reported in chapter 7 tell us much more than simply the extent to which individuals are *susceptible* to change at various times over their biographies. They also tell us something about the *opportunities for change* at a particular time and within a particular sociohistorical context (see Sears, 1983:84).[3]

2. Here we view the question of the sources of stability and sources of change as intimately related. As we have conceptualized these processes, stability is defined as the absence of change, and change is defined in terms of departures from stability. Thus, our efforts to explain levels of stability in these data also involve the simultaneous pursuit of the question of attitude change.

3. There are serious methodological problems with the automatic interpretation of the above findings in terms of life-cycle processes implicating differences in susceptibility to attitude change linked to life course experiences. Without extended elaboration, the problem is essentially one of separating "age," "period," and "cohort" (APC) interpretations of patterns of attitude stability and change. As in the study of simple averages of means (which is what the majority of APC analysts study), the separation of these factors in the explanation of stability estimates is fraught with significant problems of identification and interpretation (see Mason, Winsborough, Mason and Poole, 1973; Rodgers, 1982; Smith, Mason, and Fienberg, 1982). To be more specific, even though we have controlled for cohort in the Bennington analyses (because cohort is essentially constant), we still cannot separate aging and period interpretations of our stability estimates because of their confounding. Similarly, in the synthetic-cohort NES data, we have held period constant, but it is impossible to separate aging and cohort differences in these estimates. So, from a technical statistical perspective, our results are ambiguous because of this confounding of sources of variation in attitude stabilities. Our purpose in this book is to argue that by combining both types of designs, some better purchase can be made on the general theoretical issues of life course variation in the stability of sociopolitical attitudes.

ANALYTIC STRATEGIES

Our results to this point tell us something simultaneously about the tendencies of individuals' attitudes to persist and the opportunities for change presented by the society at a particular historical time. However, because of the *sociohistorical* limitations of these results, it is difficult to arrive at a very firm generalization about life-cycle processes of stability and change. Even the NES synthetic cohort data exist for only two time periods of the past, and they are periods representing relative stability in the sociopolitical history of the United States: the 1950s and 1970s. This historical boundedness of these results places important limitations upon the extent to which one might be able to generalize from our results to a life-cycle model of attitude stability and change.

Despite these limitations and the important difficulties in separating aging, cohort, and period factors in our estimated stabilities, it is possible to obtain further empirical evidence to assist in drawing conclusions about the sources of stability and change. There are two general strategies for coping with these problems. One, which we are not able to pursue here, but which is worth mentioning, is to generate more data across the broad spectrum of human experience regarding the stabilities of aspects of personality and cognitive variables, as well as other types of attitudes. One can easily imagine the synthetic-cohort approach being used to develop a much larger sample of stability estimates by gathering more panel data of the type exemplified by the NES designs. By replicating some of the previously obtained panel results in different time periods and by generating a richer set of stability estimates for some of the same cohorts at different times, one would be in a much stronger position to draw generalizations about life-cycle patterns of stability and change across a broader range of human experience (see Alwin, 1992). Such a strategy is likely to be very expensive and time-consuming, and for obvious reasons cannot be pursued here.

There is a second strategy, more closely within our grasp, which focuses on the causal factors that might be responsible for levels of stability and change. In this chapter and the next we conceptualize the influences of two major sources of stability in sociopolitical attitudes. First, we consider factors linked to individual differences in *susceptibility* to attitude change, particularly the concepts of personality and cognitive organization. We refer to these as *personological* explanations, since the critical factors invoked in explaining the stability of orientations are stable aspects of individual personality and/or cognitive organization that are thought to promote stability of attitudes. Then in chapter 9 we consider factors that might implicate differences in environmentally-based experiences in the processes of attitude change and stability. By contrast, we refer to these as *sociological* explanations, inasmuch as they invoke the social environment, external to the individual, to account for stability and change. In considering these environmental factors, we focus significant attention on the interpretations given by Newcomb and his colleagues (1967) regarding the importance of reference-group support in explaining both change and stability of attitudes.

INDIVIDUAL DIFFERENCES IN THE POTENTIAL FOR CHANGE

As our above conceptualization suggests, factors leading to persistence, or stability, of orientations over time may reside either in the person or in the environment. Thus, individual differences in predispositions to persistence or differences in one's social environment that form and sustain persistent attitudes and perspectives each contribute to change and stability of attitude orientations. An example of the distinctions we are making may be useful. On the one hand, people may be more susceptible to attitude change when they are young, as we have argued in chapter 1, during the impressionable years; or they may be so because of personality factors or other aspects of individual differences (see also chapter 2). On the other hand, differential exposure to certain events and experiences, such as hearing public speeches in favor of a particular political viewpoint or being exposed to a changing network of social support, may bring about change that is independent of factors linked to the individual (see chapter 3).

These sets of factors define two broad components of stability and change: one having to do with what we have called *susceptibility,* or *openness to change* (e.g., being young), the other with exposure to stabilizing influences of the environment and/or change-inducing events (e.g., changing social networks). When both components are present, however, the effects of either are likely to be more potent. This essentially captures the phenomenon Newcomb described at Bennington: young, impressionable people coming to grips with their expanding sociohistorical world, one which itself was undergoing turmoil, and doing so in a societal microcosm on the vanguard of social change, emphasizing relatively radical or progressive ideas about the direction that change should take. These same principles can be applied to the understanding of change and stability over the life course. In the most general terms, both individual predispositions and exposure to change-inducing events (public speeches on particular political issues, or divorce and remarriage) are likely to produce change.

176

Here we explore the idea of the stability of individual differences more concretely. We examine several theoretical arguments concerning the *constancy of personality and value orientations* and derive some testable hypotheses that are then examined in our Bennington data. We consider the possibility that there are *personality differences* in openness to stability and change, and that attitude change may be more likely among some people than others.[4] In this regard, we consider Rokeach's (1968:117) concept of the *centrality of attitudes* as a way of conceptualizing the nature and organization of attitudes and their likelihood of change. Rokeach argues that some attitude issues or domains of ideation are more central to the individual than others because of their salience or importance. As such, central attitudes are more resistent to change (see Judd and Krosnick, 1982). Before pursuing the *centrality* hypothesis in considerable detail, we first summarize the existing theoretical perspectives on the constancy of personality.

The Constancy of Personality

Psychologists have argued for many years that despite individual growth and development, continuity exists in personality development, although there is considerable diversity in theoretical perspectives on the nature of this continuity (e.g., Neugarten, 1964, 1973, 1977). Theories concerning life span development of personality can be grouped into three distinct categories: one that regards personality as a set of stable predispositions to behave in a particular way; one that views personality in terms of a set of systematic changes that result from traversing an ordered sequence of epigenetic stages; and a view of personality as inherently flexible and able to take on a variety of different forms over the lifecourse (Gergen, 1980).

The relative lack of agreement among life span psychologists regarding the constancy of personality is noteworthy, given the presumed relationship among political orientations, personality dispositions, and conceptions of self. As Moss and Susman note: "The very concept of personality implies a differentiated and organized hierarchy of psychological sets and behavioral dispositions that are manifested as consistent and enduring patterns in denoting the uniqueness of the individual" (1980:53). Indeed, the idea that individuals are predictable beings who are capable of a high degree of consistency across situations is a deeply held cultural belief. But, as

---

4. We use the term *personality* in its most general meaning, referring to individual differences in behavioral predispositions. Any theoretically relevant differences among individuals in predispositions to behave or react in particular ways are here considered to be personality differences (e.g., House, 1981).

noted above, there is a diversity of opinion among life span psychologists regarding the pervasiveness of these human constancies.

Many types of empirical evidence support the tenet that some individual differences, that is, some aspects of personality, are highly stable. Considerable evidence exists, for example, that many cognitive and intellective variables are highly stable over most of the adult life span, with changes due to differential aging setting in only very late in the adult years. For example, Schaie concludes that "reliably replicable age changes in psychometric abilities of more than trivial magnitude cannot be demonstrated prior to age 60." He goes on to say that, if anything, a decrement is shown in old age, noting that a "reliable decrement can be shown to have occurred for all abilities by age 74" (1983:127). His results are based on a 21-year longitudinal study of Seattle adults, and his conclusions are supported by other longitudinal studies (e.g., Cunningham and Owens, 1983).

When one considers the domains of personality and interpersonal behavior, the evidence of consistency is much harder to establish. Mischel argues that in character traits such as rigidity, social conformity, aggression, attitudes toward authority, and on virtually any other nonintellective personality dimension, a great deal of "behavioral specificity has been found regularly" (1969:1014). This point of view, in other words, suggests that considerable flexibility or potential for change exists in many aspects of personality (see also Gergen, 1980; Lerner, 1984).

On the other hand, one might argue that the lack of consistency pointed out by Mischel (1969) and others reflects not a state of nature, but the state of measurement imprecision (see Block, 1977; Moss and Susman, 1980). Indeed, some have suggested that Mischel's (1969) arguments are overdrawn and based on a selective review of the literature (e.g., Block, 1977; Moss and Susman, 1980:531). A somewhat more balanced view of this literature would perhaps give greater emphasis to possibilities of human constancy. Moss and Susman (1980:590), for example, note that empirical consistency over time is "most obvious for personality characteristics that are endowed with positive cultural and societal valences" (1980:590). They indicate that such things as achievement motivation, and "culturally prescribed appropriate sex role behaviors and interests" are found to be stable from middle childhood to adulthood. By contrast, they suggest that attitudes are the least stable personality characteristics (1980:590–91). Others question the validity of findings from longitudinal studies of personality (Nesselroade and Baltes, 1974), including a concern with the reliability of measurement (Block, 1977; Moss and Susman, 1980).

Some empirical data exist on the stability of aspects of personality, although available studies do not produce consistent results, nor are the findings altogether robust from the perspective of research design. There

178

are findings of stability and instability across various ages, using a variety of methods and measures and a variety of remeasurement intervals, and sampling a variety of different populations of interest (e.g., Block, 1971, 1981; Costa and McCrae, 1976, 1978, 1980; Costa, McCrae, and Arenberg, 1980; Costa, Fozard, McCRae, and Bosse, 1976; Douglas and Arenberg, 1978; Siegler, George, and Okun, 1979; Woodruff and Birren, 1972). The main problems with this body of evidence are that the samples are generally very small, there is little or no attention to representativeness and selectivity issues (see Nesselroade, 1988), and there is virtually no attention to the problem of measurement error (for an exception see Costa, McCrae, and Arenberg, 1983). Further, often too few stages of the life cycle are studied in such research, and frequently the issue of life course stability gets lost in the consideration of other issues, such as structural invariance, correlations and constraint among concepts, and the like. Thus, few generalizations are possible regarding the fundamental role of personality in promoting stability and change in attitude orientations.

Individual Differences in Openness to Change and Attitude Stability

One of the most important aspects of personality that is theoretically linked to attitude stability and change is the concept of *openness to change*. Such a dimension of personality may be conceptualized to provide a source of stability to attitudes, beliefs, and opinions (Rokeach, 1960). This suggests that there may be a more fundamental personality orientation that reflects an openness or a resistence to change. Indeed, this dimension of personality is often linked to sociopolitical orientations.[5] Wilson (1973), for example, argues that there is a general response predisposition, called *conservatism*, which involves a fundamental tendency to avoid change. He associates this type of conservatism with fundamentalism in religion, identification with the establishment, support of the status quo, the insistence on strict rules and punishments; such people tend to favor militarism, to be ethnocentric and intolerant of minority groups, to prefer what is conventional, traditional, and familiar, to favor restriction of sexual behavior, to oppose scientific progress, and to be fatalistic and superstitious (see Feather, 1979: 1617). The implications of this are that there is a more general value orientation, or "type of person," who is resistent to change and who is also conservative ideologically in terms of political issues.

---

5. It is perhaps worth noting that, as Rokeach (1960) defines it, the *open* versus *closed* way of thinking can be associated with any ideology, regardless of content. Thus, we extend this notion of a personality orientation concerning a mode of thought or way of thinking to one that is open versus closed to change.

Our own approach to defining *conservatism* has attempted to keep its *two* meanings distinct. That is, we have remained open to the notion that liberal political ideas can be held quite conservatively, and the issue of the rigidity with which ideas are held should best be phrased within the framework of attitude persistence and change (see chapter 1). In other words, we have not made the same theoretical assumptions made by Wilson (1973) that these two dimensions are necessarily linked. Indeed, we would question this assumption on the basis of existing theory and empirical evidence.

While we reject the notion that political conservatism is necessarily related to a personality orientation of the same name, the literature provides some support for the idea that there is a type of personality or value orientation embodied by the above qualities which is correlated with political conservatism in the ideological sense. Some of Feather's data from Australia suggest that political conservatism is positively linked to aspects of value orientations emphasizing attachment to authority and personal insecurity. The higher the conservatism, the greater the importance placed on "salvation, security, cleanliness and rule following," whereas less conservatism was found to be linked to values such as "equality, freedom, love and pleasure, as well as open-minded, intellectual, and imaginative ways of thinking" (Feather, 1979:1627). We can explore this explanation further in the present context by examining available measures of the extent of openness to change or similarity in value orientations over the life span. However, as we point out in greater detail below, the available measures do not necessarily tap the same dimensions of values examined by Feather (1979). Our analysis, which we describe later in this chapter, does permit, nonetheless, some greater purchase on this issue.

COGNITIVE ORGANIZATION AND THE CENTRALITY OF ATTITUDES

In contrast to the personality model for conceptualizing attitude stability and change, one might argue for an alternative conceptual scheme, based on theories of cognitive organization and the importance of attitudes. In other words, there may be other dimensions of individual differences which stand in stronger relation to attitudes and attitude change than the type of conservatism just discussed. One such dimension is the centrality of sociopolitical issues to the individual's cognitive organization. Rokeach (1968:117) argued that the cognitive and affective components of attitudes can be organized along a *central-peripheral* dimension wherein the more central elements are more salient or important, more resistant to change, and, if changed, exert relatively greater effects on other elements. We assume in the present context that there is a linkage between the im-

180

portance, or centrality, of attitudes toward sociopolitical objects and the extent of investment of interest, time, and effort in political activities and organizations.[6]

On the basis of this theoretical line of argument, one would expect that those women for whom sociopolitical attitudes were most central over the life span would show less attitude change than those for whom sociopolitical attitudes were less central. As noted in chapter 7, one interpretation for the high degree of stability in political attitudes among the Bennington women was the centrality of the ideological component of their sociopolitical attitudes. This, we argued, was one aspect of the Bennington College experience that was unique; that is, Bennington's emphasis on contemporary public affairs created a climate in which sociopolitical attitudes were central to most of its students in those early years. If this is true, one would expect that those women for whom political issues were (and have been) most salient would be the most resistent to change, revealing the highest levels of stability in our data. Here we address the question within the Bennington sample, asking whether the levels of attitude change and stability witnessed earlier differ among women for whom social and political issues and associated attitudes vary in centrality.

The Measurement of Attitude Centrality

We can explore the centrality hypothesis further in the present context by examining available measures of the centrality of political attitudes in the Bennington sample. As indicated in chapter 2, one of the important measures obtained and interpreted in both of Newcomb's earlier studies was the Allport-Vernon index of values and interests (Allport and Vernon, 1931). Newcomb (1943:41–42) used this as a device for better understanding his measures of political orientations, concluding that there was a relationship between some of the dimensions assessed by the Allport-Vernon measures and political orientations. We do not have the data for the original measures of values obtained by Newcomb (1943), since these data were not retained, but we can analyze the responses given in 1960 to an adaptation of the original Allport-Vernon measure and a replication of this measure obtained in 1984.

The adapted version of the Allport-Vernon scale (1931) used in our research asks people to rank six "important areas, or interests in life." The

---

6. There is some evidence based on the NES panel data collected during the 1980 and 1984 American presidential election campaigns that important attitudes change less than unimportant ones (Krosnick, 1988). Unfortunately, these results were based on relatively short periods of time (four months), and are consequently of less interest to us here. We are interested in differences in stability over major periods of the life course.

qualities to be ranked are as follows: (1) *Theoretical:* empirical, critical, or rational matters—observing and reasoning, ordering and systematizing, discovering truths; (2) *Economic:* that which is useful and practical, especially the practical affairs of the business world, preference for judging things by their tangible utility; (3) *Aesthetic:* beauty, form, and harmony for their own sake, an artistic interpretation of life; (4) *Social:* human relationships and love, interest in human beings for their own sake; (5) *Political:* power and influence, leadership and competition; (6) *Religious:* religious experience as providing satisfaction and meaning, interest in relating oneself to the unity of the universe as a whole.[7]

In his 1939 survey Newcomb found, based on a sample of 40 seniors, that theoretical, social, and aesthetic interests were the most highly valued in the Bennington community. Of least importance were economic, political, and religious interests. He also found that those who were high on political and economic values were also high on the PEP scale. At the same time, those with higher scores on theoretical and social values were among the lowest on the PEP. While it was initially surprising to Newcomb to find that economic and political values were related to conservatism (Newcomb, 1943:42), he indicated that when one considers the traits embodied by these values (practicality, utility, power, and influence), the finding may be somewhat less curious. However, because these results were reported for only a small sample of Bennington students, it is unwise to overgeneralize these distributions and relationships.

Table 8.1 presents the Allport-Vernon rankings for the 1960s and 1984 based on respondents who had data present for both time points ($n = 229$). For purposes of our analysis, we have reversed the scoring of these items, giving a high score (6) to those interests selected as most important, with the lowest score (1) assigned to that domain selected as the least important. It is worth noting that these findings for the most part replicate Newcomb's (1943) results. In both 1960 and 1984 social, aesthetic, and theoretical values were consistently the most highly valued, and economic, political, and religious values were less important.

Table 8.2 presents the correlations of the 1960s and 1984 value rank-

7. The 1960s and 1984 replicate questions were as follows: "Here are listed six important areas, or interests in life. People differ in the emphasis or degree of importance that they attribute to each of these interests. Please read the six areas and then *rank* the six interests in terms of their IMPORTANCE TO YOU at this time. Insert '1' before the area of greatest importance, '2' before the next most important one, and so on down to '6', representing the least important of all to you.

PLEASE NOTE: Your response should be made to the *complete* statement about each of the interests, and not just to the first word, which is only a convenient label; what that word means to you may not correspond at all to the statement following."

Table 8.1. Means and Standard Deviations of Rankings of Values in Allport-Vernon Scale for Respondents in 1960 and 1984 Surveys ($n = 229$)

Values	1960s		1984	
	Mean	S.D.	Mean	S.D.
Theoretical	3.808	1.438	3.493	1.532
Economic	2.825	1.339	3.044	1.459
Aesthetic	3.908	1.265	4.192	1.357
Social	5.463	0.910	5.188	1.153
Political	1.948	1.123	2.498	1.369
Religious	3.066	1.691	2.664	1.711

ings with our major measures of political orientations. These results confirm the relationship Newcomb reported between political conservatism and economic values, but they show a somewhat different relationship between political conservatism and political, aesthetic, and theoretical values. Given the larger sample sizes involved and the strong consistency in these relationships in both 1960 and 1984 as compared with the 1939 study, we weigh the later results more heavily. We conclude from the results in this table that sociopolitical conservatism, as assessed by our principal measures, is positively linked to interests involving economic values, whereas it is negatively linked to political, theoretical, and aesthetic values. However, these relationships are not as strong in the 1984 data. Indeed, the importance of political values assessed in 1984 is virtually independent of sociopolitical attitudes assessed at that time.

The Salience of Political Interests

According to Rokeach's (1968) theory, the more salient or important an attitude domain, the more central are those attitudes expected to be. And, as noted above, more central attitudes are hypothesized to be more stable and less susceptible to change. We can test this hypothesis by comparing those Bennington respondents who profess highly salient political interests on the Allport-Vernon measure of values with those for whom political interests are considerably less salient.

In order to draw this comparison, we first divided the Bennington sample into two groups according to their rankings of the political domain of interests and values.[8] Then we examined the critical parameters of one of

8. We defined this categorization by creating a sum of rankings of the political domain from the 1960 and 1984 surveys and partitioning the sample at the median of this index.

Table 8.2. Correlations of Rankings of Values in Allport-Vernon Scale with Measure of Political Orientations, 1960s and 1984

Values	1960s (n = 322)				1984 (n = 303)			
	1930 PEP	1960 PEP	PCI	L/C Scale	1930 PEP	1984 PEP	1984 PCI	L/C Scale
Theoretical	−.0941	−.1913**	−.1009	−.1952***	−.1003	−.0272	−.1012	−.1092
Economic	.2211***	.2757***	.1213*	.2111***	.1979***	.1362*	.3725***	.3432***
Aesthetic	−.0901	−.2071**	−.1384*	−.1970***	−.0244	.0256	−.1294*	−.0842
Social	.0221	−.0405	−.0034	.0331	.0068	−.0629	−.0626	−.1352*
Political	−.1976***	−.1937**	−.1899***	−.1741**	−.1263*	−.0995	−.0640	−.0449
Religious	.0867	.2374***	.2218***	.2486***	.0065	.0331	−.0255	−.0016

*$p < .05$ **$p < .01$ ***$p < .001$

the key models we relied upon in chapter 7 to describe attitude persistence and change. This model, presented in table 7.8, was estimated separately within these two categories of respondents—those for whom the political domain was highly salient and those for whom it was less so. We hypothesized, based on Rokeach's (1968) theorizing, that attitude change would be less likely to occur among those for whom political issues were the most salient.[9] These results are presented in tables 8.3 and 8.4.

These results show some differences in the direction predicted, in that the low salience category does reveal more change between the 1930s and 1984 than the high-salience group. However, the differences are not substantial enough for us to conclude that they are significant. The coefficients of stability linking the 1930s and 1984 in the two categories of salience are .688 (i.e., .807 × .853) in the case of high salience group and .589 (i.e., .682 × .863) for low salience. Inspection of the components of these results, as noted, reveals higher levels of stability in the high-salience group only in the period between college and mid-life, and though the difference is not statistically significant, this may be viewed nonetheless as support for the hypothesis.[10]

The Stability of Values

By their nature, values are central to the cognitive organization of the individual, as noted above, and because of this centrality, they are assumed to be quite stable (e.g., Rokeach, 1968, 1973). Thus, given the consistent relationship between political liberalism/conservatism and value orientations witnessed by Newcomb and reproduced above (with the changes noted), one might expect the stability of values to contribute to stability in ideological domains, inasmuch as values are linked to political attitudes. There are two sets of issues here. First, is there any evidence that values have a stability of their own? An answer to this would provide some confirmation of the notion of *constancy* of values as an aspect of personality. Second, if there is a constancy of values, are those with the most stable values also consistently more stable in their sociopolitical attitudes?[11]

9. We selected model 3, given in table 7.8, because of its relatively good fit to the data and because it involved relatively few model parameters. In estimating this model within categories of theoretically relevant other variables, we used a conservative sample size, a procedure we followed in chapter 7 as well.

10. A test of the difference between this stability parameter—linking the 1930s to the 1960s—in the two salience groups does not produce a statistically significant result $[\Delta\chi^2 = 1.66, df = 1, p = .198]$.

11. There is a third issue, to which we return later in this chapter, concerning the relationship between the constancy of values and political conservatism. Specifically, is there any evidence that those who are more likely to hold to a constant set of values over time are also more likely to be politically conservative?

Table 8.3. Parameter Estimates for a Linear Structural Equations Model of Sociopolitical Orientations across the Life Span: Bennington Women with High Salience of Political Interests in the 1960s and 1984 ($N = 64$)

Predictor Variable	Dependent Variable								
	PEP30	PID30	SPO30	PEP60	PID60	SPO60	PEP84	PID84	SPO84
η_1 1930s sociopolitical orientation	.633**	.721**	—	—	—	.807**	—	—	—
η_2 1960s sociopolitical orientation	—	—	—	.890**	.823**	—	—	—	.853**
η_3 1984 sociopolitical orientation	—	—	—	—	—	—	.532**	.756**	—
x_1 Year entered Bennington	—	—	.163	—	—	-.186*	—	—	0.0f
x_2 Number of years at Bennington	—	—	-.048	—	—	0.0f	—	—	0.0f
x_3 Parental orientations	—	—	.668**	—	—	0.0f	—	—	0.0f
R-squared	.404	.520	.457	.817	.677	.648	.281	.575	.727

Note: Based on a model with 18 *df* and a χ^2 of 12.51 ($p = .820$). The model assumed all measurement disturbances were uncorrelated over time, except that the disturbance for the PEP30 was correlated with the disturbances for PEP60 and PEP84, and the disturbance for PID60 was correlated with the disturbance for PID84.

*$p < .05$ **$p < .01$ f = parameter fixed at zero

Table 8.4. Parameter Estimates for a Linear Structural Equations Model of Sociopolitical Orientations across the Life Span: Bennington Women with Low Salience of Political Interests in the 1960s and 1984 ($N = 112$)

Predictor Variable	Dependent Variable								
	PEP30	PID30	SPO30	PEP60	PID60	SPO60	PEP84	PID84	SPO84
η_1 1930s sociopolitical orientation	.735**	.752**	—	—	—	—	—	—	—
η_2 1960s sociopolitical orientation	—	—	—	.788**	.913**	.682**	—	—	—
η_3 1984 sociopolitical orientation	—	—	—	—	—	—	.485**	.835**	.863**
x_1 Year entered Bennington	—	—	.231**	—	—	-.039	—	—	0.0f
x_2 Number of years at Bennington	—	—	-.145*	—	—	0.0f	—	—	0.0f
x_3 Parental orientations	—	—	.677**	—	—	0.0f	—	—	0.0f
R-squared	.539	.566	.607	.626	.833	.446	.244	.698	.745

Note: Based on a model with 18 df and a χ^2 of 9.17 ($p = .956$). The model assumed all measurement disturbances were uncorrelated over time, except that the disturbance for the PEP30 was correlated with the disturbances for PEP60 and PEP84, and the disturbance for PID60 was correlated with the disturbance for PID84.

*$p < .05$ **$p < .01$ f = parameter fixed at zero

187

Table 8.5. Rankings of Values in Allport-Vernon Scale for Respondents in 1960 and 1984 Surveys ($N = 303$)

Subject	Agreement				1984 Mean for Same Ranking in 1960s	1984 Mean for Diff. Ranking in 1960s	χ^2
	Percent with Similar Rank	Percent with Same Rank	Coeffi-cient	Corre-lation			
Theoretical	69.9%	33.6%	.389	.4055	3.779	3.349	103.70*
Economic	67.7	33.6	.424	.4348	2.753	3.191	76.00*
Aesthetic	74.2	36.7	.442	.4600	4.202	4.186	84.66*
Social	80.3	53.7	.163	.1885	5.764	4.519	91.88*
Political	73.4	36.7	.322	.3938	1.762	2.924	74.72*
Religious	69.0	41.0	.575	.5975	2.489	2.785	131.46*

*$p < .001$

In order to address the first of these issues, we computed the percentage of respondents ranking the Allport-Vernon values similarly and in exactly the same ways on both the 1960 and 1984 occasions of measurement. These results are given in table 8.5. The table also gives the bivariate correlation and the coefficient of agreement (see Krippendorff, 1970) between the actual value rankings, scored from 6 (most important) to 1 (least important). By whichever of these indicators one wishes to measure the stability of value rankings between the two time points, there is an indication of some stability. Some 30 to 50 percent of respondents rank a given value in exactly the same way at both times, and nearly 70 percent or more rank them similarly across this 25-year period.[12] On the other hand, the coefficients of agreement and correlation show only modest stability between the two time points.

In order to assess the extent to which the stability of individual differences in values contributes to the stability of sociopolitical orientations, and in order to clarify the nature of the relationship of values to sociopolitical orientations, we examined the properties of our above model describing attitude persistence and change (see chapter 7) within two categories of our Bennington respondents: those experiencing little change in value rankings between the 1960s and 1984 and those showing much less stability.[13]

12. We defined *similar* as having the same score, ± 1 point.

13. We divided the Bennington sample into two roughly equal-sized categories, one having more similar values between the 1960s and 1980s than the other. If the 1984 Allport-Vernon item rankings were all within one rank (plus or minus) of the 1960s item rankings, the respondent was defined as having stable values, whereas those whose rankings were less close were defined as having less stable values.

Specifically, we reestimate the model associated with table 7.8 within these two categories of respondents.[14] The rationale for this analysis lies in the expectation, based on the above reasoning, that those with more stable values will show the most attitude stability, and those with less stable values will show the least attitude stability. Tables 8.6 and 8.7 present these results.

These results reveal very similar patterns of stability across the two categories of value similarity. The coefficients of stability linking the 1930s and 1984 in the two categories of value similarity/difference are .632 (i.e., .763 × .828) in the case of the high-similarity group and .679 (i.e., .785 × .865) in the case of the low-similarity group. Inspection of these results, as well as the formal statistical tests of similarity between the model parameters (see appendix E), provides virtually no evidence that would support the interpretation that the stability of sociopolitical attitudes is linked to the stability of more general value orientations. The coefficients of stability linking the 1960s with the 1930s measures and those relating the 1960s to the 1980s are obviously quite uniform across the two groups. Other aspects of the model are also quite similar, and there is no statistical basis for concluding that the two groups vary in estimated stability ($\chi^2 = .38$, $df = 2$, $p = .827$) (see Table E.1).

Thus, we find very little support for the notion that stability of sociopolitical orientations is linked to the stability of values and interests, at least as indexed by the Allport-Vernon scale. This leads to one of several possible conclusions: (1) values themselves are not stable; (2) values are relatively stable, but their stability is independent of the stability of sociopolitical attitudes; or (3) values are stable—they are linked to attitude stability—but we have not adequately assessed the relevant aspects of values that link them to attitudes. Unfortunately, we are unable to address the plausibility of any one of these interpretations. We can only conclude that there is no support here for the argument that attitude stability is due to the more deeply rooted stability of values as an aspect of personality. Clearly, further research is needed to clarify these relationships between personality and the likelihood of attitude change.

---

14. We can perhaps be faulted for not treating these value rankings as fallible measures, as we have consistently treated attitude measures throughout this analysis. We have no choice in this case, since it is not possible to categorize the sample according to an unmeasured or latent variable representing values. Thus, for all of the analyses reported in this chapter where we partition the sample into categories for further analysis, we partition the sample according to a measure which itself may contain error, and we thus admit that in some cases we will misclassify our respondents. Given the level of precision needed for these analyses, we suspect that the extent of misclassification will not invalidate our procedures, but will simply make our inferences more conservative.

Table 8.6. Parameter Estimates for a Linear Structural Equations Model of Sociopolitical Orientations across the Life Span: Bennington Women Most Similar in Value Rankings between the 1960s and 1984 ($N = 83$)

Predictor Variable	Dependent Variable								
	PEP30	PID30	SPO30	PEP60	PID60	SPO60	PEP84	PID84	SPO84
η_1 1930s sociopolitical orientation	.756**	.750**	—	—	—	.763**	—	—	—
η_2 1960s sociopolitical orientation	—	—	—	.916**	.879**	—	—	—	.827**
η_3 1984 sociopolitical orientation	—	—	.121	—	—	—	.473**	.868**	—
x_1 Year entered Bennington	—	—	.121	—	—	-.152*	—	—	0.0f
x_2 Number of years at Bennington	—	—	-.119	—	—	0.0f	—	—	0.0f
x_3 Parental orientations	—	—	.635**	—	—	0.0f	—	—	0.0f
R-squared	.574	.562	.441	.842	.772	.562	.230	.757	.685

Note: Based on a model with 18 df and a χ^2 of 11.69 ($p = .863$). The model assumed all measurement disturbances were uncorrelated over time, except that the disturbance for the PEP30 was correlated with the disturbances for PEP60 and PEP84, and the disturbance for PID60 was correlated with the disturbance for PID84.

*$p < .05$ **$p < .01$ f = parameter fixed at zero

Table 8.7. Parameter Estimates for a Linear Structural Equations Model of Sociopolitical Orientations across the Life Span: Bennington Women Most Different in Value Rankings between the 1960s and 1984 ($N = 89$)

Predictor Variable	Dependent Variable								
	PEP30	PID30	SPO30	PEP60	PID60	SPO60	PEP84	PID84	SPO84
η_1 1930s sociopolitical orientation	.650**	.763**	—	—	—	.785**	—	—	—
η_2 1960s sociopolitical orientation	—	—	—	.763**	.884**	—	—	—	.863**
η_3 1984 sociopolitical orientation	—	—	—	—	—	—	.464**	.735**	—
x_1 Year entered Bennington	—	—	.328**	—	—	−.133	—	—	0.0f
x_2 Number of years at Bennington	—	—	−.020	—	—	0.0f	—	—	0.0f
x_3 Parental orientations	—	—	.752**	—	—	0.0f	—	—	0.0f
R-squared	.409	.583	.712	.601	.782	.553	.222	.542	.745

Note: Based on a model with 18 *df* and a χ^2 of 20.52 ($p = .305$). The model assumed all measurement disturbances were uncorrelated over time, except that the disturbance for the PEP30 was correlated with the disturbances for PEP60 and PEP84, and the disturbance for PID60 was correlated with the disturbance for PID84.
*$p < .05$ **$p < .01$ *f* = parameter fixed at zero

Intensity of Political Activity

On the basis of Rokeach's (1968) theoretical arguments and attendant research results, it can also be argued that those who are most active in political organizations and activities have more central attitudes regarding sociopolitical issues. There is some weak evidence that people are more likely to commit themselves publicly to attitude issues which they consider to be important (Schuman and Presser, 1981:242). We therefore hypothesize that those in the Bennington sample who were the most politically active are the least likely to have changed their sociopolitical attitudes over the life span, whereas those who were less active are the most likely to have changed.

In order to assess this hypothesis, we compared respondents who were different in terms of political activity over the life span. We asked the respondents to indicate whether they were active or not in the 1940s, 1950s, 1960s, 1970s, and since 1980 in three domains: (1) whether they worked or not for a political party or candidate, (2) whether they had been involved in other political activities or public issues, and (3) whether or not they had been active in activities or organizations whose major purpose was a change in the status of women (see questions F4a–e in appendix B). We measured the intensity of political activity by summing the number of times the respondent indicated she had been active in these domains across the decades listed. This score was then used as a basis for dividing the sample into two groups: one which was relatively more active in political affairs, and one which was less active.

In table 8.8 we reproduce some of the data presented in table 5.4, along with the mean of our score measuring the intensity of political activity over the life span. These results indicate that the intensity of political activity grew systematically from the 1940s through the 1970s, with an apparent decline into the decade of the 1980s. Our measure of political activity summarizes all of this information, providing the basis for categorizing our sample into groups of respondents demonstrating differences in the intensity of political activity over the life span. In other words, the highest scores on this index reflect highly consistent interest in political affairs throughout one's entire life.

In tables 8.9 and 8.10 we present our estimates of the properties of the model of attitude persistence and change, as above, for these two categories of respondents in our Bennington sample. That is, we reestimated this model (see table 7.8) separately for those scoring above the median on our measure of the intensity of political activity and those scoring below the median. These results show that the degree of attitude change over the life span is relatively uniform across categories of political involvement.

Table 8.8. Distribution of Responses to Questions about
Political Activity between the 1940s and 1984

	Women's Status (N = 307)	Parties and Candidates (N = 335)	Other (N = 335)
None	77%	40%	42%
1940s	3	22	15
1950s	3	32	21
1960s	10	36	36
1970s	17	34	36
1980s	14	30	36
Mean	0.52	1.54	1.44

The 1930s to 1984 stability coefficient for those with the most central attitudes is .653 (i.e., .764 × .855), whereas the estimated stability is .707 (i.e., .859 × .823) for those with the least central attitudes. The results of a formal statistical test for differences in stability between these two groups reveals a nonsignificant test statistic ($\chi^2 = 1.35$, $df = 2$, $p = .509$). Thus, using this measure of attitude centrality, we find that the degree of stability of attitudes among the Bennington women is independent of their level of political activity. On this basis, we are forced to conclude that there is little support for the hypothesis that attitude change is greater among those for whom political issues are least central.

Level of Political Interest

As one last test of the centrality hypothesis we rely on what is perhaps a better measure of political interest than that based on the Allport-Vernon measure of values. That measure expressly asked for interest in *power and influence* and *leadership and competition* rather than *political interests* in the sense of following political issues and public affairs. To better tap this domain, we asked our 1984 Bennington respondents to tell us about their level of interest in political activities over the years. Specifically, we inquired into whether they had maintained, increased, or decreased their level of political *interest* over the periods discussed in our questionnaire: between the 1930s–40s and the 1960s, between the 1960s and the 1970s, and between the 1970s and 1984. We assumed that social and political issues were more central for those reporting continued and increased levels of interest in such issues, and that attitude change would be less among this group compared to those for whom such interest was less apparent.[15]

15. Table 5.3 presents distributional data for the questions we asked about political interest since college.

193

Table 8.9. Parameter Estimates for a Linear Structural Equations Model of Sociopolitical Orientations across the Life Span: Bennington Women Most Politically Active between the 1940s and 1984 ($N = 134$)

Predictor Variable	Dependent Variable								
	PEP30	PID30	SPO30	PEP60	PID60	SPO60	PEP84	PID84	SPO84
η_1 1930s sociopolitical orientation	.719**	.768**	—	—	—	.764**	—	—	—
η_2 1960s sociopolitical orientation	—	—	—	.826**	.872**	—	—	—	.856**
η_3 1984 sociopolitical orientation	—	—	—	—	—	—	.509**	.755**	—
x_1 Year entered Bennington	—	—	.252**	—	—	-.154*	—	—	0.0f
x_2 Number of years at Bennington	—	—	-.068	—	—	0.0f	—	—	0.0f
x_3 Parental orientations	—	—	.674**	—	—	0.0f	—	—	0.0f
R-squared	.506	.589	.544	.696	.761	.538	.265	.568	.732

Note: Based on a model with 18 *df* and a χ^2 of 29.44 ($p = .043$). The model assumed all measurement disturbances were uncorrelated over time, except that the disturbance for the PEP30 was correlated with the disturbances for PEP60 and PEP84, and the disturbance for PID60 was correlated with the disturbance for PID84.

*$p < .05$ **$p < .01$ f = parameter fixed at zero

Table 8.10. Parameter Estimates for a Linear Structural Equations Model of Sociopolitical Orientations across the Life Span: Bennington Women Least Politically Active between the 1940s and 1984 ($N = 118$)

Predictor Variable	Dependent Variable								
	PEP30	PID30	SPO30	PEP60	PID60	SPO60	PEP84	PID84	SPO84
η_1 1930s sociopolitical orientation	.670**	.728**	—	—	—	.859**	—	—	—
η_2 1960s sociopolitical orientation	—	—	—	.884**	.829**	—	—	—	.823**
η_3 1984 sociopolitical orientation	—	—	—	—	—	—	.537**	.804**	—
x_1 Year entered Bennington	—	—	.354**	—	—	-.232**	—	—	0.0f
x_2 Number of years at Bennington	—	—	-.072	—	—	0.0f	—	—	0.0f
x_3 Parental orientations	—	—	.663**	—	—	0.0f	—	—	0.0f
R-squared	.435	.530	.611	.786	.688	.625	.308	.654	.677

Note: Based on a model with 18 df and a χ^2 of 47.33 ($p = .000$). The model assumed all measurement disturbances were uncorrelated over time, except that the disturbance for the PEP30 was correlated with the disturbances for PEP60 and PEP84, and the disturbance for PID60 was correlated with the disturbance for PID84.

$*p < .05$ $**p < .01$ f = parameter fixed at zero

Tables 8.11 and 8.12 present our estimates of the properties of the attitude change model for these two categories of respondents: those with a high level of political interest over this period and those with less political interest. Again, these results show little difference in attitude stability estimates across the two groups; if anything, the group with the highest level of interest in politics shows the most attitude change. The 1930s to 1984 stability estimate for the high-interest group is .572 (i.e., .725 × .790), which is lower than the comparable estimate for the low-interest group, .766 (i.e., .845 × .906). The significance test of the differences in stability (see table E1) shows no statistically significant differences, however $(\Delta\chi^2 = .37, df = 2, p = .831)$. Thus, even when we refine the measure of political interest as an indicator of attitude centrality, we find no strong support for the hypothesis that more central attitudes are more stable.

STABILITY OF PERSONALITY AND POLITICAL CONSERVATISM

As we have noted at several points, it is commonly assumed that those who hold more rigidly to a particular value stance may also be more ideologically conservative. By contrast, we have argued that these are separate issues and that the stability of attitudes and values is not necessarily linked to political orientations. We nonetheless believe it is important to provide a test of this hypothesis to the extent our data permit, and we devote the remainder of this chapter to this issue. We cannot directly test this hypothesis on its own terms because we lack adequate measures of conservatism in the sense of personality differences in openness to change. However, some aspects of our data permit us to address these issues in a somewhat different way. Table 8.13 presents the correlations of our several measures of constancy of personality and/or centrality of political attitudes with each of the measures of political conservatism obtained on our Bennington sample in the 1930s, 1960s, and 1984.

As can be seen from the correlations presented, there is some support for the hypothesis. Some of the 1960s measures of political conservatism are significantly correlated to a small degree with our measure of value similarity. Specifically, there is a relationship between the degree of similarity in the values measures over time and political conservatism, in that "Allport-Vernon similarity" correlates positively with all of the 1960s measures of political conservatism, two of which correlations are significant. Such a pattern also exists for the 1930s and 1984 party identification measures, but it is not statistically significant. Thus, although the evidence is weak and not consistent over the life span, there is some support for

Table 8.11. Parameter Estimates for a Linear Structural Equations Model of Sociopolitical Orientations across the Life Span: Bennington Women Most Interested in Social and Political Issues between the 1940s and 1984 ($N = 85$)

Predictor Variable	Dependent Variable								
	PEP30	PID30	SPO30	PEP60	PID60	SPO60	PEP84	PID84	SPO84
η_1 1930s sociopolitical orientation	.682**	.631**	—	—	—	.725**	—	—	—
η_2 1960s sociopolitical orientation	—	—	—	.901**	.845**	—	—	—	.790**
η_3 1984 sociopolitical orientation	—	—	—	—	—	—	.504**	.923**	—
x_1 Year entered Bennington	—	—	.344**	—	—	-.145	—	—	0.0f
x_2 Number of years at Bennington	—	—	-.067	—	—	0.0f	—	—	0.0f
x_3 Parental orientations	—	—	.662**	—	—	0.0f	—	—	0.0f
R-squared	.453	.398	.606	.827	.714	.459	.276	.845	.625

Note: Based on a model with 18 df and a χ^2 of 33.43 ($p = .015$). The model assumed all measurement disturbances were uncorrelated over time, except that the disturbance for the PEP30 was correlated with the disturbance for the PEP60 was correlated with the disturbances for PEP60 and PEP84, and the disturbance for PID60 was correlated with the disturbance for PID84.

*$p < .05$ **$p < .01$ f = parameter fixed at zero

Table 8.12. Parameter Estimates for a Linear Structural Equations Model of Sociopolitical Orientations across the Life Span: Bennington Women Least Interested in Social and Political Issues between the 1940s and 1984. (N = 138)

Predictor Variable	Dependent Variable								
	PEP30	PID30	SPO30	PEP60	PID60	SPO60	PEP84	PID84	SPO84
η_1 1930s sociopolitical orientation	.702**	.804**	—	—	—	.845**	—	—	—
η_2 1960s sociopolitical orientation	—	—	—	.857**	.849**	—	—	—	.906**
η_3 1984 sociopolitical orientation	—	—	—	—	—	—	.532**	.709**	—
x_1 Year entered Bennington	—	—	.261**	—	—	−.245**	—	—	0.0f
x_2 Number of years at Bennington	—	—	−.113	—	—	0.0f	—	—	0.0f
x_3 Parental orientations	—	—	.675**	—	—	0.0f	—	—	0.0f
R-squared	.482	.646	.561	.739	.721	.644	.290	.507	.820

Note: Based on a model with 18 df and a χ^2 of 14.53 (p = .694). The model assumed all measurement disturbances were uncorrelated over time, except that the disturbance for the PEP30 was correlated with the disturbances for PEP60 and PEP84, and the disturbance for PID60 was correlated with the disturbance for PID84.

*p < .05   **p < .01   f = parameter fixed at zero

Table 8.13. Product-Moment Correlations between Measures of Sociopolitical Conservatism and Aspects of Personality

	1930s			
	PEP30	PID30		
Allport-Vernon similarity	.037	.152		
Political salience	−.128*	−.175*		
Political activity	−.135*	−.021		
Political interest	.076	.022		

	1960s			
	PEP60	PID60	PCI60	L/C60
Allport-Vernon similarity	.158	.143*	.125	.136*
Political salience	−.185*	−.102	−.113	−.032
Political activity	−.187*	−.185**	−.118	−.294***
Political interest	.101	.044	.052	−.008

	1980s			
	PEP84	PID84	PCI84	L/C84
Allport-Vernon similarity	.002	.124	.080	.041
Political salience	.009	−.062	−.056	−.043
Political activity	−.140**	−.195***	−.225***	−.241***
Political interest	−.009	.026	.043	.037

*$p < .05$ **$p < .01$ ***$p < .001$

the idea that there is a relationship between the permanence of value
orientations and political conservatism, especially during mid-life.

It is interesting to note, however, that our other measures of the constancy of personality, namely our various indicators of attitude centrality,
do not show this type of relationship to political conservatism. Indeed,
the opposite is the case—generally, those with more central attitudes are
more likely to hold liberal political views. Those for whom political issues
were more salient and those who were most active in political organizations
and activities were significantly more liberal on a number of indicators.
In the 1960s and 1984 data, especially, our measure of political activity is
significantly related to almost all of our indicators of liberalism/conserva-
tism, indicating that those who are the most liberal on social and political
issues are also the most active politically. By contrast, our measure of political interest is unrelated to political conservatism, and our measure of the
salience of political matters is related primarily to the 1930s indicators.
Thus, while there is some evidence that political conservatism is linked to
our various indicators of the stability of personality, including our measures
of attitude centrality, the nature of this relationship varies over indicators

and over time points. We therefore find ourselves in a somewhat tenuous empirical situation, unable to offer much consistent evidence regarding this relationship and unwilling to generalize very far beyond our data.

INDIVIDUAL DIFFERENCES IN SUSCEPTIBILITY TO ATTITUDE CHANGE

In this chapter we have examined the hypothesis that differences in the constancy of personality and cognitive organization help produce differences in attitude stability and change. We have looked at several different aspects of individual differences in susceptibility to attitude change—differences that are centered on the more fundamental aspects of personality, such as the stability of values or the centrality of attitudes. Our examination of this set of issues relied on measures of aspects of individual differences assumed to be fundamentally linked to cognitive and affective organization and hypothesized to be linked to the stability of sociopolitical attitudes. We reasoned, following Rokeach (1968), that those Bennington women for whom social and political attitude issues were the most central would show the highest levels of attitude stability, whereas those with less central attitudes would have changed the most. Our results did not provide widespread support for this hypothesis.

In order to summarize the results of our examination of these personological explanations of attitude stability and change, we separately assemble our estimates of attitude persistence in table 8.14. This table arrays the stability estimates already presented in the tables discussed earlier in this chapter. The table first presents estimates of the differences in attitude stability with respect to differences in the salience of political interests, as assessed by the Allport-Vernon index of values and interests. These are followed in the table by our estimates of life span stability of political orientations within the other categories of centrality considered, including Allport-Vernon value similarity over time, the intensity of political activity, and the extent of interest in social and political affairs.

Using the ranking of the political domain offered by the Allport-Vernon index as a measure of the centrality of political attitudes, we found some modest support for the centrality hypothesis, in that more attitude change was observed between the 1930s and 1960s for the low-salience group. This result, however, was not consistently present over the later time period. Also, our other analyses using additional measures of attitude centrality—the intensity of political activity and the level of political interest— also produced no systematic differences in attitude stability over levels of centrality. From these results, we must conclude that our measures of

200

Table 8.14. Summary of Life Span Stability Estimates among Subgroups of the Bennington Sample Defined by Differences in Susceptibility to Attitude Change

	1930s to 1960	1960s to 1984	1930s to 1984
Allport-Vernon political salience			
High salience	.807	.853	.688
Low salience	.682	.863	.589
Allport-Vernon value similarity			
Similar values	.763	.828	.632
Different values	.785	.865	.679
Political activity			
More active	.764	.855	.653
Less active	.859	.823	.707
Political interest			
More interest	.725	.790	.572
Less interest	.845	.906	.766
Total (from table 7.8)	.908	.860	.781

centrality of political attitudes produced little systematic differentiation of attitude stability across levels of centrality.

We also failed to find any differences in attitude stability with respect to the concept of the stability of values. Using a measure of the similarity of values over the 1960s to 1984 time period we tried to approximate differences among women in our sample in the extent to which value orientations were stable over time. We found little support for the constancy of personality explanation of attitude stability. This analysis, as summarized in table 8.14, produced virtually no differentiation in our estimates of life span attitude persistence and change.

What accounts for this general failure to find differences in susceptibility to attitude change across levels of stability of personality and/or attitude organization? We suspect that the answer to this question lies not in the inadequacy of the theoretical argument but in something we alluded to earlier. We noted that while we expected that the high levels of stability in the Bennington sample might be due to the peculiar salience of political issues for these women, this uniqueness in and of itself might prevent us from finding support for this explanation in that sample. In short, we suggest that the amount of variation in our various centrality measures may not be sufficient to isolate extremes of attitude change. For example, we noted in chapter 5 that in our 1984 data the Bennington women revealed themselves to hold attitudes more intensely than the population generally. It may therefore be that our attempt to differentiate levels of attitude cen-

201

trality in this sample was undermined to some extent by the uniformly high levels of attitude importance. Such differences at this level of attitude intensity may not be sensitive to theoretical distinctions that would otherwise predict differences in attitude persistence and change in a more heterogeneous sample. Thus, our tentative conclusion is that there is little support for the centrality hypothesis in the Bennington sample, but that our several tests may have been insufficient because of the high salience of sociopolitical issues in that sample.

9

Reference Groups, Social Support, and the Stability of Sociopolitical Orientations

Introduction

As we suggested in the previous chapter, people vary in the extent to which they experience stabilizing influences in the environment, stemming from differential exposure to change-inducing events and the protective features of the social settings they inhabit. We argued that a higher rate of exposure to stabilizing experiences theoretically tends to produce greater persistence of attitudes, just as a lower susceptibility to change theoretically produces more stability. We used the concept of *vulnerability to attitude change* to embody both of these sets of factors, the individual's openness to change and the opportunities she experiences through exposure to the risks of change-inducing events.[1] And, of course, there is a potential interaction between susceptibility (openness to change) and exposure to such opportunities which also influences the likelihood of change, such that the effects of both are potentially magnified. This, as we noted earlier, essentially captures the phenomenon Newcomb described at Bennington: young, impressionable people coming to grips with their expanding sociopolitical environment in a setting that supported a particular perspective on the events and change occurring in the broader world.[2]

Stated a bit more formally, we theorized earlier that the likelihood of change is affected by a set of "individual-level" factors, which we have re-

---

1. Recall that in chapter 8 we used the term *susceptibility* to refer to attitude change resulting from the individual's propensity or openness to change, holding constant opportunities for change from the environment. Thus, *susceptibility* refers to the potential for change coming from the individual. By contrast, we use the term *vulnerability* to refer to the net result of the combined propensities for change stemming from both the individual and the environment. That is, the term *vulnerability* is intended to refer to the general phenomenon of change or stability resulting from both individual propensities and the likelihood of change-inducing experiences from the environment.

2. In chapter 2 we reviewed Newcomb's (1943) interpretation of the processes by which the informational environment of the Bennington College community exerted its influence on the opportunities for change.

ferred to generally here as factors affecting susceptibility or openness to change, and by a set of "social-level" factors that are reflected in the individual's exposure to "attitude-change-inducing" events in the environment and the existence of "protective" mechanisms of social support that help the individual resist such change. In theory, the relevant environmental factors can be tied to a number of different facets of the environment, from micro-settings in which the person is embedded, such as the family, to meso-environments in which the person is not an actor, but which can have indirect influences via relevant others, or to macro-environments existing at the societal and cultural level (see Bronfenbrenner, 1979; Merelman, 1968).

In this chapter we focus on several types of environmental factors that shape the opportunities for attitude persistence and change. We give special attention to two sets of factors: those linked to differential exposure to potentially change-inducing life experiences and those tied to the supportiveness of social environments. Our consideration of the latter set of factors focuses specifically on the hypothesis of Newcomb and his colleagues (1967) regarding the importance of social network support for maintaining attitudes and influencing their direction of change. In pursuing these tasks, our primary research strategy follows that used in chapter 8, namely to partition our Bennington sample into theoretically relevant categories reflecting differential opportunities for change, and then to examine differences in the extent of attitude persistence and change within these categories. Specifically, we seek evidence of different levels of attitude change within different types of social environments.

EXPOSURE TO CHANGE-INDUCING EXPERIENCES

If, as we have argued, there are differences in opportunities for change linked to exposure to change-inducing events that contribute to the extent of attitude stability and change, then we should in theory be able to specify these environmental sources of change. There are a number of possible *ecological transitions*—changes in key features of the environment—that are important from the perspective of assessing stability and change (Bronfenbrenner, 1979). One important type of environmental change relevant to the development of attitudes involves *changes in roles and role relationships*, which may produce exposure to different informational environments and reference-group norms.

In chapter 2 we noted that the notion of the *reference group* (Hyman, 1942) had been central to Newcomb's (1943) analysis and interpretation of the Bennington student's adjustment to the collegiate environment. Newcomb argued that "whatever the manner in which public issues come to be related to individual values, the relationship will be established through the medium of whatever group or groups of which the individual is a member" (1943:12). Thus, theoretically, changes in reference-group membership can potentially create opportunities for changes in attitudes on social and public issues.

Recently, Steckenrider and Cutler argued that "the most promising and still uncharted paths to the mysteries connecting aging and political dispositions lie in the sequence of roles associated with adult maturation and aging, e.g., student, spouse, wage-earner, parent, retiree, and—increasingly in today's age-conscious society—'old person'" (1989:56). Clearly, the acquisition of new roles and life experiences connected to them can be a significant factor in sociopolitical attitude change. Not only do shifts in roles and their associated rights and obligations create new interests and values (Lipset et al., 1954); they also bring about changing relationships with others (Neugarten and Hagestad, 1976). Thus, role transitions may change the nature and composition of the individual's social networks, as well as mark changes in roles and role relationships.

Role Transitions over the Life-Cycle

Several theoretical statements have been made about the key ordered changes involving role transitions across the life-cycle. Neugarten and Peterson (1957) identify four major adult life stages, each involving differing developmental tasks and life course issues: young adulthood, maturity, middle age, and old age. The first is, of course, the stage in which we have found the most instability in attitudes, and the last is one in which there is some empirical suggestion of lowered stability in attitudes, especially the stability of attitude intensity (see Sears, 1981; Alwin and Krosnick, 1991a). These variations in levels of stability may coincide with the most frequent life-cycle experiences of role transitions. One might therefore hypothesize that attitude stability will be lowest among those experiencing the most numerous and frequent role transitions.

Glenn suggests that one of the important reasons for expecting young people to be more vulnerable to change than older people is that there is a greater density of significant life events in early adulthood and a wider spacing of such events later on in life: "During a period of a few years beginning in late adolescence, the person typically experiences important status changes, assumes important new roles, and changes in many social relationships" (1980:603). Typically, Glenn argues, the person leaves home, completes her formal schooling, chooses a vocation, enters an occupation or job, gets married, and becomes a parent all within a relatively short period of the life span. This argument, thus, proposes not that an individual loses a certain susceptibility to change with aging, but instead experiences a decline in exposure to the risk of experiencing change-inducing events.

As Steckenrider and Cutler (1989:63) note, however, the connections between age and role transitions are not as obvious as they may seem. Some relevant role transitions are very clearly linked to age; others are not. One of the types of changes induced by some role transitions (e.g., those linked to employment status) is a change in socioeconomic well-being. Bengtson, Kasschau, and Ragan (1977) suggest, for example, that there are socioeconomic differences in the aging process. If so, socioeconomic factors might be related to levels of attitude stability. For example, factors linked to differences in schooling and employment may be involved in differential attitude change both because of the differential vulnerability of different groups to change-inducing experiences and the differential exposure of socioeconomic groups to such experiences.

Role Transitions and the Stability of Attitudes

The role-transition argument seems plausible as far as it goes. Its relevance in the present case depends on the linkage of the number of role transitions per se and the likelihood of attitude change. It may be difficult, however, to find evidence of it in the present context because there is considerable uniformity in the life experiences of the Bennington women. At the same time, this uniformity could account for the relatively high level of attitude stability among these women, and our inability in chapter 8 to find many extremes of attitude change may reflect this uniformity of experience.

Table 9.1 presents some information on the life course experiences of the Bennington women. This table reveals that most (some 70 percent) of the Bennington women completed college, and nearly one-third gained some postgraduate experience. Virtually all of them (95 percent) were married at least once, with about one-quarter experiencing divorce, and nearly one-quarter experiencing widowhood. Almost all of these women experienced motherhood, and many had more than one or two children. Finally, almost all these women had some labor-force experience, and almost one-half had a career (defined here and throughout this chapter as being employed in the same type of job for more than 10 years). Thus, there may be too little variation in life course experiences in the Bennington sample to suppose that we could find differences in attitude stability that result from differences in role transitions. Still, we thought it would be revealing to examine the role-transition hypothesis somewhat further.

Based on the above descriptive information about the extent of life course transitions experienced by the women in our Bennington sample,

Table 9.1. Role Transitions in the Bennington Sample

Event	Number	Percent
Schooling		
Did not complete college	69	20.6%
College completed	168	50.1
Postgraduate experience	98	29.3
Family		
Ever married	317	94.6
Ever widowed	75	22.4
Ever divorced	88	26.3
Number of children		
None	31	9.3
1 or 2	94	28.1
3	98	29.3
4+	112	33.4
Work		
Ever worked for pay	285	85.1
Occupational career	154	46.9

we developed an index measuring the *number of role transitions* experienced over the life course. Our index was computed by adding the following events into a scale summarizing the exposure to life course transitions: (1) completion of college, (2) following a course of postgraduate study, (3) number of marriages, (4) ever being divorced, (5) ever being widowed, (6) ever raising children, (7) ever being employed full-time outside the home, and (8) following an occupational career. Each of these life-cycle events involves movement in and out of roles (i.e., role transitions), and as suggested by Steckenrider and Cutler (1989), each may increase the individual's exposure to attitude-change-inducing experiences.

Of course, it may be naive to think that the sheer volume of such transitions is relevant, even if we can isolate enough variation in life experiences to test this hypothesis. It may be, as we suggest later in the chapter, that the critical aspect of such role transitions involves not just the event connected with role change, but the risk of exposure to change-inducing experiences. Nonetheless, before proceeding on to this more fine-grained analysis, we first explore the role-transition hypothesis.

In order to test the hypothesis that the number of role transitions over the life course is related to the stability of sociopolitical attitudes, we partitioned our Bennington sample into two groups: those who were high versus those who were low in the number of role transitions experienced. We divided our sample into two groups based on the median-split of this index. Tables 9.2 and 9.3 present the results for our attitude-change model within each of these two groups.

Table 9.2. Parameter Estimates for a Linear Structural Equations Model of Sociopolitical Orientations across the Life Span: Bennington Women with Most Role Transitions between the 1940s and 1984 ($N = 146$)

Predictor Variable	Dependent Variable								
	PEP30	PID30	SPO30	PEP60	PID60	SPO60	PEP84	PID84	SPO84
η_1 1930s sociopolitical orientation	.692**	.829**	—	—	—	.816**	—	—	—
η_2 1960s sociopolitical orientation	—	—	—	.928**	.834**	—	—	—	.847**
η_3 1984 sociopolitical orientation	—	—	—	—	—	—	.537**	.755**	—
x_1 Year entered Bennington	—	—	.262**	—	—	-.286**	—	—	0.0f
x_2 Number of years at Bennington	—	—	-.036	—	—	0.0f	—	—	0.0f
x_3 Parental orientations	—	—	.692**	—	—	0.0f	—	—	0.0f
R-squared	.476	.687	.560	.861	.696	.616	.299	.587	.718

Note: Based on a model with 18 df and a χ^2 of 27.87 ($p = .064$). The model assumed all measurement disturbances were uncorrelated over time, except that the disturbance for the PEP30 was correlated with the disturbances for PEP60 and PEP84, and the disturbance for PID60 was correlated with the disturbance for PID84.

*$p < .05$ **$p < .01$ f = parameter fixed at zero

Table 9.3. Parameter Estimates for a Linear Structural Equations Model of Sociopolitical Orientations across the Life Span: Bennington Women with Least Role Transitions between the 1940s and 1984 ($N = 105$)

Predictor Variable	Dependent Variable								
	PEP30	PID30	SPO30	PEP60	PID60	SPO60	PEP84	PID84	SPO84
η_1 1930s sociopolitical orientation	.691**	.645**	—	—	—	.806**	—	—	—
η_2 1960s sociopolitical orientation	—	—	—	.793**	.850**	—	—	—	—
η_3 1984 sociopolitical orientation	—	—	—	—	—	—	.485**	.836**	.817**
x_1 Year entered Bennington	—	—	.329**	—	—	−.121	—	—	0.0f
x_2 Number of years at Bennington	—	—	−.131	—	—	0.0f	—	—	0.0f
x_3 Parental orientations	—	—	.607**	—	—	0.0f	—	—	0.0f
R-squared	.459	.415	.532	.649	.723	.583	.241	.692	.668

Note: Based on a model with 18 df and a χ^2 of 22.65 ($p = .204$). The model assumed all measurement disturbances were uncorrelated over time, except that the disturbance for the PEP30 was correlated with the disturbances for PEP60 and PEP84, and the disturbance for PID60 was correlated with the disturbance for PID84.

$*p < .05$ $**p < .01$ f = parameter fixed at zero

209

These results provide little support for the hypothesis that the volume of role transitions over the life course is linked in any way to the stability of attitudes. Inspection of the stability estimates in tables 9.2 and 9.3 reveals no significant differences. Attitude stability between the 1930s and 1980s is estimated at .691 (i.e., .816 × .847) among those with the highest volume of role transitions and .659 (i.e., .806 × .817) among those with the lowest. An attitude-change model assuming equivalent levels of stability does not reduce the fit to the data significantly relative to one that permits differences in stability ($\chi^2 = .17$, $df = 2$, $p = .918$). Thus, there is no statistical basis for rejecting the null hypothesis of no differences in stability by volume of role transitions.

Role Transitions and Liberalism/Conservatism

Despite the absence of a relationship between the amount of attitude change and the volume of role transitions, there is some evidence that certain role shifts are associated with the nature of political orientations. Table 9.4 presents the correlations among the measures of sociopolitical attitudes in our data set and the role-transitional experiences summarized in our index. We also include the correlation of the dichotomy—more versus fewer transitions—we used to partition the sample in the above analysis.

The volume of role transitions is related to political liberalism/conservatism, although this is due primarily to the experience of educational and occupational transitions. Those Bennington women who completed college and/or pursued postgraduate study and those who were ever employed and/or pursued an occupational career were the most liberal in their orientations. Of course, these two sets of factors are not independent, since educational certification is often a precursor of employment and occupational pursuits.

Moreover, it is not possible for us to sort out the nature of the relationships between these socioeconomic role experiences and political attitudes from these correlations alone. There is undoubtedly considerable reciprocity in the influences that produce this relationship; that is, involvement in educational and occupational careers may have influenced these women in the direction of acquiring more liberal attitudes, or it could be that those women with more liberal attitudes at the outset were those most likely to pursue such careers. We cannot begin to decipher the message regarding causality contained in these relationships without turning to a somewhat more complicated model.

210

Table 9.4. Product-Moment Correlations between Measures of Sociopolitical Orientations and Role Transitions

Role Transitions	1930s	
	PEP30	PID30
Completed college	−.195**	−.143*
Postgraduate study	−.128*	−.170*
Number of marriages	−.038	−.021
Ever divorced	−.090	−.022
Ever widowed	−.009	−.033
Ever worked	−.111*	−.113
Occupational career	−.161**	−.161*
Ever had children	.048	.150*
Total of role transitions	−.194**	−.138
More vs. fewer transitions	−.187**	−.141*

	1960s			
	PEP60	PID60	PCI60	L/C60
Completed college	−.321**	−.164**	−.184**	−.261**
Postgraduate study	−.173*	−.160**	−.044	−.129*
Number of marriages	.112	−.013	−.045	−.018
Ever divorced	.038	−.027	−.075	.034
Ever widowed	.100	.012	.027	.038
Ever worked	−.260**	−.176**	−.170**	−.186**
Occupational career	−.185*	−.247**	−.219**	−.229**
Ever had children	.103	.105	.031	.094
Total of role transitions	−.067*	−.185**	−.184**	−.159*
More vs. fewer transitions	−.137	−.156**	−.152*	−.074

	1980s			
	PEP84	PID84	PCI84	L/C84
Completed college	−.166**	−.178**	−.230**	−.266**
Postgraduate study	−.094	−.145**	−.082	−.147**
Number of marriages	.009	.047	−.069	−.007
Ever divorced	−.042	−.031	−.093	−.011
Ever widowed	.023	.055	−.012	.043
Ever worked	−.136*	−.149**	−.104	−.125*
Occupational career	−.093	−.207**	−.190**	−.213**
Ever had children	.086	.113*	.138*	.099
Total of role transitions	−.114*	−.135*	−.184**	−.188**
More vs. fewer transitions	−.083	−.125*	−.174**	−.138**

$*p < .05$ $**p < .01$

Socioeconomic Experiences and Attitude Change

Because of the strong relationship between socioeconomic experiences and sociopolitical orientations, and because of the ambiguity in the meaning of this relationship, we pursued further the question of the possible independent contribution of postcollegiate educational and occupational experiences to attitude change in later life. In order to examine this question, we incorporated two additional variables into our models for attitude persistence and change. We included a measure of schooling experiences, coded 3 if the respondent reported having pursued postgraduate study, 2 if the respondent completed college, and 1 if not. We also included a measure of occupational career involvement, coded 3 if the respondent reported having an occupational career (holding a similar job over at least 10 years over the life course), 2 if the respondent had ever worked, but had not had an occupational career, and 1 if the respondent had never worked.

These two variables summarize much of the information we collected in our 1984 survey concerning schooling and work experiences. We include them in our model as "intervening" variables, recording experiences that took place in time between the years at Bennington College and the follow-up surveys. In figure 9.1 we depict the causal sequence of these variables within the framework of the model we have considered for attitude persistence and change.[3] These variables are thus conceptualized as temporally subsequent to the exogenous variables in our model and to the latent attitude construct assessed in the late 1930s and early 1940s (SPO30), and are thought to depend upon all of these prior factors. In addition (and important for our present purposes) these socioeconomic variables are thought to represent change-inducing experiences, and are therefore posited in our model as sources of causation and change in subsequent attitudes (SPO60 and SPO84). We conceptualize these influences in terms of an *induced-variable* model (see Alwin, 1988b), which means that we constrain the effects of the schooling and work variables on subsequent attitudes to be proportional to their joint contributions (see also Heise, 1972; Hauser and Goldberger, 1971; Jöreskog, and Sörbom, 1981). To the extent that these factors have effects on later attitudes, independent of initial postcollegiate attitudes and other exogenous factors, we can conclude that socioeconomic experiences contribute to the nature and direction of attitude change.

In table 9.5 we present the coefficient estimates of the parameters implied by the model depicted in figure 9.1. These results reveal several interesting interpretations of the relationships considered heretofore (in

---

3. In keeping with our previous practice, we have used the model presented initially in table 7.8, in which we employ similar indicators at all three time points.

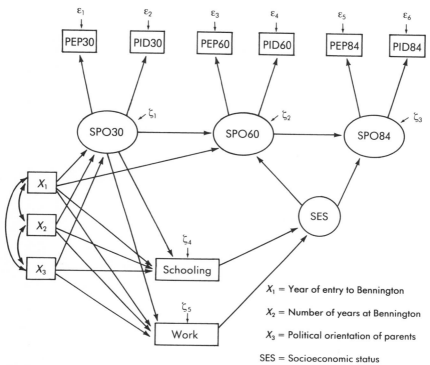

Figure 9.1. Linear Structural Equations Model of the Influences of Socioeconomic Experiences on Sociopolitical Orientations

table 9.4). First, the achievement of more schooling and an occupational career depend to a significant extent on political orientations, in that those women who were the most liberal in sociopolitical orientations upon leaving Bennington College were more likely to experience postgraduate study and an occupational career. If Newcomb (1943) was correct about the nature of the relationship between political orientations and success in the Bennington College status system, then it should not be surprising that those who were successful in one sphere might also be successful in another (see Kemper, 1968). The characteristics associated with achievement and success in the Bennington College community may transfer to success in the broader world. Thus, it is the type of person who became politically liberal at Bennington, in part because of processes linked to the achievement of status in the Bennington community, who also later became socioeconomically successful, which accounts for this relationship, rather than the experience of socioeconomic success by itself.

Table 9.5. Parameter Estimates for a Linear Structural Equations Model of the Influences of Socioeconomic Experiences on Sociopolitical Orientation

Predictor Variable	Dependent Variable											
	PEP30	PID30	SPO30	SCHOOL	WORK	SEEXP	PEP60	PID60	SPO60	PEP84	PID84	SPO84
η_1 1930s sociopolitical orientation	.682**	.742**	—	-.502**	-.465**	—	—	—	.765**	—	—	—
η_2 1960s sociopolitical orientation	—	—	—	—	—	—	.884**	.826**	—	—	—	.808**
η_3 1984 sociopolitical orientation	—	—	—	—	—	—	—	—	—	.520**	.764**	—
x_1 Year entered Bennington	—	—	.299**	.192**	.193**	.	—	—	-.211**	—	—	0.0f
x_2 Number of years at Bennington	—	—	-.072	.552**	.142**	—	—	—	0.0f	—	—	0.0f
x_3 Parental orientations	—	—	.686**	.321**	.202*	—	—	—	0.0f	—	—	0.0f
η_4 Schooling	—	—	—	—	—	.631	—	—	—	—	—	—
η_5 Work	—	—	—	—	—	.664	—	—	—	—	—	—
η_6 Socioeconomic experience	—	—	—	—	—	—	—	—	-.144*	—	—	.066
R-squared	.448	.550	.595	.439	.129	1.00	.791	.682	.612	.284	.589	.701

Note: Based on a model with 26 df and a χ^2 of 42.07 ($p = .024$). The model assumed all measurement disturbances were uncorrelated over time, except that the disturbance for the PEP30 was correlated with the disturbances for PEP60 and PEP84, and the disturbance for PID60 was correlated with the disturbance for PID84.

*$p < .05$ **$p < .01$ f = parameter fixed at zero

At the same time, these results indicate that socioeconomic experiences may modestly affect later sociopolitical development. Specifically, table 9.5 indicates that there is a significant effect of socioeconomic experiences on 1960s sociopolitical attitudes, suggesting that those women who attained greater educational and occupational success were more likely to continue to change their attitudes in a liberal direction after college. This is an important finding because it confirms the general hypothesis that exposure to change-inducing experiences—in this case experiences linked to socioeconomic careers—contributes to continued attitude change.

We also explored the relationship of specific marital events to attitude change, as we expected that divorce and widowhood specifically might be among the most potent role transitions in generating attitude change because of their potential for exposing a person to dissonant social environments. There were no relationships between the experience of divorce and widowhood and the propensity for attitude change.[4] Again, however, we would expect that by looking only at the occurrence of role transitions and not at the nature of the change or constancy in the political nature of the person's social environment, we are unlikely to see a relationship between role transitions and attitude change.

THE SUPPORTIVENESS OF SOCIAL NETWORKS

As we noted above, it is possible that the notion of role transitions does not precisely represent the critical social influences that affect levels of attitude stability and change. While attitude change and stability may not be linked to the volume of role transitions, as our above results indicated, they may be more subtly related to the experiences associated with such life changes. We can perhaps better understand the nature of attitude stability and change if we focus attention on the contextual aspects of role transitions, that is, whether role shifts are accompanied by changes in the political composition of the social environment experienced by the individual. If, for example, people experience many such transitions but generally maintain a high degree of similarity to the sociopolitical composition of their social networks, then the sheer volume of such transitions is immaterial. Such an argument suggests that we might best clarify the critical

4. These results were based on a regression analysis in which *number of marriages, ever widowed,* and *ever divorced* variables were included as predictors of 1984 political attitudes, controlling for 1930s PEP score, years of schooling completed, number of years spent working, and husband's political attitudes. These results were presented in Naomi Levan's honors thesis mentioned in the preface.

factors linked to attitude stability and change in adult life by specifying the nature of *social support* for existing attitudes.

From this perspective, the number of role transitions is irrelevant if the individual can maintain the nature of her social networks and the sociopolitical context of social support. Indeed, one of the principal interpretations of the stability of orientations given by Newcomb and his colleagues (1967) in their restudy of the Bennington women in the 1960s was that these women tended to select environments in later life that reinforced their Bennington orientations (see chapter 3). Newcomb and his colleagues (1967:53–66) argued that these women were attracted to others who agreed with their attitudes, and through further association with these others, their attitudes were reinforced through social support. They presented considerable evidence that the social support provided by the social networks in which the Bennington women were embedded did much to explain the stability and lack of change of political attitudes over the life course.[5]

Social Selection and the Similarity of Social Networks

There is widespread support for the theoretical assumption that the social structuring of human activity leads people to develop relationships with others who are similar to them in a number of respects. Structural proximity leads to increased frequency of interaction, which leads to increased interpersonal attraction. Such interpersonal attraction leads to more frequent interaction and attraction (e.g., Homans, 1974). It is therefore not very surprising that people are attracted to others who are similar to them in various ways (Byrne, 1971; Cohen, 1977; Feld, 1981, 1982; Fischer, 1982; Lazarsfeld and Merton, 1954; Richardson, 1940; Tedin, 1980; Verbrugge, 1977).

Furthermore, experimental evidence reveals that people confront new situations with a motivation to maintain self-conceptions and to avoid information that requires accommodation and change (e.g., Darley and Fazio, 1980; Secord and Backman, 1965; Snyder, 1984; Swann, 1983). Caspi and Elder summarize this research literature this way:

5. Newcomb and his colleagues were among the first social psychologists in recent years to use the concept of *social support* to account for human attitudes and behavior. The concept of social support has been an important tool for understanding well-being. Lowenthal (1964) and Lowenthal and Haven (1968), for example, used the concept to interpret the better mental health of people in more intimate social relationships, and in recent years research on the role of social support in promoting health and psychological well-being has emerged as a cottage industry (e.g., House, Laudis, and Umberson, 1988; House, Umberson and Laudis, 1988). Its importance for other aspects of human functioning has been neglected.

People preferentially search for evidence that confirms propositions they are testing, whether these are about objects, other people, or themselves. Moreover, they act in ways that generate behavioural disconfirmation for hypotheses that challenge or threaten central aspects of their self-concept. And because the strategies people employ in the quest for self-confirming evidence are quite successful, there is often little need to accommodate new experiences. (1988:237)

Thus, there may be strong conservative tendencies within individuals that would explain why people find themselves in social environments that are compatible with their own dispositions.

However, as Feld (1982) argues, the neglect of social structural factors in explaining the sources of such similarities among persons and their social environments may lead to an overestimation of the extent to which they result from individual preferences. He shows that among the most common sources of relationships, those that originate from the neighborhood, work, or voluntary associations tend to be relatively homogeneous. Of course, these structural sources of network composition may change relatively dramatically at critical periods in the life cycle.

Network Similarity over the Life Course

It would seem that any argument about the importance of social support for the maintenance of attitudes must clarify the extent to which social networks are stable in their composition over the life cycle. What evidence is there that social networks change or remain the same over the life course, and what evidence is there that network similarity is linked to other, more structural changes in social networks over the life course? Such questions are difficult to address because of the absence of appropriate panel data on network composition and network similarity.

There is some empirical evidence, however, suggesting that social networks and the level of social integration may change in significant ways over the life course. Using data from the 1985 General Social Survey, Morgan (1988) shows that the number of network ties declines with age. He also examined the extent to which age-based declines in social network participation were due to age-related changes in social resources (income, education, and health), which are known to differ by age. He found that the lower education, income, and health of older age groups accounted for some of the age-linked shrinkage of network size, but a relationship was still present even after controlling for declines in resources.

Of course, shrinkage of network size by itself may not have any implications for the composition of social networks, although there are clearly some compositional shifts that cannot be avoided. For example, in addi-

217

tion to changes in the extensiveness of social networks, Morgan (1988) also found age to be related to the composition of network membership. He found that with age the amount of age-homophily in one's social network declines. These results help verify the conclusion of Bengtson, Rosenthal, and Burton that "family structures, roles, and relationships of contemporary elderly Americans are increasingly diverse," due to the "intersection of changing patterns of mortality, fertility, and divorce with race, socioeconomic status, and gender" (1990:280).

But even if these aspects of network composition change, this does not necessarily mean that the political complexion of that network changes as well. What is the relationship between age and the political composition of one's social network? There are additional data from the General Social Survey (GSS) (National Opinion Research Center, 1989) regarding social networks that can be used to address this question. The 1987 GSS posed some questions directed toward the political composition of the respondent's social networks.[6] The GSS questions asked (among other things) about two characteristics of social networks: (1) the extent to which the respondent's social network is similar in political orientation to the respondent in terms of party identification, and (2) the extent to which the respondent talks to members of her network "about political matters."[7]

In table 9.6 we present figures for white respondents relating age to these two variables from the 1987 GSS—the extent of network similarity with regard to party identification, and the extent to which the respondent converses with network members about political matters.[8] In both instances these trajectories of network intactness seem to increase with age through age 64 and then decline in older age. Network similarity reaches a peak similarity of nearly 50 percent of the network in the 55–64 age range. It declines systematically beyond that point. Similarly, the extent of political interchange seems to peak in the 55–64 age range, declining to earlier levels from that point onward. However, if we follow Morgan's (1988) strategy of controlling statistically for several measures of social resources

6. These network questions were designed by a committee made up of Duane Alwin, Larry Bobo, James Davis, David Knoke, Thomas Gutterbach, and Tom Smith on behalf of the GSS Board of Overseers. See Marsden (1987) for a discussion of survey-based measures of social network composition.

7. The 1987 GSS network data are not as extensive as the 1985 GSS data analyzed by Morgan (1988; see also Marsden, 1987). However, the 1987 series of questions does deal with the political composition of the network and is therefore more useful for our present purposes.

8. We follow the practice established in chapter 5 of limiting our analyses to white respondents only because of the virtual absence of minority-group members in the Bennington sample. This provides a more precise comparison point for our analysis of the Bennington data.

Table 9.6. Age and Political Network Variables:
General Social Survey, 1987
($N = 1,179$)

Age	Percent with Same Party ID		Frequency of Talking Politics	
	Mean	Adj. Mean	Mean	Adj. Mean
18–24	39.9	39.9	1.8	1.8
25–34	37.8	39.8	1.8	1.8
35–44	43.2	39.9	2.2	1.9
45–54	49.4	40.0	2.0	1.9
55–64	48.4	39.9	2.5	1.9
65–74	44.4	39.9	2.4	1.9
75+	43.7	39.9	1.9	1.9
Total				
F	2.00	1.15	4.20	1.94
df	1,154		1,154	
P	.03		.00	

Note: Increment to R^2 was *ns* for both party ID ($F = 1.15$) and talking politics ($F = 1.94$).

(income, schooling, and health) that differentiate these age categories, the observed differences are removed. In other words, the *adjusted means* in table 9.6 show very few significant differences once age-group differences in compositional factors are taken into account, suggesting that the nature of political networks may be relatively constant over the life cycle.

Unfortunately, because of the nature of these data, we are not able to sort out the complex reciprocal influences that produce these correlations. We cannot tell, for example, whether the correlations between significant others and the respondent are present because people *select* compatible environments, or whether these measures correlate because the respondent's environments are primarily supportive and not a major source of attitude change. Moreover, we cannot tell whether this similarity between attitudes of the person and the attitudes in her environment is due to the lessened role of change coming from *incompatible* environments, or because such selected environments help maintain attitudes over time. Thus, as above, we approach the problem of assessing the role of environmental factors somewhat differently. Instead of trying to sort out the causality involved, we rely on available theory to help specify levels of theoretically relevant factors, which act as "conditioning" variables in the sense that they identify subgroups in our sample that theoretically should show different degrees of attitude change. In the remainder of the chapter we consider three sets of factors thought to affect the extent of attitude change: (1) the supportiveness of the marital relationship in helping maintain existing attitudes, (2) similarity to friends and its consequences for supporting attitudes, and (3) intergenerational differences and the persistence of attitudes.

THE SIMILARITY OF SOCIAL NETWORK TIES

As we indicated above, as well as in chapter 3, the main lines of argument which Newcomb and his colleagues (1967) advanced for the high degree of stability in sociopolitical orientations between college and midlife involved the supportive nature of the social environment. They looked carefully at two different aspects of the political complexion of the social networks: the attitudes of husbands and those of best friends. They concluded that "the women who had not changed their political attitudes since college had, to a greater extent, moved into a social environment which supported their existing political viewpoints" (1967:65).

Similarity to Spouses

Newcomb and his colleagues (1967) argued that the influence of the husband on the attitudes of the wife was most frequently indirect—via providing support for wives' existing attitudes—rather than direct, in the sense of causing their wives' attitudes to change. They noted that "very few couples, as of 1960–61, held opposing preferences for political parties" (1967:65), suggesting that both processes of support and change resulted in a substantial amount of harmony in political views between wives and husbands.[9]

This harmony between wives and husbands is demonstrated by the figures presented in table 9.7, which result from the cross-tabulation of the respondent's candidate preferences with those she reported for her spouse for the presidential elections since 1940. We present results based on both the 1960s and 1984 reports for the 1940 through 1960 elections. These results indicate a high degree of similarity of candidate preference between married respondents and their husbands, especially among those respondents reporting conservative orientations, where with few exceptions, 90

9. We should point out that Newcomb and his colleagues' (1967) analysis of social support was based on the interview follow-up data only, and was therefore based on data from about 90 couples. Also, recall that the interview subsample was composed of graduates from the classes of 1938, 1939, and 1940. For both of these reasons, we caution against overgeneralizing the conclusions of Newcomb and his colleagues (1967).

Table 9.7. Respondent and Husband Candidate Preference, 1940 through 1980

	Respondent			
	Obtained in 1984		Obtained in 1960s	
Husband	Liberal	Conservative	Liberal	Conservative
1940				
Liberal	80.9%	4.1%	81.0%	13.3%
Conservative	19.1%	95.9%	19.0%	86.7%
Total n	(68)	(49)	(105)	(128)
1944				
Liberal	84.1%	11.9%	81.1%	16.0%
Conservative	15.9%	88.1%	18.9%	84.0%
Total n	(132)	(59)	(159)	(100)
1948				
Liberal	82.1%	9.1%	85.7%	8.9%
Conservative	17.9%	90.9%	14.3%	91.1%
Total n	(151)	(77)	(133)	(135)
1952				
Liberal	81.8%	8.5%	80.7%	8.2%
Conservative	18.2%	91.5%	19.3%	91.8%
Total n	(137)	(117)	(135)	(159)
1956				
Liberal	80.0%	7.0%	87.1%	5.2%
Conservative	20.0%	93.0%	12.9%	94.8%
Total n	(150)	(100)	(139)	(153)
1960				
Liberal	83.3%	6.7%	85.0%	8.8%
Conservative	16.7%	93.3%	15.0%	91.2%
Total n	(180)	(75)	(153)	(136)
1964				
Liberal	85.3%	9.8%	—	—
Conservative	14.7%	90.2%	—	—
Total n	(184)	(51)		

(continued on following page)

221

Table 9.7. Respondent and Husband Candidate Preference, 1940
through 1980 *(continued)*

| | Respondent | | | |
| | Obtained in 1984 | | Obtained in 1960s | |
Husband	Liberal	Conservative	Liberal	Conservative
		1968		
Liberal	82.5%	7.3%	—	—
Conservative	17.5%	92.7%	—	—
Total *n*	(154)	(82)		
		1972		
Liberal	81.3%	7.5%	—	—
Conservative	18.7%	92.5%	—	—
Total *n*	(155)	(80)		
		1976		
Liberal	83.9%	3.7%	—	—
Conservative	16.1%	96.3%	—	—
Total *n*	(149)	(81)		
		1980		
Liberal	81.8%	10.2%	—	—
Conservative	18.2%	89.8%	—	—
Total *n*	(159)	(59)		

percent or more of those respondents report the same preference for the spouse. A high degree of similarity obtains among those respondents with a liberal orientation in each election year, some 80 percent or more of whom are married to men with the same candidate preference.

Generally speaking, the spouses of the Bennington women tend to be more conservative than their wives by our indicators of political orientations. This can be seen for both the 1960s and 1980s periods using our liberal/conservative rating scales for both surveys in which the respondents rated themselves and their husbands.[10] Table 9.8 presents the percentage of our Bennington respondents with *similar* and *different* husbands, where the distinction is based on whether the respondent's self-rating and her rating of the spouse were identical or not. These results are presented

10. Recall that in the 1960s questionnaire, a five-point rating scale was used, whereas in 1984 we used a seven-point rating scale. For present purposes this difference is probably not important.

Table 9.8. Respondent Estimates of Similarity of
Husband's Liberalism/Conservatism by
Respondent's Candidate Preference, 1960
and 1984 Surveys

	Respondent Candidate Preference, 1960	
	Democrat	Republican
Husband similar	63.6%	53.1%
Husband different		
R more liberal	29.5	27.2
R more conservative	6.8	19.8
Total	100.0%	100.0%
N	(88)	(81)

	Respondent Candidate Preference, 1984	
	Democrat	Republican
Husband similar	39.9%	40.0%
Husband different		
R more liberal	53.2	45.0
R more conservative	6.9	15.0
Total	100.0%	100.0%
N	(203)	(80)

Note: R indicates respondent.

separately by respondent's party preferences in 1960 and 1984. Where the spouse and the respondent are rated as different, we have recorded whether the respondent was more liberal or more conservative than the spouse. In both the 1960s and 1984 data, regardless of their party preference, respondents describe their spouses as more conservative than themselves. Note, however, that roughly 20 percent of those Bennington women who preferred the Republican party in 1960 saw themselves as more conservative than their husbands. This figure was 15 percent in 1984; thus, even though there is a strong tendency for respondents to describe themselves as more liberal than their spouses, there is a significant minority who report the opposite situation.

Similarity to Friends

Newcomb and his colleagues (1967) advanced a similar argument with regard to the political attitudes of friends. They noted that respondents tended to report that most of their friends had political orientations similar to their own, indicating that "women who had friends who were interested

Table 9.9. Respondent Estimates of Similarity of
Friends' Liberalism/Conservatism by
Respondent's Party Preference, 1960
Surveys

	Respondent Party Preference, 1960	
	Democrat	Republican
Friends similar	59.7%	55.1%
Friends different	20.4	18.8
Friends mixed	19.9	26.1
Total	100.0%	100.0%
N	(186)	(138)

in public affairs and who agreed with their own points of view tended to maintain their previous political orientations." Those who had friends who disagreed with them "tended to defend and question their points of view and sometimes changed them" (1967:65).

In the 1960s mailed questionnaire and personal interviews, Newcomb and his colleagues (1967) asked their respondents to indicate the extent to which (1) most of their close friends had political opinions which were similar to theirs, or were they different, and (2) if different, in what way? Table 9.9 presents the results of responses to the first question separately by categories of respondents' party preference in 1960.[11] These results indicate substantial similarities between the respondents and their friends, but not the same degree of similarity seen between the Bennington women and their husbands in the 1960s. Regardless of party preference, upwards of 55 percent of the Bennington women perceive their friends as having the same political orientation as themselves. Another 20–26 percent see a mixture of political orientations among their friends, and roughly one-fifth see their friends as different.

By replicating the procedures concerning similarity to husbands, we can use our 1984 seven-point liberal/conservative rating scale to assess similarity to friends. In the 1984 questionnaire we asked respondents to rate three of their closest friends or relatives (not including their spouses or children) on our seven-point scale. We also asked respondents to indicate whether these close friends tended to agree or disagree with them on political matters and their party identification. In table 9.10 we present the responses to these questions.

These results indicate once again the high degree of similarity between

11. Party preference in 1960 is assessed via candidate preference in the 1960 presidential election.

Table 9.10. Reports of Political Orientations of Friends, Bennington Respondents (R), 1984

Friend	R Republican			R Independent			R Democrat		
	1	2	3	1	2	3	1	2	3
Talk about politics?									
% Yes	67.5%	60.3%	70.1%	62.3%	70.0%	70.0%	89.7%	82.1%	75.9%
Agree about politics?									
% Agree	80.5	84.7	77.0	62.5	58.9	66.3	79.7	78.4	76.2
Friend's party ID									
Republican	71.1	77.8	64.9	41.5	38.3	39.6	11.5	16.1	22.8
Independent	15.8	12.5	14.9	37.2	34.0	30.8	22.3	13.9	14.7
Democrat	13.2	9.7	20.3	21.3	27.7	29.7	66.2	70.1	62.5
R's L/C vs. friend's									
Friend same	35.5	32.9	24.7	21.4	28.0	29.8	39.9	41.3	32.4
R more conservative	36.8	34.2	54.8	16.3	23.0	16.0	11.8	11.6	11.8
R more liberal	27.6	32.9	20.5	62.2	49.0	54.3	49.3	47.1	55.9
N	(80)	(78)	(77)	(106)	(106)	(100)	(146)	(145)	(141)

the Bennington women and their close friends in 1984. Certainly among those classified as Republican and Democrat, the overwhelming majority of friends have an identical party identification. Moreover, the Bennington respondents indicate that there is a high degree of agreement about politics amongst them and their friends and that frequent discussions of political issues go on between these women and their friends. Interestingly, among those women who identify themselves as independent there is genuine heterogeneity in the party preferences of their best friends.

Thus, our results confirm those presented earlier by Newcomb and his colleagues (1967): close friends represent a potential source of support for sociopolitical attitudes. Of course, similarity to friends can result from one or both of two processes: either the friendship formation process helps select friends according to their similarity to the individual in terms of political ideas, or the incompatibility of political attitudes creates a basis for the inducement of attitude change toward increased similarity. It could be, for example, that people change their attitudes to bring them into line with those around them, when efforts to change others have failed. Whatever its source, however, there is a substantial amount of similarity between our Bennington women and their social network ties in terms of sociopolitical orientations.

Political Attitudes of Husbands, Friends, and Children

Finally, in order to show the degree of similarity between the sociopolitical attitudes of our Bennington respondents and significant others in their en-

Table 9.11. Correlations between Respondent's Measures of Political Conservatism and Measures of Significant Others' Political Conservatism in 1960 and 1984

Respondent	Husband's 1940s Measures					
	HPID40					
PEP30	.346					
PID40	.471					

	Friends' and Husband's 1960s Measures					
	FRPCI60	HBL/C60	HBPCI60	HBPID60		
PEP60	.533[a]	.620	.553[a]	.568		
PCI60	.593	.433	.796	.404		
PID60	.443	.597	.687	.671		
L/C60	.479	.717	.644	.562		

	Friends', Husband's, and Children's 1984 Measures					
	FRI/C84	FRPID84[b]	HBI/C84	HBPID84	CHL/C84	CHPID84[b]
PEP84	.319	.325	.302	.326	.311	.369
PCI84	.508	.504	.564	.611	.523	.507
PID84	.481	.541	.585	.731	.567	.698
L/C84	.604	.550	.632	.623	.603	.596

Note: $p < .001$ for all measures.
[a]PEP60 for these two correlations is based on the retrospective PEP60 obtained in 1984.
[b]These are actual party ID coded: 1 = Democrat, 2 = independent and no preference, 3 = Republican.

vironments, we present in table 9.11 correlations between the respondent's political attitudes and her reports of those of her husband, her friends, and (in 1984) her children. For the period of the 1930s and 1940s, the only indicator we have of the attitudes of others is the respondent's report of the party preference of her husband.[12] The 1960s survey includes three measures of the husband's political attitudes: respondent's rating of husband's political orientation on the five-point liberal/conservative scale (HBLC60), husband's score on the political conservatism scale (HBPCI60) (see chapter 4), and husband's political party preference (HBPID60), defined in the same manner as the measure of respondent's political party preference (see chapter 4). In the 1960s survey we also have a measure of the respondent's friends' political conservatism index (FRPCI60) (see chapter 4). In the 1984 questionnaire we included several measures of friends' and husbands'

12. We use the candidate preference in the 1940 presidential election as a measure of the husband's party preference. Here we use the 1960s report if it is available; if not, we use the 1984 report of husband's preference.

attitudes toward social and political affairs. We included the respondents' ratings of their husbands and their friends on the seven-point rating scale (FRL/C84 and HBL/C84), and husbands' and friends' political party preference (FRPID84 and HBPID84).[13] In 1984 we included measures of the liberal/conservative rating for the respondent's children (CHL/C84) and the respondent's children's political party preferences (CHPID84).[14]

The correlations presented in table 9.11 are uniformly positive and highly significant from a statistical point of view. They all indicate a high degree of similarity between the respondent and her significant others in terms of political orientations. Of course, these correlations would be even higher if we had corrected for measurement error. There is some indication that correlations between the person's attitudes and those of her significant others increase with time. Specifically, the data from the 1940s reveal the lowest correlations. The correlations in the later years are slightly higher but are roughly the same between time periods.

The similarities reported and discussed throughout this chapter depend, of course, on our respondents' *reports* of the attitudes of spouses, friends, and children. We must always consider the possibility that respondents report much more similarity than there actually is; that is, they may perceive those close to them as having more similar attitudes than they actually do. Though we cannot assess the degree to which this may be the case, such a possibility is consistent with our earlier finding that respondents distort their own retrospective reports of their attitudes (candidate preferences) in the service of consistency (see chapter 6). In addition, though our own evidence on centrality suggests otherwise, it is possible that this tendency to overestimate similarity may be particularly characteristic of those for whom political attitudes are most salient or central—those who have the greatest "stake" in them.

These patterns, coupled with the common assumption that constancy in social networks may contribute to homophily in attitudes and behaviors (Feld, 1982), lead to the expectation that there is considerable potential for social networks to support substantial amounts of attitude persistence into the mature years and that, with aging, network instabilities do not necessarily reduce the supportiveness of that set of micro-environments. Indeed, assuming that the figures in table 9.6 represent the social network characteristics of the Bennington women, these results support the notion of persistence in the Bennington sample through our period of observa-

13. Husbands' and friends' political party preference are measured for present purposes as follows: 3 = Republican preference, 2 = independent or no preference, 1 = Democratic preference.

14. Children's measures are averaged over the respondent's reports for each of her children.

tion, as the Bennington women were roughly between 65 and 70 years of age at the time we interviewed them in 1984 (see table 5.9).

SOCIAL SUPPORT AND ATTITUDE STABILITY

To this point we have discussed two main sources of network similarity—similarity to spouse and similarity to close friends—and have shown that there is a substantial amount of correlation between the sociopolitical orientations of our respondents and those of members of their social networks. As noted, the nature of our data makes it very difficult to pinpoint the direction of this influence; that is, it is not possible to interpret these high levels of similarity and/or correlation among our various measures of respondent's sociopolitical orientations and those of their network members in causal terms. However, regardless of the causal mechanisms that produced these similarities, there is a basis in theory for the hypothesis that greater support for attitudes will exist in environmental contexts exhibiting more similarity to the respondent in terms of the others' political outlooks. Indeed, we would expect greater attitude change over time where there is evidence of an incompatibility between the attitudes of the person and the attitudes represented in the environment. If this is true, we expect it to result from the dual processes of *social selection* and *social support*.

Marriage and the Persistence of Attitudes

One of the most important aspects of social support for attitudes inheres in the marital relationship. The intimacy of marriage and the opportunities it provides for exchanging ideas, opinions, and perspectives generate relatively potent sources of stability and/or change (see Buss, 1984, 1987; Caspi and Herbener, 1990). Virtually all of our Bennington women were married at some point, so it is not possible to compare married versus unmarried respondents. But it is possible to draw comparisons among women in terms of the potential for supportive interchange between themselves and their spouses. In the preceding discussion we referred to the high degree of similarity between the Bennington women and their husbands in terms of political party preferences (see table 9.7). Here we examine the extent of attitude change separately for two categories of women: those whose party preferences were the same as their husbands' over the entire marital history, and those whose party preferences were to some extent different from their husbands' at some time or other.

Using the above units of comparison—similarity of respondent's and husband's party preferences in each presidential election—we can partition our sample into two groups.[15] Then we can estimate our primary model of attitude persistence and change (the same model for which results were presented in table 7.8) for each of these groups, comparing the results. Tables 9.12 and 9.13 present these estimates for those most similar to their husbands in terms of party preferences and those least similar to their husbands, respectively.

Comparing the parameter estimates for our model of attitude change for these two groups of Bennington women, we see that those women whose candidate preferences are identical to their husbands' have, by far, the most stable attitudes over the time period we studied. The coefficient linking the 1930s period with 1984 is .752 (i.e., .829 × .908). This coefficient is considerably higher than the comparable coefficient for the group of women whose husbands were less similar to themselves in party preferences over the life span. The 1930s–1984 stability coefficient for this latter group is .430 (i.e., .658 × .653). Thus, our hypothesis that similarity of social networks is linked to the extent of attitude change is strongly supported. The differences between the two models are statistically significant ($\Delta \chi^2 = 8.1$, $df = 2$, $p = .017$). Indeed, the differences reported here are the largest we have yet witnessed in our examination of the sources of stability and change.

We conclude, therefore, that those women inhabiting marital environments with little political disagreement are much less likely to change their attitudes over their lives than those whose marital environments contain some significant political disagreement. Such disagreement over the preferred presidential candidate is, we suggest, an important basis for attitude change, especially when the discrepancy is long-standing. And, as our evidence indicates, those women with dissimilar spouses were more likely to change their attitudes at some point in their lives. We conclude that perhaps two types of processes working in tandem have helped produce the high degree of attitude stability witnessed throughout our earlier analyses. We suspect that the Bennington women and their husbands made supportive choices through the process of assortative mating, wherein political orientations were a basis of mate selection. That is, men and women are very likely to choose mates who share their own viewpoints on various social and political issues. Then, once selected, spouses play an extremely

---

15. One group of respondents included those whose candidate preferences were always the same as those of their husbands (regardless of the number of elections involved or the number of different husbands). The other group included the remaining respondents, for whom there was at least one election in which their candidate preference and those of their spouses differed.

Table 9.12. Parameter Estimates for a Linear Structural Equations Model of Sociopolitical Orientations across the Life Span: Bennington Women Most Similar to Their Husbands, 1940–80 ($N = 130$)

Predictor Variable	Dependent Variable								
	PEP30	PID30	SPO30	PEP60	PID60	SPO60	PEP84	PID84	SPO84
η_1 1930s sociopolitical orientation	.723**	.739**	—	—	—	.830**	—	—	—
η_2 1960s sociopolitical orientation	—	—	—	.856**	.875**	—	—	—	.917**
η_3 1984 sociopolitical orientation	—	—	—	—	—	—	.601**	.779**	—
x_1 Year entered Bennington	—	—	.258**	—	—	−.201**	—	—	0.0f
x_2 Number of years at Bennington	—	—	−.142*	—	—	0.0f	—	—	0.0f
x_3 Parental orientations	—	—	.642**	—	—	0.0f	—	—	0.0f
R-squared	.509	.547	.543	.736	.765	.616	.371	.606	.841

Note: Based on a model with 18 *df* and a χ^2 of 22.30 ($p = .219$). The model assumed all measurement disturbances were uncorrelated over time, except that the disturbance for the PEP30 was correlated with the disturbances for PEP60 and PEP84, and the disturbance for PID60 was correlated with the disturbance for PID84.

*$p < .05$ **$p < .01$ f = parameter fixed at zero

Table 9.13. Parameter Estimates for a Linear Structural Equations Model of Sociopolitical Orientations across the Life Span: Bennington Women Least Similar to Their Husbands, 1940–1980 (N = 95)

Predictor Variable	Dependent Variable								
	PEP30	PID30	SPO30	PEP60	PID60	SPO60	PEP84	PID84	SPO84
η_1 1930s sociopolitical orientation	.573**	.780**	—	—	—	.658**	—	—	—
η_2 1960s sociopolitical orientation	—	—	—	.892**	.784**	—	—	—	.653**
η_3 1984s sociopolitical orientation	—	—	—	—	—	—	.354**	.860**	—
x_1 Year entered Bennington	—	—	.354**	—	—	−.203	—	—	0.0f
x_2 Number of years at Bennington	—	—	−.107	—	—	0.0f	—	—	0.0f
x_3 Parental orientations	—	—	.609**	—	—	0.0f	—	—	0.0f
R-squared	.322	.609	.563	.813	.614	.360	.145	.753	.426

Note: Based on a model with 18 df and a χ^2 of 36.45 (p = .006). The model assumed all measurement disturbances were uncorrelated over time, except that the disturbance for the PEP30 was correlated with the disturbances for PEP60 and PEP84, and the disturbance for PID60 was correlated with the disturbance for PID84.

$*p < .05$ $**p < .01$ f = parameter fixed at zero

231

important role in helping to maintain a person's attitudes and helping to protect the person from the influences of sources of attitude change.[16] Of course, to the extent that either of these processes does not work to embed the person in a supportive environment, more attitude change is likely, a fact to which our results strongly attest.

Similarity to Friends and Attitude Stability

We assume that, in addition to spouses, friendship ties provide considerable support for sociopolitical attitudes. Friends may represent a weaker set of social influences in this sense, since friendships are more likely to change than ties to spouses. And people may be somewhat more tolerant of differences between friends than among family members. Some friendships may be created out of involvement in political organizations and political activities, which would provide considerable structural basis for social support of sociopolitical orientations. Other friendship ties may result from other social contacts, but regardless of their source, as we indicated above (see table 9.10), there is a substantial amount of similarity in political orientations between members of our Bennington sample and their closest friends.

In order to draw a comparison between those Bennington women with the most politically similar friendships and those with somewhat less similar environments, we divided the Bennington sample into two groups according to their degree of political similarity in 1960 and 1984. We based our index of political similarity in this case simultaneously on information from the 1960s and 1984 questionnaires. As noted above, Newcomb and his colleagues (1967) relied on their 1960s respondents to assess the similarity of these respondents to their friends (see table 9.9). In 1984 we asked our respondents to report their friends' political preferences and then used this as a basis for assessing the degree of similarity. Combining these two sources of information, we partitioned our sample into two groups, estimating our models of attitude change separately within each.[17] These results are presented in tables 9.14 and 9.15.

We hypothesized, as above, that those members of the Bennington

16. These results are corroborated by recent research analyzing married couples from the Berkeley Guidance Study and the Oakland Growth Study. Caspi and Herbener (1990) report that marriage to a similar other promotes greater within-marriage consistency across middle adulthood.

17. We created this index by assigning a 3 in each survey year to those respondents who were judged to have the same party preference, a 2 to those who had friends with a mixture of party preferences, and a 1 to those whose friends' party preferences were all the same, but different from those of the respondents.

Table 9.14. Parameter Estimates for a Linear Structural Equations Model of Sociopolitical Orientations across the Life Span: Bennington Women Most Similar to Their Friends, 1960–80 ($N = 160$)

Predictor Variable	Dependent Variable								
	PEP30	PID30	SPO30	PEP60	PID60	SPO60	PEP84	PID84	SPO84
η_1 1930s sociopolitical orientation	.749**	.762**	—	—	—	.794**	—	—	—
η_2 1960s sociopolitical orientation	—	—	—	.785**	.924**	—	—	—	—
η_3 1984 sociopolitical orientation	—	—	—	—	—	—	.504**	.918**	.967**
x_1 Year entered Bennington	—	—	.208**	—	—	-.158*	—	—	0.0f
x_2 Number of years at Bennington	—	—	-.154*	—	—	0.0f	—	—	0.0f
x_3 Parental orientations	—	—	.690**	—	—	0.0f	—	—	0.0f
R-squared	.553	.581	.544	.627	.854	.601	.268	.843	.935

Note: Based on a model with 18 df and a χ^2 of 30.49 ($p = .033$). The model assumed all measurement disturbances were uncorrelated over time, except that the disturbance for the PEP30 was correlated with the disturbances for PEP60 and PEP84, and the disturbance for PID60 was correlated with the disturbance for PID84.
$*p < .05$ $**p < .01$ f = parameter fixed at zero

233

Table 9.15. Parameter Estimates for a Linear Structural Equations Model of Sociopolitical Orientations across the Life Span: Bennington Women Least Similar to Their Friends, 1960–80 ($N = 158$)

Predictor Variable	Dependent Variable								
	PEP30	PID30	SPO30	PEP60	PID60	SPO60	PEP84	PID84	SPO84
η_1 1930s sociopolitical orientation	.657**	.720**	—	—	—	.804**	—	—	—
η_2 1960s sociopolitical orientation	—	—	—	.911**	.722**	—	—	—	.783**
η_3 1984 sociopolitical orientation	—	—	.394**	—	—	—	.521**	.653**	0.0f
x_1 Year entered Bennington	—	—	—	—	—	−.212**	—	—	0.0f
x_2 Number of years at Bennington	—	—	−.069	—	—	0.0f	—	—	0.0f
x_3 Parental orientations	—	—	.579**	—	—	0.0f	—	—	0.0f
R-squared	.426	.518	.587	.842	.521	.516	.274	.429	.613

Note: Based on a model with 18 *df* and a χ^2 of 25.39 ($p = .114$). The model assumed all measurement disturbances were uncorrelated over time, except that the disturbance for the PEP30 was correlated with the disturbances for PEP60 and PEP84, and the disturbance for PID60 was correlated with the disturbance for PID84.

*$p < .05$ **$p < .01$ f = parameter fixed at zero

sample who were most similar to their friends would show the least attitude change by our estimated parameters, whereas those with the least similar friendship ties would show the most attitude change. This hypothesis is strongly supported in these results. Attitude stability between the 1930s and 1984 is significantly higher for those women with relatively similar friendship networks than for those women with less similar networks ($\Delta\chi^2 = 13.93$, $df = 2$, $p = .001$).

The 1930s–1984 estimated stability coefficient for those women with the least similar friends is .630 (i.e., .804 × .783), whereas the comparable coefficient for those with the most similar friends is .768 (i.e., .794 × .967). This difference is, however, primarily linked to the 1960s–1984 time period, since the 1930s–1960s components of these coefficients are virtually identical. This probably reflects the timing of our measurement rather than anything more fundamental about the processes of attitude persistence and change. Specifically, our measurement of similarity to friends (in contrast to our measures of spouses' similarity) pertains to the 1960s and 1984. We have no measures of friendship similarity prior to 1960. Thus, we suspect that our inability to locate much difference in attitude stability between the two groups formed by our measures during the 1930s and 1960s stems from the imprecision of measuring friendship similarity during this period. For the period we have more precisely assessed—the 1960s and 1984—we find substantial differences in attitude stability and change.

Intergenerational Influences and Attitude Change

We concluded in chapter 7 that one of the most important influences on young people's sociopolitical orientations is the parental family. Although offspring in their young adult years, such as the young Bennington women, clearly form distinct and autonomous ideas about the social and political issues of their day, there is a substantial amount of transmission of basic values and orientations across generations. In the Bennington data, the strongest estimated influence on 1930s sociopolitical orientations in our earlier models (see chapter 7) was from parents' political liberalism/conservatism. As we indicated previously, this finding is consistent with a growing body of literature which suggests that there is considerable value similarity across generations (e.g., Bengtson, 1975; Glass, Bengtson, and Dunham, 1986).

We believe that intergenerational influences are transmitted from child to parent as well as from parent to child (Bronfenbrenner, 1979). Thus, the Bennington women were not only influenced by their parents (and presumably vice versa), they were also potentially influenced by their children. In

Table 9.16. Distribution of Birth Years for Children Born to the
Bennington Sample, Based on 1984 Survey Reports

Birth Cohort	Age in 1984	N	Percent
1930–34	50–54	3	0.3%
1935–39	45–49	30	3.3
1940–44	40–44	216	23.4
1945–49	35–39	316	34.3
1950–54	30–34	239	25.9
1955–59	25–29	96	10.4
1960–64	20–24	18	2.0
1965 and after	<20	4	0.4
Total		922	100.0%

the case of the Bennington women, this is a unique set of potential influences, since their children became politically aware during a rather volatile historic period, namely the 1960s. Of course, it is very difficult to sort out the causal directionality of the intergenerational similarities observed empirically. Correlational similarity between the Bennington women and their children, as revealed in table 9.11, could indicate either that these women had some influence on the development of the sociopolitical orientations of their children, or that their children developed distinct attitudes and had some influence on their parents in later life, or both.

In chapter 5 we suggested that in addition to the cohorts born between 1915 and 1924 (the birth cohorts to which the Bennington women belong), the 1945–54 birth cohorts reveal a considerable concentration of liberal attitudes. We indicated that since the children of the Bennington women were mainly born during these years, and because these were the age groups that achieved political maturity during the 1960s, the liberal views of this generation may have acted to help maintain the attitudes of their mothers over the mature years of life. We suspect therefore that those Bennington women who had children growing up during that period are more likely to have maintained liberal attitudes than those who had less exposure to the children of this generation.

The overwhelming majority of the children born to the Bennington women were born between 1940 and 1955—some 84 percent (table 9.16). Sufficient numbers of the Bennington sample had children—more than 90 percent—that we concluded that intergenerational similarities and differences are important potential sources of attitude stability and change.

We estimated the extent of liberalism/conservatism in the children of the Bennington women. In anticipation of the importance of the attitudes of children in promoting attitude stability, in our 1984 survey we asked respondents to provide information on the nature of their children's attitudes. We asked them to rate (for up to six children) each child's standing on our seven-point liberal/conservative scale. We also asked them to indicate whether they thought their children agreed with them on political matters, the extent to which they talked to their children about political issues, and the party identification of their children.

By and large, the children of the Bennington women are slightly more liberal than the larger birth cohorts of which they are a part. This can be seen by comparing the *percent Republican* figures given in table 9.17 with pertinent figures from table 5.12. For example, while 35 percent of the birth cohorts born in 1945–54 prefer the Republican party (fewer than all other cohorts; see table 5.12), only 24 percent of the children of the Bennington women from the 1945–54 cohorts have a Republican preference. Generally speaking, the children of the Bennington women can be considered slightly more liberal than others in their age groups, which are themselves slightly more liberal than other cohorts.

These patterns could be considered evidence that the Bennington women had some influence on their children, but proof of such influence is very difficult to establish in this context. Perhaps more interesting in this regard, however, is the potency of the influence of the children on their mothers' sociopolitical orientations. Is it possible that this generation's influence was an important component of the process of attitude persistence and change we have here uncovered? Such influence could be felt directly, in the sense that children may stimulate attitude change, or it could be felt indirectly, through providing support for parental attitudes.

Similarity to Children and Attitude Stability

Table 9.17 presents the data we obtained from our inquiries into the political orientations of our respondents' children *by birth order*. These results indicate that the children of the Bennington women are by no means as liberal as their mothers, despite the fact that they are predominantly liberal in their orientations. But, as we observed above, there is a substantial extent of intergenerational persistence of political orientations. In sum, there is a considerable amount of similarity between these women and their children. Extremely high levels of perceived intergenerational agreement is registered broadly in the reports of party identification, perceived agreement, and the liberal/conservative 1–7 rating scale. Using our seven-point liberal/conservative ratings, the children of Bennington Republicans (as registered in 1984 party preference) tend to be more liberal, if they are different from their mothers. Children of Bennington Democrats tend to be either the same political orientation, or slightly more conservative. In

Table 9.17. Reports of Political Orientations of Children, Bennington Respondents (R), 1984

	Respondent Party ID, 1984											
	Republican				Independent				Democrat			
Child	1st	2nd	3rd	4th	1st	2nd	3rd	4th	1st	2nd	3rd	4th
Talk about politics?												
% Yes	57.1%	65.3%	60.0%	54.8%	64.3%	49.5%	56.9%	53.6%	80.3%	78.6%	80.0%	72.4%
Agree about politics?												
% Agree	81.4	81.7	81.8	76.7	70.0	73.5	83.6	86.4	83.1	86.2	84.5	95.7
Child's party ID												
Republican	69.8	64.1	75.6	66.7	12.7	16.2	12.3	21.2	12.8	5.7	8.3	12.1
Independent	12.7	16.2	12.3	22.7	58.2	62.2	64.9	59.1	29.9	26.7	25.0	18.2
Democrat	12.8	5.7	8.3	0.0	29.9	21.6	22.8	23.1	57.3	67.6	66.7	76.9
Child's political viewpoint												
Child same	27.3	33.8	26.5	31.3	36.7	39.7	34.9	36.4	36.1	47.7	45.6	40.0
R more conservative	56.1	53.3	46.9	40.6	16.7	12.8	17.5	31.8	16.8	14.0	11.8	8.0
R more liberal	16.7	12.3	26.5	28.1	46.7	47.4	47.6	31.8	47.1	38.3	42.6	52.0
N	(77)	(72)	(55)	(31)	(98)	(91)	(72)	(28)	(127)	(117)	(75)	(29)

Note: Column heads (1st, 2nd, etc.) refer to birth order.

both cases there is a tendency for children to be seen as more aligned with the center: children of conservatives more likely to be liberal, and children of liberals more likely to be seen as more conservative. This should not be surprising, given the modest levels of absolute agreement with regard to this 1–7 liberal/conservative scale.

In order to examine the linkage between the supportiveness of children's sociopolitical orientations and the extent of attitude stability and change, we partitioned the Bennington sample into two groups: one in which mother and children had the same political orientation, and one in which they were dissimilar. We defined intergenerational similarity in terms of agreement between mother and all of her children with respect to the three-ply party preference designation: Democrat, Republican, or independent.[18] Then, in order to test the hypothesis of social support with respect to similarity of children, we defined a variable that was made up of the percentage of children who agreed with the individual.[19]

Tables 9.18 and 9.19 present our separate estimates of our model of attitude stability and change for these two groups of respondents. These results indicate some difference in the attitude-change process between these groups, though not in the predicted direction. Among those with very similar children, the 1930s to 1984 stability coefficient is .593 (i.e., .698 × .849), whereas the comparable coefficient for the dissimilar groups is .713 (i.e., .857 × .832). (The difference is not statistically significant $[\Delta\chi^2 = 3.72, df = 2, p = .156]$.) Moreover, the main component of difference between these two groups shows a lower level of attitude stability among those most similar for the 1930s–1960s time period, which is of limited relevance to the consideration of the influence of children on their mothers. The 1960s had not yet happened to affect this time period, and the children of the Bennington women would have been too young to have had any influence on that period. Thus, we conclude that the overall results indicate a high degree of uniformity in the patterns of attitude change across categories defined in terms of similarity to children.

18. In this analysis, as elsewhere in this chapter, we include those who responded *no preference* in the category of independents, as this was a very small number and will not affect the proportions substantially.

19. Our index measured the extent of agreement between the respondent and the children with whom she talked politics. We defined the relevant network of children as those with whom the respondent talked about politics. Then, using a three-category party identification variable (Democratic, Republican or independent), we calculated the percentage of the child network that was exactly the same as the respondent. A similarity of 100 percent would exist if every one of the respondent's children had exactly the same party identification as the respondent. Approximately one-half of our sample had exactly the same party identification; the remainder had some dissimilarity between mother and children.

Table 9.18. Parameter Estimates for a Linear Structural Equations Model of Sociopolitical Orientations across the Life Span: Bennington Women Most Politically Similar to Their Children ($N = 106$)

Predictor Variable	Dependent Variable								
	PEP30	PID30	SPO30	PEP60	PID60	SPO60	PEP84	PID84	SPO84
η_1 1930s sociopolitical orientation	.591**	.747**	—	—	—	.698**	—	—	—
η_2 1960s sociopolitical orientation	—	—	—	.766**	.994**	—	—	—	.849**
η_3 1984 sociopolitical orientation	—	—	—	—	—	—	.580**	.939**	—
x_1 Year entered Bennington	—	—	.248**	—	—	−.067	—	—	0.0f
x_2 Number of years at Bennington	—	—	−.094	—	—	0.0f	—	—	0.0f
x_3 Parental orientations	—	—	.656**	—	—	0.0f	—	—	0.0f
R-squared	.342	.558	.540	.604	.988	.461	.362	.883	.721

Note: Based on a model with 18 df and a χ^2 of 44.78 ($p = .000$). The model assumed all measurement disturbances were uncorrelated over time, except that the disturbance for the PEP30 was correlated with the disturbances for PEP60 and PEP84, and the disturbance for PID60 was correlated with the disturbance for PID84.

*$p < .05$ **$p < .01$ f = parameter fixed at zero

Table 9.19. Parameter Estimates for a Linear Structural Equations Model of Sociopolitical Orientations across the Life Span: Bennington Women Least Politically Similar to Their Children ($N = 129$)

Predictor Variable	Dependent Variable								
	PEP30	PID30	SPO30	PEP60	PID60	SPO60	PEP84	PID84	SPO84
η_1 1930s sociopolitical orientation	.831**	.792**	—	—	—	.857**	—	—	—
η_2 1960s sociopolitical orientation	—	—	—	.939**	.760**	—	—	—	.832**
η_3 1984 sociopolitical orientation	—	—	—	—	—	—	.462**	.701**	—
x_1 Year entered Bennington	—	—	.247**	—	—	−.318**	—	—	0.0f
x_2 Number of years at Bennington	—	—	−.045	—	—	0.0f	—	—	0.0f
x_3 Parental orientations	—	—	.684**	—	—	0.0f	—	—	0.0f
R-squared	.683	.628	.557	.879	.577	.670	.215	.491	.692

Note: Based on a model with 18 *df* and a χ^2 of 25.73 ($p = .106$). The model assumed all measurement disturbances were uncorrelated over time, except that the disturbance for the PEP30 was correlated with the disturbances for PEP60 and PEP84, and the disturbance for PID60 was correlated with the disturbance for PID84.

*$p < .05$ **$p < .01$ f = parameter fixed at zero

Exposure to the 1960s Generation

The overwhelming majority of the children of the Bennington women were born between 1940 and 1954 and were liberal in their orientation to political matters (see tables 9.16 and 9.17). Thus, it is important to examine the effect of the number of children *born in this period*, since we assume that the amount of influence is proportional to the volume of exposure, which varies with the number of children. We approached the question of the influence of children on attitude change of the Bennington women by partitioning our sample into three groups: those with no children or one, those with two or three children, and those with four or more children *born between 1940 and 1954*. It was thought that the influence of the children would be the greatest among those women with the most children growing up during this period and least among those women with the fewest (or no) children.

In table 9.20 we present data from our inquiries about children's political orientations arrayed by birth cohort, again for categories of mother's party preference in 1984. These data provide some hint of a liberal bias among the cohort of "Bennington children" born between 1945 and 1954. For example, children of Republican mothers born between 1945 and 1954 are slightly less Republican in their orientation than other cohorts, and substantially more Democratic choices occur among the children of independent and Democratic mothers for this cohort of children than for the others. The evidence in this regard, however, is not overwhelming, and we therefore claim only a "hint" of support for the hypothesis that the children had an influence on the attitudes of their mothers. Thus, as noted, we hypothesized that those women more exposed to the 1960s generation would reveal the greatest amount of attitude change.

As in the previous analyses, we here compare the parameter estimates for our model of attitude persistence and change (see table 7.8) for the three categories of exposure to children from the 1960s generation. Tables 9.21 and 9.22 present the results for the two extreme categories: those with most exposure to this generation versus those with the least exposure. As hypothesized, those with the most exposure to children maturing during this era show the greatest attitude change between the 1960s and 1984. The path coefficient representing stability between these times for women with the greatest exposure to this generation is .71, whereas those with least exposure show a high degree of stability, a coefficient of .94. These results are not statistically significant ($\Delta\chi^2 = 1.69$, $df = 4$, $p = .793$), however. We, thus, conclude that while children seem to have the potential to influence the development of political attitudes in their mothers, we have not been able to find strong evidence for such an effect. We suspect that

Table 9.20. Reports of Political Orientations of Children by Birth Cohort, Bennington Respondents (R), 1984

	Respondent Party ID, 1984								
	Republican			Independent			Democrat		
Child Birth Cohort	1955–64	1945–54	1934–44	1955–64	1945–54	1934–44	1955–64	1945–54	1934–44
Talk about politics?									
% Yes	52.2%	63.2%	59.4%	59.5%	55.2%	34.6%	87.2%	77.4%	71.4%
Agree about politics?									
% Agree	75.0	83.2	84.8	75.8	79.4	82.4	94.1	85.5	84.4
Child's party ID									
Republican	78.9	61.9	74.3	34.2	13.6	18.2	8.1	5.6	12.9
Independent	10.5	24.8	11.4	57.9	61.2	68.2	45.9	24.6	22.6
Democrat	10.5	13.3	14.3	7.9	25.2	13.6	45.9	69.7	64.5
Child's political viewpoint									
Child same	36.4	29.2	28.6	35.1	36.2	52.4	55.9	47.2	34.4
R more conservative	40.9	50.9	45.7	16.2	18.1	4.8	14.7	12.7	6.2
R more liberal	22.7	19.8	25.7	48.1	45.7	42.8	29.4	40.1	59.4
N	(23)	(117)	(37)	(42)	(134)	(26)	(39)	(155)	(35)

Table 9.21. Parameter Estimates for a Linear Structural Equations Model of Sociopolitical Orientations across the Life Span: Bennington Women Most Exposed to Children of the 1960s Era ($N = 83$)

Predictor Variable	Dependent Variable								
	PEP30	PID30	SPO30	PEP60	PID60	SPO60	PEP84	PID84	SPO84
η_1 1930s sociopolitical orientation	.746**	.604**	—	—	—	.869**	—	—	—
η_2 1960s sociopolitical orientation	—	—	—	.951**	.688**	—	—	—	.712**
η_3 1984 sociopolitical orientation	—	—	—	—	—	—	.549**	.729**	—
x_1 Year entered Bennington	—	—	.188	—	—	−.013	—	—	0.0f
x_2 Number of years at Bennington	—	—	−.127	—	—	0.0f	—	—	0.0f
x_3 Parental orientations	—	—	.602**	—	—	0.0f	—	—	0.0f
R-squared	.549	.365	.438	.905	.474	.749	.299	.590	.506

Note: Based on a model with 18 df and a χ^2 of 23.24 ($p = .181$). The model assumed all measurement disturbances were uncorrelated over time, except that the disturbance for the PEP30 was correlated with the disturbances for PEP60 and PEP84, and the disturbance for PID60 was correlated with the disturbance for PID84.

*$p < .05$ **$p < .01$ f = parameter fixed at zero

Table 9.22. Parameter Estimates for a Linear Structural Equations Model of Sociopolitical Orientations across the Life Span: Bennington Women Least Exposed to Children of the 1960s Era ($N = 86$)

Predictor Variable	Dependent Variable								
	PEP30	PID30	SPO30	PEP60	PID60	SPO60	PEP84	PID84	SPO84
η_1 1930s sociopolitical orientation	.729**	.858**	—	—	—	.828**	—	—	—
η_2 1960s sociopolitical orientation	—	—	—	.838**	.932**	—	—	—	—
η_3 1984 sociopolitical orientation	—	—	—	—	—	—	.560**	.844**	.944**
x_1 Year entered Bennington	—	—	.394**	—	—	-.338**	—	—	0.0f
x_2 Number of years at Bennington	—	—	-.064	—	—	0.0f	—	—	0.0f
x_3 Parental orientations	—	—	.677**	—	—	0.0f	—	—	0.0f
R-squared	.373	.737	.620	.699	.868	.577	.315	.712	.891

Note: Based on a model with 18 df and a χ^2 of 67.78 ($p = .000$). The model assumed all measurement disturbances were uncorrelated over time, except that the disturbance for the PEP30 was correlated with the disturbance for the PEP60 and PEP84, and the disturbance for PID60 was correlated with the disturbance for PID84.

*$p < .05$ **$p < .01$ f = parameter fixed at zero

the process may be more complicated than our measurements have been able to specify. Clearly, further work is needed on this question.

Similarity to Social Networks in 1984 and Attitude Stability

Interest in a final comparison of those Bennington women with supportive social environments and those with somewhat less supportive environments led us to divide the sample into two groups based on a measure of political similarity to their entire social network obtained in 1984. In order to test this hypothesis in the present context, we defined a variable that was comprised of the information regarding the respondent estimates of husbands', best friends', and children's political liberalism/conservatism, along with information obtained in 1984 regarding whether the respondent discussed political matters with each of these people. Our index of similarity to social networks was based on a weighted sum of these estimates.[20] Then, as above, we examined the key parameters of our primary model of attitude persistence and change, which we have relied upon heretofore. This model was estimated separately in the two groups: those with politically similar networks and those without. These results are presented in tables 9.23 and 9.24.

Our hypothesis that there would be substantially more attitude change among those with less similar social networks is upheld in these results. They show that attitude stability is generally higher for those most similar to members of their network than it is for those less politically similar. In the high-similarity group (see table 9.23) the coefficient of stability linking the 1930s and 1984 is .713 (i.e., .772 × .924), whereas in the low-similarity group (see table 9.24) the comparable coefficient is .550 (i.e., .767 × .717). Inspection of the components of these stability estimates reveals that the lower degree of stability in the low-similarity category is due primarily to the difference between the groups in the stability of attitudes between the 1960s and 1984. The difference is highly significant ($\Delta\chi^2 = 6.90$, $df = 2$, $p = .032$). Again, we suspect that the finding of significant differences only in the degree of stability and change in the period between the 1960s and 1984, not in the period from the 1930s to the 1960s, stems from the fact

20. Our index was defined as follows: we defined the relevant social network as those family and friends with whom the respondent talked about political matters (husband, children, and best friends). Then using a three-category party identification variable (Democratic, Republican, or independent), we calculated the percentage of the network that had exactly the same party identification as the respondent. A similarity of 100 percent would exist if every member of the respondent's social network was identical to her in terms of party identification. Zero similarity would exist if none of the respondent's social network agreed with her in terms of party identification.

Table 9.23. Parameter Estimates for a Linear Structural Equations Model of Sociopolitical Orientations across the Life Span: Bennington Women with Most Politically Similar Networks in 1984 ($N = 120$)

Predictor Variable	Dependent Variable								
	PEP30	PID30	SPO30	PEP60	PID60	SPO60	PEP84	PID84	SPO84
η_1 1930s sociopolitical orientation	.685**	.761**	—	—	—	.773**	—	—	—
η_2 1960s sociopolitical orientation			—	.855**	.940**	—	—	—	.924**
η_3 1984 sociopolitical orientation—			—			—	.558**	.946**	—
x_1 Year entered Bennington			.333**			−.121			0.0f
x_2 Number of years at Bennington			−.098			0.0f			0.0f
x_3 Parental orientations			.658**			0.0f			0.0f
R-squared	.471	.579	.590	.751	.884	.537	.329	.898	.853

Note: Based on a model with 18 df and a χ^2 of 44.65 ($p = .000$). The model assumed all measurement disturbances were uncorrelated over time, except that the disturbance for the PEP30 was correlated with the disturbances for PEP60 and PEP84, and the disturbance for PID60 was correlated with the disturbance for PID84.

*$p < .05$ **$p < .01$ f = parameter fixed at zero

247

Table 9.24. Parameter Estimates for a Linear Structural Equations Model of Sociopolitical Orientations across the Life Span: Bennington Women with Least Politically Similar Networks in 1984 ($N = 124$)

Predictor Variable	Dependent Variable								
	PEP30	PID30	SPO30	PEP60	PID60	SPO60	PEP84	PID84	SPO84
η_1 1930s sociopolitical orientation	.719**	.755**	—	.866**	.772**	.767**	—	—	—
η_2 1960s sociopolitical orientation	—	—	—	—	—	—	.573**	.624**	.717**
η_3 1984 sociopolitical orientation	—	—	.244**	—	—	—	—	—	—
x_1 Year entered Bennington	—	—	.244**	—	—	−.276**	—	—	0.0f
x_2 Number of years at Bennington	—	—	−.097	—	—	0.0f	—	—	0.0f
x_3 Parental orientations	—	—	.657**	—	—	0.0f	—	—	0.0f
R-squared	.486	.571	.529	.740	.595	.539	.338	.368	.514

Note: Based on a model with 18 df and a χ^2 of 49.41 ($p = .000$). The model assumed all measurement disturbances were uncorrelated over time, except that the disturbance for the PEP30 was correlated with the disturbances for PEP60 and PEP84, and the disturbance for PID60 was correlated with the disturbance for PID84.

$*p < .05$ $**p < .01$ f = parameter fixed at zero

that our measures explicitly focus on network composition in 1984, and not necessarily any time earlier. This adds even stronger support to our hypothesis, in that the difference in attitude change is tied to the time specificity of our measures.

OPPORTUNITIES FOR ATTITUDE STABILITY AND CHANGE

In this chapter we have examined the hypothesis that differences in opportunities for attitude change help explain differences in attitude stability and change. We have examined two broad sets of factors: those linked to differential exposure to change-inducing experiences and those linked to the supportiveness of social environments for maintaining attitudes and influencing their direction of change. We looked primarily at the experience of role transitions and various aspects of social support.

We found that while the role-transition hypothesis suggested an explanation of attitude stability and change, there were no differences in attitude change between groups exposed to differing volume of role transitions. We concluded that rather than the sheer amount of role change over the life span, the critical aspect of such role transitions involves the risk of exposure to change-inducing experiences. We argued that the notion of role transitions does not precisely represent the contextual aspects of role shifts, that is, whether such transitions are accompanied by changes in the supportiveness of the social environment in its political complexion. We suggested that the number of role transitions, or *life-events* as they are referred to in other relevant literature, is irrelevant if the individual can maintain the nature of her social networks and the sociopolitical context of support.

Using several different ways of operationalizing the concept of social support in terms of different domains of support—spouses, friends, and children—we found that we could explain differences in the extent of attitude change in terms of the concept of social support. Our main finding was that attitude change was greater among those who inhabited a dissonant political environment, and attitude persistence was greatest when similarity existed between the individual and significant others. All of these results are summarized in table 9.25.

Perhaps the strongest evidence in this regard pertains to the extent of supportiveness of the marital relationship. We noted that there was a substantial agreement in political views between the Bennington women and their husbands, and we found that where agreement on political party preferences was the greatest, the persistence of political orientations was greatest. We concluded from these findings that the marital relationship

249

Table 9.25. Summary of Life Span Stability Estimates among
Subgroups of the Bennington Sample Defined by
Differences in Opportunities for Attitude Change

	1930s to 1960	1960s to 1984	1930s to 1984
Role transitions			
Most transitions	.816	.847	.691
Fewest transitions	.806	.817	.659
Similarity to husband			
Same party preferences	.830	.917	.761
Different party preferences	.658	.653	.430
Similarity to friends			
Similar friends	.794	.967	.768
Dissimilar friends	.804	.783	.630
Similarity to children			
Similar children	.698	.849	.593
Dissimilar children	.857	.832	.713
Exposure to 1960s generation			
Most exposure	.869	.712	.619
Least exposure	.828	.944	.782
1984 Network similarity			
Similar networks	.772	.924	.713
Dissimilar networks	.767	.717	.550
Total (from table 7.8)	.908	.860	.781

provides considerable potential for support for the maintenance of political attitudes.

We also found support for the hypothesis that similarity to one's close friends in terms of political orientations was supportive of attitude stability. Although it was more difficult to operationalize such a test, given the absence of information on social networks over the life span—our data were limited to the 1960s and 1984 time periods—we nonetheless found support for the hypothesis where measures were available. Indeed, our findings confirmed the notion that similarity to friends along dimensions of political identification and preference helps promote attitude persistence, and dissimilarity to friends is linked to change.

In both of these instances—that of husbands and that of friends—we are unable to sort out the causal mechanisms involved because of the nature of our data. However, we think two explanations are quite plausible for the similarities we observed between our respondents and their significant others, both of which are theoretically tied to the notion of social support. First, we think that assortative mating occurs in both mate selection and friendship choice to an important extent, and this suggests that individuals actively seek support for their own viewpoints and perspectives. Then, we suggested, once spouses and/or friends are selected, they play an important role in helping to maintain a person's attitudes and in helping to protect the person from sources of attitude change (see Caspi and Herbener, 1990). In both of these instances, our results suggest that the greater the extent to which social processes embed an individual in supportive social environments which do not disrupt her attitudinal perspectives on political issues and actors and which contribute important support and verification to these views, the less will be the amount of attitude change throughout the life span.

Finally, we also considered children as an important source of potential attitude persistence and change. We reasoned, first, that the influence of children would operate in a manner consistent with that of spouses and close friends, and that similarity to children would reveal the same manner of differences. For this hypothesis, we found very little support. We found that the intergenerational influences operated somewhat differently, if at all. We found that attitude change was greatest among those women most exposed to children of the 1960s generation, and considerably more persistence was found among those with the least exposure to children born between 1940 and 1954.

Although these results were not statistically significant, they do fit with one interpretation of the relation between generations. They suggest that children may have a substantial influence on parental attitudes directly, rather than merely acting as supportive influences. The greater attitude change among those women most exposed to children who grew to political maturity during the 1960s may reflect the intensity of the times in which these children were growing up and during which their mothers were completing their middle years.

There were, after all, considerable attitude changes occurring among the Bennington women over this period. Recall that, by our 1960s estimates, nearly one-half of these women preferred the Republican Party in presidential elections between 1940 and 1960. Many of these women were supporters of Dwight Eisenhower and Richard Nixon during the 1950s and 1960s, but became more liberal in their orientations with time. In the 1980 and 1984 presidential elections, 75–80 percent supported Democratic candidates (Jimmy Carter and Walter Mondale). We argued above that the general weight of partisanship among the children of the Bennington women was in the liberal or Democratic direction, and that, if anything, their influence was felt in changing maternal attitudes in this direction as much as it was in supporting the attitudes of mothers who were already leaning in this direction.

Our strongest conclusions regarding the factors influencing the extent of attitude persistence and change emphasize the role of factors tied to the *social environment,* that is, opportunities for change, rather than factors tied to personality and/or cognitive organization. We have uncovered several instances in which the supportiveness of social environments for sociopolitical orientations emerges as a critical factor in the maintenance and preservation of attitudes. This position is strongly compatible with the emphasis placed by Newcomb and his colleagues (1967) on the important role of social support in attitude development over the life span.

Our results are consistent with the emergent view of human development that conceives of the relationship between the individual and her environment in dynamic rather than static terms. Bronfenbrenner (1979) has, for example, conceptualized human development in terms of the reciprocal relationship between the person and the environment—in which the person is an active participant in shaping her environment, while at the same time various aspects of the environment (interpersonal relations, roles, and molar activities) provide the potential for transforming the individual.

This view is also articulated by Mortimer and her colleagues in their study of parallel issues surrounding stability and change in the self-concept (Mortimer, Finch, and Kumka, 1982, 1986) and in work involvement and job satisfaction (Lorence and Mortimer, 1985; Mortimer, Finch, and Maruyama, 1988). In that work several examples are presented of what Mortimer et al. call *dynamic stability:* the process by which the individual constructs circumstances which help maintain prior orientations and which in turn feed back on the person so as to maintain stability over time. The person is thus not only the recipient of influences from the environment; she is also an active agent in the shaping of that environment.

The findings presented in this chapter reinforce this dynamic perspective on human development. They suggest that the Bennington women to some extent selected environments that were compatible with their own political orientations, which in turn helped reinforce those orientations. Their supportive choices in marriage and friendship helped maintain their attitudes in part by immunizing them from the influences of environmental sources of change. And to the extent that the environment did not provide opportunities for dynamic stability, the individual was more likely to experience attitude change.

10

Social Change and the Stability of Individuals: A Review and Interpretation

INTRODUCTION

We began this monograph with three objectives. The first was to describe the results of a three-wave longitudinal study of political attitude persistence and change in several cohorts of Bennington College women from the 1930s to the present. Second, we sought to interpret and explain the patterns of stability and change exhibited in the lives of these women. And third, we wanted to assess the extent to which our interpretations and explanations might be useful in understanding the processes of the lifelong development of attitudes more generally. In addition to the primary objectives of analyzing and interpreting our own Bennington data, we also examined the 1984 National Election Study data in order to provide a benchmark comparison for our Bennington sample. Our search for a generational interpretation of the early Bennington results led us to consider all of the NES data since 1952 with respect to a few key measurements. Further, our interest in the question of persistence and change in the lives of the Bennington women led us to consider the more representative panel data from the 1950s and 1970s NES studies.

In this final chapter we return to the theoretical concerns with which we began, assessing the extent to which our findings have any measure of external validity or generality. Consistent with our earlier expressed concerns about the historical uniqueness of the Bennington sample, we ask whether our findings might be peculiar to the Bennington cohorts and uniquely tied to the historical period in which they lived their lives. We are particularly interested in the ways in which our views of life course development—the "typical" or "average" ways of growing to adulthood—are interpretable in terms of the historical periods sampled in our data.

Our interest in the extent to which our interpretation of the life span development of attitudes might be understood from a sociohistorical perspective is important because different historical periods present differing opportunities for individuals to change. The period of the mid-1930s was a period of rapid social change in which the electorate was moving toward the acceptance of Roosevelt's New Deal. In such periods of rapid social change, the young may be even more open to change, as we have argued in chapter 9. Thus, it is important for purposes of generalizing from the experiences of the Bennington women that we resolve the question of whether youth is universally an impressionable period, with growing persistence of attitudes after such an initial period, or whether such patterns as are identifiable in our results reflect only the influences of certain sociohistorical circumstances.

In this final chapter we first review the theoretical and conceptual issues that guided our research into the life span development of sociopolitical orientations. We then summarize what we consider to be the central findings from this research. Within that context and on the basis of those empirical findings, we pose the broader question of their *historical durability*, given the admitted limitations of historically unique samples such as ours. In this context we again review our findings from the synthetic cohort analysis of the NES national panel studies. Following that discussion, we suggest several avenues for further research which we believe would contribute to an understanding of attitude development and change over the life course. Included in our set of recommendations for future research is a plea for a *historically oriented* study of life course development (see Elder, and Caspi, 1988).

THEORETICAL AND CONCEPTUAL ISSUES

In order to examine the historical durability of generalizations about aging and levels of stability of adult sociopolitical orientations over the life span, we must again clarify the nature of the sociopolitical orientations of interest to us. We must also clarify the critical issues regarding the nature of individual development and our specific questions aimed at understanding change and stability in sociopolitical orientations. As in any research endeavor, we must also address the problems of measuring the types of factors that influence attitude development and their role in sociopolitical attitude stability and change. In this regard we have tried to be sensitive to the fact that we are dealing with self-report data, which may be strongly affected by subjective factors, and that our basis for inference, which in some cases is essentially retrospective, is often relatively fragile.

The Nature of Sociopolitical Orientations

We have conceived of sociopolitical orientations in terms of cognitive and affective beliefs about social and political systems, the institutional structures they constitute, and the individual and collective actors that populate these systems and structures. We have defined the concept of *political ideology* in terms of a coherent set of cognitive and affective responses to political matters (see Sniderman and Tetlock, 1986). We have tried to distinguish more basic *ideological* orientations from less fundamental aspects of sociopolitical orientations, such as object-specific attitudes tied to particular political issues and actors. This is important theoretically because our concerns about life span development transcend such particularistic matters, referring instead to more fundamental aspects of the individual's stance toward the social and political system. Moreover, for practical reasons, we have tried to tap more basic orientations because of our inability to study the same political issues and actors over the entire biography of the individual in which the social and political objects in the environment change.

Most important for our purposes, the conception of sociopolitical orientations adopted in the study of life span development must allow for the possibility of constancy *or* change over time. Attitudes toward specific sociopolitical actors or issues are subject to perturbations in time, which limit their utility in studying human development over long spans of biographical time. Thus, our approach to defining the nature of sociopolitical attitudes has been to attempt to identify conceptually a latent construct which reflects such a *basic stance* toward social and political systems, political parties, and generalized political actors.

Models of the Development of Political Orientations

Theoretical conceptions of human development differ in their images of the influences of the social environment and their lasting effects. Two theoretical perspectives that present somewhat contrasting images are what we call *primacy* models and *critical-stage* models. The *primacy principle,* referred to by Searing et al., (1976), suggests the importance of orientations developed early in life, assuming that later development is strongly tied to these early developments. The critical-stage image, by contrast, suggests first the existence of distinct stages or spans of development, which may or may not be the earliest stages, and second, the unique importance of one or more of these stages for establishing individual orientations. Following Sears (1981, 1983), we have suggested the possible appropriateness of the generational/persistence model, which portrays a version of an intersection of these two contrasting images of development: one emphasizing the primacy of influence of the early adult years, and the other the importance of historical, or generational, influences occuring at this critical stage (i.e., the impressionable years).

255

A second line of contrast among images of the influence of the social environment, in contrast to when these influences are most felt, is the extent to which that influence lasts. The assumption of persistence, as suggested by the generational/persistence model, conveys the idea that attitudes are rigidly held to throughout the life span. But as Glenn (1980) indicates, it is not clear whether this stability is always monotonically increasing, or whether it follows some other form. The contrasting image, conveyed by the lifelong openness perspective, is one that suggests a long-term process of change and adaptation, unaffected by the more conservative tendencies to maintain a constant self-image and a constant personality (see Gergen, 1980).

Neither of these contrasts really captures the textured reality that we have examined in our empirical work above. Indeed, we suggested that what may be needed is a hybrid version of the generational/persistence model—one which acknowledges the potential for generational differences and a tendency for these to persist, but at moderate rather than high levels of persistence. There seems, in other words, to be some support for both a persistence model and a lifelong openness model. We have seen extremely high levels of persistence in the Bennington sample, but in the synthetic cohort models we derived from the NES panel data, we see substantially lower levels. We return to these issues later in the chapter.

The Definition and Measurement of Attitude Strength

Our approach to studying the strength of attitudes departs significantly from analytic strategies used with considerable frequency in the literature on aging and political orientations. The conventional logic is that measures of political orientations, especially partisan identifications, contain two main dimensions or aspects of political orientations: direction and strength (see Converse, 1976; Converse and Pierce, 1987). We have followed these conventions with respect to defining ideological orientations in terms of identification with the liberal versus the conservative poles of the political spectrum. Operationally, we have distinguished this dimension in a number of ways, using party identification, candidate preferences, self-assessments on continua of liberalism/conservatism, and stance on contemporary social and political issues.

In addition to direction of party identification, the common approach in the research literature includes an assessment of the strength of party identification. The traditional definition of the strength component of party identification refers to the intensity with which attitudes are held. In the case of party identification, the strength of identification is measured by asking the respondent to characterize herself in terms of how strongly she

256

identifies with a particular party. What the conventional literature calls *attitude strength* we thus prefer to call *attitude intensity;* we reserve the concept of *attitude strength* for the phenomenon of attitude stability and durability in the face of opportunities for change. We are able to define the concept of attitude strength in this way—in a manner that seems un-questionably more precise—specifically because we have had access to longitudinal data, with attitudes assessed at several points over the course of life. Thus, we have addressed the question of attitude strength within a framework that assesses the extent of attitude change. We have assumed, therefore, that those attitudes are strongest which are relatively most re-sistant to change. Within this framework it is conceivable to assess the potential and extent of change, that is, attitude strength, in either the direction or intensity of attitudes (see Alwin and Krosnick, 1991a).

ATTITUDE STABILITY AND CHANGE OVER THE LIFE SPAN

Within the framework of these considerations, the analyses contained in the foregoing chapters focused on a number of theoretical issues concerned with the development of sociopolitical attitudes. Before we consider the historical generality of these findings, we briefly summarize the basic con-clusions to which our findings lead us. We first review our reassessment of the extent to which there are impressionable years in early adulthood during which individuals are particularly susceptible to changes in their attitudes and orientations. We then juxtapose our assessment of this set of issues with our results regarding the influence of the family in politi-cal socialization. Third, we consider the extent to which our data lend themselves to a generational interpretation of political attitude develop-ment, and the extent to which different cohorts may be said to have differ-ent sociopolitical orientations. Fourth, we reconsider the results we have amassed on the question of persistence and one particular version of the persistence hypothesis: namely, that aging induces greater stability of atti-tudes (Glenn, 1980). Fifth, we address the veracity of Sears's (1981, 1983) generational/persistence model of life course variation in sociopolitical attitudes.

The Impressionable Years

It is commonly believed, and with strong justification, that the earliest years are the most important for development in many cognitive, affec-tive, and moral domains. David Sears (1981:79) recounts a story told about the Jesuits, who believed they could control a person's thinking for life if

257

they were able to control their education up to the age of five. This view is compatible with many perspectives emerging from developmental psychology, which emphasize the early establishment of individual differences that have a high degree of continuity throughout later life (e.g., Block, 1971, 1981; Moss and Susman, 1980; Thomas and Chess, 1977).

We have emphasized throughout this discussion that the extent of persistence in human beings may vary quite dramatically across behavioral, cognitive, and affective domains. Thus, it is important to recognize the possibility that although some aspects of human functioning may be quite stable from early childhood, others do not become stable until early adulthood, and still others may never stabilize. In their discussion of the development of *temperament*, or *styles of behaving*, thought to be basic predispositional orientations to the environment, Thomas and Chess (1977), for example, return to a model of *behavioral individuality*, or uniqueness of individual functioning, in which individual differences established early in life show a strong degree of continuity throughout later life.[1] This view is consistent with much that has been written in developmental psychology affirming that the early period(s) of socialization lays the foundation for basic patterns of individual functioning. According to such a view (e.g., Block, 1971, 1981; Moss and Susman, 1980), individual cognitive, emotional, interpersonal, political, ideological, moral, and other aspects of human functioning become quite stable over biographical time.

For others, the establishment of personality, or character, is not fully accomplished until early adulthood, and vulnerability to influence or change persists through early adulthood. But at that stage, many scholars argue, stability or constancy characterizes one's orientation to the environment. As we noted in chapter 1, Mannheim argued, for example, that "even if the rest of one's life consisted of one long process of negation and destruction of the natural world view acquired in youth, the determining influence of these early impressions would still be predominant" (1952:298). Of course, it is not always clear from such discussions whether these patterns are thought to reflect something inherent in people that indicates their ability to change, or whether they reflect something about the opportunities for

---

1. The evidence presented by Thomas and Chess (1977:161) is, however, relatively weak. They report correlations (uncorrected for unreliability) over one-year intervals of about .3 (on the average) for nine scores over the first five years of life. Even allowing for measurement error, this does not appear to reflect much constancy of personality. Interestingly, they base their argument for the consistency of personality on the "significance" of these interyear correlations, despite the fact that they are of only moderate magnitude. A conclusion that over one year the correlational consistency of a behavioral trait is not significantly different from zero is a far cry from arguing that the trait reflects a stable underlying predisposition to respond in a consistent way.

change. It is probably most correct at this stage in the development of our understanding to assume *both* that greater opportunities for change extend into early adulthood, and that greater inherent openness to influence on the part of the individual persists through that stage.

At several points in our earlier discussions we considered whether there are impressionable years in which people are more vulnerable to changing their basic sociopolitical orientations, due either to greater susceptibility to change and/or greater opportunities for change. We asked whether the young are truly more impressionable, as the literature consistently maintains, or whether there are other periods in the life-cycle when people are more vulnerable to change. In answering this question we retraced the main contours of Newcomb's (1943) pioneering study of attitude change at Bennington College (see chapter 2), concluding that the evidence he had assembled clearly supported the view that attitudes continue to be quite malleable through young adulthood. We also tested the impressionable years hypothesis using synthetic cohort data from the National Election Study panels. These results provided considerable support for this hypothesis, in that levels of attitude stability were substantially lower in the youngest age groups (see also Alwin and Krosnick, 1991a).

Our findings thus reinforce the view that considerable flexibility and potential for change lasts into the period of late adolescence and early adulthood. While it is important to recognize the possibility that some aspects of human functioning, such as certain cognitive skills and aspects of temperament, may demonstrate significant stability from early childhood, it is equally important to recognize that the acquisition of ideas, attitudes, and political ideologies that are likely to remain stable does not take place until early in adulthood. This, of course, corresponds with the assumption that a certain degree of maturity, experience, and basic knowledge is required before young people can absorb the factual and procedural knowledge of social and political life.

For those concerned with the developmental trajectories of sociopolitical attitudes and orientations, the issues then become not whether there are impressionable years, followed by some lengthy period of growing stability of attitudes, but rather, what are the important influences on the young? Which influences shape the attitudes that will then remain relatively stable over the entire life course, and what is the relative importance of these various factors? In this regard, we have identified two major sets of factors as relevant: the influences stemming from the family of origin and the influences of one's generation.[2]

---

2. Of course, we are aware of the fact that life course stages change as society changes, and that not all historical periods necessarily give normative definition to a period of *ado-*

The Family and Early Political Socialization

According to most theorists of the contemporary political world, explicit political socialization begins in late childhood and early adolescence, but attitudes continue to be formed into early adulthood (Jennings and Niemi, 1974; Kinder and Sears, 1985). Given the early susceptibility to influence and the variety of opportunities for influence in these early years, there are a number of theoretical viewpoints about the relative importance of various agencies of socialization. More than 30 years ago, Hyman argued that the family was "foremost among agencies of socialization into politics" (1959: 69). This view was supported by a number of early theoretical discussions of political socialization (e.g., Davies, 1965). By contrast, Hess and Torney (1967) argued that it was the school that was the most important and effective instrument of political socialization in the United States. The family, they conceded, promotes early and basic attachment to the social system, including its political and governmental institutions, thereby insuring the stability of basic institutions and basic partisan identification. The family's effect does not, according to this view, extend to "idiosyncratic attitudes" that develop in the course of a child's personal experiences with the social system and its institutions.

In chapter 7 we considered the role of the family in the development of socio-political attitudes. We were interested in whether there is any support for the primacy principle, which postulates that there is considerable political learning in the family of origin, and that families are relatively effective in transmitting sociopolitical orientations across generations. We inquired about the relative influence of the family compared to extrafamilial influences on the development of social and political orientations. In this regard, we provided some reinterpretation of the original Bennington research. The emphasis in that study was on the relative malleabilty of attitudes in young adulthood, and while this emphasis had strong theoretical and empirical support, we noted that the equally forceful influence of the parental generation had been somewhat overshadowed in the original interpretation. We reexamined this question within the framework of the theoretical and empirical research literature that has followed.

Our results suggest the strong influence of the parental generation. In this regard we concluded that, contrary to what has commonly been

---

lescence, a youthful stage in which the individual experiences a prolonged period of semi-independence and a period of flexibility and openness to change. As Elder (1980) notes, in a society characterized by a rather abrupt transition from childhood to adulthood, there may be no impressionable years after childhood. Thus, we are careful to limit our understanding of the impressionable years as a phenomenon that may be circumscribed by a particular set of social, cultural, economic, and historical circumstances.

viewed as the essential import of the early Bennington research, the family of origin is one of the most important influences on political attitudes. We were not able to compare the influences of parental orientations with the Bennington experience in terms of magnitude, since within our data most aspects of the Bennington experience are a constant. Thus, we cannot conclude that parental influences are more important than collegiate experiences—only that parental influence seems to be strong and consistent throughout the life span.

Early Adulthood and Generational Influences

The transition to adulthood in Western society is characterized by the confluence of many significant changes in opportunities for self-expression and autonomous behavior.[3] As the child moves to some extent away from the parental sphere of influence, other forces begin to complement these intergenerational influences. One of the most important of these is the peer group, and as we have emphasized throughout earlier discussions, peer influences are often summarized by the concept of *generation*. The assumption is that one of the structural mechanisms by which generations emerge is through the existence of generational peers who interpret social events and cultural phenomena.

In chapter 5 we considered to what extent generational or, more precisely, cohort experiences help shape sociopolitical orientations. Are there substantial enough differences in the historical factors affecting each new generation as it passes through the impressionable period of youth to argue that generational differences play a significant role in political socialization? We noted that generational explanations are an especially popular interpretive device for understanding social change, and we wanted to extend this possibility toward a potential reinterpretation of the original "Bennington effect" as a cohort phenomenon. That is, we wondered whether the pattern of findings identified by Newcomb (1943) at Bennington College might really be explained by the fact that these young women achieved political consciousness during the 1930s, and that their change in the direction of the New Deal might be seen as part of a cohort phenomenon. To manage an examination of this hypothesis, we turned to cohort data from the National Election Study, available since 1952.

As we noted in chapter 5, with the possible exception of the 1960s

3. There is evidence that parental values emphasizing independence or autonomy are increasing relative to preferences for obedience and conformity (see Alwin, 1988a, 1990a, 1990b). Regardless of trends in parental valuation of autonomy, the concept of adolescence has historically been defined as a period in which the individual gains a high degree of autonomy and independence of thought and action.

generation (see Gitlin, 1987), the generation from which the Bennington College women of the 1930s and 1940s came was clearly more liberal in its orientations than either earlier or later ones. And regardless of the direction of political loyalty, this generation appears to hold more intense attitudes than the younger cohorts. At the same time, the Bennington women were themselves even more intensely liberal than women of their own generation. We noted in chapter 5 that the Bennington women seemed to be more a part of the "New Deal generation" than many of their peers, and in some sense they were more intensely affected by the events of the 1930s and 1940s than their collegiate contemporaries. We found that educated women of the 1930s generation are likely to carry allegiances to the Republican party to a much greater extent than their age-mates. Even on this score, the Bennington women could be seen as quite distinct: in their attachment to the New Deal and to Democratic political loyalties since the 1930s and 1940s, they differed significantly from other educated women of comparable age. Thus, we argued, they could be seen as more typical of their generation than their college-educated peers. We suggested that other women receiving an education in the 1930s and 1940s were probably more likely to be shielded from social events and social change, whereas the Bennington experience was one in contemporary education amidst a set of actors that had shaped a particularly progressive informational environment (see chapter 2).

Although we favor a generational interpretation to some extent in accounting for the early Bennington College phenomenon identified by Newcomb, we do not intend to discount the role of the unique influences of the Bennington College environment. The two phenomena are not mutually exclusive. One could argue, for example, that what Newcomb (1943) identified in terms of change at Bennington College in the 1930s and 1940s was an embodiment of the larger historical environment. We should note, however, that while most available research suggests that cohort or generational differences in sociopolitical orientations are typically seen in only weak forms, those residues which are seen to exist between cohorts typically single out the 1930s generation as distinctive (e.g., Knoke and Hout, 1974).

Persistence versus Lifelong Openness to Change

One of the principal motives we had for engaging in the present research was to assess the trajectory of the stability or persistence of sociopolitical orientations over the life course. Do basic attitudes grow in strength with age? Does attitude stability level off at some point in the life span, or do attitudes continue to grow in strength with age? And is there a point later in the life span when attitudes experience a process of destabilization?

There are contrasting images of human development emphasizing the human capacity for adaptation and change. Citing a theme that has been continuously reiterated in life span research, and noting the lack of evidence for high degrees of continuity in early life, Gergen (1973, 1980) proposes an *aleatoric account* of human constancy—a perspective on development that calls attention to the *inherent* potential for adjustment and adaptation to changes in the social environment. Gergen argues that existing development patterns are "potentially evanescent, the unstable result of the particular juxtaposition of contemporary historical events" (1980: 34–35). At the level of individuals, the life course is "fundamentally open-ended." Even with full knowledge of the individual's past experience, Gergen argues, "one can render little more than a probabalistic account of the broad contours of future development" (1980:35).

Any rendering of the extent of persistence in human ideation, emotion, and behavioral orientations may thus be seen as falling somewhere along this continuum subtended by two extreme points of view. On the one hand, human characteristics may be only randomly linked over time—following Gergen's aleatoric image that developmental trajectories are traceable to the accidental composite of existing circumstances. On the other hand, after some early period of vulnerability to change, human tendencies become highly stabilized patterns of consistent responses to the environment, characterized by resistence to change. According to this view, the individual's orientations exhibit a great degree of stability, even in the face of experiences that stimulate reevaluation and change.

There is little evidence in the present set of findings that bears out Gergen's claims. We find political attitudes to be highly persistent from early adulthood to old age. These results, of course, apply primarily to those more ideological aspects of political self-conceptions and identifications, but there is a high degree of stability nonetheless. Beyond the early adult years, there is hardly any other period which we could characterize in terms of *impressionable years*. The entire life span certainly cannot be characterized accurately as a continual period of intense influence and change, at least insofar as political ideology is concerned. Whether "human developmental trajectories *may* be virtually infinite in their variegation" (Gergen, 1980:37; emphasis added), our research provides no evidence that they are.

While most theorists agree that there is an early period of great vulnerability to influence and changes in behavioral traits and dispositions, it is not clear exactly when the impressionable years end. However, with respect to later periods of life, most available evidence strongly supports the *aging/stability* thesis, which posits a growing persistence of attitudes with age (see Glenn, 1980). This is demonstrated by the results presented in chapter 7. Our results (see also Alwin and Krosnick, 1991a) show that except for the intensity of partisan attitudes, which show some slight decline in old age, the directional elements of partisan identification seem to hold quite firmly throughout the life span.

Reevaluating the Generational/Persistence Model

At several points in our previous discussions we have noted that in general our data fit well with some of the main elements of Sears's (1981, 1983) generational/persistence model of attitude development. This model combines three critical components: first, the notion of a period of vulnerability to influence occurring in late adolescence and early adulthood; second, the notion that each new cohort experiences that time of life differently, and that there are unique residues within the individual because of those generational experiences; and third, the idea that after some early period of influence and change, attitudes become crystallized and increasingly stable with age.

We believe this is a useful model for summarizing what is known about the formation and development of sociopolitical attitudes, particularly with respect to the data we have assembled here. However, there are a number of qualifications we would make in considering the general applicability of this model to the development of attitude phenomena. The first, and perhaps the most serious, shortcoming of this model stems from the fact that only rarely have sociologists and political scientists been able to demonstrate strong cohort effects on social and political attitude variables. Our reading of the existing research literature leads to the conclusion that evidence for cohort, or generational, effects on sociopolitical attitudes is to be found in only meagre amounts (e.g., Abramson, 1976, 1983; Converse, 1976, 1979; Glenn, 1980; Knoke and Hout, 1974; Oppenheim, 1970; Roberts and Lang, 1985). Thus, this model may give too much emphasis to generational phenomena, to the neglect of other important influences on development.

Of course, we would point out that most discussions of cohort phenomena emphasize that cohort influences represent only a *potential* set of influences and are not necessitated by differences in historical experiences. Even though there are not wide differences between cohorts in social and political attitudes, and there is considerably more *intracohort* variation than *intercohort* variation, this does not invalidate other aspects of the model. At this stage in the development of our knowledge, one can usually identify some small differences in attitudes that span relatively longer periods and are typical of several categories of cohorts, but in general these differences do not seem to be as important as differences within cohorts.

Even if we were to remove this generational component, the remaining aspects of this model provide a useful interpretation of the life span development of attitudes. Indeed, the notion that there is an early period of vulnerability—years of greatest malleability of attitudes and orientations to life—coupled with increasing persistence, or what Glenn (1980) calls *aging/stability*, seems to fit our data very nicely. Thus, even if generational differences represent just one of several influences on the formation of attitudes, we can still speak about the impressionable years, followed by a long period of decreasing flexibility of attitudes. Such a modification of the model would de-emphasize the generational component, recognizing the potency of other within-cohort influences on sociopolitical attitudes, while at the same time maintaining that attitudes grow in strength with age. However, these *critical-stage* and *aging/stability* components of the model also need some qualification and reevaluation.

While we have described our results—from both the Bennington sample and the NES panels—as supporting the idea that attitudes tend to be highly stable after early adulthood, we have also noted that there is evidence of a substantial amount of attitude change as well. In fact, we estimated that over the nearly fifty-year period covered by our Bennington data, some 60 percent of the variance in our latent attitude variables in 1984 could be predicted on the basis of 1930s attitudes, whereas 40 percent of that variation reflected attitude change. Thus, while we believe it is appropriate to emphasize the persistence thesis, the extent of continuity of attitudes can easily be exaggerated. In other words, the generational-persistence model of attitude development risks putting too great an emphasis on attitude stability, to the neglect of understanding the nature and extent of attitude change.

We earlier suggested a hybrid version of the persistence thesis—one that would give substantially more emphasis to flexibility and change. In other words, it is certainly not at all the case that people's attitudes simply become fixed at some early stage and are impervious to the sources of attitude change. While demonstrating considerable stability, our results also confirm a nontrivial degree of attitude change over the life span. Both stability and change are present.

Finally, the generational-persistence model needs to be qualified in terms of its scope. Sears (1983) has argued that the model is perhaps most suited to explaining the development of more *symbolic* dispositions—those orientations which contain more affective information—such as party identification and scales reflecting ideological liberalism/conservatism. The results of the present research are consistent with this suggestion, as we have sought to distinguish more basic or central ideological orientations from less fundamental aspects of sociopolitical orientations. However, we also

265

recognize that this model may not apply to other types of attitude or cognitive variables (see Alwin, 1992). Indeed, one might expect that some types of attitudes would show high degrees of stability in early adulthood, but increase in flexibility with time.

SOCIAL CHANGE AND HISTORICAL CONSIDERATIONS

In venturing an interpretation of the Bennington data, we cannot ignore the unique historical circumstances in which these women first acquired their political viewpoints. As we noted earlier, most of these women were born between 1913 and 1921. They reached age 18 roughly during the 1930s. Of course, women's suffrage had only finally come into existence in 1920, and the social meaning of gender was undergoing substantial change. Our earlier discussion emphasized the fact that the Bennington women were part of a historical process begun in the nineteenth century that made available to women the skills and knowledge linked to higher education, which American society had previously extended only to men. Viewed from this perspective, women's liberal arts colleges like Bennington played a central role in breaking down these barriers (see Horowitz, 1984). It is difficult, therefore, to generalize confidently from the lives of the Bennington women, not just because they are unlikely to be representative in a sampling sense, but, more important, because of the uniqueness of the female collegiate experience, especially the Bennington College experience, during this historical period.

Moreover, these women experienced the transition from mid-life to older age during an extremely volatile decade, the 1960s. Thus, their levels of stability into old age may not be typical or representative of others experiencing part of the life course during a different historical period. Even the data we presented earlier from the National Election Study panels are somewhat limited, in that they pertain to historical periods mainly characterized by political stability: the 1950s and 1970s. We return nonetheless to these data subsequently in order to reexamine the patterns of attitude change we found there.

The Historical Durability of Life-Cycle Differences in Stability

In what has become a frequently cited paper, Gergen argued that "contemporary" theories of social behavior are "primarily reflections of contemporary history" (1973:309). In a more recent essay, elaborating upon this same point, Gergen suggests that evidence of cohort differences in developmental trajectories of a wide range of human characteristics are invariably found among cohorts born in different historical eras within the same culture. In his view, "depending on the sociohistorical circumstances, differing age-related trajectories are found in value commitments, personality characteristics, mental capabilities, political ideology, communication patterns, and so on" (1980:37). In support of this claim Gergen cites Elder's (1974) detailed analysis of the life span effects of growing up in the Great Depression as opposed to a more stabilized economic period. He also cites evidence from the developmental literature of cohort effects on aspects of cognitive functioning (cf. Baltes and Schaie, 1973; Baltes and Reinert, 1969; Huston-Stein and Baltes, 1976; Nesselroade and Baltes, 1974; Woodruff and Birren, 1972).

From the perspective of the research we reported in the previous chapters, we believe that Gergen (1980) may have confused the possibility of cohort (or generational) effects on individuals at critical stages with the question of the persistence or stability of those influences. As we have noted throughout previous chapters, it is entirely possible for intercohort differences in typical values in sociopolitical attitudes to coexist with high degrees of intracohort constancy in individual differences.[4] Thus, contrary to what Gergen (1980) seems to be arguing, there is no necessary connection between the possibility of cohort effects of the form Mannheim, Ryder, and others have suggested might exist, and the degree of stability of those cohorts over biographical time. Indeed, those who have argued most strongly that generational differences, or cohort effects, exist in sociopolitical orientations have also argued that these differences persist over the lifetimes of individuals (Carlsson and Karlsson, 1970; Mannheim, 1952; Ryder, 1965).

Most social scientists tend to agree that one must be cautious to limit conclusions concerning age patterns to the period in which the data were gathered (e.g., Glenn, 1980:635), but the historical specificity of the results is seen as an issue for empirical investigation. Throughout our own analyses we have emphasized the *historical boundedness* of these results. Even our stability estimates based on the NES panel studies, which contribute to a *synthetic cohort* model of life span development of political attitudes, were based on panel data from unique periods in (American) history, periods in which political stability was more characteristic of the polity than upheaval and change.

---

4. We should perhaps note that, except possibly for Elder's (1974) work, none of the work cited by Gergen (1980:37) in support of this argument (listed above) actually addressed the question of the differing age-related trajectories of value commitments, personality characteristics, political ideology, and so forth.

Historical Differences in Life-Cycle Patterns of Stability

But is there no basis in our research for trans-historical generalizations? Can we not generalize on the basis of these results to lawlike principles of life course development of attitudes?

We can examine the historical durability of one set of findings from our analyses of the National Election Study panel data. Specifically, we examine the extent to which the synthetic cohort data from the 1950s and 1970s studies tell a consistent story of life-cycle changes in the stability of attitudes over the entire life span. As we noted in chapter 7, this type of over-time comparison of cohorts is made possible because one variable—our adopted measure of political party identification—is measured over the three waves of each of the 1950s and 1970s panel studies. Therefore we can compare estimates of eight-year stabilities both across cohort groups within the same panel study and within the same cohort groups across time points. This latter intracohort comparison of levels of persistence represents the strongest information we have for evaluating the aging/stability hypothesis.

Estimates of eight-year stabilities permit us to attach an empirical reading to the amount of stability experienced by each of our birth-cohort categories, each of which spans a period of eight years. These estimates, based on the four-year stability estimates given in table 7.15, are presented in table 10.1, separately for (1) the seven-point measure of party identification, (2) its Republican-independent-Democrat directional component, and (3) its *intensity* component.[5] The stability estimates are also presented graphically for the party identification variable and its directional component in figures 10.1, 10.2 and 10.3 respectively.

These data indicate that political party identification can be characterized by two different types of historical durability. In the first instance, these results reinforce a notion of durability consistent with the processes characterized in the earlier chapters as stability, or persistence, of attitudes over biographical time. With one remarkable exception, these data reveal a second, more important type of historical durability: both sets of estimates of life span stability of partisan identification follow virtually the same trajectory. In fact, with that one exception, the estimates of individual-level stability for the age categories are identical across the two studies. For example, both panels produce an estimate of roughly .45–.55 for the estimated eight-year stability of the 1–7 scale for the youngest age group—those 18–25—and so forth for virtually all comparable age groups.

5. These figures are based on *estimated* eight-year stability coefficients for each age group obtained by squaring the four-year estimates presented in table 7.15.

Table 10.1. Estimates of Eight-Year Stability Parameters for Party Identification and Direction of Party Identification: National Election Study Panels

Age in				Party ID 1–7		Dem/Ind/Rep 1–3		Intensity 0–3	
1956	n	1972	n	1956–60	1972–76	1956–60	1972–76	1956–60	1972–76
		18–25	(191)		.441		.430		.356
		26–33	(219)		1.000		.982		.706
18–25	(83)	34–41	(181)	.534	.953	.442	.922	.370	.511
26–33	(212)	42–49	(191)	.637	.927	.623	.817	.476	.646
34–41	(227)	50–57	(158)	.996	.998	.920	1.000	.661	.872
42–49	(174)	58–65	(132)	1.000	.910	.976	.869	.656	.808
50–57	(125)	66–83	(151)	.893	.755	.819	.736	.746	.444
58–65	(94)			.933		.766		.366	
66–83	(92)			.832		.721		.410	
Total	(1,045)		(1,237)	.869	.893	.824	.872	.579	.581

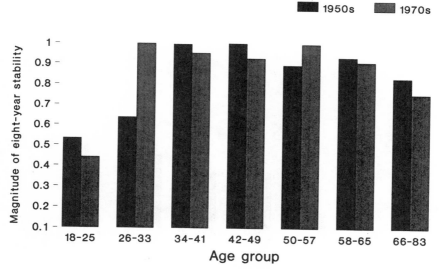

Figure 10.1. Stability of Party Identification

The major exception to this nearly identical pattern of life span estimates of the growing stability of attitudes is the set of stability estimates for the 26–33 age category. In the 1950s data the stability estimate for this group is roughly midway between the estimate for the 18–25 and 34–41 age groups—in the range .6—whereas in the 1970s data the comparable estimate is very high—in excess of the theoretical limit. What accounts for

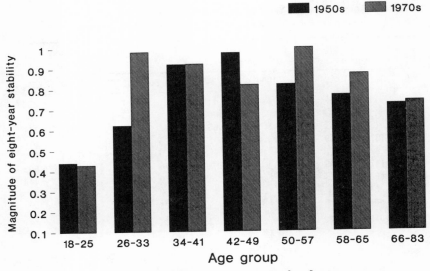

Figure 10.2. Stability of Direction of Party Identification

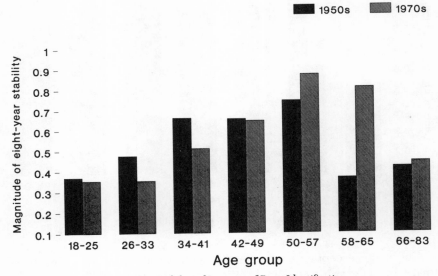

Figure 10.3. Stability of Intensity of Party Identification

this disparity? Is it possible that, while the general pattern of life span stability estimates follows an aging stability course that is relatively general, there are historical circumstances that explain the deviations?

We believe there is an explanation for the unusually high degree of stability among those who were 26–33 in the 1970s panel data. This exception may represent a unique cohort effect on attitude stability. This cohort was born in the years between 1939 and 1946, and its members were 16–23 years old in the early 1960s. Coming of age in the decade of the 1960s, this cohort experienced its impressionable years during one of the most turbulent periods in recent American political history. It seems likely, then, that this cohort may have entered the 1970s with highly crystallized partisan attitudes, generating highly stable attitudes somewhat prematurely over the early life course. Unlike their 1950s counterparts—those 26–33 in the mid-1950s—who grew to political maturity in the stable years following World War II, the 1960s cohort entered mid-life with their political minds made up. The group that grew to political maturity during the 1950s, as indicated above, reveals an increasing level of persistence, compared to their survey-mates who were eight years their juniors; and they are not as highly persistent as those who were older—those 34–41 in the 1950s study. By contrast, those 26–33 in the 1970s study reveal a level of stability similar to the 34–41 year olds in both studies, again suggesting a premature, historically unique crystallization of attitudes.

Despite this important and interesting exception, our main results lead us to emphasize the presence of relatively durable life-cycle factors in the development of the directional component of sociopolitical attitudes. The interpretation of these findings, while recognizing the possibility of unique cohort departures from the main lines of aging/stability shown here, suggests that our results have greater generality than we have heretofore claimed. Our Bennington data also suggest that the stability of attitudes increases over biographical time, although we have only three time points and cannot easily gauge more precise shifts in attitude stability. Our Bennington data further suggest that an important set of mechanisms that contributes to stability is the development and maintenance of networks of social support that have stabilizing influences on sociopolitical attitudes. (See Alwin (1992) for further interpretation of these eight-year stability estimates.)

UNRESOLVED ISSUES: AVENUES FOR FUTURE RESEARCH

At several points throughout this research, we realized there were issues we could not address, either because of the limitations in the scope of what we had sought to investigate or imperfections in our data. Several of these are impossible to address given the absence of appropriate data or the ambiguities in existing data. Others can be addressed within the context of existing data. Most of the unresolved research issues, however, will require new data resources. In this final section of this chapter we briefly lay out what we believe are the issues that can be productively addressed in future research.

Aging and Attitude Crystallization

Throughout this volume we have used the term *attitude crystallization* in such a way as to suggest that it was a natural accompaniment of *attitude persistence*. Indeed, it is common in the literature on political socialization to find such terms used in conjunction, with authors frequently referring to the lack of attitude stability and crystallization in young adults, and the tendencies toward the growth of both attitude stability and attitude crystallization with age (see Sears, 1987).

In fact, issues of attitude persistence and attitude crystallization are separate and separable questions. If we define attitude crystallization in terms of the constraint or cohesiveness of various indicators of latent attitude constructs, then it can easily be seen that the extent of stability in these latent attitudes is independent of the extent to which indicators of such a construct are interrelated (see Alwin, 1991).

The concept of *political ideology* used here assumes a common underlying dimension to political attitudes and behavior. Following Sniderman and Tetlock (1986), we have assumed that individuals are variously characterized as having a set of weakly organized, or at least minimally connected, set of cognitive and affective beliefs about social and political systems, the institutional structures they constitute, and the individual and collective actors that populate them.

There has been considerable discussion and debate about the extent to which sociopolitical orientations are characterized by *attitude constraint* (see Converse, 1964, 1980; Judd and Milburn, 1980; Judd, Krosnick, and Milburn, 1981). This general connectedness of sociopolitical attitudes is thought to vary across levels of elite status. Converse (1964) argued that the average person's understanding of abstract political ideas and issues as well as the details of the political process is remarkably limited, and that the belief systems of "mass publics" are characterized by little coherence and consistency, with views on one set of issues only loosely tied to beliefs on other issues. By contrast, Converse (1964) argued, elites are much more knowledgeable about public issues; they think in terms of abstract principles of political ideology, and they have thought about the basic stances of political actors and institutions. Elites are said to have a much more coherent or connected set of political beliefs and attitudes about public issues.

We have relied on this set of ideas in our effort to account for the high degree of stability in the orientations of the Bennington women, since Converse (1964) argued that connected sets of attitudes and beliefs are much more stable than less coherent structures. We reasoned (see chapter 7) that the family background and educational status of these women, as well as their Bennington College experience, made social and political affairs much more salient to them. However, we have not been able to assess hypotheses regarding the relationship of time to the changing structure of attitudes because we have not been able to rely on a constant set of measures. By opting for conceptual rather than literal replication of the sociopolitical orientations we assessed, we realized we could not compare correlations among indicators at any given occasion of measurement.

Much of the debate surrounding this issue (see reviews by Kinder and Sears, 1985; Sniderman and Tetlock, 1986) has focused first on the extent to which attitude constraint can be said to exist, and second on differences across social categories (e.g., levels of schooling and other measures of elite status) in the extent of attitude constraint. Virtually none of this literature has focused on the relationship between aging and attitude constraint (see Sears, 1983). Some empirical evidence shows that with age (time), attitudes become more crystallized around a common theme. Measuring attitude change in sex-role attitudes in a sample of women between 1962 and 1977, Thornton, Alwin, and Camburn (1983) found that a more coherent set of attitudinal responses existed in 1977 in comparison to 1962. This change in the structure of attitudes might be due to processes inherent in aging, which may stimulate the greater coherence of attitudes over time, or it might be due to historical events. Thornton, Alwin, and Camburn (1983) attribute the change to the sharp increase in the public interest in sex roles associated with the rise of the women's movement and media attention to the Equal Rights Amendment in the late 1960s and early 1970s.

Little is actually known about the relationship between age and attitude constraint, and there is little empirical basis for sorting out the potential explanations. We hope that future research will address this general set of issues. It seems to us that there are two bedrock issues that need to be addressed: the extent to which age groups differ with respect to attitude constraint, and the question of interpreting variations in attitude constraint over time. In the type of analysis suggested above, it would be extremely useful to be able to control for cohort in the same manner as we have in our analysis of attitude stability in the NES panel data. Such a design permits the separation of aging and cohort influences, since by following a cohort

273

(or set of cohorts) over time, we can gain a better understanding of the uniquenesses of individual cohorts. However, this design does not allow us cleanly to separate aging and period effects, although to the extent the patterns are predictable on the basis of a life-cycle model, a better purchase on these issues can be obtained. Suffice it to say at this stage that the extension of our above models to include multiple indicators of latent constructs over time within the framework of a *repeated-synthetic-cohort panel design* would provide a preliminary basis for grappling with this set of issues.

Gender and Attitude Change

It is not clear to what extent it is important to consider the results based on our Bennington data as reflecting processes specific to women's political development. The combined facts of substantial change in these women's attitudes during their years at Bennington, the intensity and importance of that change in their lives, and the overall persistence of these changed orientations, all could be understood (at least in part) in terms of the social meaning of gender, the meaning of women's higher education during the 1930s and 1940s, the gender structure of the early Bennington environment (an all-female student body and a primarily male faculty), and changes in the roles of women of the past half-century.

Little research has provided direct comparisons of males and females in their potential differences in individual-level stabilities of the type examined here. There is, however, a large experimental literature dealing with gender differences in influenceability (see Eagly, 1978, 1983, 1987; McGuire, 1985). Although there are differences in interpretations of what the research literature shows (compare Eagly, 1978, 1983, 1987 and Maccoby and Jacklin, 1974, with McGuire, 1985), there is some support for the view that women tend to be more influenceable, an asymmetry found in a number of different studies (see Eagly and Carli, 1981). If these results are accurate, the greater potential to yield to pressure on the part of women suggests a hypothesis that women will exhibit less persistence of attitudes over the life cycle. Indeed, Eagly (1978:105–108) suggests that if women are more susceptible to social influences, it is because of role behavior structured into the female sex role, or because of women's greater orientation to interpersonal goals.

Our findings are, of course, at odds with most of what this research suggests, as we find the Bennington women to be strongly resistant to change in later adulthood and not at all passive recipients of influence. And even in their young adult years, during the time they were students at Bennington, their degree of attitude change should perhaps be understood in terms of the meaning of gender in the late 1930s and early 1940s.

While one might understand that change as a passive acceptance of influence from the college environment, a perspective that is consistent with the view of women as susceptible to change, we would argue that it makes more sense to understand it as a process of actively seeking autonomy and independence from their parents.

To our knowledge, no study using sufficiently large and representative samples has attempted to investigate stability differences by gender in any of the variables proposed for analysis here. The Bennington sample contained only women, so the conclusions drawn from that study may not be applicable to men. As we noted above in our discussion of role transitions, there is some suggestion that the uniformity of many role transitions over the life span may have created the potential for the persistence of attitudes. Is it conceivable that the attitude change Sears (1981) and others find after age 65 is differentially characteristic of women and men, given that the data in the upper age ranges contain predominantly women? We have found no significant linkage between attitude change and the experience of widowhood (see chapter 9), but could it be that in a more broadly representative sample of women, one more socioeconomically diverse, we might find the experience of such losses more disruptive of attitudinal perspectives?

In any case, future research needs to establish whether there are any significant differences between men and women in the estimated magnitude of stability in attitudes over the life span. In fact, such research can be done using existing data and can be performed in a relatively straightforward fashion. Of course, as we note in the following, such research should be carried out within the context of a model that specifies the variables that provide opportunities for attitude change. If Eagly (1978, 1983, 1987) is correct that women are more vulnerable to attitude change because they experience more of the change-inducing behaviors as a function of the female sex role, such research should be able to determine the extent to which this is true. Again, however, we would note that no extant data would permit the investigation of models involving gender-role experiences, as the existing panel data do not provide precise measures of significant live events.

Aging and the Constancy of Personality

Our assumption has been that if we could find evidence of stability in dimensions of personality which could be said to define fundamental aspects of the person—theoretically more fundamental to individual functioning than political ideology or social attitudes—then this might serve as an explanatory device for understanding our empirical assessments of stability. There is actually little agreement among developmental psychologists regarding the extent to which basic aspects of personality, those related to cognitive functioning and affective orientations, remain constant over time.

There is a high degree of consensus regarding the early development and constancy of individual differences in certain cognitive and intellective skills (e.g., Bloom, 1964; Schaie, 1983), suggesting substantial constancy of behavior. On the other hand, concerning other aspects of personality and individual functioning there is virtually no agreement. Some perspectives, such as Gergen's aleatoric account of life span development (1980), cite the individual's potential for change and adaptation to new circumstances. Others view personality and basic individual orientations (to other actors, social institutions, and social life generally) as more stable phenomena, suggesting considerable basis for a stability account of individual differences (e.g., Moss and Susman, 1980).

As we indicated earlier in this chapter, our research evidence has provided little support for explanations of attitude stability that rely on notions of individual differences in susceptibility to attitude change (see chapter 8). We noted that one reason for this could be that we have been unable to measure precisely the differences that have been conceptualized to explain constancies of personality and cognitive organization. Another reason lies at the heart of one of the interpretations we have given the unusually high level of stability found among the Bennington women: the unusually high level of salience they assign to social and political issues. There may, of course, be other, more important factors tied to individual differences that might account for the high level of stability witnessed here.

We have very little theoretical understanding of the relationship between *personality*—defined in terms of a more or less stable set of predispositions to act and respond with respect to the environment—on the one hand, and *political ideology* on the other. We have here stretched the notion of personality to include individual differences in such things as values, interests, and attitude organization. We do not, as yet, have much evidence that stabilities in these aspects of individuals are linked in any coherent way to stabilities in attitudes and political behavior. It is important nonetheless to reach some theoretical and empirical understanding regarding how basic aspects of personality become stable over biographical time. The meaning one attributes to much of our data depends upon the extent to which we can assume a basic constancy of personality and consistency of self-images over time.

Thus, we propose that some systematic attention be given to the question of how constancies in basic aspects of personality develop and how these are related to constancies in sociopolitical orientations. Specifically, we propose that research be devoted to the question of how individual differences in susceptibility, or openness, to change in basic personality orientations—differences in the type of conservatism referred to earlier in terms of a generally rigid orientation to life and a resistence to change— are developed, and how these are linked to stabilities in other domains of life. By studying the individual-level stability of a wide range of aspects of personality, and by examining life-cycle differences in such stabilities within the synthetic-cohort framework introduced here, greater empirical clarity can be brought to the presently diverse speculative terrain regarding constancy and change in human behavior (see Alwin, 1992).

Social Networks and the Social Environment

We indicated earlier that in addition to differences in individual susceptibility to change, it is important to understand the relationship of constancies in social environments and the opportunities for attitude change. We were unable to demonstrate that changes in social networks due to major life events, role transitions, or life course changes were linked in any coherent fashion to long-term stabilities in attitudes. However, we were able to show a dramatic relationship between attitude stability and many different indicators of the supportiveness of social environments.

We speculated that the dual processes of social selection and social support served to maintain the compatibility between the individual's attitudes and those of members of her social network. Unfortunately, our data do not permit us to achieve any further clarity regarding the complex reciprocal influences that produce these correlations. We cannot tell whether the consistencies between our respondents and their significant others are present because people select compatible environments, or whether they exist because individuals' environments are primarily supportive and not an important source of attitude change.

Little is known about the relationship between age and the compatibility of one's social environment with respect to political matters. We cited Morgan's (1988) careful analysis of the relation of age to network composition, which indicates a significant decline in network size in older age, independent of changes in resources and health. But we also were able to show that, despite these changes, the political complexion of one's social network seems to be quite similar over most of the life span. In other words, there are no obvious points of deflection in changes in network composition that are linked to similar shifts in the political composition of those networks.

Unfortunately, pertinent information on role transitions over the life-cycle is only sparsely available in extant data, such as the NES panels, and the material that does exist in these surveys does not contain information on social networks, their composition, and change. Thus, within the confines of existing data, a more rigorous investigation of this set of issues is not possible. We propose that future research address the question of the relative importance of social selection and social support in the development and change of sociopolitical attitudes over time. More data are needed to ascertain the extent to which changes in social relationships and social networks can be linked interpretively to patterns of aging and attitude change.

Historical Differences in Life-Cycle Patterns of Stability and Change

Our research has shown that there seem to be definite life course patterns that can be recovered from panel data, either by studying a single cohort through time, as in our Bennington research, or by creating synthetic cohorts of estimated stabilities by categories of age. We have noted previously that there are some severe problems with these types of designs. We noted in particular that there is a historical boundedness to all of our results, although we provide some evidence in this chapter that the processes operating to produce these data seem relatively uniform with respect to historical time.

Still, while these results are relatively convincing, there is a need for more data. One way to generate a stronger basis for inference is to obtain comparable data across more recent time periods. We propose specifically that the four-year, three-wave NES panel studies be replicated during the 1990s in order to investigate the extent to which various measures of attitudes might replicate the life span developmental patterns witnessed here. Existing longitudinal comparisons of cohort-specific stabilities are limited to estimates from the 1950s and 1970s NES panel studies and exist for only a single variable: political party identification. Due to these limitations, we propose that new data be collected to provide cohort-specific comparisons for many more variables. This would provide a much stronger inferential basis for determining the nature of life-cycle patterns in attitude stabilities.

Indeed, one of the most basic issues in life span development is the extent to which age-grading in a given society changes as the society changes historically. For example, Neugarten and Datan (1973) argue that as society changes, the rhythm of the life cycle also changes. Specifically, they note that the timing of major life events principally affecting young people has changed significantly over the last century: the age of leaving school has increased, age at marriage has declined, and the age at the birth of the first child has declined. Events affecting people in the older years have also changed in their average age of occurrence: the age of women at the death of their spouses has increased dramatically, and the marriage of a person's youngest child occurs at a younger age, presumably a function of changes in the age at first marriage.

278

Neugarten and Datan (1973:69), in fact, suggest a hypothesis that would have implications for our findings regarding the impressionable years of late adolescence and early adulthood. They wrote that as their chapter was being written, "the morning newspaper carries a story about high school radicals and the fact that by the time they reach college they seem to have exhausted their political energies . . . [they] have burned out and [are] leading a more conventional life as [college students]" than did previous generations. Their journalistic evidence does not, of course, do justice to the hypothesis that social change brings changes in life course patterns in attitude stability. Unfortunately, except for the evidence of uniformity in life-cycle patterns of stability and change in the stability of political party preferences derived from the NES panel studies reported above, there is little available data that can be brought to bear on this type of hypothesis. We therefore propose that these panel studies be replicated in the future so that historical variations in patterns of stability over the life span can be documented and compared with existing estimates of the critical parameters of these processes.

Concluding Comments

We began this project with the rather modest goals of conducting a third wave in a longitudinal study of attitude development and change, describing the patterns of stability and change, and interpreting these patterns in terms of theoretically relevant processes. We sought to lodge our longitudinal study within the theoretical and empirical literature on life span developmental processes, taking into account all of the factors that might contribute to patterns of stability and change in attitudes. In pursuit of these goals we have tried to shed more light on the nature of political attitude development and change over the entire life span.

This pursuit, however, has taken us in a number of different directions, and we believe there is some didactic value in underscoring certain aspects of the nature of our investigation. For a number of reasons, not the least of which was the fact that the Bennington women were obviously not a sample of any known population of interest, we sought a comparative basis in extant data from the National Election Studies. The NES data provided such a comparative framework in three different ways, which we believe strengthened our inferences considerably. First, we were fortunate to be able to compare the Bennington women with the larger population in 1984 by replicating many of the 1984 NES questions. This was a strategy also followed by Newcomb and his colleagues (1967) for obtaining a benchmark comparison of the women with the larger population in the 1960s. Second, we were able to use the entire NES series since 1952 to investigate better the comparability of the Bennington women with women born into the same cohorts, especially those who also had some college experience during the 1930s and 1940s. This led us to compare the full array of birth-cohort data in the NES with respect to certain key measures. Finally, our interest in the issue of patterns of attitude stability in the Bennington sample led us to a parallel investigation of the nationally representative panel data from the 1950s and 1970s NES studies. Using these data, we were able to estimate the parameters of a synthetic-cohort model of attitude change and stability, which provided supplementary support for the Bennington results.

As we conclude the presentation of our findings, we recall our own initial skepticism about the utility of studying attitude development and change in a historically and socially unique group of women, who are not necessarily representative of populations to which we might otherwise wish to generalize. Our own skepticism in this regard has been tempered by the apparent uniformity of results between our Bennington analyses and our analyses of the NES panel data. And while we have noted at several points the ways in which the Bennington women are truly distinct, their patterns of attitude development and change over the life span do seem to coincide in broad outline with other available evidence.

Although we are not fully prepared to dismiss the uniqueness of the Bennington data, we are encouraged that our efforts to evaluate these processes in other relevant data yielded such clear convergences. In other respects, particularly our attempts to explain the growing persistence of attitudes after young adulthood, we were not able to find other data that could be relied upon to supplement the Bennington sample. Thus, our conclusions with respect to the relative importance of the social environment and its role in providing social support and our conclusions regarding the relative unimportance of cognitive organization and the constancy of personality in explaining differences in attitude persistence and change need further confirmation in other research before they will serve as a basis for broader generalization.

We have also outlined a number of avenues which we believe future research might profitably take. We have given greatest emphasis in that discussion to studies that fit within the synthetic-cohort models we developed for the NES data. We have not mentioned the possibility of reinterviewing other existing samples which are like the Bennington sample in the sense that they embody a less-representative view of life course trajectories of attitudes and behavior, although such a course of research would no doubt be beneficial. While we obviously counsel great caution in developing research designs around such purposive samples, we believe our research on the Bennington women demonstrates how it is possible to remedy many of the problems of dealing with such unique cohorts by strategically developing comparisons with more nationally representative bodies of data.

Thus, while the Bennington studies may not by themselves provide the definitive test of hypotheses generated from the literature on life span development, they have shown themselves to be of great use in generating hypotheses that can be verified in other samples at other times. In this sense, we hope that the Bennington studies will continue to stimulate research on processes of attitude development and change over the life span, and continue their role in posing questions regarding the lifelong relationship between personality and social change.

Appendixes   References   Index

Appendix A

The Political and Economic Progressivism (PEP) Scale

On the following pages appear statements about certain contemporary public issues. You will agree with some of the statements, disagree with some, and be uncertain of others. There are no "right" or "wrong" answers. Whatever you happen to think about it is the right answer for you.

Please indicate your replies as follows:

Encircle A if you *agree* with the statement; encircle SA if you *strongly agree* with it; encircle D if you *disagree* with the statement; encircle SD if you *strongly disagree;* encircle ? if you are *uncertain.*

SA   A   ?   D   SD

THE PEP SCALE

1. The only true prosperity of the nation as a whole must be based upon the prosperity of the working class.
2. Recovery has been delayed by the large number of strikes.
3. Some form of collective society, in which profits are replaced by reimbursements for useful mental or manual work, is preferable to our present system.
4. The depression occurred chiefly because the working classes did not receive enough in wages to purchase goods and services produced at a profit.
5. A "planned economy" is not enough unless it is planned for the welfare of workers rather than of business men.
6. Most labor trouble happens only because of radical agitators.
7. The people who complain most about the depression wouldn't take a job if you gave it to them.
8. The standard of living of the working class can be kept above the poverty line only as workers force it up by the use of strikes.
9. Labor organizations have as much right to bring in outside agitators as do business men to import outside technical experts.
10. Any able-bodied man could get a job right now if he tried hard enough.
11. Most people on relief are living in reasonable comfort.
12. The budget should be balanced before the government spends any money on "social security."

285

13. Our government has always been run primarily in the interests of big business, and so it is those interests which were chiefly responsible for the depression.
14. Labor unions are justifiable only if they refrain from the use of strikes.
15. Since it is impossible for working people to make any substantial savings, they have fully earned their rights to old-age pensions.
16. It is all right to try to raise the standard of living of the lower classes, provided that existing property rights are continually safeguarded.
17. Most employers think only of profits and care little about their employees' welfare.
18. Unemployment insurance would saddle us with a nation of idlers.
19. Organizations of the unemployed are just a group of chronic complainers.
20. We have no true democracy in this country, because only business and industrial concerns have economic opportunity.
21. If the government didn't meddle so much in business, everything would be all right.
22. You can't expect democracy to work very well as long as so many uneducated and unintelligent people have the vote.
23. The vast majority of those in the lower economic classes are there because they are stupid or shiftless, or both.
24. Those who have the ability and the foresight to accumulate wealth ought to be permitted to enjoy it themselves.
25. The middle classes will never enjoy security or prosperity until they understand that their welfare is identified with that of the working class, and not with that of business and industrial groups.
26. The real threat to prosperity in this country is the repressive activity of those who wish to keep wealth and economic power in the hands of those who now possess them.

Appendix B

The 1984 Questionnaire

This appendix reproduces the questionnaire used in the personal interviews conducted with 28 members of our Bennington sample (see Chapter 4, pp. 69–70). The telephone interview, conducted with the remaining 307 respondents, was based on an abbreviated version of this questionnaire, but supplemented with a self-administered form which telephone respondents returned by mail. The following questions were deleted from the telephone interview, but were included on the self-administered form: C13, C14, C15, C16, C17, C34, D27, and D28. The following questions were included in neither the telephone interview nor the self-administered form: A27, A28, A29, A30, A31, C3, C4, C7, C8, C32, D1, D2, D16, D17, D24, D25, D26, F5, F6, F7, F8, F9, F10, F11, F12, F13, F14, F15, F20, F21, F22, F23, F24, F26 (except c, d, and h), G9, G10, G11, G13, and G21.

POLITICAL ORIENTATION OVER THE LIFE-SPAN
P. 40 (462294)
1984

For office use only

Receipt Date

SURVEY RESEARCH CENTER
INSTITUTE FOR SOCIAL RESEARCH
THE UNIVERSITY OF MICHIGAN
ANN ARBOR, MICHIGAN 48106

2. Interviewer Label OR

   NAME:_____

3. Your IW No. _____

4. Date of IW _____

5. Length of IW _____(min.)

6. Length of Edit_____(min.)

POLITICAL ORIENTATION OVER THE LIFE-SPAN

STATEMENT OF CONFIDENTIALITY MUST BE READ TO RESPONDENT:

Before we start, I would like to assure you that this interview is
confidential and completely voluntary. If we should come to any
question which you don't want to answer, just let me know and
we'll go on to the next question. May we go ahead?

EXACT TIME NOW:_____

$$\boxed{SECTION\ A}$$

A1. In what years did you first attend Bennington College? _____ TO _____
                                                              YEAR   YEAR

    A1a. Did you receive a degree from Bennington? | 1. YES | | 5. NO |

    A1c. What was your major field of study there?

_____

A2. Did you continue your formal education at any time after you left Bennington College?

        | 1. YES | | 5. NO | ----> TURN TO P.2, A4

A3. Did you receive any (additional) college degrees?

        | 1. YES | | 5. NO | ----> GO TO A3e

A3a. What degree? (Any other?)			
A3b. From which college or university?			
A3c. What year was that?			
A3d. What was your major area of study?			

    A3e. Which (other) colleges or universities did you attend? When?

      1._____When?_____

      2._____When?_____

      3._____When?_____

A4. What was the highest year of college you finally completed?

$\boxed{\text{01 YR}}$ $\boxed{\text{02 YR}}$ $\boxed{\text{03 YR}}$ $\boxed{\text{04 YR}}$ $\boxed{\text{05 YR}}$ $\boxed{\text{06 YR}}$ $\boxed{\text{07 YR}}$ $\boxed{\text{08+ YRS}}$

A5. Since you first attended college, have you <u>ever</u> followed a career or profession, or been employed either part-time or full-time?

$\boxed{\text{1. YES}}$ $\boxed{\text{5. NO}}$ ----> TURN TO P.3, A10

A6. What was the first regular job you had after leaving Bennington College?

_____

A6a. What were your main activities or duties? _____

_____

_____

A6b. What business or industry was that? _____

_____

A6c. What year did you start that job? YEAR:_____

A6c. How long did you do that kind of work? _____ # YEARS

A7. Are you doing any work for pay now?

$\boxed{\text{1. YES}}$ ----> TURN TO P. 3, A8 $\boxed{\text{5. NO}}$

A7a. When did you stop working last? _____ YEAR

A7b. What were your main reasons for no longer working?

_____

_____

290

A8. What (is your current/was your most recent) job? | SAME AS A6 | ---> GO TO A9

_____

A8a. What (are/were) your main activities or duties? _____

_____

_____

A8b. What business or industry (is/was) that? _____

_____

A8c. What year did you start that job? YEAR:_____

A8d. How long (have you done/did you do) that kind of work? _____ YEARS

A9. What job did you have the longest in your lifetime?

| SAME AS A6 | or | SAME AS A8 | ---> GO TO A10

_____

A9a. What were your main activities or duties? _____

_____

_____

A9b. What business or industry was that? _____

A9c. What year did you start that job? YEAR:_____

A9d. How long (have you done/did you do) that kind of work? _____ YEARS

A10. Are you currently married, widowed, divorced, separated or have you never been married?

| 1. MARRIED | 2. WIDOWED | 3. DIVORCED | 4. SEPARATED | 5. NEVER MARRIED |

TURN TO P. 6, A26

A12.   Altogether, how many times have you been married?

_____   1. ONCE ------> TURN TO P. 5, A20

	A. FIRST MARRIAGE	B. NEXT MARRIAGE
A13. In what year were you (first/next) married?	_____ YEAR	_____ YEAR
A14. What was your husband's main occupation?	_____	_____
A14a. What were his main activities or duties?	_____	_____
A14b. What business or industry was that?	_____	_____
A15. How many years of school did your husband complete?	_____YEARS	_____YEARS
A16. Did that marriage end in widowhood, or divorce?	1. WIDOWED 2. DIVORCED	1. WIDOWED 2. DIVORCED
A17. In what year (were you widowed/did you and your husband stop living together)?	_____ YEAR	_____ YEAR
A18. Did you have any children from that marriage?	1. YES 5. NO	1. YES 5. NO

A19. INTERVIEW CHECKPOINT: ___ 1. ONLY 2 IN A12; TURN TO P. 5, A20.   TURN TO P. 5, A20.

___ 2. MORE THAN 2 IN A12 ---> ASK A13-A19 AGAIN, NEXT MARRIAGE

[ONLY OR LAST MARRIAGE]

A20. In what year were you (last) married?   YEAR:_____

A21. Did you have any children from this marriage?

| 1. YES | | 5. NO |

A22. How many years of school did your husband complete?

NUMBER OF YEARS_____

A23. (Has/did) your husband (retired/retire) from work?

| 1. YES | | 5. NO | ------> GO TO A24

    A23a. What year was that? _____

    A23b. How did your husband's retirement affect your life?

    _____

    _____

    _____

A24. What (is/was) your husband's main job? _____

_____

    A24a. What (are/were) his main activities or duties?_____

    _____

    _____

    A24b. What business or industry (is/was) that?_____

    _____

A25. (IF NOT CURRENTLY MARRIED) In what year (were you widowed/did you and your husband stop living together?)

YEAR:_____

293

A26. How long have you lived in <u>this</u> community?

_____ YEARS | 97. ALL MY LIFE | ----> GO TO A32.

A27. Where did you live before you moved here?

_____
CITY AND STATE

A28. How many years did you live there?

_____ YEARS

A29. Where did you grow up; that is, what city and state do you consider your main residence until you were about 16 years old?

_____
CITY AND STATE

A30. About how many different communities have you lived in since leaving college?

NUMBER _____

A31. In which city and state have you lived the longest since leaving college?

_____
CITY AND STATE

A31a. During which years was that? _____

A32. Of the ten families that live closest to your home, how many would you say you know by name?

_____ NUMBER | 00. NONE | ----> TURN TO P. 10, B1

A33. Of these ten families, how many have you ever visited with, either in their home or in yours?

_____ NUMBER

294

SECTION B
BACKGROUND

B1. Please tell me a bit about your background. What was your mother's religious preference while you were growing up?

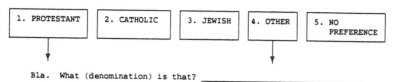

       B1a. What (denomination) is that? _____

B2. What was your father's religious preference while you were growing up?

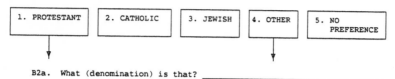

       B2a. What (denomination) is that? _____

B3. What is your religious preference now?

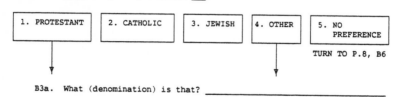

       B3a. What (denomination) is that? _____

B4. (IF ANY RELIGIOUS PREFERENCE) would you say you go to (church/synagogue) every week, almost every week, once or twice a month, a few times a year, or never?]

B5. Do you listen to religious services regularly on radio or TV?

| 1. YES | | 5. NO |

B6. In general, how religious-minded would you say you are--very religious minded, more than average, average, less than average, or not at all religious minded?

| 1. VERY | 2. MORE THAN AVERAGE | 3. AVERAGE | 4. LESS THAN AVERAGE | 5. NOT AT ALL |

B7. When you were growing up, did you attend Sunday School or religious instruction classes regularly, most of the time, some of the time, or never?

| 1. REGULARLY OR PAROCHIAL SCHOOL | 2. MOST OF THE TIME | 3. SOME OF THE TIME | 4. NEVER |

B8. How many years of schooling did your <u>father</u> complete?

[IF DON'T KNOW: Well, just approximately ...] _____ YEARS

B9. What was your <u>father</u>'s main occupation or job when you were about 16?

_____

B9a. What were his main activities or duties?

_____

_____

_____

B9b. What kind of industry or business was that? What did they make or do at the place where he worked?

_____

_____

B10. What political party did your father prefer when you were about 16 years old.

| 1. REPUBLICAN | 2. DEMOCRATIC | 4. NONE | 7. OTHER | 8. DK |

SPECIFY:_____

296

B11. How many years of schooling did your <u>mother</u> complete?

[IF DON'T KNOW: Well, just approximately ...] _____ YEARS

B12. Did your mother work for pay when you were about 16?

| 1. YES | | 5. NO | ----> GO TO B13

B12a. Did she work mostly full-time or part-time?

| 1. FULL-TIME | | 2. PART-TIME |

B12b. What was her main occupation or job when you were about 16?

_____

B12c. What were her main activities or duties?

_____

_____

_____

B12d. What kind of industry or business was that? What did they make or do at the place where she worked?

_____

B13. What political party did your mother prefer when you were about 16 years old.

| 1. REPUBLICAN | | 2. DEMOCRATIC | | 4. NONE | | 7. OTHER | | 8. DK |

SPECIFY:_____

297

B14. What is the month, day, and year of your birth?

$$\underline{\hspace{2cm}} - \underline{\hspace{1cm}} - \underline{\hspace{2cm}}$$
$$\text{MONTH} \quad \text{DAY} \quad \text{YEAR}$$

B15. [RB, PAGE 1] Would you give me the letter which best describes your (and your husband's) total income before taxes in 1983? Please consider all sources such as wages, profits, interest, social secruity and so on.

LETTER _____   97. REFUSED   98. DON'T KNOW

RB, PAGE 1

A. LESS THAN $10,000

B. $10,000 - $19,999

C. $20,000 - $29,999

D. $30,000 - $49,999

E. $50,000 - $74,999

F. $75,000 - $99,999

G. $100,000 OR MORE

298

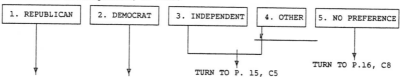

```
                    ┌──────────────────────────────┐
                    │          SECTION C           │
                    │  CURRENT POLITICAL ATTITUDES  │
                    └──────────────────────────────┘
```

C1. Generally speaking, do you usually think of yourself as a Republican, a
     Democrat, an independent, or what?

1. REPUBLICAN	2. DEMOCRAT	3. INDEPENDENT	4. OTHER	5. NO PREFERENCE

TURN TO P. 15, C5

TURN TO P.16, C8

C2. Would you call yourself a <u>strong</u> (Republican/Democrat) or a <u>not very strong</u>
     (Republican/Democrat)?

1. STRONG		2. NOT VERY STRONG	----> TURN TO P. 14, C4

C3. Do any of these statements come close to what you mean when you say you are a <u>strong</u> (Republican/Democrat)?	1. YES	5. NO
C3a. I involve myself in what the (Republican/Democratic) Party is doing.		
C3b. My parents were (Republican/Democrat) and I am too.		
C3c. I am enthusiastic about what the (Republican/ Democratic) Party stands for.		
C3d. I almost always support the (Republican/Democratic) candidates.		
C3e. I really mean that I liked the (Republican/Democratic) candidate very much in the last presidential election.		
C3f. I'm a strong (Republican/Democrat) because of the way I feel about what Ronald Reagan has been doing.		
C3g. With me it's more a matter of strongly disliking the opposite party than anything else.		
C3h. Any other reason why you say you are <u>a strong</u> (Republican/Democrat)? (What is that?)		

TURN TO P. 17, C9

C4. Do any of these statements come close to what you mean when you say you are <u>not a strong</u> (Republican/Democrat)?	1. YES	5. NO
C4a. I usually think of myself as a (Republican/Democrat), but I don't agree completely with what the party stands for.		
C4b. I usually prefer (Republican/Democratic) candidates but sometimes I support candidates of other parties.		
C4c. I vote for the person not the party.		
C4d. I usually support (Republican/Democratic) candidates, but I don't much like the (Republican/Democrats) in this predidential election.		
C4e. I don't involve myself in what the (Republican/Democratic) party is doing.		
C4f. I'm a (Republican/Democrat) but it isn't very important to me.		
C4f. I'm a not very strong (Republican/Democrat) because of the way I feel about what Ronald Reagan has been doing.		
C4g. With me it's more a matter of <u>not liking</u> the opposite party than anything else.		
C4h. Any other reason why you say you are <u>not a strong</u> (Republican/Democrat)? (What is that?)		

TURN TO P. 17, C9

300

C5. (FOR INDEPENDENTS or OTHER - 3-4 in C1): Do you think of yourself as closer to the Republican Party or to the Democratic Party?

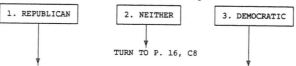

| 1. REPUBLICAN | 2. NEITHER | 3. DEMOCRATIC |

TURN TO P. 16, C8

C6. Do you think of yourself as much closer or only a little closer to the (Republican/Democratic) party?

| 1. MUCH CLOSER | 2. A LITTLE CLOSER |

C7. Do any of these statements come close to what you mean when you say you think of yourself as closer to the (Republican/Democratic) Party?	1. YES	5. NO
C7a. More often than not, I find myself supporting what the (Republican/Democratic) Party stands for.		
C7b. Most of the time I prefer (Republican/Democratic) Candidates.		
C7c. I prefer the (Republican/Democratic) candidates in the coming presidential election.		
C7d. I've always lived around (Republicans/Democrats).		
C7e. I don't involve myself in what the other party is doing.		
C7f. I feel closer to the (Republican/Democratic) Party because of the way I feel about what Ronald Reagan has been doing.		
C7g. I like the other party even less than I like the (Republican/Democratic) Party.		
C7h. Any other reason why you feel closer to the (Republican/Democratic) Party? (What is that?)		

TURN TO P. 17, C9

C8. (FOR NO PREFERENCE [5 in C1] or CLOSE TO NEITHER PARTY [2 in C5]):

C8. Do any of these statements come close to what you mean when you say you (have no preference/are close to neither party)?	1. YES	5. NO
C8a. I support both Democrats and Republicans.		
C8b. I decide on the <u>person</u> not the party.		
C8c. I decide on the <u>issues</u> not the party label.		
C8d. Neither major party stands for what I think is important.		
C8e. I dislike both major parties.		
C8f. I'm not much interested in politics.		
C8g. The parties almost never deliver on their promises.		
C8f. I don't know enough to make a choice.		
C8h. I like both parties about the same.		
C8i. I'm independent because of the way I feel about what Ronald Reagan has been doing.		
C8j. My parents were independent and I am too.		
C8k. Any other reason why you have no preference? (What is that?)		

302

C9. Some people seem to follow what's going on in government and public affairs most of the time, whether there's an election going on or not. Others aren't that interested. Would you say you follow what's going on in government and public affairs most of the time, some of the time, only now and then, or hardly at all?

1. MOST OF THE TIME	2. SOME OF THE TIME	3. ONLY NOW AND THEN	4. HARDLY AT ALL	8. DON'T KNOW

C10. How about the presidential campaign in 1984. Would you say that you are very much interested, somewhat interested, or not much interested in following the presidential campaign in 1984?

1. VERY MUCH INTERESTED	3. SOMEWHAT INTERESTED	5. NOT MUCH INTERESTED

C11. In the present presidential campaign do you prefer Reagan, Mondale, Hart or Jackson?

1. REAGAN	2. MONDALE	3. HART	4. JACKSON

C12. Would you say that you personally care a good deal which party wins the presidential election in the fall of 1984, or that you don't care very much which party wins?

1. CARE A GOOD DEAL	5. DON'T CARE VERY MUCH	8. DON'T KNOW

C13. In general, which do you rely on most for news about politics and current events -- television, newspapers, magazines or radio?

1. TV	2. NEWSPAPER	3. MAGAZINE	4. RADIO	5. ALL EQUAL	6. NONE

C14. How often do you watch the national network news on TV -- every evening, 3 or 4 times a week, once or twice a week, or less often?

| 1. EVERY EVENING | 2. 3 OR 4 TIMES A WEEK | 3. ONCE OR TWICE A WEEK | 4. LESS OFTEN |

C14a. When you watch the news on TV, do you pay a great deal of attention to news about government and politics, do you pay some attention, or don't you pay much attention to news about government and politics?

| 1. GREAT DEAL OF ATTENTION | 2. SOME ATTENTION | 3. DON'T PAY MUCH ATTENTION |

C15. Do you regularly read a news magazine such as Time, Newsweek, or U.S. News and World Report?

| 1. YES | | 5. NO | ---->GO TO C15c

C15a. What news magazines do you read regularly?

_____

_____

C15b. When you read news magazines, do you pay a great deal of attention to news about government and politics, do you pay some attention, or don't you pay much attention to news about government and politics?

| 1. GREAT DEAL OF ATTENTION | 2. SOME ATTENTION | 3. DON'T PAY MUCH ATTENTION |

C15c. What other magazines do you read regularly?

_____

_____

_____

304

C16.   Do you read any newspapers regularly?

| 1. YES | | 5. NO | ----->GO TO C17 |

    C16a.   When you read the newspapers, do you pay a great deal of attention to news about government and politics, do you pay some attention, or don't you pay much attention to news about government and politics?

| 1. GREAT DEAL OF ATTENTION | 2. SOME ATTENTION | 3. DON'T PAY MUCH ATTENTION |

    C16b.   What newspapers do you read on a regular basis?

_____

_____

_____

C17.   Do you regularly listen to national news on the radio?

| 1. YES | | 5. NO | ----> TURN TO P. 20, C18 |

    C17a.   And when you listen to national news on the radio, how much attention do you generally pay to news about government and politics: A great deal of attention, some attention, or not much attention?

| 1. GREAT DEAL OF ATTENTION | 2. SOME ATTENTION | 3. DON'T PAY MUCH ATTENTION |

305

C18. Please indicate the candidate whom you <u>preferred</u> in each of the 11 presidential campaigns since 1939. I'll help you recall their names.

C18. In ... did you prefer:		C19. Did you <u>vote</u> in...?	C18. In ... did you prefer:		C19. Did you <u>vote</u> in...?
C18a. 1980	1. Carter		C18g. 1956	1. Stevenson	
	2. Reagan	1. YES		2. Eisenhower	1. YES
	3. Anderson	5. NO		7. OTHER:	5. NO
	7. OTHER:				
C18b. 1976	1. Carter		C18h. 1952	1. Stevenson	
	2. Ford	1. YES		2. Eisenhower	1. YES
	7. OTHER:	5. NO		7. OTHER:	5. NO
C18c. 1972	1. McGovern		C18i. 1948	1. Truman	
	2. Nixon	1. YES		2. Dewey	1. YES
	7. OTHER:	5. NO		3. Thurmond	5. NO
				7. OTHER:	
C18d. 1968	1. Humphrey				
	2. Nixon	1. YES	C18j. 1944	1. Roosevelt	
	3. Wallace	5. NO		2. Dewey	1. YES
	7. OTHER:			7. OTHER:	5. NO
C18e. 1964	1. Johnson		C18k. 1940	1. Roosevelt	
	2. Goldwater	1. YES		2. Wilkie	1. YES
	7. OTHER:	5. NO		7. OTHER:	5. NO
C18f. 1960	1. Kennedy				
	2. Nixon	1. YES			
	7. OTHER:	5. NO			

306

APPENDIX B

C20. INTERVIEWER CHECKPOINT: ☐ 1. R WAS <u>NEVER</u> MARRIED ---> TURN TO P. 22, C22

☐ 2. ALL OTHERS ---> ASK C21

C21. If you were married at the time, please indicate your husband's preference in the past presidential elections.

In ... did your husband prefer:			In ... did your husband prefer:	
C21a. 1980	1. Carter		C21g. 1956	1. Stevenson
0. NOT	2. Reagan		0. NOT	2. Eisenhower
MARRIED	3. Anderson		MARRIED	7. OTHER:
	7. OTHER:			
C21b. 1976	1. Carter		C21h. 1952	1. Stevenson
0. NOT	2. Ford		0. NOT	2. Eisenhower
MARRIED	7. OTHER:		MARRIED	7. OTHER:
C21c. 1972	1. McGovern		C21i. 1948	1. Truman
0. NOT	2. Nixon		0. NOT	2. Dewey
MARRIED	7. OTHER:		MARRIED	3. Thurmond
				7. OTHER:
CC21d. 1968	1. Humphrey			
0. NOT	2. Nixon		C21j. 1944	1. Roosevelt
MARRIED	3. Wallace		0. NOT	2. Dewey
	7. OTHER:		MARRIED	7. OTHER:
C21e. 1964	1. Johnson		C21k. 1940	1. Roosevelt
0. NOT	2. Goldwater		0. NOT	2. Wilkie
MARRIED	7. OTHER:		MARRIED	7. OTHER:
C21f. 1960	1. Kennedy			
0. NOT	2. Nixon			
MARRIED	7. OTHER:			

307

C22. [RB, PAGE 2] Let's talk about your feelings toward some of the groups of people who are often active in politics.

I'll read the name of a group and I'd like you to rate this group using a feeling thermometer. You may use any number from 0 to 100 for rating. Ratings between 50 degrees and 100 degrees mean that you feel favorable and warm toward the group. Ratings between 0 degrees and 50 degrees mean that you don't feel too favorable toward the group.

If you don't feel particularly warm or cold toward the group, you would rate the group at the 50 degree mark.

At what number on the thermometer would you place . . .	RATING
C22a. Big business?	
C22b. Poor people?	
C22c. Liberals?	
C22d. Southerners?	
C22e. Hispanics?	
C22f. Radical students?	
C22g. The elderly?	
C22h. The present US Supreme Court?	
C22i. People seeking to protect the environment?	
C22j. The Federal government in Washington?	
C22k. At what number on the thermometer would you place the military?	
C22l. Businessmen and businesswomen?	
C22m. Blacks?	
C22n. Democrats?	
C22p. People on welfare?	
C22q. Republicans?	
C22r. Labor unions?	
C22s. Civil rights leaders?	

At what number on the thermometer would you place . . .	RATING
C22t. Young people?	
C22u. Conservatives?	
C22v. The Women's Liberation Movement?	
C22w. Working men and working women?	
C22x. Congress -- that is the US Senate and the House of Representatives?	
C22y. Evangelical groups active in politics, such as the Moral Majority?	
C22z. Middle-class people?	

Now, would you think about some of the issues in our country today.

C23. During the past year, would you say that the United States' position in the world has grown weaker, stayed about the same, or has it grown stronger?

1. WEAKER	3. STAYED SAME	5. STRONGER	8. DON'T KNOW

C24. How worried are you about our country getting into a <u>conventional war</u>, one in which nuclear weapons are <u>not</u> used? Are you very worried, somewhat worried, or not worried at all?

1. VERY WORRIED	3. SOMEWHAT WORRIED	5. NOT WORRIED	8. DK

C25. How worried are you about our country getting into a <u>nuclear war</u>? Are you very worried, somewhat worried, or not worried at all?

1. VERY WORRIED	3. SOMEWHAT WORRIED	5. NOT WORRIED	8. DK

309

C26. Some people think the government in Washington should provide **fewer** services, even in areas such as health and education, in order to reduce spending. Other people feel it is important for the government to provide **more** services even if it means an increase in spending.

Do you have an opinion on this issue, or haven't you thought much about this?

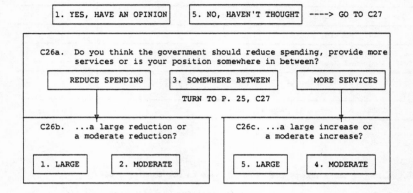

| 1. YES, HAVE AN OPINION | 5. NO, HAVEN'T THOUGHT | ----> GO TO C27 |

C26a. Do you think the government should reduce spending, provide more services or is your position somewhere in between?

| REDUCE SPENDING | 3. SOMEWHERE BETWEEN | MORE SERVICES |

TURN TO P. 25, C27

C26b. ...a large reduction or a moderate reduction?

| 1. LARGE | 2. MODERATE |

C26c. ...a large increase or a moderate increase?

| 5. LARGE | 4. MODERATE |

C27. Some people feel that the government in Washington should make every effort to improve the social and economic position of blacks and other minority groups. Others feel that the government should not make any special effort to help minorities because they should help themselves.

Do you have an opinion on this issue, or haven't you thought much about this?

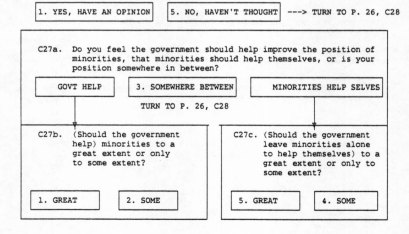

| 1. YES, HAVE AN OPINION | 5. NO, HAVEN'T THOUGHT | ---> TURN TO P. 26, C28 |

C27a. Do you feel the government should help improve the position of minorities, that minorities should help themselves, or is your position somewhere in between?

| GOVT HELP | 3. SOMEWHERE BETWEEN | MINORITIES HELP SELVES |

TURN TO P. 26, C28

C27b. (Should the government help) minorities to a great extent or only to some extent?

| 1. GREAT | 2. SOME |

C27c. (Should the government leave minorities alone to help themselves) to a great extent or only to some extent?

| 5. GREAT | 4. SOME |

C28. Some people think that the United States should become more involved in the internal affairs of Central American countries. Others believe that the U.S. should become less involved in this area.

Do you have an opinion on this issue, or haven't you thought much about this?

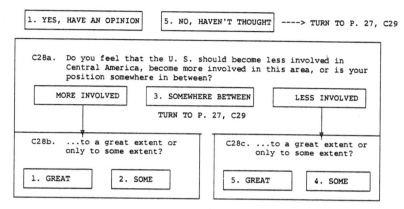

| 1. YES, HAVE AN OPINION | | 5. NO, HAVEN'T THOUGHT | ----> TURN TO P. 27, C29

C28a. Do you feel that the U. S. should become less involved in Central America, become more involved in this area, or is your position somewhere in between?

MORE INVOLVED   3. SOMEWHERE BETWEEN   LESS INVOLVED

TURN TO P. 27, C29

C28b. ...to a great extent or only to some extent?

1. GREAT   2. SOME

C28c. ...to a great extent or only to some extent?

5. GREAT   4. SOME

C29. Some people believe that we should spend less money for defense. Others feel that defense spending should be increased.

Do you have an opinion on this issue, or haven't you thought much about this?

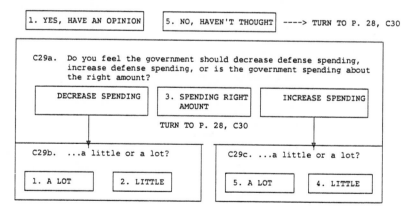

| 1. YES, HAVE AN OPINION | | 5. NO, HAVEN'T THOUGHT | ----> TURN TO P. 28, C30

C29a. Do you feel the government should decrease defense spending, increase defense spending, or is the government spending about the right amount?

DECREASE SPENDING   3. SPENDING RIGHT AMOUNT   INCREASE SPENDING

TURN TO P. 28, C30

C29b. ...a little or a lot?

1. A LOT   2. LITTLE

C29c. ...a little or a lot?

5. A LOT   4. LITTLE

311

C30. Some people feel it is important for us to try to cooperate more with Russia, while others believe we should be much tougher in our dealings with Russia.

Do you have an opinion on this issue, or haven't you thought much about this?

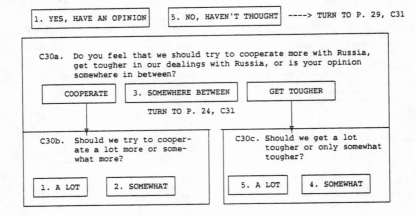

| 1. YES, HAVE AN OPINION | | 5. NO, HAVEN'T THOUGHT | ----> TURN TO P. 29, C31 |

C30a. Do you feel that we should try to cooperate more with Russia, get tougher in our dealings with Russia, or is your opinion somewhere in between?

| COOPERATE | 3. SOMEWHERE BETWEEN | GET TOUGHER |

TURN TO P. 24, C31

C30b. Should we try to cooperate a lot more or somewhat more?

| 1. A LOT | 2. SOMEWHAT |

C30c. Should we get a lot tougher or only somewhat tougher?

| 5. A LOT | 4. SOMEWHAT |

C31. Some people feel the government in Washington should make every effort to improve the social and economic position of older Americans. Others feel that the government is already doing as much as it can and families should do more to care for their older adults.

Do you have an opinion on this issue, or haven't you thought much about this?

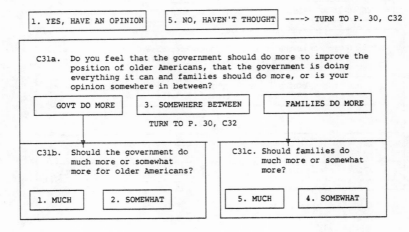

| 1. YES, HAVE AN OPINION | | 5. NO, HAVEN'T THOUGHT | ----> TURN TO P. 30, C32 |

C31a. Do you feel that the government should do more to improve the position of older Americans, that the government is doing everything it can and families should do more, or is your opinion somewhere in between?

| GOVT DO MORE | 3. SOMEWHERE BETWEEN | FAMILIES DO MORE |

TURN TO P. 30, C32

C31b. Should the government do much more or somewhat more for older Americans?

| 1. MUCH | 2. SOMEWHAT |

C31c. Should families do much more or somewhat more?

| 5. MUCH | 4. SOMEWHAT |

C32. Some people feel that the government in Washington should make every effort to improve the social and economic position of women. Others feel that the government should not make any special effort to help women because they should help themselves.

Do you have an opinion on this issue, or haven't you thought much about this?

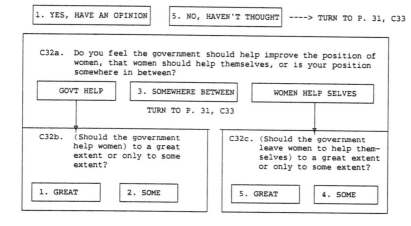

| 1. YES, HAVE AN OPINION | 5. NO, HAVEN'T THOUGHT | ----> TURN TO P. 31, C33

C32a. Do you feel the government should help improve the position of women, that women should help themselves, or is your position somewhere in between?

| GOVT HELP | 3. SOMEWHERE BETWEEN | WOMEN HELP SELVES |

TURN TO P. 31, C33

C32b. (Should the government help women) to a great extent or only to some extent?

1. GREAT   2. SOME

C32c. (Should the government leave women to help themselves) to a great extent or only to some extent?

5. GREAT   4. SOME

C33. Please tell me how much you agree or disagree with the following statements. These statements are like those that Ted Newcomb asked you about several times while you were at Bennington.

Do you strongly agree, agree, disagree, strongly disagree or are you uncertain?	1. STRONGLY AGREE	2. AGREE	4. DISAGREE	5. STRONGLY DISAGREE	8. UN-CERTAIN
C33a. The prosperity of the nation as a whole must be based upon the prosperity of working class people.					
C33b. Some form of collective society is preferable to our present system.					

Do you strongly agree, agree, disagree, strongly disagree or are you uncertain?	1. STRONGLY AGREE	2. AGREE	4. DISAGREE	5. STRONGLY DISAGREE	8. UN-CERTAIN
C33c. Most labor trouble happens only because of radical agitators.					
C33d. Any able-bodied person could get a job right now if he or she tried hard enough.					
C33e. The budget should be balanced before the government spends any money on social programs.					
C33f. Our government has always been run primarily in the interests of big business.					
C33g. Labor unions are justifiable only if they refrain from the use of strikes.					
C33h. Most employers think only of profits and care little about their employees' welfare.					
C33i. Organizations of the unemployed are just a group of chronic complainers.					
C33j. We have no true democracy in this country, because only business and industrial concerns have economic opportunity.					
C33k. If the government did not meddle so much in business, things would be alright.					
C33m. You can't expect democracy to work very well as long as so many uneducated and unintelligent people have the vote.					
C33n. The vast majority of those in the lower economic classes are there because they are stupid or shiftless, or both.					

314

C34. Here are listed six important areas, or interests, in life. People differ in
the emphasis or degree of importance that they attribute to each of these
interests.

Please (read/follow along as I read) the six areas and then <u>rank</u> the six
interests in terms of their IMPORTANCE TO YOU at this time. Insert "1" before
the area of greatest importance, "2" before the next most important one, and
so on down to "6", representing the least important of all to you.

PLEASE NOTE: Your response should be made to the <u>complete</u> statement about
each of the interests, and not just to the first word, which is only a
convenient label; what that word means to you may not correspond at all to
the statement following.

   <u>RANK</u>   (Use <u>each</u> of the numbers from 1 - 6)

C34a. _____ Theoretical: empirical, critical, or rational matters -- observing and
reasoning, ordering and systematizing, discovering
truths.

C34b. _____ Economic: that which is useful and practical, especially the
practical affairs of the business world; preference for
judging things by their tangible utility.

C34c. _____ Aesthetic: beauty, form and harmony for its own sake, an artistic
interpretation of life.

C34d. _____ Social: human relationships and love; interest in human beings
for their own sake.

C34e. _____ Political: power and influence; leadership and competition.

C34f. _____ Religious: religious experience as providing satisfaction and
meaning; interest in relating oneself to the unity of the
universe as a whole.

SECTION D
SELF-ASSESSED CHANGE IN POLITICAL ATTITUDES

D1. Many of the women whom we have interviewed have spontaneously used such terms as conservative, moderate, or liberal in describing their general political points of view.

People have different things in mind when they say that someone's political views are liberal or conservative. We'd like to know more about this. Let's start with liberal. What sorts of things do you have in mind when you say that someone's political views are liberal? (PROBE: Can you give me an example?) (Any other?)

_____

_____

_____

_____

_____

_____

_____

_____

_____

_____

_____

_____

_____

_____

_____

D2. And what do you have in mind when you say that someone's political views are conservative? (PROBE: can you give me an example?) (Any other?)

_____

_____

_____

_____

_____

_____

_____

_____

_____

_____

_____

_____

_____

_____

_____

_____

_____

_____

317

[RB, page 3] Now, let's talk about your general political viewpoint at various points in your life from the 1930s until the present. Please just try to remember and describe your general political viewpoint as best you can. In the questions that follow, please describe your general political view on a scale of 1 to 7 where 1 is very conservative, 2 is somewhat conservative, and 3 is moderate, but leaning toward conservative. Four would be moderate. Five is moderate, but leaning toward liberal, 6 is somewhat liberal and 7 is very liberal.

```
     1            2            3            4            5            6            7
 |-----------|-----------|-----------|-----------|-----------|-----------|

   Very      Somewhat     Leaning      Moderate    Leaning      Somewhat      Very
Conservative Conservative toward                  toward       Liberal     Liberal
                          Conservative            Liberal
```

D3. Which category (from 1 to 7) best describes your general political viewpoint when you first entered Bennington College?

                    Number: _____   8. DK

D4. Which category (from 1 to 7) best describes your general political viewpoint when you left Bennington College?

                    Number: _____   8. DK

D5. INTERVIEWER CHECKPOINT:

     1. [ ] THE ANSWERS TO D3 AND D4 ARE THE SAME NUMBER. ---> GO TO D6

     2. [ ] THE ANSWERS TO D3 AND D4 ARE DIFFERENT. ---> GO TO D6

     3. [ ] D3 AND D4 ARE BOTH DK. -----> TURN TO P. 36, D7

D6. You have described your general political viewpoint as having (changed/stayed the same) during the time you were a Bennington student. Why do you think your viewpoint (changed/stayed the same) during that time?

_____

_____

_____

_____

_____

_____

318

D7. [RB, Page 3] Please think for a moment about events in 1960. Which category (from 1 through 7) best describes your general political viewpoint in the year 1960? (PROBE: That was when Kennedy and Nixon ran for president.)

Number: _____ | 8. DK |

D8. INTERVIEWER CHECKPOINT:

1. [ ]   THE ANSWERS TO D4 AND D7 ARE THE SAME NUMBER. ---> GO TO D9

2. [ ]   THE ANSWERS TO D4 AND D7 ARE DIFFERENT. ---> GO TO D9

3. [ ]   D4 AND D7 ARE BOTH DK. -----> TURN TO P. 37, D10

D9. You have described your general political viewpoint as having (changed/stayed the same) between the time you left Bennington and the year 1960. Why do you think your viewpoint (changed/stayed the same) during that time period?

_____

_____

_____

_____

_____

_____

_____

D10. [RB, PAGE 3] Please think for a moment about events in 1972. Which category (from 1 through 7) best describes your general political viewpoint <u>in 1972</u>? (PROBE: That was when McGovern and Nixon ran for president.)

Number: _____ | 8. DK |

D11. INTERVIEWER CHECKPOINT:

1. [ ]   THE ANSWERS TO D7 AND D10 ARE THE <u>SAME NUMBER</u>. ---> GO TO D12

2. [ ]   THE ANSWERS TO D7 AND D10 ARE <u>DIFFERENT</u>. ---> GO TO D12

3. [ ]   D7 AND D10 ARE BOTH DK. -----> TURN TO P. 38, D13

D12. You have described your general political viewpoint as having (changed/stayed the same) between 1960 and 1972. Why do you think your viewpoint (changed/ stayed the same) during that time?

_____

_____

_____

_____

_____

_____

_____

D13. [RB, PAGE 3] Which category (from 1 to 7) best describes your general
political viewpoint today?

Number: _____ | 8. DK |

D14. INTERVIEWER CHECKPOINT:

1. [   ]   THE ANSWERS TO D10 AND D13 ARE THE SAME NUMBER. ---> GO TO D15

2. [   ]   THE ANSWERS TO D10 AND D13 ARE DIFFERENT. ---> GO TO D15

3. [   ]   D10 AND D13 ARE BOTH DK. -----> TURN TO P. 39, D16

D15. You have described your general political viewpoint as having (changed/stayed
the same) between 1972 and today. Why do you think your viewpoint (changed/
stayed the same) during that time?

_____

_____

_____

_____

_____

_____

_____

_____

_____

_____

_____

D16. Are there any ways in which your present political viewpoint is the same as the viewpoint you had while at college?

_____

_____

_____

_____

_____

D17. What seem to be the most important factors that have influenced your present political viewpoint--such things as national or international events or conditions, your work or family experience, people, travel, and so on.?

_____

_____

_____

_____

_____

_____

_____

_____

_____

_____

Personal or external events often have varying effects on people's _interest_ in public affairs.

D18. First, did you become more interested, remain the same or become less interested in public affairs while you were in college?

| 1. MORE INTERESTED | 2. REMAIN SAME | 3. LESS INTERESTED |

D18a. Why do you think that was so?

_____

_____

D19. From the period 1940 to 1960 did you become more interested, remain the same or become less interested in public affairs than when you were in college?

| 1. MORE INTERESTED | 2. REMAIN SAME | 3. LESS INTERESTED |

D19a. Why do you think that was so?

_____

_____

D20. From the period 1960 to 1972 did you become more interested, remain the same or become less interested in public affairs?

| 1. MORE INTERESTED | 2. REMAIN SAME | 3. LESS INTERESTED |

D20a. Why do you think that was so?

_____

_____

_____

D21. From the period <u>1972 to the present</u> did you become more interested, remain the same or become less interested in public affairs?

| 1. MORE INTERESTED | 2. REMAIN SAME | 3. LESS INTERESTED |

D21a. Why do you think that was so?

_____

_____

_____

D22. [RB, PAGE 3] Now, the following estimates of political viewpoints are a little more difficult. Would you try to estimate what <u>you think</u> were the viewpoints of your contemporaries at Bennington--that is, the women you attended college with--in comparison with your <u>own</u> viewpoint at various times.

Which category (from 1 to 7) do you think best describes the general political viewpoint of your classmates when they <u>first entered</u> Bennington College?

Number: _____ | 8. DK |

D23. Which category (from 1 to 7) do you think best describes the general political viewpoint when your classmates <u>left</u> Bennington College?

Number: _____ | 8. DK |

D24. Which category (from 1 to 7) do you think best describes the general political viewpoint of your classmates in <u>the year 1960</u>?

Number: _____ | 8. DK |

D25. Which category (from 1 to 7) do you think best describes the general political viewpoint of your classmates in <u>the year 1972</u>?

Number: _____ | 8. DK |

D26. Which category (from 1 to 7) do you think best describes the general political viewpoint of your classmates <u>at the present time</u>?

Number: _____ | 8. DK |

324

USE HANDOUT - page 2-4

D27. Here are 26 statements about public issues of the 1930s. These are the same
ones Ted Newcomb asked you to reply to, perhaps several times, while you were
a student at Bennington. Please try to answer them in terms of how <u>you think
you might have answered them when you left Bennington</u>. We don't really expect
you to remember after all these years, of course; just make the best guesses
you can. Some of these statements may sound outdated; after all, the way we
talk about public issues changes over time. Please respond by circling the
category -- whether you think you strongly agreed, agreed, disagreed, strongly
disagreed or were uncertain about each statement -- at <u>that</u> time.

In the 1930's, do you think you strongly agreed, agreed, disagreed or strongly disagreed?	STRONGLY AGREED (1)	AGREED (2)	UN-CERTAIN (3)	DISAGREED (4)	STRONGLY DISAGREED (5)
D27a. The only true prosperity of the nation as a whole must be based upon the prosperity of the working class.					
D27b. Recovery has been delayed by the large number of strikes.					
D27c. Some form of collective society, in which profits are replaced by reimbursements for useful mental or manual work, is preferable to our present system.					
D27d. The depression occurred chiefly because the working classes did not receive enough in wages to purchase goods and services produced at a profit.					
D27e. A "planned economy" is not enough unless it is planned for the welfare of workers rather than of business men.					
D27f. Most labor trouble happens only because of radical agitators.					
D27g. The people who complain most about the depression wouldn't take a job if you gave it to them.					

In the 1930's, do you think you strongly agreed, agreed, disagreed or strongly disagreed?	STRONGLY AGREED (1)	AGREED (2)	UN-CERTAIN (3)	DISAGREED (4)	STRONGLY DISAGREED (5)
D27h. The standard of living of the working class can be kept above the poverty line only as workers force it up by the use of strikes.					
D27i. Labor organizations have as much right to bring in outside agitators as do business men to import outside technical experts.					
D27j. Any able-bodied man could get a job right now if he tried hard enough.					
D27k. Most people on relief are living in reasonable comfort.					
D27l. The budget should be balanced before the government spends any money on "social security".					
D27m. Our government has always been run primarily in the interests of big business, and so it is those interests which were chiefly responsible for the depression.					
D27n. Labor unions are justifiable only if they refrain from the use of strikes.					
D27o. Since it is impossible for working people to make any substantial savings, they have fully earned their rights to old-age pensions.					
D27p. It is all right to try to raise the standard of living of the lower classes, provided that existing property rights are continually safeguarded.					
D27q. Most employers think only of profits and care little about their employees' welfare.					

In the 1930's, do you think you strongly agreed, agreed, disagreed or strongly disagreed?	STRONGLY AGREED (1)	AGREED (2)	UN- CERTAIN (3)	DISAGREED (4)	STRONGLY DISAGREED (5)
D27r. Unemployment insurance would saddle us with a nation of idlers.					
D27s. Organizations of the unemployed are just a group of chronic complainers.					
D27t. We have no true democracy in this country, because only business and industrial concerns have economic opportunity.					
D27u. If the government didn't meddle so much in business everything would be all right.					
D27v. You can't expect democracy to work very well as long as so many uneducated and unintelligent people have the vote.					
D27w. The vast majority of those in the lower economic classes are there because they are stupid or shiftless, or both.					
D27x. Those who have the ability and the foresight to accumulate wealth ought to be permitted to enjoy it themselves.					
D27y. The middle classes will never enjoy security or prosperity until they understand that their welfare is identified with that of the working class, and not with that of business and industrial groups.					
D27z. The real threat to prosperity in this country is the repressive activities of those who wish to keep wealth and economic power in the hands of those who now possess them.					

USE HANDOUT - page 5-7

D28. Here are the 26 statements about public issues of the 1930s again. Would you please try to answer them this time in terms of how you think you might have answered them in 1960. Again, we don't really expect you to be able to know after all these years; just make the best guesses you can by circling the category -- whether you think you strongly agreed, agreed, disagreed, strongly disagreed or were uncertain about each statement -- in 1960.

In 1960, do you think you strongly agreed, agreed, disagreed or strongly disagreed?	STRONGLY AGREED (1)	AGREED (2)	UN-CERTAIN (3)	DISAGREED (4)	STRONGLY DISAGREED (5)
D28a. The only true prosperity of the nation as a whole must be based upon the prosperity of the working class.					
D28b. Recovery has been delayed by the large number of strikes.					
D28c. Some form of collective society, in which profits are replaced by reimbursements for useful mental or manual work, is preferable to our present system.					
D28d. The depression occurred chiefly because the working classes did not receive enough in wages to purchase goods and services produced at a profit.					
D28e. A "planned economy" is not enough unless it is planned for the welfare of workers rather than of business men.					
D28f. Most labor trouble happens only because of radical agitators.					
D28g. The people who complain most about the depression wouldn't take a job if you gave it to them.					
D28h. The standard of living of the working class can be kept above the poverty line only as workers force it up by the use of strikes.					

328

In 1960, do you think you strongly agreed, agreed, disagreed or strongly disagreed?	STRONGLY AGREED (1)	AGREED (2)	UN-CERTAIN (3)	DISAGREED (4)	STRONGLY DISAGREED (5)
D28i. Labor organizations have as much right to bring in outside agitators as do business men to import outside technical experts.					
D28j. Any able-bodied man could get a job right now if he tried hard enough.					
D28k. Most people on relief are living in reasonable comfort.					
D28l. The budget should be balanced before the government spends any money on "social security".					
D28m. Our government has always been run primarily in the interests of big business, and so it is those interests which were chiefly responsible for the depression.					
D28n. Labor unions are justifiable only if they refrain from the use of strikes.					
D28o. Since it is impossible for working people to make any substantial savings, they have fully earned their rights to old-age pensions.					
D28p. It is all right to try to raise the standard of living of the lower classes, provided that existing property rights are continually safeguarded.					
D28q. Most employers think only of profits and care little about their employees' welfare.					
D28r. Unemployment insurance would saddle us with a nation of idlers.					
D28s. Organizations of the unemployed are just a group of chronic complainers.					

In 1960, do you think you strongly agreed, agreed, disagreed or strongly disagreed?	STRONGLY AGREED (1)	AGREED (2)	UN-CERTAIN (3)	DISAGREED (4)	STRONGLY DISAGREED (5)
D28t. We have no true democracy in this country, because only business and industrial concerns have economic opportunity.					
D28u. If the government didn't meddle so much in business everything would be all right.					
D28v. You can't expect democracy to work very well as long as so many uneducated and unintelligent people have the vote.					
D28w. The vast majority of those in the lower economic classes are there because they are stupid or shiftless, or both.					
D28x. Those who have the ability and the foresight to accumulate wealth ought to be permitted to enjoy it themselves.					
D28y. The middle classes will never enjoy security or prosperity until they understand that their welfare is identified with that of the working class, and not with that of business and industrial groups.					
D28z. The real threat to prosperity in this country is the repressive activities of those who wish to keep wealth and economic power in the hands of those who now possess them.					

E1. INTERVIEWER CHECKPOINT:

☐ 1. R HAS NEVER BEEN MARRIED ----> TURN TO P. 54, E14

☐ 2. R IS <u>NOT CURRENTLY</u> MARRIED ----> Let's talk about your
family and friends.

☐ 3. R IS CURRENTLY MARRIED ----> Let's talk about your
family and friends.

E2a. How old is your husband? _____

E2b. [RB, PAGE 4] How close do you feel to him: extremely close, very
close, quite close, not too close, or not close at all?

| 1. EXTREMELY | 2. VERY | 3. QUITE | 4. NOT TOO | 5. NOT AT ALL |

<u>E2c.</u> (Do/did) you ever talk about politics with (him/your husband)?

| 1. YES | 5. NO |

E2d. In general, would you say you (agree/agreed) with him on politics or (do/did)
you disagree?

| 1. AGREE | 2. DISAGREE |

E2e. (Does/did) he consider himself a Republican, a Democrat, an independent, or
what?

| 1. REPUBLICAN | 2. DEMOCRAT | 3. INDEPENDENT | 4. NO PREFERENCE | 5. OTHER |

SPECIFY: _____

E2f. [RB, PAGE 3] On a scale from 1 to 7, with 1 meaning very conservative and 7 meaning very liberal, what number would you say (represents/represented) his general political viewpoint?

NUMBER:_____

E2g. As far as you know, (has/had) he changed his basic political viewpoint (since you have been/while you were) married?

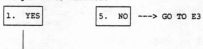

E2h. (Has/had) he become more conservative or more liberal?

| 1.   MORE CONSERVATIVE | 2.   MORE LIBERAL |

E3.   Altogether how many children have you <u>raised</u>? Please include any step-children, adopted children and long-term foster children you raised.

NUMBER:_____ | 00. NONE | --->TURN TO P. 54, E14

E3a.   How many of those children are living?

NUMBER:_____ | 00. NONE | --->TURN TO P. 54, E14

Lets talk more about (these living children/your child).

| TURN TO GRID P. 52 (E4-E13) |

CIRCLE RESPONSE IN GRID FOR CHILD MENTIONED.	1ST	2ND
E4. Is the (oldest, 2nd, 3rd, etc.) male or female?	M F	M F
E5. And how old is (he/she) now?	YRS	YRS
E6. What was the highest year of school (he/she) completed?		
E7. [RB, PAGE 4] How close do you feel to (him/her): 1. extremely close 2. very close 3. quite close, 4. not too close, or 5. not close at all.	1. EXTREME 2. VERY 3. QUITE 4. NOT TOO 5. NOT ALL	1. EXTREME 2. VERY 3. QUITE 4. NOT TOO 5. NOT ALL
E8. Do you ever talk about politics with (him/her)?	Y N	Y N
E9. In general, would you say you agree with (him/her) on politics or do you disagree?	1. AGREE 5. DISAG	1. AGREE 5. DISAG
E10. As far as you can tell, does (he/she) consider (himself/herself) a Republican, a Democrat, an independent, or what?	1. REPUB 2. DEM 3. IND 7. OTHER: _____	1. REPUB 2. DEM 3. IND 7. OTHER: _____
E11. [RB, PAGE 3] On a scale from 1 to 7, (with 1 meaning very conservative and 7 meaning very liberal), what number would you say represents (his/her) general political viewpoint?		
IF CHILD IS 26 YRS OR OLDER:		
E12. As far as you know, has (he/she) changed (his/her) basic political viewpoint since (he/she) was about 20 years old?	Y N	Y N
E13. (IF YES) Has (he/she) become more conservative or more liberal?	1. CON 2. LIB 0. INAP	1. CON 2. LIB 0. INAP

3rd	4th	5th	6th
M F	M F	M F	M F
YRS	YRS	YRS	YRS
1. EXTREMELY 2. VERY 3. QUITE 4. NOT TOO 5. NOT ALL	1. EXTREMELY 2. VERY 3. QUITE 4. NOT TOO 5. NOT ALL	1. EXTREMELY 2. VERY 3. QUITE 4. NOT TOO 5. NOT ALL	1. EXTREMELY 2. VERY 3. QUITE 4. NOT TOO 5. NOT ALL
Y N	Y N	Y N	Y N
1. AGREE 5. DISAG	1. AGREE 5. DISAG	1. AGREE 5. DISAG	1. AGREE 5. DISAG
1. REPUB 2. DEM 3. IND 7. OTHER:	1. REPUB 2. DEM 3. IND 7. OTHER:	1. REPUB 2. DEM 3. IND 7. OTHER:	1. REPUB 2. DEM 3. IND 7. OTHER:
_____	_____	_____	_____
IF CHILD IS 26 YRS OR OLDER:			
Y N	Y N	Y N	Y N
1. CON 2. LIB 0. INAP	1. CON 2. LIB 0. INAP	1. CON 2. LIB 0. INAP	1. CON 2. LIB 0. INAP

APPENDIX B

E14. How many households of your relatives--parents, grown children, other relatives, and in-laws--are within a couple of hours driving time from your home? Count each household as one unit.

_____ NUMBER OF HOUSEHOLDS | 00. NONE | ---> GO TO E15

E14a. [RB, PAGE 5] About how often do you see any of these relatives, either in their home or in your own? (Would you say almost daily, once a week or more, once a month or more, once every three or four months or less than once a year?)

| 1. ALMOST DAILY | 2. ONCE A WEEK OR MORE | 3. ONCE A MONTH OR MORE | 4. ONCE EVERY 3 OR 4 MONTHS | 5. LESS THAN ONCE A YEAR |

E15. Other than relatives, about how many friends do you have in this area that you feel you can call on for advice or help in time of need? Count each household as one unit.

_____ NUMBER OF HOUSEHOLDS | 00. NONE | ---> GO TO E16

E15a. [RB, PAGE 5] About how often do you see any of these friends, either in their home or in your own? (Would you say almost daily, once a week or more, once a month or more, once every three or four months or less than once a year?)

| 1. ALMOST DAILY | 2. ONCE A WEEK OR MORE | 3. ONCE A MONTH OR MORE | 4. ONCE EVERY 3 OR 4 MONTHS | 5. LESS THAN ONCE A YEAR |

E16. Would you say that you have a good many very good friends that you could count on if you had any sort of trouble, an average number, or not too many very good friends?

| 1. GOOD MANY | 3. AVERAGE NUMBER | 5. NOT TOO MANY |

E17. Some people feel that they have too many friends--more than they can keep up with--while other people feel they would like to have more. How about you: do you feel that you have too many friends, too few, or is the number about right?

| 1. TOO MANY | 3. ABOUT RIGHT | 5. TOO FEW |

335

E18. Now, please think about three of your close friends or relatives. (PAUSE) Do you have three in mind?

REPEAT E18a-E18i FOR EACH FRIEND	1ST	2ND	3RD
E18a. Is the (1st/2nd/3rd) male or female?	M F	M F	M F
E18b. And how old is (he/she) now?			
E18c. How many years have you known (him/her)?			
E18d. Do you ever talk about politics with (him/her)?	Y N	Y N	Y N
E18e. In general, would you say you agree with (him/her) on politics or do you disagree?	1. AGREE 2. DISAG	1. AGREE 2. DISAG	1. AGREE 2. DISAG
E18f. As far as you can tell, does (he/she) consider (himself/herself) a Republican, a Democrat, an independent, or what?	1. REPUB 2. DEM 3. IND 7. OTHER: _____	1. REPUB 2. DEM 3. IND 7. OTHER: _____	1. REPUB 2. DEM 3. IND 7. OTHER: _____
E18g. [RB, PAGE 3] On a scale from 1 to 7, (with 1 meaning very conservative and 7 meaning very liberal), what number would you say represents (his/her) general political viewpoint?			
E18h. As far as you know, has (he/she) changed (his/her) basic political viewpoint since you have known (him/her)?	Y N	Y N	Y N
E18i. (IF YES) Has (he/she) become more conservative or more liberal?	1. CON 2. LIB 0. INAP	1. CON 2. LIB 0. INAP	1. CON 2. LIB 0. INAP

```
                    SECTION F
          CURRENT INTERESTS AND ACTIVITIES
```

Now would you tell me about your general interests and activities.

F1. In general, would you say you have become more active and interested in organizations, activities, and causes since you left Bennington College, less active or about the same?

| 1. MORE ACTIVE | | 2. ABOUT SAME | | 3. LESS ACTIVE | | 8. DK |

I have a list of clubs and organizations that many people are active in. Please tell me which of these kinds of organizations you are active in now.

F2. Are you active in fraternal organizations or lodges?

| 1. YES | | 5. NO | -----> GO TO F3

F2a. How long have you been active?   YEARS: _____

F3. Are you active in labor unions?

| 1. YES | | 5. NO | -----> GO TO F4

F3a. How long have you been active?   YEARS: _____

F4. Are you active in church-sponsored groups?

| 1. YES | | 5. NO | -----> GO TO F5

F4a. How long have you been active?   YEARS: _____

F5. Are you active in business or civic groups?

| 1. YES | | 5. NO | -----> GO TO F6

F5a. How long have you been active?   YEARS: _____

F6. Are you active in educational groups?

| 1. YES | | 5. NO | -----> TURN TO P. 58, F7

F6a. How long have you been active?   YEARS: _____

337

F7. Are you active in <u>literary, art, music or other cultural groups</u>?

| 1. YES | 5. NO | -----> GO TO F8 |

    F7a. How long have you been active?   YEARS: _____

F8. Are you active in <u>youth serving groups</u>?

| 1. YES | 5. NO | -----> GO TO F9 |

    F8a. How long have you been active?   YEARS: _____

F9. Are you active in <u>sports or recreational groups</u>?

| 1. YES | 5. NO | -----> GO TO F10 |

    F9a. How long have you been active?   YEARS: _____

F10. Are you active in <u>professional associations or organizations</u>?

| 1. YES | 5. NO | -----> GO TO F11 |

    F10a. How long have you been active?   YEARS: _____

F11. Are you active in <u>neighborhood improvement groups</u>?

| 1. YES | 5. NO | -----> GO TO F12 |

    F11a. How long have you been active?   YEARS: _____

F12. Are you active in <u>social clubs or card clubs</u>?

| 1. YES | 5. NO | -----> GO TO F13 |

    F12a. How long have you been active?   YEARS: _____

F13. Are you active in <u>charitable or welfare organizations</u>?

| 1. YES | 5. NO | -----> TURN TO P. 59, F14 |

    F13a. How long have you been active?   YEARS: _____

338

F14. Are you active in <u>political clubs or organizations</u>?

| 1. YES | | 5. NO | -----> GO TO F15 |

   F14a. How long have you been active? YEARS: _____

F15. Are there any other types of organizations in which you are active?

| 1. YES | | 5. NO | -----> GO TO F16 |

   F15a. What are those?

_____

_____

_____

_____

F16. Whether they belong to organizations or not, many people at some time in their lives work for various political committees, causes, or fund raising groups.

Have you worked for a political party or candidate since leaving Bennington College?

| 1. YES | | 5. NO | -----> TURN TO P. 59, F17 |

F16a. Did you do that in the <u>1940s</u>?   1. YES   5. NO

F16b. Did you do that in the <u>1950s</u>?   1. YES   5. NO

F16c. In the <u>1960s</u>?   1. YES   5. NO

F16d. In the <u>1970s</u>?   1. YES   5. NO

F16e. Since <u>1980</u>?   1. YES   5. NO

F17. Have you been involved in other political activities or public issues?

| 1. YES | | 5. NO | -----> TURN TO P. 61, F18 |

F17a. Were you active in the <u>1940s</u>? | 1. YES | | 5. NO |

F17b. Were you active in the <u>1950s</u>? | 1. YES | | 5. NO |

F17c. In the <u>1960s</u>? | 1. YES | | 5. NO |

F17d. In the <u>1970s</u>? | 1. YES | | 5. NO |

F17e. Since <u>1980</u>? | 1. YES | | 5. NO |

F17f. What activities were those?

_____

_____

_____

_____

Next, let's talk about how you are feeling these days.

F18. How would you rate your health at the present time: would you say it is
      excellent, very good, good, fair or poor?

| 1. EXCELLENT | 2. VERY GOOD | 3. GOOD | 4. FAIR | 5. POOR |

F19. Do you have any major medical problems at the present time?

| 1. YES | | 5. NO |------> GO TO F20

    F19a. What is that? (Any other?)

    _____

    _____

    _____

F20. [RB, PAGE 6] How much difficulty do you have seeing things up close, for
      example for reading (with your glasses): no difficulty, a little difficulty,
      some difficulty, a lot of difficulty, or can you not do it at all?

| 1. NO DIFF-ICULTY | 2. A LITTLE DIFF-ICULTY | 3. SOME DIFF-ICULTY | 4. A LOT OF DIFF-ICULTY | 5. CAN NOT DO AT ALL |

F21. [RB, PAGE 6] How much difficulty do you have hearing people when they talk to
      you (with hearing aid if you use one)?

| 1. NO DIFF-ICULTY | 2. A LITTLE DIFF-ICULTY | 3. SOME DIFF-ICULTY | 4. A LOT OF DIFF-ICULTY | 5. CAN NOT DO AT ALL |

F22. [RB, PAGE 6] How much difficulty do you have in walking up a flight of stairs?

1. NO DIFF-ICULTY	2. A LITTLE DIFF-ICULTY	3. SOME DIFF-ICULTY	4. A LOT OF DIFF-ICULTY	5. CAN NOT DO AT ALL

F23. [RB, PAGE 6] How much difficulty do you have getting around your house?

1. NO DIFF-ICULTY	2. A LITTLE DIFF-ICULTY	3. SOME DIFF-ICULTY	4. A LOT OF DIFF-ICULTY	5. CAN NOT DO AT ALL

F24. [RB, PAGE 6] How much difficulty do you have remembering things?

1. NO DIFF-ICULTY	2. A LITTLE DIFF-ICULTY	3. SOME DIFF-ICULTY	4. A LOT OF DIFF-ICULTY	5. CAN NOT DO AT ALL

F25. (No longer using RB) Some people worry about their health a lot. How about you--how worried are you about your health: very worried, quite worried, a little worried or not at all worried?

1. VERY WORRIED	2. QUITE WORRIED	3. A LITTLE WORRIED	4. NOT AT ALL WORRIED

342

F26. [RB, PAGE 7] Could you tell me how satisfied you are with different parts of your life, using a scale from one to seven. One means completely dissatisfied, four is neutral (equally dissatisfied and satisfied, and seven means completely satisfied. As I read each one, please tell me what number best describes how satisfied you are.

```
     1          2          3          4          5          6          7
     |          |          |          |          |          |          |
  Very                              Neutral                          Very
Dissatisfied                                                      Satisfied
```

F26a. [RB, PAGE 7] First, (from 1 to 7) how satisfied are you with your home?

NUMBER_____

F26b. How satisfied are you with your means of transportation?

NUMBER_____

F26c. How satisfied are you with your relationships with your good friends?

NUMBER_____

F26d. Taken all in all, how satisfied are you with your health at the present time?

NUMBER_____

F26e. How satisfied are you with your (and your husband's) present income?

NUMBER_____

F26f. How satisfied are you with your (and your husband's) savings and investments?

NUMBER_____

F26g. How satisfied are you with your safety from crime?

NUMBER_____

F26h. How satisfied are you with your life as a whole these days?

NUMBER_____

F27. [RB, PAGE 8] We are interested in how people are feeling these days. During the past few weeks how often did you feel relaxed and free of tension: would you say always, often, sometimes, rarely or never?

| 1. ALWAYS | 2. OFTEN | 3. SOMETIMES | 4. RARELY | 5. NEVER |

F28. During the past few weeks how often did you feel particularly excited or interested in something?

| 1. ALWAYS | 2. OFTEN | 3. SOMETIMES | 4. RARELY | 5. NEVER |

F29. During the past few weeks how often was your sleep restless?

| 1. ALWAYS | 2. OFTEN | 3. SOMETIMES | 4. RARELY | 5. NEVER |

F30. During the past few weeks how often did you feel you had as much pep as when you were five years younger?

| 1. ALWAYS | 2. OFTEN | 3. SOMETIMES | 4. RARELY | 5. NEVER |

F31. During the past few weeks how often did you have a poor appetite?

| 1. ALWAYS | 2. OFTEN | 3. SOMETIMES | 4. RARELY | 5. NEVER |

F32. During the past few weeks how often did you feel bored?

| 1. ALWAYS | 2. OFTEN | 3. SOMETIMES | 4. RARELY | 5. NEVER |

F33. During the past few weeks how often did you feel so restless you couldn't sit long in a chair.

| 1. ALWAYS | 2. OFTEN | 3. SOMETIMES | 4. RARELY | 5. NEVER |

F34. During the past few weeks how often did you feel things were going your way?

| 1. ALWAYS | 2. OFTEN | 3. SOMETIMES | 4. RARELY | 5. NEVER |

344

```
┌─────────────────────────────┐
│        SECTION G            │
│  OTHER POLITICAL ISSUES     │
└─────────────────────────────┘
```

G1. Do you agree or disagree with the following statement, or don't
     you know: Most of the important decisions in the life of the
     family should be made by the man of the house.

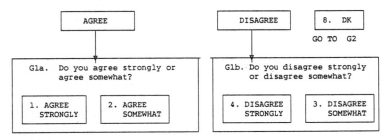

G2. Do you agree or disagree with the following statement, or don't
     you know: It's perfectly all right for women to be very active
     in clubs, politics, and other outside activities before the
     children are grown up.

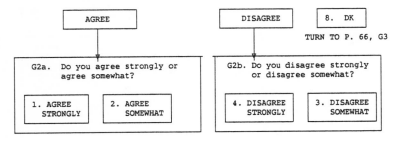

G3. And this statement: There is some work that is men's work and some that is women's, and they should not be doing each other's.

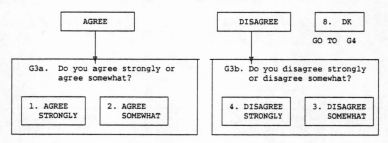

G4. Do you agree or disagree with this statement: A wife should not expect her husband to help around the house after he comes home from a hard day's work.

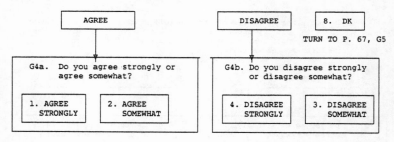

346

G5. And this statement: A working mother can establish as warm and secure a relationship with her children as a mother who does not work.

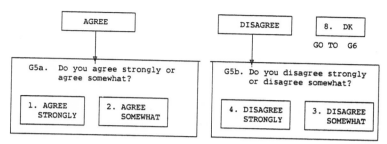

G6. Women are much happier if they stay at home and take care of their children. Do you agree, disagree, or don't you know?

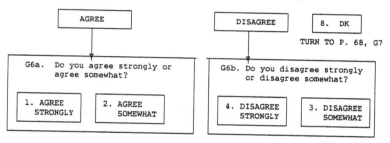

347

G7. And this statement: It is much better for everyone if the man earns the main living and the woman takes care of the home and family.

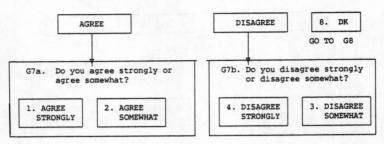

G8. It is more important for a wife to help her husband's career than to have one herself. Do you agree, disagree or don't you know?

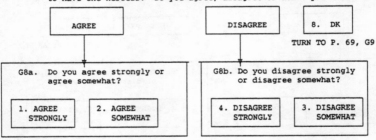

348

G9.   Social Security should be paid for work done in the home, including housework and child care.

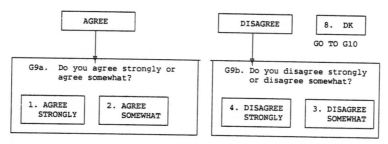

```
┌──────────────┐              ┌──────────────┐      ┌────────────┐
│    AGREE     │              │   DISAGREE   │      │  8.  DK    │
└──────────────┘              └──────────────┘      └────────────┘
                                                     GO TO G10

┌─────────────────────────┐   ┌──────────────────────────┐
│ G9a.  Do you agree       │   │ G9b. Do you disagree      │
│   strongly or            │   │   strongly or disagree    │
│   agree somewhat?        │   │   somewhat?               │
│                          │   │                           │
│ ┌──────────┐ ┌─────────┐ │   │ ┌───────────┐ ┌─────────┐ │
│ │1. AGREE  │ │2. AGREE │ │   │ │4. DISAGREE│ │3. DISAGREE│
│ │ STRONGLY │ │SOMEWHAT │ │   │ │  STRONGLY │ │ SOMEWHAT │
│ └──────────┘ └─────────┘ │   │ └───────────┘ └─────────┘ │
└─────────────────────────┘   └──────────────────────────┘
```

G10. Parents should be notified if a daughter under 18 is diagnosed as pregnant.

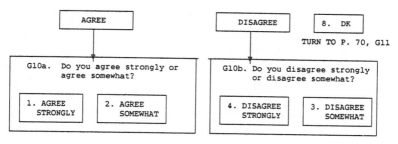

```
┌──────────────┐              ┌──────────────┐      ┌────────────┐
│    AGREE     │              │   DISAGREE   │      │  8.  DK    │
└──────────────┘              └──────────────┘      └────────────┘
                                                     TURN TO P. 70, G11

┌─────────────────────────┐   ┌──────────────────────────┐
│ G10a.  Do you agree      │   │ G10b. Do you disagree     │
│   strongly or            │   │   strongly or disagree    │
│   agree somewhat?        │   │   somewhat?               │
│                          │   │                           │
│ ┌──────────┐ ┌─────────┐ │   │ ┌───────────┐ ┌─────────┐ │
│ │1. AGREE  │ │2. AGREE │ │   │ │4. DISAGREE│ │3. DISAGREE│
│ │ STRONGLY │ │SOMEWHAT │ │   │ │  STRONGLY │ │ SOMEWHAT │
│ └──────────┘ └─────────┘ │   │ └───────────┘ └─────────┘ │
└─────────────────────────┘   └──────────────────────────┘
```

G11. Birth control should qualify for payment by Medicare/Medicaid.

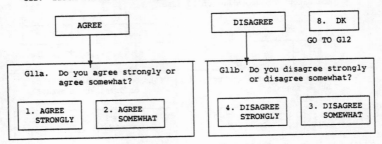

G12. A woman's job should be kept for her when she is having a baby.

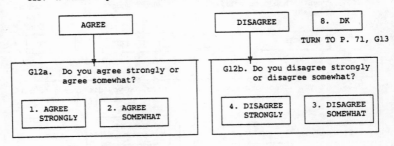

350

G13. Federally-funded day care should be available for working mothers. Do you agree, disagree or don't you know.

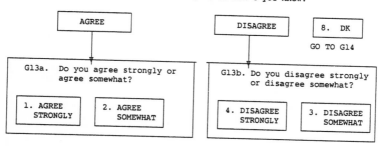

G14. Women generally have a very difficult time when all their children have left home.

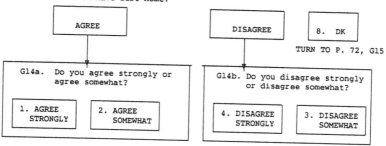

351

G15. Do you agree or disagree with this statement: a woman can live a full and happy life without marrying?

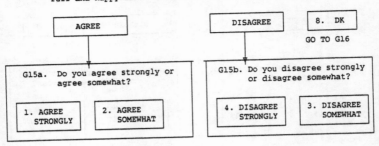

G16. Men and women should be paid the same money if they do the same work.

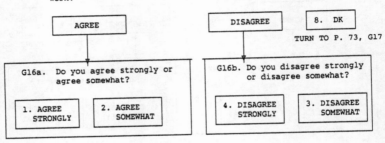

G17. A woman should have exactly the same job opportunities as a man.

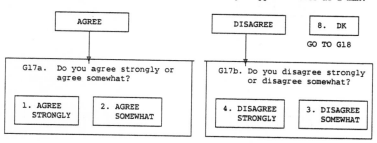

G18. Women should be considered as seriously as men for jobs as executives or politicians or even President.

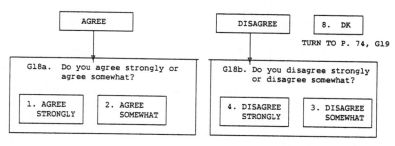

353

G19. Parents should encourage just as much independence in their daughters as in their sons.

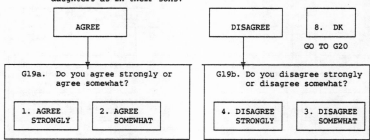

```
┌─────────────────┐              ┌─────────────────┐   ┌─────────────┐
│     AGREE       │              │   DISAGREE      │   │   8.  DK    │
└─────────────────┘              └─────────────────┘   └─────────────┘
         │                                │                  GO TO G20
         ▼                                ▼
┌─────────────────────────┐    ┌──────────────────────────┐
│ G19a. Do you agree       │    │ G19b. Do you disagree     │
│       strongly or        │    │       strongly or         │
│       agree somewhat?    │    │       disagree somewhat?  │
│ ┌──────────┐ ┌─────────┐ │    │ ┌──────────┐ ┌──────────┐ │
│ │1. AGREE  │ │2. AGREE │ │    │ │4. DISAGREE│ │3. DISAGREE│ │
│ │ STRONGLY │ │ SOMEWHAT│ │    │ │ STRONGLY │ │ SOMEWHAT │ │
│ └──────────┘ └─────────┘ │    │ └──────────┘ └──────────┘ │
└─────────────────────────┘    └──────────────────────────┘
```

G20. Have you personally experienced any forms of sex discrimination?

          1. YES   5. NO ----> GO TO G21

G20a. Please describe the one that was most important to you.

_____

_____

_____

G21. Have you personally been involved in any activities or organizations whose major purpose was a change in the status of women?

          1. YES   5. NO ----> TURN TO P. 75, G22

G21. Which ones and when?

a. _____   b. When? _____

c. _____   d. When? _____

G22. Why did you choose to attend a women's college?

_____
_____
_____
_____
_____
_____
_____

G22a. If you had it to do again, would you still choose to attend a women's college?

| 1. YES | | 5. NO |

G22b. Would you encourage a granddaughter to attend a women's college?

| 1. YES | | 5. NO |

G23.   Please name three women or groups of women whom you have admired or who have
        had an important impact on your life, whether you have known them personally
        or not.

   G23a. _____

   G23b. How would you describe her impact on your life?

        _____

        _____

        _____

   G23c. _____

   G23d. How would you describe her impact on your life?

        _____

        _____

        _____

   G23e. _____

   G23f. How would you describe her impact on your life?

        _____

        _____

        _____

Those are all the questions I have. Thank you very much for your time and help.

EXACT TIME NOW:_____

$$\boxed{\textit{POST-INTERVIEW INFORMATION}}$$

X1. Race of respondent:

| 1. WHITE | | 2. BLACK | | 3. OTHER |

X2. R's understanding of the questions was . . .

| 1. EXCELLENT | 2. GOOD | 3. FAIR | 4. POOR |

X3. R's interest in providing useful answers was . . .

| 1. EXCELLENT | 2. GOOD | 3. FAIR | 4. POOR |

X4. How tiring did the interview seem to be to R?

| 1. VERY TIRING | 2. A LITTLE TIRING | 3. NOT TIRING |

X5. Were there any serious problems with the interview, such as R's difficulty in hearing or understanding the questions, etc., which you think affected the quality of the interview?

| NONE | _____

_____

_____
_____
_____

Appendix C

*Comparison of Political Affect of the Bennington Sample
with the 1984 National Election Study Respondents*

As indicated in the text, our 1984 survey also included a series of "feeling thermometers" measuring the respondent's affective responses to several social and political stimulus objects, which were replicates of questions in the 1984 NES survey. These responses were given on a nine-point scale, as indicated in appendix B. In the analyses presented here we collapse the responses to these questions into five categories, presenting the percentage of respondents falling into these five categories.

Table C.1. Comparison of Political Affect of Bennington Respondents and 1984 National
Elections Study Respondents (Feeling Thermometers)

	1984 NES White Respondents				
Question	Total NES	Women	Women 60+	Women 60+ w/College	Bennington
C22a. Big business					
0–20	8.4%	7.6%	8.2%	12.2%	6.4%
21–40	21.4	20.6	19.7	24.4	17.8
41–60	47.1	48.1	42.9	46.3	43.5
61–80	15.8	15.9	20.4	14.6	34.6
81–100	7.3	7.8	8.8	2.4	7.7
n	1,591	859	147	41	325
C22b. Poor people					
0–20	0.8%	0.6%	0.6%	2.5%	0.6%
21–40	3.0	2.4	1.9	2.5	2.2
41–60	35.2	30.5	28.6	32.5	23.0
61–80	30.7	32.8	28.6	40.0	37.6
81–100	30.3	33.7	40.3	22.5	36.6
n	1,624	886	154	40	309

Table C.1. Comparison of Political Affect of Bennington Respondents and 1984 National Elections Study Respondents (Feeling Thermometers) *(continued)*

| Question | 1984 NES White Respondents | | | | |
	Total NES	Women	Women 60+	Women 60+ w/College	Bennington
C22c. Liberals					
0–20	5.8%	4.5%	4.9%	2.6%	1.2%
21–40	17.4	14.1	16.9	30.8	6.8
41–60	46.9	48.4	47.9	43.6	22.4
61–80	18.9	20.6	19.0	15.4	38.8
81–100	11.0	12.4	11.3	7.7	30.8
n	1,552	839	142	39	321
C22e. Hispanics					
0–20	4.2%	3.3%	5.1%	0.0%	0.6%
21–40	11.3	10.3	9.5	10.5	7.1
41–60	47.8	46.7	54.0	52.6	50.2
61–80	22.0	22.7	21.2	26.3	24.7
81–100	14.8	17.0	10.2	10.5	17.4
n	1,536	827	137	38	312
C22h. The present U.S. Supreme Court					
0–20	2.7%	1.5%	1.4%	2.5%	8.1%
21–40	9.3	7.6	6.2	12.5	24.5
41–60	41.9	42.2	37.7	35.0	48.4
61–80	30.1	31.6	37.7	32.5	20.2
81–100	16.0	17.1	17.1	17.5	6.8
n	1,597	860	146	40	322
C22k. Military					
0–20	2.5%	1.8%	1.3%	4.9%	27.4%
21–40	6.5	5.8	2.0	0.0	29.1
41–60	33.4	33.2	27.5	34.1	29.3
61–80	28.2	27.9	33.3	39.0	10.4
81–100	29.4	31.4	35.9	22.0	29.1
n	1,627	883	153	41	317
C22m. Blacks					
0–20	2.9%	1.9%	2.7%	0.0%	0.3%
21–40	9.0	8.0	10.1	12.8	2.0
41–60	43.2	40.2	39.2	35.9	34.9
61–80	26.3	27.3	27.7	33.3	33.7
81–100	18.6	22.6	20.3	17.9	3.8
n	1,622	886	148	39	309
C22n. Democrats					
0–20	8.2%	7.1%	7.3%	10.0%	0.9%
21–40	18.4	16.2	19.9	25.0	5.1
41–60	40.0	39.9	37.1	35.0	31.9
61–80	21.2	21.6	15.9	20.0	38.8
81–100	12.2	15.2	19.9	10.0	23.3
n	1,627	883	151	40	313

(continued on following page)

Table C.1. Comparison of Political Affect of Bennington Respondents and 1984 National Elections Study Respondents (Feeling Thermometers) *(continued)*

	1984 NES White Respondents				
Question	Total NES	Women	Women 60+	Women 60+ w/College	Bennington
C22p. People on welfare					
0–20	9.0%	8.1%	7.5%	7.7%	1.3%
21–40	22.3	22.1	17.0	12.8	8.5
41–60	46.2	45.1	48.3	56.4	42.5
61–80	14.6	15.4	17.7	17.9	32.7
81–100	8.0	9.3	9.5	5.1	15.0
n	1,599	869	147	39	306
C22q. Republicans					
0–20	7.5%	7.8%	10.6%	10.3%	10.5%
21–40	12.7	12.8	9.3	15.4	22.0
41–60	34.0	34.5	31.1	23.1	39.4
61–80	26.0	25.0	24.5	30.8	19.8
81–100	19.8	20.0	24.5	20.5	8.3
n	1,630	885	151	39	313
C22r. Labor unions					
0–20	10.8%	8.9%	9.9%	10.0%	3.9%
21–40	21.0	17.7	17.2	27.5	22.0
41–60	38.4	40.8	40.4	45.0	49.0
61–80	17.6	20.0	17.9	12.5	21.3
81–100	12.2	12.7	14.6	5.0	3.8
n	1,603	866	151	40	313
C22s. Civil rights leaders					
0–20	11.2%	9.9%	13.0%	4.9%	1.8%
21–40	17.4	15.9	24.0	26.8	6.5
41–60	45.0	45.9	44.5	41.5	26.5
61–80	16.1	18.0	13.7	24.4	34.4
81–100	10.3	10.3	4.8	2.4	30.4
n	1,599	862	146	41	316
C22u. Conservatives					
0–20	3.3%	3.4%	2.2%	2.6%	16.0%
21–40	11.5	10.2	10.1	10.3	25.5
41–60	45.5	45.5	48.6	43.6	35.7
61–80	24.1	24.8	28.3	35.9	16.6
81–100	15.5	16.2	10.9	7.7	5.8
n	1,553	835	138	39	313
C22v. The women's liberation movement					
0–20	9.2%	9.4%	11.4%	4.9%	4.0%
21–40	12.8	12.4	10.1	9.8	7.8
41–60	43.2	40.8	46.3	48.8	25.0
61–80	20.4	20.6	18.8	19.5	36.2
81–100	14.4	16.8	13.4	17.1	27.0
n	1,609	870	149	41	320

Table C.1. Comparison of Political Affect of Bennington Respondents and 1984 National Elections Study Respondents (Feeling Thermometers) *(continued)*

Question	Total NES	Women	Women 60+	Women 60+ w/College	Bennington
		1984 NES White Respondents			

C22y. Evangelical groups active in politics, such as the Moral Majority

	Total NES	Women	Women 60+	w/College	Bennington
0–20	20.5%	17.5%	15.4%	20.0%	75.9%
21–40	20.8	20.0	22.1	27.5	14.8
41–60	39.6	41.1	43.4	42.5	6.9
61–80	12.2	13.9	14.0	7.5	.9
81–100	6.9	7.5	5.1	2.5	1.5
n	1,534	827	136	40	318

C22z. Middle-class people

0–20	0.5%	0.6%	0.0%	0.0%	0.3%
21–40	1.5	0.9	0.6	0.0	1.2
41–60	28.8	26.4	22.1	22.5	33.5
61–80	33.9	32.7	39.0	30.0	31.3
81–100	35.3	39.4	38.3	47.5	28.7
n	1,630	895	154	40	310

Appendix D

Comparison of the Bennington Sample with the 1952–84 NES Respondents

Table D.1. Comparison of the Bennington Respondents and the 1952–84 National Election Study Respondents: Political Party Preference (C1)

Question: Generally speaking do you usually think of yourself as a Republican, a Democrat, an independent or what?

	NES Total Sample	NES Women	NES Women Born 1910–24	NES Women Born 1910–24 w/College	Bennington Women
1952					
Democrat	46.4%	47.0%	49.4%	34.1%	
Republican	28.7	30.2	28.5	36.4	
Independent	22.9	20.0	19.1	29.5	
Other	0.4	0.3	0.0	0.0	
None	1.6	2.5	3.0	0.0	
n	1,615	878	298	44	
1956					
Democrat	42.8%	41.6%	48.4%	34.4%	
Republican	30.1	33.5	29.2	45.9	
Independent	24.4	21.3	20.1	19.7	
Other	0.2	0.0	0.0	0.0	
None	2.5	3.6	2.3	0.0	
n	1,610	881	335	61	
1958					
Democrat	48.4%	49.0%	54.2%	44.0%	
Republican	29.4	30.0	26.4	42.0	
Independent	19.3	17.5	15.9	14.0	
Other	0.5	0.4	0.8	0.0	
None	2.4	3.1	2.7	0.0	
n	1,310	701	259	50	

Table D.1. Comparison of the Bennington Respondents and the 1952–84 National Election
Study Respondents: Political Party Preference (C1)

Question: Generally speaking do you usually think of yourself as a Republican, a Democrat, an independent or what? *(continued)*

	NES Total Sample	NES Women	NES Women Born 1910–24	NES Women Born 1910–24 w/College	Bennington Women
1960					
Democrat	46.9%	48.3%	48.7%	29.6%	
Republican	30.4	32.3	27.2	47.7	
Independent	21.5	17.9	21.5	20.5	
Other	0.3	0.2	0.5	2.2	
None	0.9	1.3	2.1	0.0	
n	992	524	195	44	
1962					
Democrat	45.3%	43.0%	46.5%	34.8%	
Republican	29.6	32.0	29.1	56.6	
Independent	22.2	20.5	18.8	8.6	
Other	0.1	0.0	0.0	0.0	
None	2.8	4.5	5.6	0.0	
n	1,168	639	196	46	
1964					
Democrat	49.0%	50.2%	57.0%	36.2%	
Republican	26.5	27.6	24.0	38.3	
Independent	23.4	20.9	18.1	25.5	
Other	0.7	0.5	0.4	0.0	
None	0.4	0.8	0.5	0.0	
n	1,394	750	221	47	
1966					
Democrat	43.7%	44.4%	46.5%	44.1%	
Republican	26.9	27.4	28.1	32.4	
Independent	28.2	26.8	24.3	23.5	
Other	0.2	0.3	0.0	0.0	
None	1.0	1.1	1.1	0.0	
n	1,131	633	189	34	
1968					
Democrat	40.9%	42.5%	42.7%	13.0%	
Republican	26.7	26.1	30.1	43.5	
Independent	31.0	29.6	27.2	43.5	
Other	0.2	0.1	0.0	0.0	
None	1.2	1.7	0.0	0.0	
n	1,387	769	216	46	

(continued on following page)

Table D.1. Comparison of the Bennington Respondents and the 1952–84 National Election
Study Respondents: Political Party Preference (C1)

Question: Generally speaking do you usually think of yourself as a Republican, a Democrat,
an independent or what? *(continued)*

	NES Total Sample	NES Women	NES Women Born 1910–24	NES Women Born 1910–24 w/College	Bennington Women
1970					
Democrat	39.0%	40.2%	44.2%	40.0%	
Republican	26.6	27.5	30.4	48.6	
Independent	33.4	31.4	24.4	11.4	
Other	0.2	0.0	0.0	0.0	
None	0.8	0.9	1.0	0.0	
n	1,395	784	197	35	
1972					
Democrat	37.0%	39.3%	46.7%	35.1%	
Republican	25.4	26.3	28.4	42.1	
Independent	36.0	32.6	24.0	22.8	
Other	0.3	0.4	0.0	0.0	
None	1.3	1.4	0.9	0.0	
n	2,394	1,345	324	57	
1974					
Democrat	35.9%	38.5%	42.6%	33.4%	
Republican	25.5	26.5	26.2	44.5	
Independent	36.2	31.6	27.7	19.9	
Other	0.3	0.5	0.0	0.0	
None	2.1	2.9	3.5	2.2	
n	1,400	796	202	45	
1976					
Democrat	35.5%	37.3%	44.2%	36.8%	
Republican	26.6	29.1	30.0	33.8	
Independent	36.7	32.3	24.7	29.4	
Other	0.4	0.3	0.7	0.0	
None	0.8	1.0	0.4	0.0	
n	1,959	1,113	267	68	
1978					
Democrat	36.3%	37.7%	46.5%	35.6%	
Republican	22.5	25.2	21.4	28.9	
Independent	38.6	33.7	30.3	35.5	
Other	0.2	0.3	0.0	0.0	
None	2.4	3.1	1.8	0.0	
n	2,016	1,096	211	45	

Table D.1. Comparison of the Bennington Respondents and the 1952–84 National Election
　　　　Study Respondents: Political Party Preference (C1)
Question: Generally speaking do you usually think of yourself as a Republican, a Democrat,
　　　　an independent or what?

	NES Total Sample	NES Women	NES Women Born 1910–24	NES Women Born 1910–24 w/College	Bennington Women
1984					
Democrat	32.3%	35.6%	41.0%	35.7%	44.2%
Republican	30.1	28.9	32.3	37.1	24.2
Independent	36.7	34.4	26.5	27.2	30.4
Other	0.0	0.0	0.0	0.0	0.3
None	0.9	1.1	0.2	0.0	0.9
n	4,990	2,750	471	143	335
1980					
Democrat	37.2%	40.5%	46.7%	34.2%	
Republican	26.2	26.3	29.6	45.6	
Independent	35.1	31.5	22.6	20.2	
Other	0.1	0.1	0.0	0.0	
None	1.4	1.6	1.1	0.0	
n	3,143	1,758	368	79	
1982					
Democrat	40.3%	44.0%	49.8%	38.7%	
Republican	26.6	25.5	25.2	34.1	
Independent	31.0	28.3	23.8	27.2	
Other	0.1	0.0	0.0	0.0	
None	2.0	2.2	1.2	0.0	
n	1,248	679	163	44	

Table D.2. Comparison of the Bennington Respondents and the 1964–84 National Election Study Respondents: Follow Government Affairs (C9)

Question: Some people seem to follow what's going on in government and public affairs most of the time, whether there's an election going on or not. Others aren't that interested. Would you say you follow what's going on in government and public affairs most of the time, some of the time, only now and then, or hardly at all?

	NES Total Sample	NES Women	NES Women Born 1910–24	NES Women Born 1910–24 w/College	Bennington Women
1964					
Most of time	31.0%	25.5%	25.0%	36.6%	
Some of time	41.2	40.5	46.7	53.7	
Now and then	17.0	20.3	16.8	7.3	
Hardly at all	10.8	13.7	11.5	2.4	
n	1,288	699	208	41	
1966					
Most of time	36.7%	29.7%	37.6%	55.9%	
Some of time	30.0	32.4	32.3	35.3	
Now and then	17.2	19.5	14.2	0.0	
Hardly at all	16.1	18.4	15.9	8.8	
n	1,136	636	189	34	
1968					
Most of time	34.7%	28.5%	37.9%	62.8%	
Some of time	30.3	30.7	23.2	30.2	
Now and then	18.4	21.6	21.6	2.3	
Hardly at all	16.6	19.2	17.3	4.7	
n	1,195	667	185	43	
1972					
Most of time	37.4%	30.5%	36.7%	59.2%	
Some of time	36.2	37.3	32.4	32.7	
Now and then	15.2	17.6	16.6	6.1	
Hardly at all	11.2	14.6	14.3	2.0	
n	1,943	1,094	259	49	
1974					
Most of time	39.9%	35.5%	44.8%	64.5%	
Some of time	37.3	38.0	35.8	28.9	
Now and then	13.8	16.2	10.4	4.4	
Hardly at all	9.0	10.3	9.0	2.2	
n	1,394	794	201	45	
1976					
Most of time	39.9%	35.0%	46.6%	66.7%	
Some of time	31.5	30.8	29.0	17.5	
Now and then	18.0	19.9	12.0	9.5	
Hardly at all	10.6	14.3	12.4	6.3	
n	1,675	968	241	63	

Table D.2. Comparison of the Bennington Respondents and the 1964–84 National Election
Study Respondents: Follow Government Affairs (C9)

Question: Some people seem to follow what's going on in government and public affairs
most of the time, whether there's an election going on or not. Others aren't that
interested. Would you say you follow what's going on in government and public
affairs most of the time, some of the time, only now and then, or hardly at all?
(continued)

	NES Total Sample	NES Women	NES Women Born 1910–24	NES Women Born 1910–24 w/College	Bennington Women
1980					
Most of time	37.8%	31.5%	39.4%	56.8%	
Some of time	35.9	37.5	34.3	32.4	
Now and then	16.8	19.0	14.8	9.5	
Hardly at all	9.5	12.0	11.5	1.3	
n	2,948	1,640	338	74	
1982					
Most of time	28.4%	22.9%	28.8%	50.0%	
Some of time	35.7	35.4	33.1	34.1	
Now and then	21.2	24.9	22.1	13.6	
Hardly at all	14.7	16.8	16.0	2.3	
n	1,242	678	163	44	
1984					
Most of time	38.3%	32.3%	49.5%	66.3%	74.0%
Some of time	33.1	35.4	28.5	24.6	20.9
Now and then	19.4	21.1	13.7	7.7	3.9
Hardly at all	9.2	11.2	8.3	1.4	1.2
n	4,728	2,599	445	142	335

Table D.3. Comparison of the Bennington Respondents and the 1952–84 National Election
Study Respondents: Interest in Election Campaigns (C10)

Question: How about the presidential campaign in 1984? Would you say that you are very
much interested, or not much interested in following the presidential campaign
in 1984?

	NES Total Sample	NES Women	NES Women Born 1910–24	NES Women Born 1910–24 w/College	Bennington Women
1952					
Very much	37.9%	35.2%	28.3%	59.1%	
Somewhat	34.5	35.8	43.7	36.4	
Not much	27.6	29.0	28.0	4.5	
n	1,595	869	293	44	
1956					
Very much	30.4%	26.5%	26.2%	43.3%	
Somewhat	39.5	40.5	42.5	46.7	
Not much	30.1	33.0	31.3	10.0	
n	1,603	878	332	60	
1958					
Very much	27.1%	22.7%	21.8%	30.0%	
Somewhat	34.7	34.2	35.0	44.0	
Not much	38.2	43.1	43.2	26.0	
n	1,307	699	257	50	
1960					
Very much	40.9%	36.5%	33.3%	43.2%	
Somewhat	39.2	40.1	42.1	50.0	
Not much	19.9	23.4	24.6	6.8	
n	973	524	195	44	
1962					
Very much	37.1%	33.5%	34.8%	39.1%	
Somewhat	37.6	37.1	38.4	47.9	
Not much	25.3	29.4	26.8	13.0	
n	1,172	638	198	46	
1964					
Very much	40.5%	39.4%	40.4%	58.6%	
Somewhat	54.4	55.2	55.3	39.0	
Not much	5.1	5.4	4.3	2.4	
n	1,288	698	208	41	
1966					
Very much	30.7%	26.3%	28.8%	54.5%	
Somewhat	40.7	43.1	46.7	36.4	
Not much	28.6	30.6	24.5	9.1	
n	1,122	624	184	33	

Table D.3. Comparison of the Bennington Respondents and the 1952–84 National Election
Study Respondents: Interest in Election Campaigns (C10)

Question: How about the presidential campaign in 1984? Would you say that you are very
much interested, or not much interested in following the presidential campaign
in 1984? *(continued)*

	NES Total Sample	NES Women	NES Women Born 1910–24	NES Women Born 1910–24 w/College	Bennington Women
1968					
Very much	39.6%	36.3%	37.7%	53.3%	
Somewhat	39.7	41.6	42.8	40.0	
Not much	20.7	22.1	19.5	6.7	
n	1,380	766	215	45	
1970					
Very much	34.2%	30.8%	38.1%	57.2%	
Somewhat	42.6	42.7	38.1	37.1	
Not much	23.2	26.5	23.8	5.7	
n	1,396	785	197	35	
1972					
Very much	31.1%	26.9%	30.6%	50.9%	
Somewhat	41.9	43.4	37.0	42.1	
Not much	27.0	29.7	32.4	7.0	
n	2,392	1,346	324	57	
1976					
Very much	37.0%	35.1%	44.2%	63.3%	
Somewhat	42.9	44.5	39.0	27.9	
Not much	20.1	20.4	16.8	8.8	
n	1,956	1,113	267	68	
1978					
Very much	21.6%	20.5%	33.0%	42.2%	
Somewhat	45.2	43.6	35.9	42.2	
Not much	33.2	35.9	31.1	15.6	
n	2,013	1,101	212	45	
1980					
Very much	32.5%	30.2%	42.3%	62.0%	
Somewhat	45.0	47.0	37.6	32.9	
Not much	22.5	22.8	20.1	5.1	
n	3,108	1,740	364	79	
1982					
Very much	24.9%	23.0%	31.9%	38.6%	
Somewhat	44.4	45.2	39.9	47.8	
Not much	30.7	31.8	28.2	13.6	
n	1,247	679	163	44	

(continued on following page)

Table D.3. Comparison of the Bennington Respondents and the 1952–84 National Election Study Respondents: Interest in Election Campaigns (C10)

Question: How about the presidential campaign in 1984? Would you say that you are very much interested, or not much interested in following the presidential campaign in 1984? *(continued)*

	NES Total Sample	NES Women	NES Women Born 1910–24	NES Women Born 1910–24 w/College	Bennington Women
1984					
Very much	40.8%	38.7%	52.9%	64.1%	75.2%
Somewhat	41.7	43.2	32.6	29.6	18.5
Not much	17.5	18.1	14.5	6.3	6.3
n	5,009	2,759	473	142	335

Table D.4. Comparison of the Bennington Respondents and the 1952–84 National Election
Study Respondents: Candidate Preference (C11)

Question: In this year's presidential campaign, do you prefer Reagan or Mondale?

	NES Total Sample	NES Women	NES Women Born 1910–24	NES Women Born 1910–24 w/College	Bennington Women
1952					
Republican	57.1%	59.0%	57.4%	64.3%	42.6%
Democrat	42.7	40.7	41.8	35.7	57.4
Other	0.2	0.3	0.8	0.0	0.0
n	1,370	717	251	42	326
1956					
Republican	79.3%	79.7%	76.5%	87.7%	37.7%
Democrat	20.6	20.2	23.5	12.3	62.3
Other	0.1	0.1	0.0	0.0	0.0
n	1,417	756	289	57	329
1960					
Republican	57.6%	59.3%	60.0%	75.0%	26.0%
Democrat	42.1	40.7	40.0	25.0	74.0
Other	0.3	0.0	0.0	0.0	0.0
n	767	391	150	36	331
1964					
Republican	9.9%	11.6%	12.6%	9.8%	20.2%
Democrat	90.0	88.4	87.4	90.2	76.5
Other	0.1	0.0	0.0	0.0	0.3
n	1,253	663	198	41	321
1968					
Republican	79.0%	78.2%	82.0%	79.1%	32.9%
Democrat	20.6	21.3	16.9	18.6	66.5
Other	0.4	0.5	1.1	2.3	0.6
n	1,170	624	177	43	328
1972					
Republican	94.9%	94.0%	95.5%	98.2%	30.6%
Democrat	5.1	5.9	4.5	1.8	69.4
Other	0.0	0.1	0.0	0.0	0.0
n	2,192	1,203	287	55	330
1976					
Republican	52.4%	54.0%	54.2%	54.9%	31.2%
Democrat	47.5	45.9	45.8	45.1	68.8
Other	0.1	0.1	0.0	0.0	0.0
n	1,672	893	212	51	330
1980					
Republican	45.7%	45.0%	35.4%	48.8%	23.4%
Democrat	54.2	54.9	64.1	51.2	76.0
Other	0.1	0.1	0.5	0.0	0.6
n	1,777	965	195	43	333

(continued on following page)

371

Table D.4. Comparison of the Bennington Respondents and the 1952–84 National Election
Study Respondents: Candidate Preference (C11)

Question: In this year's presidential campaign, do you prefer Reagan or Mondale?
(*continued*)

	NES Total Sample	NES Women	NES Women Born 1910–24	NES Women Born 1910–24 w/College	Bennington Women
1984					
Republican	81.1%	79.1%	76.9%	73.0%	26.4%
Democrat	18.5	20.5	22.3	25.7	73.3
Other	0.4	0.4	0.8	1.3	0.3
n	3,006	1,623	260	74	307

372

Table D.5. Comparison of the Bennington Respondents and the 1952–84 National Election Study Respondents: Interest in the Election Outcome (C12)

Question: Would you say that you personally care a good deal which party wins the presidential election in the fall of 1984, or that you don't care very much which party wins?

	NES Total Sample	NES Women	NES Women Born 1910–24	NES Women Born 1910–24 w/College	Bennington Women
1952					
A good deal	68.5%	67.0%	64.4%	81.0%	
Not very much	31.5	33.0	35.6	19.0	
n	1,567	842	284	42	
1956					
A good deal	65.5%	63.6%	61.7%	82.0%	
Not very much	34.5	36.4	38.3	18.0	
n	1,539	836	321	61	
1964					
A good deal	67.5%	67.4%	67.8%	69.8%	
Not very much	32.5	32.6	32.2	30.2	
n	1,322	714	205	43	
1968					
A good deal	58.7%	57.6%	59.3%	65.1%	
Not very much	41.3	42.4	40.7	34.9	
n	1,303	726	199	43	
1972					
A good deal	61.5%	61.8%	65.0%	81.5%	
Not very much	38.5	38.2	35.0	18.5	
n	2,305	1,292	309	54	
1976					
A good deal	58.1%	57.3%	60.9%	58.2%	
Not very much	41.9	42.7	39.1	41.8	
n	1,899	1,076	256	67	
1980					
A good deal	52.5%	52.4%	58.8%	64.0%	
Not very much	47.5	47.6	41.2	36.0	
n	3,004	1,666	352	75	
1984					
A good deal	67.7%	67.3%	72.6%	75.4%	88.4%
Not very much	32.3	32.7	27.4	24.6	11.6
n	4,921	2,697	456	138	327

Table D.6. Comparison of the Bennington Respondents and the 1974–84 National Election
Study Respondents: Attention to Television News (C14)
Question: How often do you watch the national network news on TV—every day, three or
four times a week, once or twice a week, or less often?

	NES Total Sample	NES Women	NES Women Born 1910–24	NES Women Born 1910–24 w/College	Bennington Women
1974					
Every day	59.6%	59.4%	72.3%	68.9%	
3 or 4 times per week	22.8	22.0	13.4	13.3	
1 or 2 times per week	9.0	8.7	8.9	11.1	
Less often	8.6	9.9	5.4	6.7	
n	1,389	791	202	45	
1976					
Every day	54.6%	54.1%	74.3%	73.0%	
3 or 4 times per week	23.2	24.3	15.8	9.5	
1 or 2 times per week	13.9	13.5	6.6	12.7	
Less often	8.3	8.1	3.3	4.8	
n	1,681	970	241	67	
1980					
Every day	39.2%	43.7%	63.1%	68.4%	
3 or 4 times per week	23.5	21.3	17.5	16.5	
1 or 2 times per week	17.5	16.9	8.2	7.6	
Less often	19.8	18.1	11.2	7.5	
n	3,116	1,742	365	79	
1984					
Every day	45.1%	45.4%	72.1%	76.2%	53.2%
3 or 4 times per week	20.7	20.1	14.5	11.9	22.1
1 or 2 times per week	18.5	18.5	7.5	7.1	9.6
Less often	15.7	16.0	5.9	4.8	15.1
n	1,940	1,072	186	42	312

Note: In 1974 and 1976 offered response categories were *Frequently, Sometimes, Rarely,*
and *Never.*

Table D.7. Comparison of the Bennington Respondents and the 1980–84 National Election
Study Respondents: Attention to Political News (C14)

Question: When you watch the news on TV, do you pay a great deal of attention to news
about government and politics, do you pay some attention, or don't you pay much
attention to news about government and politics?

	NES Total Sample	NES Women	NES Women Born 1910–24	NES Women Born 1910–24 w/College	Bennington Women
1980					
A great deal	48.0%	43.8%	53.1%	69.3%	
Some	43.8	47.1	38.2	28.0	
Not much	8.2	9.1	8.7	2.7	
n	2,908	1,634	343	75	
1984					
A great deal	35.6%	29.2%	41.3%	46.3%	67.9%
Some	51.2	56.5	47.8	48.8	31.1
Not much	13.2	14.3	10.9	4.9	1.0
n	1,872	1,040	184	41	305

Table D.8. Comparison of the Bennington Respondents and the 1958–84 National Election
Study Respondents: Perception of Strength of U.S. Position (C23)

Question: During the past year, would you say that the United States' position in the world
has grown weaker, stayed about the same, or has it grown stronger?

	NES Total Sample	NES Women	NES Women Born 1910–24	NES Women Born 1910–24 w/College	Bennington Women
1958					
Weaker	29.0%	29.4%	24.3%	39.1%	
Stayed same	45.6	49.8	52.0	45.7	
Stronger	25.4	20.8	23.7	15.2	
n	1,112	548	202	46	
1960					
Weaker	40.4%	40.9%	41.0%	47.8%	
Stayed same	36.6	37.9	39.9	29.5	
Stronger	23.0	21.2	19.1	22.7	
n	858	433	173	44	
1964					
Weaker	25.5%	24.2%	22.9%	37.2%	
Stayed same	43.8	46.4	46.8	55.8	
Stronger	30.7	29.4	30.3	7.0	
n	1,194	615	188	43	
1968					
Weaker	58.7%	59.3%	61.8%	68.9%	
Stayed same	34.1	33.9	30.9	31.1	
Stronger	7.2	6.8	7.3	0.0	
n	1,184	628	178	45	
1984					
Weaker	27.8%	29.8%	33.4%	36.2%	63.1%
Stayed same	40.4	45.1	43.2	44.0	22.2
Stronger	31.8	25.1	23.4	19.8	14.7
n	4,927	2,702	461	141	325

Table D.9. Comparison of the Bennington Respondents and the 1956–84 National Election
Study Respondents: Perceived Likelihood of Conventional War (C24)

Question:

Wording in 1956 and 1960: "Now I'd like to ask you some questions about the chances of our
country getting into war. Would you say that at the present time you are pretty worried about
this country getting into another war, somewhat worried, or not worried at all?"

Wording in 1982 and 1984: "How about the chances of our country getting into a conventional war, one in which neither side uses nuclear weapons? Are you pretty worried about
this country getting into such a war at the present time, somewhat worried, or not worried
at all?"

	NES Total Sample	NES Women	NES Women Born 1910–24	NES Women Born 1910–24 w/College	Bennington Women
1956					
Very worried	11.4%	12.2%	13.9%	11.7%	
Somewhat worried	44.6	47.8	51.4	50.0	
Not worried	44.0	40.0	34.7	38.3	
n	1,590	869	329	60	
1960					
Very worried	21.3%	25.1%	22.2%	20.5%	
Somewhat worried	48.4	54.4	60.3	56.8	
Not worried	30.3	20.5	17.5	22.7	
n	966	521	194	44	
1982					
Very worried	20.1%	22.7%	25.9%	11.6%	
Somewhat worried	45.4	46.9	48.2	41.9	
Not worried	34.5	30.4	25.9	46.5	
n	1,242	677	162	43	
1984					
Very worried	18.9%	22.3%	22.4%	18.9%	38.9%
Somewhat worried	45.9	49.9	49.4	50.3	47.2
Not worried	35.2	27.8	28.2	30.8	13.9
n	4,995	2,752	472	143	331

Table D.10. Comparison of the Bennington Respondents and the 1982–84 National Election
Study Respondents: Attitude toward Government Spending (C26)

Question: Some people think the government in Washington should provide fewer services, even in areas such as health and education, in order to reduce spending. Other people feel it is important for the government to provide more services, even if it means an increase in spending. Do you think the government should reduce spending, provide more services, or is your position somewhere in between?

	NES Total Sample	NES Women	NES Women Born 1910–24	NES Women Born 1910–24 w/College	Bennington Women
1982					
Reduce	43.1%	36.8%	40.8%	46.4%	
Between	30.1	32.8	34.3	34.1	
More services	26.8	30.4	24.9	19.5	
n	994	519	108	41	
1984					
Reduce	32.8%	26.4%	29.0%	36.3%	13.3%
Between	35.3	36.2	39.7	36.2	50.3
More services	31.9	37.4	31.3	27.5	36.4
n	4,061	2,138	348	127	324

Table D.11. Comparison of the Bennington Respondents and the 1970–84 National Election Study Respondents: Attitude toward Aid to Minorities (C27)

Question: Some people feel that the government in Washington should make every effort to improve the social and economic position of blacks and other minority groups. Others feel that the government should not make any special effort to help minorities because they should help themselves. Do you feel the government should help improve the position of minorities, that minorities should help themselves, or is your position somewhere in between?

	NES Total Sample	NES Women	NES Women Born 1910–24	NES Women Born 1910–24 w/College	Bennington Women
1970					
Government help	24.6%	24.4%	22.1%	32.3%	
Between	27.0	29.6	34.7	29.0	
Help themselves	48.4	46.0	43.2	38.7	
n	1,250	692	176	31	
1972					
Government help	28.9%	29.1%	23.5%	22.4%	
Between	24.9	24.8	26.5	34.7	
Help themselves	46.2	46.1	50.0	42.9	
n	1,781	978	234	49	
1974					
Government help	25.0%	26.2%	22.5%	28.6%	
Between	26.0	27.8	27.2	14.3	
Help themselves	49.0	46.0	50.3	57.1	
n	1,194	663	169	42	
1976					
Government help	29.3%	29.6%	20.6%	23.4%	
Between	22.6	24.5	25.7	28.1	
Help themselves	48.1	45.9	53.7	48.5	
n	1,616	878	218	64	
1978					
Government help	23.0%	25.2%	26.7%	20.4%	
Between	25.9	25.5	25.7	25.0	
Help themselves	51.1	49.3	47.6	54.6	
n	1,802	959	183	44	
1980					
Government help	16.6%	17.1%	14.6%	13.4%	
Between	27.7	29.0	29.0	35.8	
Help themselves	55.7	53.9	56.4	50.8	
n	2,454	1,334	259	67	
1982					
Government help	21.1%	21.4%	16.7%	19.0%	
Between	30.3	31.0	40.5	45.3	
Help themselves	48.6	47.6	42.8	35.7	
n	1,062	577	131	42	

(continued on following page)

379

Table D.11. Comparison of the Bennington Respondents and the 1970–84 National Election
Study Respondents: Attitude toward Aid to Minorities (C27)

Question: Some people feel that the government in Washington should make every effort
to improve the social and economic position of blacks and other minority groups.
Others feel that the government should not make any special effort to help
minorities because they should help themselves. Do you feel the government
should help improve the position of minorities, that minorities should help themselves, or is your position somewhere in between? *(continued)*

	NES Total Sample	NES Women	NES Women Born 1910–24	NES Women Born 1910–24 w/College	Bennington Women
1984					
Government help	30.2%	30.7%	27.5%	26.6%	53.6%
Between	29.1	30.6	31.7	37.5	38.2
Help themselves	40.7	38.7	40.8	35.9	8.2
n	4,210	2,271	375	128	330

Table D.12. Comparison of the Bennington Respondents and the 1980–84 National Election Study Respondents: Attitude toward Defense Spending (C29)

Question: Some people believe that we should spend less money for defense. Others feel that defense spending should be increased. Do you feel the government should decrease defense spending, increase defense spending, or is the government spending about the right amount?

	NES Total Sample	NES Women	NES Women Born 1910–24	NES Women Born 1910–24 w/College	Bennington Women
1980					
Decrease	9.4%	10.8%	5.3%	6.9%	
Right amount	17.0	20.1	20.6	15.1	
Increase	73.6	69.1	74.1	78.0	
n	2,709	1,435	301	73	
1982					
Decrease	34.0%	37.1%	30.3%	24.4%	
Right amount	32.5	36.5	41.3	56.1	
Increase	33.5	26.4	28.4	19.5	
n	1,010	523	109	41	
1984					
Decrease	35.9%	38.0%	34.0%	30.4%	75.2%
Right amount	30.9	30.4	36.1	36.8	20.3
Increase	33.2	31.6	29.9	32.8	4.5
n	4,313	2,234	364	125	311

Appendix E

Structural Equation Models

Throughout this book we employ structural equation modeling techniques to obtain estimates of the magnitudes of causal relationships among variables. These techniques are quite useful in studying the role of theoretically relevant factors in processes of human development and change within the context of fallible indicators (see Alwin, 1988c, Campbell and Mutran, 1982; Jöreskog, 1979; Kessler and Greenberg, 1981; Nesselroade, 1970, 1977; Nesselroade and Baltes, 1979). Structural equation modeling is, however, a somewhat arcane field of application; thus, this appendix provides a brief discussion of the technique via an explication of the models underlying our analysis of stability. This discussion attempts to present our analytic procedures in a relatively nontechnical manner, so that all readers can obtain an appreciation of our methods of analysis.

THE BASIC MODELS

In chapter 7 we introduced a model, depicted graphically in figure 7.1, in which a *latent* variable representing sociopolitical orientations in the 1930s (or 1940s) was dependent upon three causally prior *exogenous* factors: year entered Bennington College (x_1), number of years at Bennington (x_2), and parental sociopolitical orientations (x_3).[1] The impact or influence of these factors on 1930s sociopolitical orientations (SPO30) can be represented as a set of parameters in a linear structural equation model.[2]

The model in figure 7.1 can be represented by two sets of linear structural equations: one expressing the measurement assumptions, or *measurement model*, for the linkage between the latent construct defining 1930s sociopolitical orientations,

---

1. *Exogenous* factors are those whose sources of variation are not the focus of the model, and variables for which the sources of variation arise outside the system of variables under consideration. By contrast, *endogenous* variables are those whose sources of variation arise in part from amongst the set of variables being considered. In our analysis the latent variables representing sociopolitical orientations are endogenous variables.

2. Discussions of structural equation models, also called *path models*, can be found in a number of different sources (see e.g., Alwin and Hauser, 1975; Duncan, 1975a).

and one expressing the effects of the x's on this latent variable. The structural equations expressing the relationship between the 1930s measures of sociopolitical orientations, y_1 (PEP30) and y_2 (PID30), and the latent variable they measure are as follows:

$$y_1 = \lambda_{1\eta}\eta + \epsilon_1$$

$$y_2 = \lambda_{2\eta}\eta + \epsilon_2$$

where η is the latent construct representing sociopolitical orientations, the λ's express relationships of the y's to this latent variable, and the ϵ's are *disturbance* variables containing measurement error and specific variance unique to the particular measure. This model is equivalent to a *common factor* model for the two measures, in that it assumes the ϵ's are independent (i.e., uncorrelated) with respect to the latent variable. Unfortunately, in most cases it is not possible to separate the error and specific components and their separate variance.

The second part of the model involves the structural equation for the effects of the x's on this latent variable. This model, in conformance with the diagram in figure 7.1 is as follows:

$$\eta = \gamma_{\eta x_1}x_1 + \gamma_{\eta x_2}x_2 + \gamma_{\eta x_3}x_3 + \zeta$$

where the γ's (gammas) are *effect parameters* reflecting the relative effects of x_1, x_2 and x_3, while *holding constant* the effects of the other factors in the model, and ζ is a *disturbance* variable reflecting unknown sources of variation in η.[3]

Of particular interest in such equations is the sign of the γ-coefficients, indicating whether the dependent variable, in our case the latent variable η, increases or decreases as a function of increases in a particular x_i. Our estimates of these coefficients in the Bennington sample (see table 7.3), indicate that *the number of years attending Bennington* has a negative coefficient, suggesting that the longer one attended Bennington College, the *less* conservative the respondent is expected to be on the average.[4] The coefficients for x_1 and x_3 are, on the other hand, positive, since we expected more conservative children would have more conservative parents, and the later the student entered Bennington College, the more conservative she would be.[5]

In order to compare the relative sizes of the γ-coefficients, we have in all of

3. It is assumed that ζ is uncorrelated with the x's, but we have no way of evaluating this issue in the absence of strong theory. In the present case we make this assumption, knowing that we have no doubt omitted important variables that are correlated with the x's.

4. Recall that the measures of 1930s sociopolitical orientations are both scored so that a conservative orientation is given a high score; thus, in the above example, the longer the student stayed at Bennington, the less conservative she is expected to be.

5. We indicated in chapter 7 that we thought this effect was due not to the period of time the student entered, but to the relative age of the student when last measured. Recall that the attitudes of students entering the study near its termination had been at Bennington just a few years; thus, their later attitudes are censored by our design.

our analyses represented the variables in *standardized* units; that is, they are all measured from a mean of zero and scaled to have a standard deviation of unity. By putting these effects in standard form, we forego the possibility of comparing *metric*, or *unstandardized*, coefficients across groups (see below), but for our purposes we are content to make comparisons between the *standardized* coefficients. In defense of this strategy, we would argue that there is no "true" metric of sociopolitical orientations; thus, we arbitrarily define the metric of these latent variables in standardized terms. This means that all variables in our analysis—observed and unobserved alike—are scaled to have standard deviations of unity.[6]

The remaining models estimated in chapter 7 are simple extensions of the one discussed in the foregoing. Two types of extensions are to be found: extending the model by including additional latent variables, and extending the model by including additional measures. The model estimates found in table 7.5 (see figure 7.2) extend the model by including a second latent construct, representing latent sociopolitical orientations in the 1960s. This adds a second structural equation for this second latent variable, and it adds a measurement model linking the 1960s measures of sociopolitical orientations to this second latent variable.[7] The set of structural equations for this model is as follows:

$$\eta_1 = \gamma_{\eta_1 x_1} x_1 + \gamma_{\eta_1 x_2} x_2 + \gamma_{\eta_1 x_3} x_3 + \zeta_1$$

$$\eta_2 = \gamma_{\eta_2 x_1} x_1 + \beta_{21} \eta_1 + \zeta_2$$

where the γ-coefficients are defined as above, and the ζ_1 and ζ_2 variables are defined as above. There are two differences from the earlier discussion. First, the second of these equations contains an *effect* of time-1 (1930s) sociopolitical attitudes on time-2 (1960s) attitudes. This coefficient, represented by β_{21}, specifies the stability of attitudes, that is, the dependence of individual differences in latent attitudes at time 2 (the 1960s) on latent attitudes at time 1, independent of the effects of the exogenous variables. Second, the model specifies that some of the potential effects of the exogenous variables are nonexistent, or zero, because of their lack of theoretical justification. Thus, parental sociopolitical orientations (x_3) and the number of years at Bennington (x_2) affect 1960s attitudes only via their effects on 1930s attitudes.

The measurement portion of this model (see figure 7.2) is represented by the following set of equations:

$$y_1 = \lambda_{1\eta_1} \eta_1 + \epsilon_1$$

$$y_2 = \lambda_{2\eta_1} \eta_1 + \epsilon_2$$

6. See Alwin, 1988b, for a more detailed discussion of the issue of standardization.

7. We have not referred to the exogenous variables as *latent* variables because we have only a single measure of each. We could, however, also refer to such variables as *latent constructs*, but it is conventional to simply assume such latent variables are identical to their observed counterparts.

$$y_3 = \lambda_{3\eta_2}\eta_2 + \epsilon_3$$

$$y_4 = \lambda_{4\eta_2}\eta_2 + \epsilon_4$$

where the equations for y_1 and y_2 are identical to those given above, and the conventions for interpreting the model parameters are the same as specified above. This is essentially a two-factor common factor model in which each factor is measured by two observed variables replicated over time. Each measured variable is specified to be dependent upon only one common factor, (i.e., each is *univocal*), and each measure contains *random* sources of disturbance, involving errors of measurement and specific sources of variation.

In chapter 7 we estimated two different versions of the basic structural equation model including a stability coefficient linking the 1930s and 1960s. The first is the one we just discussed. The second adds more measures of the latent construct, including y_5 (PCI60) and y_6 (LC60), so that there are four univocal measures of the latent variable for the 1960s sociopolitical orientations. The model for the two additional measures is as follows:

$$y_5 = \lambda_{5\eta_2}\eta_2 + \epsilon_5$$

$$y_6 = \lambda_{6\eta_2}\eta_2 + \epsilon_6$$

We noted in chapter 7 that whether we interpret the version of the model containing all four time-2 measures, or the version containing only replicates of the 1930s measures, the estimated magnitude of stability is virtually identical; thus, our interpretation of the process of attitude stability and change is the same, regardless of how we measure the underlying latent variable for the 1960s time period. This is important because it reinforces the robustness of our conclusions regarding processes of attitude stability and change.

Our final model depicting attitude stability and change over the life course includes a latent attitude variable and its measures for the third time point in our longitudinal design. This model is depicted in figure 7.3. Estimates of the parameters of this model for two different versions, incorporating different sets of measures of the 1984 and 1960s latent variables, are given in tables 7.8, 7.9, and 7.10. This model will not be given extended treatment here, as we have already discussed its basic components. As can be seen in figure 7.3, this model adds a third structural equation for the latent attitude at time 3. This equation is as follows:

$$\eta_3 = \beta_{32}\eta_2 + \zeta_3$$

In this model the latent variable representing sociopolitical orientations at time 3 (SPO84) depends *only* on the time-2 embodiment of the latent attitude. In other words, in this model the time-3 latent attitude orientation does not depend directly on any of the exogenous factors, nor on the time-1 attitude. These prior factors influence the time-3 attitude only *indirectly*, via the time-2 latent attitude. To the extent that attitudes are stable, these early influences can be said to influence later attitudes via their impact on earlier attitudes. In this sense, the model specifies that early influences on attitudes exert an effect on later attitudes via processes of attitude continuity rather than change.[8] This assumption builds upon those theoretical models that credit early influences for attitude constancy over the life span.

STATISTICAL FIT OF MODELS

Because we have followed a multiple indicator approach to the study of attitude persistence and change, our models are *overidentified*, in the sense that our multiple indicators provide several estimates of the causal parameters of our models (see Alwin, 1988c:108–10). This means that by using certain statistical estimation techniques—specifically, maximum-likelihood estimation—it is possible to use the overidentified nature of the model to our advantage in testing the fit of the model to the data. Such tests do not help us evaluate the fundamental truth of our causal and measurement assumptions—these assumptions can only be assessed on the basis of theory and prior literature. But we can evaluate how well the model fits the data using *goodness-of-fit* information; that is, we can evaluate how well the empirical estimates help reproduce the data structure from which they were derived.

Maximum-likelihood estimation requires some relatively strong assumptions of a multinormal distribution among the measured variables, and under these assumptions a test statistic can be derived (the *likelihood-ratio* statistic), which under certain conditions of sampling is characterized by the χ^2 distribution with df degrees of freedom. The data gathered in the Bennington research are, we think, of unusually high quality, but we doubt nonetheless that the data meet the requirements of the interpretation of maximum-likelihood estimates in the most rigorous and precise manner. We thus interpret the fit statistics reported in chapters 7, 8, and 9 as a rough guide to the adequacy of the fit of the data to the model.

For all of our models we present the estimated likelihood-ratio χ^2, the degrees of freedom (df), and the calculated probability of a Type I statistical error, that is, the probability of falsely rejecting the null hypothesis of no difference between the observed covariance matrix for the variables and the comparable covariance matrix reproduced on the basis of the model's estimated coefficients. A high p-value indicates a high likelihood that one would be wrong if the null hypothesis were rejected.

Using the model depicted in figure 7.3 as an example, for which empirical estimates of the coefficients of the model are given in table 7.8, we can illustrate the

8. One way in which to illustrate this point, which we do not elaborate upon here, is to write the *reduced-form* equations for the time-2 and time-3 latent attitude variables, that is, to write the equations in terms of the three exogenous variables, omitting the latent attitude variables that act as intervening variables (see Duncan, 1975a). This would show that later attitudes are dependent upon the exogenous variables; then by tracing through their effects, it would become clear that these exogenous factors depend upon the intervening early attitude variables to transmit their effects into later life. In this sense the influences of early experiences contribute to continuity in attitudes via their impact on fixing attitude orientations in early adulthood.

interpretation of these quantities. As indicated at the bottom of table 7.8, this model has an estimated χ^2 value of 20.97 on the theoretical χ^2 distribution with 18 degrees of freedom. On this theoretical distribution, such an estimated χ^2 value for our model has a p-value of .281. This is interpreted as meaning that if we were to reject the null hypothesis that our model fits the data, there would be a probability of .281 that we would be wrong. Obviously the higher such a p-value, the more confidence one would have that one's model fits the data. If one wanted to reject the null hypothesis—that there is no difference between the empirical data and the estimates produced by the model—one would want to have a small p-value.

In this example we seem to be in a relatively good position, that is, fitting the data with a nontrivial p-value. This suggests that the model fits the data relatively well, although a higher p-value would reflect a better overall fit to the data. Generally speaking, experience suggests that it is usually more difficult to fit the covariance structure of the data when there are more and diverse measures involved and when there are multiple groups involved. Thus, for example, as we add measures in tables 7.9 and 7.10, the fit to the data declines. In both cases the test statistics indicate that we could easily reject the null hypothesis—that the model fits the data—with a very low probability of being wrong. The p-value for the model estimates presented in table 7.9 is .012, and in table 7.10 it is .006. Thus, our model fits these data significantly less well. Nonetheless, we believe the consistency in our estimates of the basic stability parameters across these various models encourages us to put greater weight on the theoretical interpretation of these data rather than on the degree of statistical fit to the data. Throughout the text, we present these estimates of the goodness-of-fit of our models to the data, although we consider these as just one criterion for evaluating the plausibility of a particular model.[9]

COMPARING STRUCTURAL EQUATION MODELS ACROSS GROUPS

Our primary research strategy for investigating sources of attitude stability and change in chapters 8 and 9 involves (1) partitioning the Bennington sample on a given theoretical variable, and (2) estimating the models described above in both groups. This analysis is aimed at detecting differences in stability parameters across theoretically relevant categories. Our expectation in those chapters is that if a given theoretical factor is useful in explaining the degree of persistence and change in latent attitudes, then there will be predictable differences in levels of stability across categories defined by our sample partition. We consider two sets of theoretically relevant factors: those tied to *personological* factors, primarily attitude centrality and constancy of personality, and those tied to *sociological* explanations, mainly differences in environmental social support for attitudes.

In making these comparisons of stability estimates across groups, we rely on statistical techniques for comparing structural equation models across groups (see Alwin and Jackson, 1979, 1981). We are essentially interested in the comparison of

9. See Bentler (1990) for a recent review of the literature on comparative fit indices in structural equation models.

a model that forces the stability parameters to be equal across categories of theoretically relevant variables with a model that does not impose such a constraint. If
the model forcing stability estimates to be equal over groups fits the data just as
well as one which allows the groups to be different in estimated stabilities, then we
conclude that there are few nontrivial differences in stability across groups. If, on
the other hand, the model imposing equal stability coefficients across groups fits
the data much less well, then we conclude that the processes of attitude change
and stability are different across groups.

In order to evaluate the hypothesis of similar vs. different coefficients of stability
across theoretically relevant categories, it is necessary to impose the assumption
that the measurement structure is the same across groups. This amounts to an
assumption that the linkage between measures and the latent variables are equivalent across groups (see Alwin and Jackson, 1981). It is possible to test this assumption, but even if the data fail to meet it, this constraint must be imposed when
comparing structural parameters representing stability and change; otherwise, the
comparison of stabilities would involve comparing quantities in different metrics.
In any case, we provide information in all cases for evaluating whether the measurement models are equivalent across groups. In most cases this assumption can
be met within our data, but in a few instances it cannot be met. We provide the
information for evaluating the extent to which such an assumption seems to place
too much of a constraint on the data.

Table E.1 provides all of the necessary information for evaluating these hypotheses in the cases considered in chapters 8 and 9. We thought it would be advisable
to present all of this information in one place, rather than scatter it throughout
the text, and table E.1 accomplishes this purpose. Our discussions in the relevant
text refer to this table. Presented in this table are estimates of the χ^2 values for
the fit of the model within each category.[10] This information is given in the first
column of table E.1. The sum of these χ^2 values across the two groups represents
the aggregate fit of the model to the data for the two groups without any constraints
being imposed on the parameters across both groups. The degrees of freedom for
this aggregate χ^2 is the sum of the *df* for each group. In all cases a *p*-value is
given for models within groups. For example, in the case of evaluating the fit of
the model within the two groups defined by the Allport-Vernon (AV) measure of
political salience, the sum of the two χ^2 values is 21.68. In both groups the model
fits extremely well, with *p*-values of .820 in the high-salience group and .956 in
the low-salience group. In this case—the imposition of the constraint of identical
measurement models across groups—the fit of the model constrained over groups

---

10. Recall that in those chapters, we reestimate only the model depicted in figure 7.3, the
results of which were presented in table 7.8. We did not estimate our more elaborate models,
which involved a greater number of measures of sociopolitical orientations, separately within
each partition of the sample because we did not think our results would be substantially
affected by the choice of indicators. We could have estimated such models as well, but we
chose to simplify matters by focusing on just one basic model. Also note that because of our
sample size, we restrict our comparison to two groups in all cases except one, *exposure to the
1960s generation*, in which we use three groups.

Table E.1. Measures of Statistical Fit of Attitude Stability Models Estimated in
 Chapters 8 and 9

	Unconstrained			Constrained Λ			Constrained Λ, β		
	χ^2	df	p	χ^2	df	p	χ^2	df	p
AV political salience									
High salience ($n = 64$)	12.51	18	.820	23.35	39	.978	25.01	41	.977
Low salience ($n = 112$)	9.17	18	.956	Δ1.67	3	.644	Δ1.66	2	.436
	21.68	36							
AV value similarity									
Similar ($n = 83$)	11.69	18	.863	33.74	39	.708	34.12	41	.768
Different ($n = 89$)	20.52	18	.305	Δ1.53	3	.675	Δ0.38	2	.827
	32.21	36							
Political activity									
High ($n = 134$)	29.44	18	.043	77.38	39	.000	78.73	41	.000
Low ($n = 118$)	47.33	18		Δ0.61	3	.894	Δ1.35	2	.509
	76.77	36							
Political interest									
High ($n = 85$)	33.43	18	.015	50.00	39	.037	50.37	41	.150
Low ($n = 138$)	14.53	18	.694	Δ2.04	3	.564	Δ0.37	2	.831
	47.96	36							
Role transitions									
High ($n = 146$)	27.87	18	.064	53.42	39	.062	53.59	41	.090
Low ($n = 105$)	22.65	18	.204	Δ2.90	3	.407	Δ0.17	2	.918
	50.52	36							
Similarity to husband									
Similar ($n = 130$)	22.30	18	.219	70.74	39	.001	78.84	41	.000
Different ($n = 95$)	36.45	18	.006	Δ11.99	3	.007	Δ8.10	2	.017
	58.75	36							
Similarity to friends									
Similar ($n = 160$)	30.49	18	.033	96.84	39	.000	110.77	41	.000
Dissimilar ($n = 158$)	25.39	18	.114	Δ40.56	3	.000	Δ13.93	2	.001
	55.88	36							
Similarity to children									
Similar ($n = 106$)	44.78	18	.000	96.62	39	.000	100.34	41	.000
Dissimilar ($n = 129$)	25.73	18	.106	Δ26.11	3	.000	Δ3.72	2	.156
	70.51	36							
Exposure to 1960s generation									
0–2 ($n = 86$)	67.78	18	.000	155.18	60	.000	156.87	64	.000
3 ($n = 74$)	58.21	18	.000						
4+ ($n = 83$)	23.24	18	.181	Δ5.95	6	.429	Δ1.69	4	.793
	149.23	54							

(continued on following page)

Table E.1. Measures of Statistical Fit of Attitude Stability Models Estimated in
        Chapters 8 and 9 *(continued)*

	Unconstrained			Constrained Λ			Constrained Λ, β		
	χ^2	df	p	χ^2	df	p	χ^2	df	p
1984 Network similarity									
Similar ($n = 120$)	44.65	18	.000	129.00	39	.000	135.90	41	.000
Dissimilar ($n = 124$)	49.41	18	.000	Δ33.06	3	.000	Δ6.90	2	.032
	94.06	36							

has a χ^2 value of 23.35. This information is presented in the second column of table E.1. The difference between this estimated χ^2 value and the aggregate unconstrained χ^2 value referred to above, 21.68, is distributed as a χ^2 as well, with degrees of freedom equal to the difference between the degrees of freedom in both cases. This χ^2 value is 1.67 with 3 *df*, which is not a significant loss of fit. We thus conclude that it does not compromise the data to impose this equality constraint on the data.

As a next step in the examination of the equivalence of stability coefficients across the groups, we estimated a model in which the groups were forced to have stability coefficients of identical magnitude, in addition to the assumption of identical measurement models. The estimated χ^2 for the multiple-group model in this case is given in the third column of table E.1, along with appropriate degrees of freedom and *p*-values. In the example given for AV *political salience,* again the difference between the estimated χ^2's for the two constrained models reflects the lack of fit to the data resulting from the imposition of the additional constraint that the stability coefficients are equal across groups. This difference, $25.01 - 23.35 = 1.66$, is again not significant, indicating that there is an insignificant loss of fit introduced by assuming the processes of stability and change are the same across groups. As we conclude in the text, the results in this example suggest that there is no difference in the degree of attitude persistence across the life course for those for whom the political domain is salient versus those for whom it is less salient.

In cases where the processes of attitude stability and change seem to be significantly different, there is a difference χ^2 in the third column of table E.1 that is statistically significant. For example, in the case of *similarity to husband* the estimated χ^2 value of 8.10 with 2 degrees of freedom is significant at the .017 level. Thus, in this case we judge the extent of attitude change to be significantly different across the two groups as defined in terms of similarity to the political orientations of husbands. As noted in the discussion of these results in chapter 9, this provides evidence in support of the hypothesis that there is greater attitude change among women who inhabit less supportive social environments, with significantly less attitude change witnessed among those with highly compatible social environments. And, as further noted in chapter 9, this type of finding is replicated when we consider similarity to friends and network similarity more generally.

We should note that our model does not fit the data well in a number of groups defined by our theoretically based partitions of the sample. Similarly, in some of our multiple-group constrained models, the p-value is so small (e.g., $p = .000$) as to support the conclusion that the model should be rejected in terms of adequate fit to the data. We would simply emphasize the fact that, while the fit to the data may not be as good as we would like, we believe our basic model is a sound one for our data. In any case, a better fit to the data could be achieved by examining areas of the covariance structure where adequate fit is not attained, and then adding parameters to more adequately reproduce the data. Such an approach would be relatively straightforward and would undoubtedly produce a more adequate fit to the data at hand. However, such an ad hoc approach to the data would not be likely to produce any different estimates of the parameters of our model and would therefore not lead us to change any of our basic interpretations of the data. Thus, in the present monograph, we forego the further examination of the issue of the fit of our model to the data, and emphasize what we take to be the most plausible interpretation for the patterns we observe therein.

Appendix F

Analyzing Synthetic Cohort Data

In our analysis of stability and change in the NES party identification measure we employ a synthetic cohort modeling strategy. Those panel data spanned only four years, which is not enough time to examine long-term persistence and change. We therefore employ an analytic strategy that is very common in cohort analysis (see Glenn, 1977), which is to compare age groups in their characteristics within a cross-sectional survey. The NES panel data are cross-sectional in the sense that they provide a set of stability estimates for each of several age groups, and we can on this basis "synthesize" the aging of a single cohort by piecing together stability estimates for groups of different age. There are obvious risks in using this technique, and we approach its use cautiously.

As in cohort analysis of means or other sample quantities, the cohort analysis of estimated stabilities is subject to a number of important pitfalls. First, in order to assume that the stability differences between age groups reflect life-cycle differences, one must assume that there are no unique cohort effects on the estimated stabilities; that is, one assumes that the stability differences between age groups reflect aging rather than cohort differences. Of course, as we argue in chapters 8 and 9, cohorts may differ in the extent of the *opportunities* for attitude change, and this assumption may compromise empirical reality somewhat. We explore this issue in chapter 7 and return to it in chapter 10 as well.

However, in addition to comparing differences between age groups within a particular NES panel study, because there are two available three-wave, four-year panel studies—one conducted in 1956–58–60 and one conducted in 1972–74–76—it is possible to estimate the stabilities for the same set of cohorts across time. Thus, it is possible to control for cohort in the sense that we can compare *the same* cohort over time (therein controlling for cohort), making inferences about the role of aging in producing differences in levels of stability assessed over time. Of course, in this case the differences in stability due to aging are confounded with differences in stability due to historical time itself. Still, our model makes quite specific predictions about the trajectories of attitude change, and we doubt that historical differences could realistically account for the patterns of growth in stability which we hypothesize exist.

We employ a class of just-identified *simplex* models that specify two structural equations for a set of three over-time measures of a given variable, y_t :

$$y_t = \tau_t + \epsilon_t$$

$$\tau_t = \beta_{t,t-1}\tau_{t-1} + v_t$$

The first equation represents a set of measurement assumptions, indicating that the over-time measures are assumed to be *tau-equivalent*, except for true attitude change, and that measurement error is random (see Alwin, 1988c; Jöreskog, 1974). The second equation specifies the causal processes involved in attitude change over time. This model assumes that the system is in *dynamic equilibrium* and that this equilibrium can be described by a lag = 1, or Markovian, process in which the distribution of the true variable at time t is dependent only on the distribution at time $t - 1$ and not directly dependent upon distributions of the true variable at earlier times.

Estimates of these structural equation parameters help assess the stability and reliability of reports of attitudes in the NES panel data.[1] In order to estimate such models, some assumptions regarding the measurement error structure and the nature of true attitude changes must be made. All estimation strategies available for three-wave data require a lag = 1 assumption regarding the nature of true attitude change, but they differ in their approach to assumptions about measurement error. One approach assumes equal reliabilities over occasions of measurement (Heise, 1969). This is often a realistic assumption and may be useful especially when the attitude process being assessed is not in dynamic equilibrium. Another approach to estimating the parameters of this model is to assume constant error variances rather than constant reliabilities (Wiley and Wiley, 1970). This is often seen as a less restrictive assumption than that made by the Heise model, but it can produce erroneous estimates if the true distributions increase or decrease in variability over time (Alwin, 1988c). We analyzed our data in both ways using Jöreskog and Sörbom's (1986) LISREL VI computer program and found results that were virtually identical for standardized parameters (see Alwin and Krosnick, 1991a).

Unfortunately, the LISREL solution exceeds the theoretical limit of 1.0 for standardized parameters (i.e., there can be negative variances for the v_t in practice) in a few instances. Thus, for purposes of estimating these models, we employ Peter Bentler's EQS program (Bentler, 1989), which estimates such models under the constraint that the variance of v_t not be less than zero. For these purposes we employ Bentler's generalized least squares approach. The results are in fact very close to those obtained using maximum-likelihood estimation in LISREL.

---

1. This, of course, depends on the robustness of the assumptions underlying the simplex model. Perhaps the most risky assumption in this particular case is the Markovian assumption, which puts rather restrictive limitations on the nature of what can be considered "true change." In this context, only change that contributes to monotonic and linear change over the three time points is true change. This essentially correlational nature of change may not capture what we might otherwise like to think of as change when the system is not in dynamic equilibrium. Change that does not fit with this model is considered measurement error, at least to the extent that it is random with respect to the "true" distribution. We are grateful to Philip Converse for drawing this to our attention.

References

Abeles, Ronald P., ed. 1987. Life-Span Perspectives and Social Psychology. Hillsdale, N.J.: Lawrence Erlbaum Associates.

Abramson, Paul R. 1975. Generational Change in American Politics. Lexington, Mass.: D. C. Heath.

Abramson, Paul R. 1976. "Generational change and the decline of party identification in America, 1952–1974." American Political Science Review 70:469–78.

Abramson, Paul R. 1979. "Developing party identification: A further examination of life-cycle, generational, and period effects." American Journal of Political Science 23:78–96.

Abramson, Paul R. 1983. Political Attitudes in America. San Francisco: W. H. Freeman.

Abramson, Paul R., and Ronald Inglehart. 1986. "Generational replacement and value change in six West European societies." American Journal of Political Science 30:1–25.

Abramson, Paul R., and Ronald Inglehart. 1987. "Generational replacement and the future of post-materialist values." Journal of Politics 49:231–41.

Achen, Christopher H. 1975. "Mass political attitudes and the survey response." American Political Science Review 69:1218–31.

Acock, Alan C., and Vern L. Bengtson. 1980. "Socialization and attribution processes: Actual vs. perceived similarity among parents and youth." Journal of Marriage and the Family 40:519–30.

Allen, Frederick Lewis. 1939. Since Yesterday: The 1930s in America. New York: Harper and Row.

Allport, Gordon W., and Philip E. Vernon. 1931. A Study of Values: A Scale for Measuring the Dominant Interests in Personality. New York: Houghton Mifflin.

Alwin, Duane F. 1973. "Making inferences from attitude-behavior correlations." Sociometry 36:253–78.

Alwin, Duane F. 1976. "Attitude scales as congeneric tests: a re-examination of an attitude-behavior model." Sociometry 41:76–77.

Alwin, Duane F. 1988a. "From obedience to autonomy: Changes in traits desired in children, 1924 to 1978." Public Opinion Quarterly 52:33–52.

Alwin, Duane F. 1988b. "Measurement and scaling of coefficients in structural equation models." In J. S. Long, ed., Common Problems/Proper Solutions: Avoiding Error in Quantitative Social Research. Beverly Hills: Sage, 15–45.

395

Alwin, Duane F. 1988c. "Structural equation models in research on human development and aging." In T. Warner Schaie et al., eds., Methodological Advances in Aging Research. New York: Springer-Verlag, 71–170.

Alwin, Duane F. 1989. "Problems in the estimation and interpretation of the reliability of survey data." Quality and Quantity 23:277–331.

Alwin, Duane F. 1990a. "Historical changes in parental orientations to children." In Nancy Mandell, ed., Sociological Studies of Child Development. Greenwich, Conn.: JAI Press, 3:65–86.

Alwin, Duane F. 1990b. "Cohort replacement and changes in parental socialization values." Journal of Marriage and the Family 52:347–60.

Alwin, Duane F. 1992. "Aging, personality, and social change." In David L. Featherman, Richard M. Lerner, and Marion Perlmutter (Eds.), Life Span Development and Behavior. Hillsdale, N.J.: Lawrence Erlbaum Associates, Inc. Forthcoming.

Alwin, Duane F., and Robert M. Hauser. 1975. "The decomposition of effects in path analysis." American Sociological Review 40:37–47.

Alwin, Duane F., and David J. Jackson. 1979. "Measurement models for response errors in surveys." In Karl F. Schuessler ed., Sociological Methodology 1980. San Francisco: Jossey-Bass, 68–119.

Alwin, Duane F., and David J. Jackson. 1981. "Applications of simultaneous factor analysis to issues of factorial invariance." In David J. Jackson and Edgar F. Borgatta, eds., Factor Analysis and Measurement in Sociological Research. SAGE Studies in International Sociology. London: Sage, 249–79.

Alwin, Duane F., and Jon A. Krosnick. 1991a. "Aging, cohorts, and the stability of socio-political orientations over the life span." American Journal of Sociology 97: 169–95.

Alwin, Duane F., and Jon A. Krosnick. 1991b. "The reliability of survey attitude measurement: the influence of question and respondent attributes." Sociological Methods and Research. 20: 139–81.

Alwin, Duane F., and Arland Thornton. 1984. "Family origins and the schooling process: Early vs. late influence of parental characteristics." American Sociological Review 49:784–802.

Andrews, Frank, and Regula Herzog. 1986. "Respondent age and survey measurement error." Journal of American Statistical Association 81:403–10.

Ann Arbor News. 27 July 1986. "The Bennington girl: Fifty years later." F1–F2.

Baltes, Paul B., and Gunther Reinert. 1969. "Cohort effects in cognitive development of children as revealed by cross-sectional sequences." Developmental Psychology 1:169–77.

Baltes, Paul B., and K. Warner Schaie. 1973. "On life-span developmental research paradigms, retrospects and prospects." In Paul B. Baltes and K. Warner Schaie, eds., Life-span Developmental Psychology: Personality and Socialization. New York: Academic Press, 365–95.

Baltes, Paul B., Steven W. Cornelius, and John R. Nessleroade. 1979. "Cohort effects in developmental psychology." In Nessleroade and Baltes, eds. (1979: 61–87).

Bem, Daryl J. 1972. "Self-perception theory." In Leonard Berkowitz, ed., Advances in Experimental Social Psychology. New York: Academic Press, 6:2–62.

Bem, Daryl J., and H. Keith McConnell. 1970. "Testing the self-perception explanation of dissonance pheomena: On the salience of premanipulation attitudes." Journal of Personality and Social Psychology 14:23–31.

Bengtson, Vern L. 1975. "Generation and family effects in value socialization." American Sociological Review 40:358–71.

Bengtson, Vern L. 1989. "The problem of generations: Age group contrasts, continuities, and social change." In Vern L. Bengtson and K. Warner Schaie, eds., The Course of Later Life: Research and Reflections. New York: Springer, 25–54.

Bengtson, Vern L., Patricia L. Kasschau, and Pauline K. Ragan. 1977. "The impact of social structure on aging individuals." In J. E. Birren and K. Warner Schaie, eds., Handbook of the Psychology of Aging. New York: Van Nostrand Reinhold, 327–47.

Bengtson, Vern L., Carolyn Rosenthal, and Linda Burton. 1990. "Families and aging: Diversity and heterogeneity." In Linda George and Robert Binstock, eds., Handbook of Aging and the Social Sciences. 3d. ed. San Diego: Academic Press, 263–87.

Bentler, Peter M. 1989. EQS: Structural Equations Program Manual. Version 3.0. BMDP Statistical Software, Inc. 1440 Sepulveda Blvd. Suite 316. Los Angeles, CA 90025.

Bentler, Peter M. 1990. "Comparative fit indexes in structural models." Psychological Bulletin 107:238–46.

Block, Jack. 1971. Lives through Time. Berkeley: Bancroft Books.

Block, Jack. 1977. "Advancing the science of personality: Paradigmatic shift or improving the quality of research?" In D. Magnusson and N. S. Endler, eds., Psychology at the Crossroads: Current Issues in Interactional Psychology. Hillsdale, N.J.: Lawrence Erlbaum Associates.

Block, Jack. 1981. "Some enduring and consequential structures of personality." In A. I. Rabin, Joel Aronoff, Andrew M. Barclay, and Robert A. Zucker, eds., Further Explorations in Personality. New York: John Wiley and Sons, 27–43.

Bloom, Benjamin. 1964. Stability and Change in Human Characteristics. New York: John Wiley and Sons.

Brim, Orville G., Jr., and Jerome Kagan. 1980. Constancy and Change in Human Development. Cambridge: Harvard Univ. Press.

Brockway, Thomas P. 1981. Bennington College: In the Beginning. Bennington, Vt.: Bennington College Press.

Bronfenbrenner, Urie. 1979. The Ecology of Human Development: Experiments By Nature and Design. Cambridge: Harvard Univ. Press.

Buss, David M. 1984. "Toward a psychology of person-environment correspondence: The role of spouse selection." Journal of Personality and Social Psychology 47:361–77.

Buss, David M. 1987. "Selection, evocation, and manipulation." Journal of Personality and Social Psychology 53:1214–21.

Byrne, Donn. 1971. The Attraction Paradigm. New York: Academic Press.

Campbell, Angus, Philip E. Converse, Warren E. Miller, and Donald E. Stokes. 1960. The American Voter. New York: John Wiley and Sons.

Campbell, Donald T., and Julian Stanley. 1963. "Experimental and quasi-experimental designs for research teaching." In N. L. Gage, ed., Handbook of Research on Teaching. Chicago: Rand McNally.

Campbell, Ernest Q. 1969. "Adolescent socialization." In David A. Goslin, ed., Handbook of Socialization Theory and Research. Chicago: Rand McNally, 821–59.

Campbell, Richard T. 1988. "Integrating conceptualization, design, and analysis in panel studies of the life course." In K. Warner Schaie, Richard T. Campbell, William Meredith, and Samuel C. Rawlings, eds., Methodological Issues in Aging Research. New York: Springer, 43–69.

Campbell, Richard T., and Elizabeth Mutran. 1982. "Analyzing panel data in studies of aging." Research on Aging 4:3–41.

Capel, W. C. 1967. "Continuities and discontinuities in attitudes of the same person measured through time." Journal of Social Psychology 73:125–26.

Carlsson, Gosta, and Katarina Karlsson. 1970. "Age, cohorts, and the generation of generations." American Sociological Review 35:710–18.

Caspi, Avshalom, and Glen Elder, Jr. 1988. "Emergent family patterns: The inter-generational construction of problem behaviour and relationships." In Robert Hinde and Joan Stevenson-Hinde, eds., Relationships Within Families. Oxford: Oxford Univ. Press, 218–40.

Caspi, Avshalom, and Ellen S. Herbener. 1990. "Continuity and change: Assortative marriage and the consistency of personality in adulthood." Journal of Personality and Social Psychology 58:250–58.

Centers, Richard. 1950. "Children of the New Deal: Social stratification and adolescent attitudes." International Journal of Opinion and Attitude Research 4: 315–35.

Claggett, William. 1981. "Partisan acquisition versus partisan intensity: Life-cycle, generation, and period effects, 1952–1976." American Journal of Political Science 25:193–214.

Clos, M. 1966. "Evaluation of mental health workshops in Kentucky." Journal of Educational Research 59:278–81.

Cohen, Jere M. 1977. "Sources of peer group homogeneity." Sociology of Education 50:227–41.

Converse, Philip E. 1964. "The nature of belief systems in mass publics." In D. E. Apter, ed., Ideology and Discontent. New York: Free Press, 206–61.

Converse, Philip E. 1969. "Of time and partisan stability." Comparative Political Studies 2:139–71.

Converse, Philip E. 1970. "Attitudes and non-attitudes: Continuation of a dialog." In E. R. Tufte, ed., The Quantitative Analysis of Social Problems. Reading, Mass.: Addison-Wesley.

Converse, Philip E. 1975. "Public opinion and voting behavior." In Fred I. Greenstein and Nelson W. Polsby, eds., Handbook of Political Science. Reading, Mass.: Addison-Wesley, 4:75–169.

Converse, Philip E. 1976. The Dynamics of Party Support: Cohort Analyzing Party Identification. Beverly Hills: Sage.

Converse, Philip E. 1979. "Rejoinder to Abramson." American Journal of Political Science 23:97–100.

Converse, Philip E. 1980. "Comment: Rejoinder to Judd and Milburn." American Sociological Review 45:644–46.

Converse, Philip E., and Gregory B. Markus. 1979. "Plus ca change . . . : The new CPS election panel study." American Political Science Review 73:32–49.

Converse, Philip E., and Roy Pierce. 1987. "Measuring partisanship." Political Methodology 11:143–66.

Costa, Paul T., Jr., James L. Fozard, Robert R. McCrae, and Raymond B. Bosse. 1976. "Relations of age and personality dimensions to cognitive ability factors." Journal of Gerontology 31:663–69.

Costa, Paul T., Jr., and Robert R. McCrae. 1976. "Age differences in personality structure: A cluster analytic approach." Journal of Gerontology 31:564–70.

Costa, Paul T., Jr., and Robert R. McCrae. 1978. "Age differences in personality structure revisited: Studies in validity, stability, and change." International Journal of Aging and Human Development 8:261–75.

Costa, Paul T., Jr., and Robert R. McCrae. 1980. "Still stable after all these years: Personality as a key to some issues in adulthood and old age." In Paul B. Baltes and Orville G. Brim, Jr., eds., Life-Span Development and Behavior. New York: Academic Press, 3:65–102.

Costa, Paul T., Jr., Robert R. McCrae, and David Arenberg. 1980. "Enduring dispositions in adult males." Journal of Personality and Social Psychology 38: 793–800.

Costa, Paul T., Jr., Robert R. McCrae, and David Arenberg. 1983. "Recent longitudinal research on personality and aging." In K. Warner Schaie, ed., Longitudinal Studies of Adult Psychological Development. New York: Guilford Press.

Crittenden, James. 1962. "Aging and party affiliation." Public Opinion Quarterly 26:648–57.

Cunningham, Walter R., and William A. Owens, Jr. 1983. "The Iowa state study of the adult development of intellectual abilities." In K. Warner Schaie, ed., Longitudinal Studies of Adult Psychological Development. New York: The Guilford Press, 20–39.

Cutler, Neal E. 1970. "Generations, maturity, and party affiliation: A cohort analysis." Public Opinion Quarterly 33:583–88.

Cutler, Neal E. 1974. "Aging and generations in politics: The conflict of explanations and inference." In Allen R. Wilcox, ed., Public Opinion and Political Attitudes. New York: John Wiley and Sons, 440–62.

Cutler, Steven J., and Robert L. Kaufman. 1975. "Cohort changes in political attitudes: Tolerance for ideological nonconformity." Public Opinion Quarterly 39: 63–81.

Dalton, Russell J. 1980. "Reassessing parental socialization: Indicator unreliability versus generational transfer." American Political Science Review 74:421–31.

Darley, John M., and Russell H. Fazio. 1980. "Expectancy confirmation processes arising in the social interaction sequence." American Psychologist 35:867–81.

Davies, James C. 1965. "The family's role in political socialization." Annals of the American Academy of Political and Social Science 361:10–19.

Davis, James A. 1975. "Communism, conformity, cohorts, and categories: American tolerance in 1954 and 1972–73." American Journal of Sociology 81:491–13.

Delli Carpini, Michael X. 1989. "Age and history: Generations and sociopolitical change." In Sigel (1989:11–55).

Douglas, Karen, and David Arenberg. 1978. "Age changes, cohort differences, and cultural change on the Guilford-Zimmerman Temperment Survey." Journal of Gerontology 33:737–47.

Duncan, Otis Dudley. 1975a. Introduction to Structural Equation Models. New York: Academic Press.

Duncan, Otis Dudley. 1975b. "Measuring social change via replication of surveys." In K. C. Land and S. Spilerman, eds., Social Indicator Models. New York: Russell Sage Foundation, 105–27.

Eagly, Alice H. 1978. "Sex differences in influenceability." Psychological Bulletin 85:86–116.

Eagly, Alice H. 1983. "Gender and social influence: A social psychological analysis." American Psychologist 38:971–81.

Eagly, Alice H. 1987. Sex Difference in Social Behavior: A Social-role Interpretation. Hillsdale, NJ: Lawrence Erlbaum.

Eagly, Alice H., and Linda L. Carli. 1981. "Sex of researchers and sex-typed communications as determinants of sex differences in influenceability: A meta-analysis of social influence studies." Psychological Bulletin 90:1–20.

Easton, D., and J. Dennis 1969. Children in the Political System: Origins of Political Legitimacy. New York: McGraw-Hill.

Elder, Glen H., Jr. 1974. Children of the Great Depression. Chicago: Univ. of Chicago Press.

Elder, Glen H., Jr. 1975. "Age differentiation and the life course." Annual Review of Sociology 1:165–90.

Elder, Glen H., Jr. 1978a. "Family history and the life course." In Tamara Hareven, ed., Transitions: The Family and the Life Course in Historical Perspective. New York: Academic Press, 17–64.

Elder, Glen H., Jr. 1978b. "Approaches to social change and the family." In John Demos and Sarane Spence Boocock, eds., Turning Points: Historical and Sociological Essays on the Family. Chicago: Univ. of Chicago Press, 1–38.

Elder, Glen H., Jr. 1979. "Historical change in life patterns and personality." In Paul Baltes and Orville Brim, eds., Life-Span Development and Behavior. New York: Academic Press, 2:117–59.

Elder, Glen H., Jr. 1980. "Adolescence in historical perspective." In Joseph Adelson, ed., Handbook of Adolescent Psychology. New York: John Wiley and Sons, 3–46.

Elder, Glen H., Jr. 1981. "History and the life course." In Daniel Bertaux, ed., Biography and Society: The Life History Approach in the Social Sciences. Beverly Hills: Sage, 77–114.

Elder, Glen H., Jr., and Avshalom Caspi. 1988. "Human development and social change: an emerging perspective on the life course." In Niall Bolger, Avshalom

Caspi, Geraldine Downey, and Martha Moorehouse, eds., Persons in Context: Developmental Processes. New York: Cambridge Univ. Press, 77–113.

Elder, Glen H., Jr., Avshalom Caspi, and Linda M. Burton. 1988. "Adolescent transitions in developmental perspective: sociological and historical insights." In M. Gunnar, ed., Minnesota Symposium on Child Psychology. Hillsdale, N.J.: Lawrence Erlbaum Associates, 21:151–79.

Erikson, Erik H. 1950. Childhood and Society. New York: W. W. Norton.

Erikson, Erik H. 1959. "Identity and the life cycle: Selected papers." Psychological Issues 1:50–100.

Feather, N. T. 1979. "Value correlates of conservatism." Journal of Personality and Social Psychology 37:1617–30.

Featherman, David L., and Richard M. Lerner. 1985. "Ontogenesis and sociogenesis: Problematics for theory and research about development and socialization across the lifespan." American Sociological Review 50:659–76.

Feld, Scott L. 1981. "The focused organization of social ties." American Journal of Sociology 86:1015–35.

Feld, Scott L. 1982. "Social structural determinants of similarity among associates." American Sociological Review 47:797–801.

Feldman, Kenneth A., and Theodore M. Newcomb. 1969. The Impact of College on Students. San Francisco: Jossey-Bass.

Feldman, Kenneth A., and John Weiler. 1976. "Changes in initial differences among major-field groups: An exploration of the 'accentuation effect.'" In William H. Sewell, Robert M. Hauser, and David L. Featherman, eds., Schooling and Achievement in American Society. New York: Academic Press, 373–407.

Fendrich, James M., and Kenneth L. Lovoy. 1988. "Back to the future: Adult political behavior of former student activists." American Sociological Review 53:780–84.

Firebaugh, Glen, and Kenneth E. Davis. 1988. "Trends in antiblack prejudice, 1972–1984: Region and cohort effects." American Journal of Sociology 94:251–72.

Fischer, Claude S. 1982. To Dwell Among Friends: Personal Networks in Town and City. Chicago: Univ. of Chicago Press.

Franklin, Charles H. 1984. "Issue preferences, socialization, and the evolution of party identification." American Journal of Political Science 28:459–78.

Gergen, Kenneth J. 1973. "Social psychology as history." Journal of Personality and Social Psychology 26:309–20.

Gergen, Kenneth J. 1980. "The emerging crisis in life-span developmental theory." In Paul B. Baltes and Orville G. Brim, Jr., eds., Life-Span Development and Behavior. New York: Academic Press, 32–65.

Gilligan, Carol. 1982. In a Different Voice: Psychological Theory and Women's Development. Cambridge: Harvard Univ. Press.

Gitlin, Todd. 1987. The Sixties: Years of Hope, Days of Rage. New York: Bantam Books.

Glass, Jennifer, Vern L. Bengtson, and Charlotte Chorn Dunham. 1986. "Attitude similarity in three-generation families: Socialization, status inheritance, or reciprocal effects?" American Sociological Review 51:685–98.

Glenn, Norval D. 1969. "Aging, disengagement, and opinionation." Public Opinion Quarterly 33:17–33.

Glenn, Norval D. 1974. "Aging and conservatism." Annals of the American Academy of Political and Social Science 33:176–86.

Glenn, Norval D. 1977. Cohort Analysis. Beverly Hills: Sage.

Glenn, Norval D. 1980. "Values, attitudes and beliefs." In Orville G. Brim, Jr., and Jerome Kagan, eds., Constancy and Change in Human Development. Cambridge: Harvard Univ. Press, 596–639.

Glenn, Norval D. 1981a. "Age, birth cohorts, and drinking: An illustration of the hazards of inferring effects from cohort data." Journal of Gerontology 36:362–69.

Glenn, Norval D. 1981b. "The utility and logic of cohort analysis." Journal of Applied Behavioral Sciences 17:247–57.

Glenn, Norval D., and Michael Grimes. 1968. "Aging, voting, and political interest." American Sociological Review 33:563–75.

Glenn, Norval D., and Ted Hefner. 1972. "Further evidence on aging and party identification." Public Opinion Quarterly 36:31–47.

Glenn, Norval D., and Richard E. Zody. 1970. "Cohort analysis with national survey data." Gerontologist 10:233–40.

Goethals, George R., and Richard F. Reckman. 1973. "The perception of consistency in attitudes." Journal of Experimental Social Psychology 9:491–501.

Greenstein, Fred I. 1965. Children and Politics. New Haven: Yale Univ. Press.

Greenwald, Anthony. 1980. "The totalitarian ego: Fabrication and revision of personal history." American Psychologist 35:603–18.

Guest, Lester. 1964. "A longitudinal study of attitude development and some correlates." Child Development 35:779–84.

Hauser, Robert M., and Arthur S. Goldberger. 1971. "The treatment of unobserved variables in path analysis." In Herbert L. Costner, ed., Sociological Methodology 1971. San Francisco: Jossey-Bass, 81–117.

Heise, David R. 1969. "Separating reliability and stability in test-retest correlation." American Sociological Review 34:93–101.

Heise, David R. 1972. "Employing nominal variables, induced variables, and block variables in path analysis." Sociological Methods and Research 1:147–74.

Hess, Robert D., and Judith V. Torney. 1967. The Development of Political Attitudes in Children. Chicago: Aldine.

Himmelweit, Hilde T., Marianne Jaeger-Biberian, and Janet Stockdale. 1978. "Memory for past vote: Implications of a study of bias in recall." British Journal of Political Science 26:312–32.

Hoge, Dean R., and Irving E. Bender. 1974. "Factors influencing value change among college graduates in adult life." Journal of Personality and Social Psychology 29:572–85.

Homans, George C. 1974. Social Behavior: Its Elementary Forms. New York: Harcourt Brace Jovanovich.

Horowitz, Helen L. 1984. Alma Mater: Design and Experience in the Women's Colleges from their Nineteenth-Century Beginnings to the 1930s. New York: Knopf.

House, James S. 1981. "Social structure and personality." In Morris Rosenberg and

Ralph H. Turner, eds., Social Psychology: Sociological Perspectives. New York: Basic Books, 525–61.

House, James S., Karl R. Landis, and Deborah Umberson. 1988. "Social relationships and health." Science 241:540–45.

House, James S., Deborah Umberson, and Karl R. Landis. 1988. "Structures and processes of social support." Annual Review of Sociology 14:293–318.

Huston-Stein, Aletha, and Paul B. Baltes. 1976. "Theory and method in life-span developmental psychology: Implications for child development." In Hayne W. Reese, ed., Advances in Child Development and Behavior. New York: Academic Press, 11:169–88.

Hyman, Herbert H. 1942. "The psychology of status." Archives of Psychology no. 269.

Hyman, Herbert H. 1959. Political Socialization. Glencoe, Ill.: The Free Press.

Hyman, Herbert H. 1960. "Reflections on reference groups." Public Opinion Quarterly 24:383–96.

Inglehart, Ronald. 1971. "The silent revolution in Europe: Intergenerational change in post-industrial societies." American Political Science Review 65:991–1017.

Inglehart, Ronald. 1977. The Silent Revolution: Changing Values and Political Styles Among Western Publics. Princeton, N.J.: Princeton Univ. Press.

Inglehart, Ronald. 1986. "Intergenerational changes in politics and culture: The shift from materialist to postmaterialist value priorities." Research in Political Sociology 2:81–105.

Inkeles, Alex. 1955. "Social change and social character: The role of parental mediation." Journal of Social Issues 11:12–23.

Jennings, M. Kent. 1979. "Another look at the life cycle and political participation." American Journal of Political Science 23:755–71.

Jennings, M. Kent, and Gregory B. Markus. 1984. "Partisan orientations over the long haul: Results from the three-wave political socialization panel study." American Political Science Review 78:1000–1018.

Jennings, M. Kent, and Richard G. Niemi. 1968. "The transmission of political values from parent to child." American Political Science Review 62:169–84.

Jennings, M. Kent, and Richard G. Niemi. 1974. The Political Character of Adolescence. Princeton, N.J.: Princeton Univ. Press.

Jennings, M. Kent, and Richard G. Niemi. 1978. "The persistence of over-time analysis of two generations." British Journal of Political Science 8:333–63.

Jennings, M. Kent, and Richard G. Niemi. 1981. Generations and Politics. Princeton, N.J.: Princeton Univ. Press.

Jones, Barbara. 1946. Bennington College: The Development of an Educational Idea. Bennington, Vt.: Bennington College Press.

Jöreskog, Karl G. 1970. "Estimation and testing of simplex models." British Journal of Mathematical and Statistical Psychology 23:121–45.

Jöreskog, Karl G. 1973. "A general method for estimating a linear structural equation system." In Arther S. Goldberger and Otis Dudley Duncan, eds., Structural Equation Models in the Social Sciences. New York: Seminar Press, 85–112.

Jöreskog, Karl G. 1974. "Analyzing psychological data by structural analysis of covariance matrices." In D. H. Kranz, R. C. Atkinson, R. D. Luce, and P. Suppes, eds., Measurement, Psychophysics, and Neural Information Processing. San Francisco: W. H. Freeman.

Jöreskog, Karl G. 1979. "Statistical estimation of structural models in longitudinal-developmental investigations." In Nesselroade and Baltes (1979:303–74).

Jöreskog, Karl G., and Dag Sörbom. 1981. "The use of LISREL in sociological model building." In David J. Jackson and Edgar F. Borgatta, eds., Factor Analysis and Measurement in Sociological Research. London and Beverly Hills: Sage.

Jöreskog, Karl G., and Dag Sörbom. 1982. "Recent developments in structural equation modeling." Journal of Marketing Research 19:404–16.

Jöreskog, Karl G., and Dag Sörbom. 1986. LISREL VI—Analysis of Linear Structural Relationships by the Method of Maximum-Likelihood. User's Guide, Version VI. Chicago: National Educational Resources.

Judd, Charles M., and Jon A. Krosnick. 1982. "Attitude centrality, organization, and measurement." Journal of Personality and Social Psychology 42:436–47.

Judd, Charles M., Jon A. Krosnick, and Michael A. Milburn. 1981. "Political involvement and attitude structure in the general public." American Sociological Review 46:660–69.

Judd, Charles M., and Michael A. Milburn. 1980. "The structure of attitude systems in the general public: comparisons of a structural equation model." American Sociological Review 45:627–43.

Kelly, E. Lowell. 1955. "Consistency of the adult personality." American Psychologist 10:659–81.

Kelley, Harold H. 1952. "The two functions of reference groups." In Guy E. Swanson, Theodore Newcomb, and Eleanor L. Hartley, eds., Readings in Social Psychology. 2d ed. New York: Holt, Rinehart and Winston.

Kemper, Theodore D. 1968. "Reference groups, socialization, and achievement." American Sociological Review 33:31–45.

Kessler, Ronald C., and David F. Greenberg 1981. Linear Panel Analysis: Models of Quantitative Change. New York: Academic Press.

Kiesler, Charles A., Barry E. Collins, and N. Miller. 1969. Attitude Change: A Critical Analysis of Theoretical Approaches. New York: John Wiley and Sons.

Kinder, Donald R., and David O. Sears. 1985. "Public opinion and political action." In Gardner Lindzey and Elliot Aronson, eds., The Handbook of Social Psychology. 3d ed. New York: Random House, 2:659–741.

Knoke, David. 1976. Change and Continuity in American Politics: The Social Bases of Political Parties. Baltimore: Johns Hopkins Univ. Press.

Knoke, David, and Michael Hout. 1974. "Social and demographic factors in American political party affiliations, 1952–72." American Sociological Review 39:700–713.

Kohlberg, Lawrence. 1966. "Stage and sequence: The cognitive-development approach to socialization." In David A. Goslin, ed., Handbook of Socialization Theory and Research. Chicago: Rand McNally.

Krippendorff, Klaus. 1970. "Bivariate agreement coefficients for reliability of data." In Sociological Methodology 1970. San Francisco: Jossey-Bass.

Krosnick, Jon A. 1988. "Attitude importance and attitude change." Journal of Experimental Social Psychology 24:240–55.

Krosnick, Jon A., and Duane F. Alwin. 1989. "Aging and the susceptibility to attitude change." Journal of Personality and Social Psychology 57:416–25.

Lang, Kurt, and Gladys Engel Lang. 1978. "Experiences and ideology: The influence of the sixties on an intellectual elite." Research in Social Movements, Conflicts, and Change, 1:197–230.

Lazarsfeld, Paul F., and Robert K. Merton. 1954. "Friendship as a social process: A substantive and methodological analysis." In Morroe Berger, Theodore Abel, and Charles H. Page, eds., Freedom and Control in Modern Society. New York: Octagon Books, 18–66.

Lerner, Richard L. 1984. On the Nature of Human Plasticity. New York: Cambridge Univ. Press.

Lipset, Seymour M., Paul F. Lazarsfeld, Allan H. Barton, and Juan Linz. 1954. "The psychology of voting: an analysis of political behavior." In Gardner Lindzey, ed., Handbook of Social Psychology. Cambridge: Cambridge Univ. Press, 2: 1124–75.

Looft, William R. 1973. "Socialization and personality throughout the life span: an examination of contemporary psychological approaches." In Paul B. Baltes and K. Warner Schaie, eds., Life-Span Developmental Psychology: Personality and Socialization. New York: Academic Press, 25–69.

Lord, Frederick M., and Melvin R. Novick. 1968. Statistical Theories of Mental Test Scores. Reading, Mass.: Addison-Wesley.

Lorence, Jon, and Jeylan T. Mortimer. 1985. "Job involvement through the life course: A panel study of three age groups." American Sociological Review 50: 618–38.

Lowenthal, Marjorie F. 1964. "Social isolation and mental illness in old age." American Sociological Review 29:54–70.

Lowenthal, Marjorie F., and Clayton Haven. 1968. "Interaction and adaptation: Intimacy as a critical variable." American Sociological Review 33:20–30.

Lykken, David T. 1968. "Statistical significance in psychological research." Psychological Bulletin 70:151–59.

Maccoby, Eleanor E., and Carol N. Jacklin. 1974. The Psychology of Sex Differences. Stanford: Stanford Univ. Press.

McGuire, William J. 1985. "Attitudes and attitude change." In G. Lindzey and E. Aronson, eds., The Handbook of Social Psychology. 3d ed. New York: Random House, 2:233–346.

Mannheim, Karl. 1952. "The problem of generations." In Paul Kecskemeti, ed., Essays on the Sociology of Knowledge. London: Routledge and Kegan Paul, 276–320.

Markus, Gregory B. 1982a. "The political environment and the dynamics of public attitudes: A panel study." American Journal of Political Science 23:338–59.

Markus, Gregory B. 1982b. "Political attitudes during an election year: A report of the 1980 NES panel study." American Political Science Review 76:538–560.

Markus, Gregory B. 1986. "Stability and change in political attitudes: Observed, recalled, and 'explained.'" Political Behavior 8:21–44.

Marsden, Peter V. 1987. "Core discussion networks of Americans." American Sociological Review 52:122–31.

405

Marwell, Gerald, Michael T. Aiken, and N. J. Demerath III. 1987. "The persistence of political attitudes among 1960s civil rights activists." Public Opinion Quarterly 51:359–75.

Mason, Karen O., Halliman H. Winsborough, William M. Mason, and William K. Poole. 1973. "Some methodological issues in cohort analysis of archival data." American Sociological Review 38:242–58.

Merelman, Richard M. 1968. "Intimate environments and political behavior." Midwest Journal of Political Science 12:382–400.

Miller, Warren E., and the National Election Studies. 1985. American National Election Study, 1984: Continuous Monitoring Survey File. Ann Arbor: Inter-University Consortium for Social and Political Research.

Miller, Warren E., and Santa Traugott. 1989. American National Election Studies Data Sourcebook, 1952–1986. Cambridge: Harvard Univ. Press.

Mills, C. Wright. 1959. The Sociological Imagination. New York: Oxford Univ. Press.

Mischel, Walter. 1969. "Continuity and change in personality." American Psychologist 24:1012–18.

Morgan, David L. 1988. "Age differences in social network participation." Journal of Gerontology 43:129–37.

Mortimer, Jeylan T., Michael D. Finch, and Donald Kumka. 1982. "Persistence and change in development: The multidimensional self-concept." In Paul B. Baltes and Orville G. Brim, Jr., eds., Life-Span Development and Behavior. New York: Academic Press, 4:263–313.

Mortimer, Jeylan T., Michael D. Finch, and Donald Kumka. 1986. Work, Family, and Personality: Transition to Adulthood. Norwood, N.J.: Ablex.

Mortimer, Jeylan T., Michael D. Finch, and Geoffrey Maruyama. 1988. "Work experience and job satisfaction: Variation by age and gender." In Jeylan T. Mortimer and Kathryn M. Borman, eds., Work Experience and Psychological Development through the Life Span. Boulder, Colo.: Westview Press.

Moss, Howard A., and Elizabeth J. Susman. 1980. "Longitudinal study of personality development." In Orville G. Brim, Jr. and Jerome Kagan, eds., Constancy and Change in Human Development. Cambridge: Harvard Univ. Press.

Moss, Louis, and Harvey Goldstein, eds. 1979. The Recall Method in Social Surveys. London: Univ. of London Institute of Education.

National Opinion Research Center. 1989. General Social Surveys, 1972–1989: Cumulative Codebook. Chicago, Ill.: National Opinion Research Center.

Nesselroade, John R. 1970. "Application of multivariate strategies to problems of measuring and structuring long-term change." In L. R. Goulet and Paul B. Baltes, eds., Life-Span Developmental Psychology. New York: Academic Press, 194–210.

Nesselroade, John R. 1977. "Issues in studying developmental change in adults from a multivariate perspective." In James E. Birren and K. Warner Schaie, eds., Handbook of the Psychology of Aging. New York: Van Nostrand Reinhold, 59–69.

Nesselroade, John R. 1988. "Sampling and generalizability: Adult development and aging research issues examined within the general methodological framework of selection." In T. Warner Schaie et al., eds., Methodological Advances in Aging Research. New York: Springer-Verlag, 13–42.

Nesselroade, John R., and Paul B. Baltes. 1974. "Adolescent personality development and historical change, 1970–1972." Monographs of the Society for Research in Child Development 39 (1, Serial No. 154).

Nesselroade, John R., and Paul B. Baltes, eds. 1979. Longitudinal Research in the Study of Behavior and Development. New York: Academic Press.

Neugarten, Bernice L. 1964. Personality in Middle and Late Life: Empirical Studies. New York: Atherton Press.

Neugarten, Bernice L. 1973. "Personality change in late life: A developmental perspective." In Carl Eisdorfer and M. Powell Lawton, eds., The Psychology of Adult Development and Aging. Washington D.C.: American Psychological Association, 311–35.

Neugarten, Bernice L. 1977. "Personality and aging." In James E. Birren and K. Warner Schaie, eds., Handbook of the Psychology of Aging. New York: Van Nostrand Reinhold, 626–49.

Neugarten, Bernice L., and Nancy Datan. 1973. "Sociological perspectives on the life cycle." In Paul B. Baltes and K. Warner Schaie, eds., Life-Span Developmental Psychology: Personality and Socialization. New York: Academic Press, 53–69.

Neugarten, Bernice L., and Gunhild O. Hagestad. 1976. "Age and the life course." In Robert H. Binstock and Ethel Shanas, eds., Aging and the Social Sciences. New York: Van Nostrand Reinhold, 35–55.

Neugarten, Bernice L., and Warren A. Peterson. 1957. "A study of the American age-grade system." Proceedings of the Fourth Congress of the International Association of Gerontology, 3:497–502.

Newcomb, Theodore M. 1943. Personality and Social Change: Attitude Formation in a Student Community. New York: Dryden Press.

Newcomb, Theodore M. 1946. "The influence of attitude climate upon some determinants of information." Journal of Abnormal and Social Psychology 41:291–302.

Newcomb, Theodore M. 1947. "Some patterned consequences of membership in a college community." In Theodore M. Newcomb, Eleanor L. Hartley, et al., eds., Readings in Social Psychology. New York: Henry Holt, 345–57.

Newcomb, Theodore M. 1952. "Attitude development as a function of reference groups: the Bennington Study." In Guy E. Swanson, Theodore M. Newcomb, and Eleanor L. Hartley, eds., Readings in Social Psychology. Rev. ed. New York: Henry Holt, 420–30.

Newcomb, Theodore M., Kathryn E. Koenig, Richard Flacks, and Donald P. Warwick. 1967. Persistence and Change: Bennington College and Its Students after 25 Years. New York: John Wiley and Sons.

Niemi, Richard G., Richard S. Katz, and David Newman. 1980. "Reconstructing past partisanship: The failure of the party identification recall questions." American Journal of Political Science 24:633–51.

Nisbett, Richard E., and Timothy D. Wilson. 1977. "Telling more than we can know: Verbal reports on mental processes." Psychological Review 84:231–59.

Noelle-Neumann, Elisabeth. 1984. The Spiral of Silence. Chicago: Univ. of Chicago Press.

Nunnally, J. C. 1978. Psychometric Theory. 2d ed. New York: McGraw-Hill.

Oppenheim, Karen. 1970. Voting in Recent American Presidential Elections. Ph.D. diss., University of Chicago.

Oskamp, Stuart. 1977. Attitudes and Opinions. Englewood Cliffs, N.J.: Prentice-Hall.

Piaget, Jean. 1932. The Moral Judgment of the Child. New York: Free Press.

Presser, Stanley. 1982. "Studying social change with survey data: Examples from Louis Harris Surveys." Social Indicators Research 10:407–22.

Richardson, Helen M. 1940. "Community of values as a factor in friendships of college and adult women." Journal of Social Psychology 11:303–12.

Riley, Matilda W. 1973. "Aging and cohort succession: Interpretations and misinterpretations." Public Opinion Quarterly 37:35–49.

Roberts, Carl W., and Kurt Lang. 1985. "Generations and ideological change: Some observations." Public Opinion Quarterly 49:460–73.

Rodgers, Willard L. 1982. "Estimable functions of age, period, and cohort effects." American Sociological Review 47:774–87, 793–96.

Rokeach, Milton. 1960. The Open and Closed Mind: Investigations into the Nature of Belief Systems and Personality Systems. New York: Basic Books.

Rokeach, Milton. 1968. Beliefs, Attitudes, and Values: A Theory of Organization and Change. San Francisco: Jossey-Bass.

Rokeach, Milton. 1973. The Nature of Human Values. New York: Free Press.

Ross, Michael, Cathy McFarland, Michael Conway, and Mark P. Zanna. 1983. "Reciprocal relation between attitudes and behavior recall: Committing people to newly formed attitudes." Journal of Personality and Social Psychology 45: 257–67.

Ross, Michael, Cathy McFarland, and Garth J. O. Fletcher. 1981. "The effect of attitude on the recall of personal histories." Journal of Personality and Social Psychology 40:627–34.

Ryder, Norman B. 1965. "The cohort as a concept in the study of social change." American Sociological Review 30:843–61.

Schaie, K. Warner. 1983. "The Seattle Longitudinal Study: A 21-year exploration of psychometric intelligence in adulthood." In K. Warner Schaie, ed., Longitudinal Studies of Adult Psychological Development. New York: The Guilford Press.

Schuman, Howard, and Stanley Presser. 1981. Questions and Answers in Attitude Surveys. Orlando, Fla.: Academic Press.

Schuman, Howard, and Jacqueline Scott. 1989. "Generations and collective memories." American Sociological Review 54:359–81.

Searing, Donald D., Joel J. Schwartz, and Alden E. Lind. 1973. "The structuring principle: Political socialization and belief systems." American Political Science Review 67:415–32.

Searing, Donald D., Gerald Wright, and George Rabinowitz. 1976. "The primacy principle: Attitude change and political socialization." British Journal of Political Science 6:83–113.

Sears, David O. 1975. "Political socialization." In Fred I. Greenstein and Nelson W.

Polsby, eds., Handbook of Political Science. Reading, Mass.: Addison-Wesley, 2:96–136.

Sears, David O. 1981. "Life-stage effects on attitude change, especially among the elderly." In Sara B. Kiesler, James N. Morgan, and Valarie K. Oppenheimer, eds., Aging: Social Change. New York: Academic Press.

Sears, David O. 1983. "On the persistence of early political predispositions: The roles of attitude object and life stage." In Ladd Wheeler, ed., Review of Personality and Social Psychology. Beverly Hills: Sage, 4:79–116.

Sears, David O. 1987. "Implications of the life-span approach for research on attitudes and social cognition." In Abeles (1987:17–60).

Sears, David O., and J. P. Weber. 1988. "Presidential campaigns as agents of pre-adult political socialization." Paper presented at the 11th annual meetings of the International Society of Political Psychology, Meadowlands, N.J., 3 July.

Secord, Paul F., and Carl W. Backman. 1965. "An interpersonal approach to personality." In Brendon Maher, ed., Progress in Experimental Personality Research. New York: Academic Press, 91–125.

Sherif, Muzafer. 1948. An Outline of Social Psychology. New York: Harper and Brothers.

Siegler, Ilene C., Linda K. George, and Morris A. Okun. 1979. "Cross-sequential analysis of adult personality." Developmental Psychology 15:350–51.

Sigel, Roberta S., ed. 1989. Political Learning in Adulthood: A Sourcebook of Theory and Research. Chicago: Univ. of Chicago Press.

Smith, Herbert L., William M. Mason, and Stephen E. Fienberg. 1982. "More chimeras of the age-period-cohort accounting framework: Comment on Rodgers." American Sociological Review 47:787–93.

Smith, Thomas E. 1983. "Parental influence: A review of the evidence of influence and theoretical models of the parental influence process." In Alan Kerckhoff, ed., Research in Sociology of Educational Socialization. Greenwich, Conn.: JAI Press, 13–45.

Smith, Tom W. 1984. "Recalling attitudes: An analysis of retrospective questions on the 1982 GSS." Public Opinion Quarterly 48:639–49.

Smith, Tom W., and D. L. Klaeser. 1983. "Looking backwards: A summary of findings and recommendations." Historical Methods 16:16–29.

Sniderman, Paul M., and Philip E. Tetlock. 1986. "Interrelationship of Political Ideology and Public Opinion." In Margaret Hermann, ed., Political Psychology: Contemporary Problems and Issues. San Francisco: Jossey-Bass, 62–96.

Snyder, Mark. 1984. "When belief creates reality." In Leonard Berkowitz, ed., Advances in Experimental Social Psychology. Orlando, Fla.: Academic Press, 18: 247–305.

Stagner, Ross. 1936. "Facist attitudes: An exploratory study." Journal of Social Psychology 7:309–10.

Steckenrider, Janie S., and Neal E. Cutler. 1989. "Aging and adult political socialization: The importance of roles and transitions." In Sigel, ed. (1989:56–88).

Stouffer, Samuel A. 1955. Communism, Conformity, and Civil Liberties: A Cross-section of the Nation Speaks Its Mind. Garden City, N.Y.: Doubleday.

409

REFERENCES

Swann, W. B., Jr. 1983. "Self-verification: Bringing social reality into harmony with the self." In J. Suls and Anthony G. Greenwald, eds., Psychological Perspectives on the Self. Vol. 2. Hillsdale, N.J.: Lawrence Erlbaum Associates.

Tedin, Kent L. 1980. "Assessing peer and parental influence on adolescent political attitudes." American Journal of Political Science 24:136–154.

Thomas, Alexander, and Stella Chess. 1977. Temperament and Development. New York: Bruner-Mazel.

Thomas, William I., and Florian Znaniecki. 1918. The Polish Peasant in Europe and America. Chicago: Univ. of Chicago Press.

Thornton, Arland, Duane F. Alwin, and Don Camburn. 1983. "Causes and consequences of sex-role attitudes and attitude change." American Sociological Review 49:784–802.

Verbrugge, Lois M. 1977. "The structure of adult friendship choices." Social Forces 56:576–97.

Watson, John B. 1925. Behaviorism. New York: W. W. Norton.

Wheaton, R. Blair, Bengt Muthen, Duane F. Alwin, and Gene F. Summers. 1977. "Assessing reliability and stability in panel models." In David R. Heise, ed., Sociological Methodology 1977. San Francisco: Jossey-Bass, 85–136.

Wiley, David E., and James A. Wiley. 1970. "The estimation of measurement error in panel data." American Sociological Review 35: 112–17.

Wilson, Glenn D. 1973. The Psychology of Conservatism. New York: Academic Press.

Woodruff, Diana S., and James E. Birren. 1972. "Age changes and cohort differences in personality." Developmental Psychology 6:252–59.

Yarrow, Marian R., John D. Campbell, and Roger V. Burton. 1970. "Recollections of childhood: A study of the retrospective method." Monographs of the Society for Research in Child Development 35, no. 138.

Name Index

Subject Index

*Political and Economic Progressivism Scale
(PEP):* (Appendix A)
and Allport-Vernon Scale of Values,
183–201
results reported in *Personality and Social
Change*
aggregate change, 36–39
Bennington students vs. students at
other colleges, 44–45
divergence from parents, 39–43
individual change, 46
relationship to personality, 51–52
relationship to social status, 50–51, 52
relationship to values and interests,
46–47
results reported in *Persistence and
Change*, 57, 137–38
use in assessing stability, 137–38
and role transitions, 206–15
scores of participants in first, second, and
third studies, 71, 73
and similarity to significant others, 225–
28
use in present study, 74, 78–79, 82, 83,
139–47, 149–62 *passim*
Political ideology, 20, 22, 77–78, 170, 171,
179, 254, 255, 265, 276. *See also*
Political liberalism/conservatism
Political issues
comparison of stances of Bennington
women and 1984 NES respondents,
105–08, Appendix D
Political liberalism/conservatism
and aging, 90–94 *passim*
and Allport-Vernon Scale of Values,
183–201
change in Bennington students in 1930's,
36–39
change from 1930's to 1960's, 55–58,
60–61
change from 1960 to 1984, political party
identification, 94–96
change from 1930's to 1984, presidential
candidate preference, 99–100
of children and attitude stability, 235–41
comparison of Bennington women to
1984 NES respondents, 102–08
comparison of Bennington women to
NES Respondents, 1952–1984,
108–11

families of Bennington students in 1930's,
33, 34, 36
parent-child divergence in 1930's, 39–43
as political ideology 77–78, 179–80
retrospections, 122–26
and role transitions, 210–14
scale of, 80, 82, 83
and similarity to significant others, 225–
28
and stability of personality, 196–200
stability, use in estimating, 144, 149,
150, 151, 154, 155, 161, 162, 163,
164, 165
Political party identification, 12–13, 19, 20,
21, 22, 55, 80–81
and aging, 90–94
in Bennington women in 1984, 94–96
Bennington women and friends, 223–25
of Bennington women's parents, 140, 148
comparison of Bennington women and
1952–1984 NES respondents, 108–
11
comparison of Bennington women and
1984 NES respondents, 102–3
distinction between direction and intensity, 90–94, fn115, 167–69, 268
intensity in NES birth cohorts 1895–
1964, 115–18
similarity to friends and attitude stability,
232–35
and similarity to significant others, 225–
28
stability of in NES panels, 167–69,
268–71
Political socialization, 6, 10–12, 14, 18,
22, 24, 61, 88, 260–61. *See also*
Sociopolitical orientations
Present study. *See also* Methodology
comparative measurement over time
(literal replications, conceptual
replications), 76–77, 77n6
controlling for factors (year entered
Bennington, number of years attended Bennington, parents' party
affiliation), 71, 73, 139–40, 149
data available over time, 75–76
measures of sociopolitical orientation
available, 78–83
questionnaire, 74
research design, 67–69

Present study (*continued*)
response rates, 70
sample, 69–70
sampling biases, 70–74
Presidential candidate preferences
and Allport-Vernon Scale of Values,
183–201
Bennington women and friends, 223–25
Bennington women and spouses, 220–23
comparison of Bennington women and
1984 NES respondents, 102–3
in midlife, 56
in midlife related to PEP, 57
in *Personality and Social Change*, 39–41
parent-child divergence, 39–41
reported in 1984, 99–100
and role transitions, 206–15
similarity to significant others, 225–28
similarity to spouses and attitude stability,
228–32
stability of, 165–66
use in present study, 82, 83
use in assessment of stability, 140,
141, 142, 143, 145, 147, 149, 150,
152, 153, 154, 155, 156, 157, 159,
161, 162

Reagan, R., 96, 103
Recall. *See* Retrospections
Reference groups, 26, 30–34, 203–52
passim. See also Roles
and explanation of Bennington effect, 101
as informational environment, 48–50,
52, 125
and perceived attitudes of others, 125–26,
126n5
and retrospections, 131–32
and stability, 203–52 *passim*
Research design
present study, 27–28
Rennington research, 37n8
Retrospections, 81, 120–134 *passim*, 160–
65
accounts of attitude change, 122–26
accounts of attitudes, 122–26
interest in political affairs, 81, 96–98
of Political and Economic Progressivism
Scale, 81, 128–31
on political liberalism/conservatism, 81,

122–24, 128–31
political viewpoint of Bennington contemporaries, 81
presidential candidate preferences, 81,
99–100, 131–32, 165–66
stability of, 160–65
validity of, 22n15, 100, 120n1, 121,
126–32 *passim*, 160–65, 160n17, 166
Reuther, W., 56, 57
Roles. *See also* Reference groups; Social
networks; Social support
role transitions, 204–11
life-cycle, 205–6
and political liberalism/conservatism,
210–11
and stability of attitudes, 206–10
Roosevelt, F. D., 26, 35, 39n10, 44, 56, 57,
78, 92, 254

Social change, 5, 16, 17, 89
and historical considerations, 266–71
and sociopolitical orientations, 25, 26
Social environment. *See also* Reference
groups
dynamic stability, 252
early environmental influences, 140–49
ecological transitions, 204–15
informational environment, 50–51, 125
stability/change in attitudes, 176, 215–20,
228, 252, 255, 277
Social networks. *See also* Roles; Social
support
similarity of ties, 218
similarity of ties and stability, 220–28,
246–48
to friends, 223–25
to significant others, 225–28
to spouses, 220–23
and social environment, 277–78
and social selection, 216–17
supportiveness of, 215–20
similarity over life course, 217–20
Social selection, 216–17
Social support, 216n5 *See also* Roles; Social
networks
relationship to attitude change from
college to mid-life, 58–60
and stability, 203–52 *passim*
similarity to children, 235–45

420

Symbolic predispositions. *See* Political
    ideology
Synthetic cohorts, 8, 9, 167, 175, 267, 274,
    Appendix F

Taft, R., 56, 57
Thomas, N., 39*n10*
Truman, H. S., 56, 57

Values. *See* Allport-Vernon scale of values
Vietnam War, 15, 69, 112, 119, 242–45

Widowhood. *See also* Roles, role transitions
    and attitude change, 215
    in Bennington sample, 206, 207
Women's suffrage, 266

Life Course Studies
David L. Featherman
David I. Kertzer
    Series Editors

Nancy W. Denney
Thomas J. Espenshade
Dennis P. Hogan
Jennie Keith
Maris A. Vinovskis
    Associate Series Editors

DISCARD

DATE DUE			
JUN 30 1993			
sent 3-20-03			
GAYLORD			PRINTED IN U.S.A.